ROUND BARNS OF AMERICA

75 Icons of History

ROBERT KROEGER

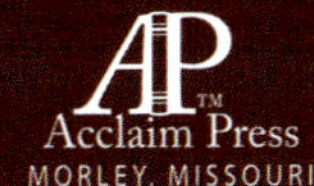

Acclaim Press
MORLEY, MISSOURI

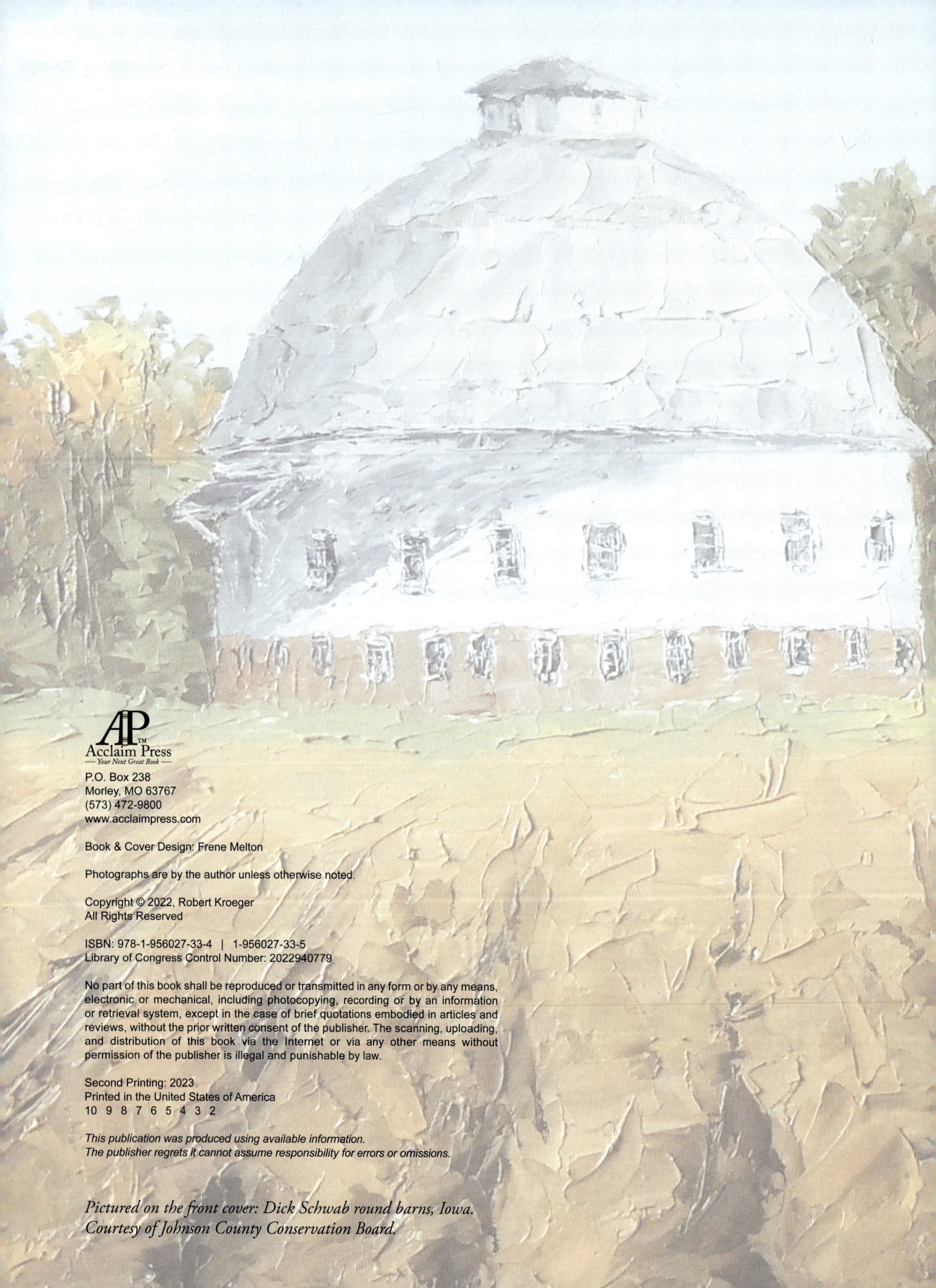

Acclaim Press
Your Next Great Book

P.O. Box 238
Morley, MO 63767
(573) 472-9800
www.acclaimpress.com

Book & Cover Design: Frene Melton

Photographs are by the author unless otherwise noted.

ISBN: 978-1-956027-33-4 | 1-956027-33-5
Library of Congress Control Number: 2022940779

Second Printing: 2023
Printed in the United States of America
10 9 8 7 6 5 4 3 2

Pictured on the front cover: Dick Schwab round barns, Iowa.
Courtesy of Johnson County Conservation Board.

CONTENTS

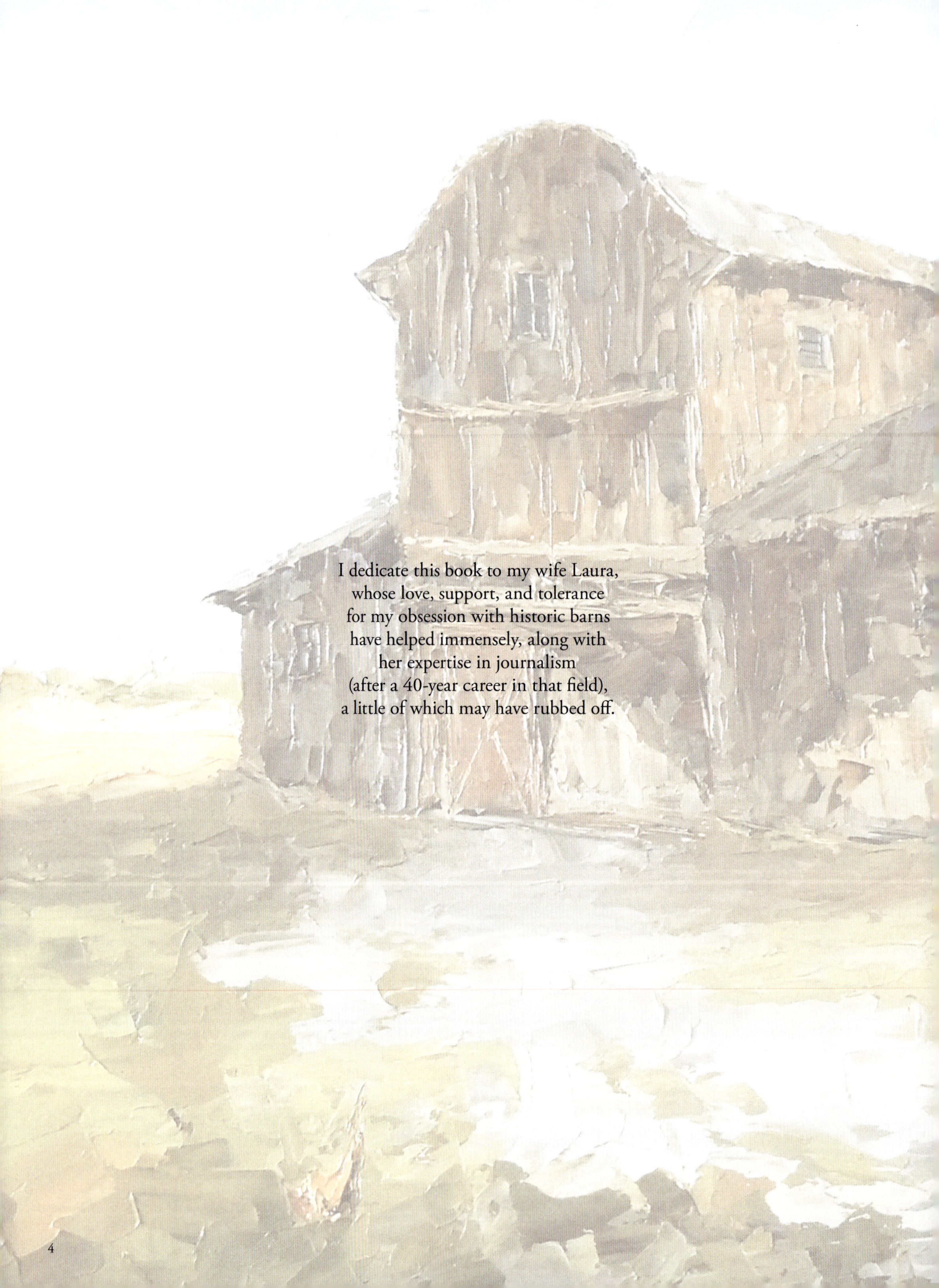

I dedicate this book to my wife Laura,
whose love, support, and tolerance
for my obsession with historic barns
have helped immensely, along with
her expertise in journalism
(after a 40-year career in that field),
a little of which may have rubbed off.

FOREWORD

I like to think of round barns as the fireworks show at the end of an era of incredible craftsmanship. If you stand in the haymow of an old round barn and gaze upwards, you can witness firsthand the fireworks — with rafters overhead emanating — seemingly exploding — from the center apex.

The craft of the rectangular barn was its massive timbers — hand-hewn with mortise and tenon joinery. By the time the round barn came along, one aspect of the carpentry work had been simplified. Inside was smaller dimensional lumber, oftentimes precut at a local sawmill; simple balloon framing had become popular. But the intricacy of the round barn lies in its shape. Many carpenters were perplexed by the angles. Generally, only the most skilled carpenters would tackle a round barn project. Indeed, only a small number really understood what a beautiful shape round could be.

Beyond the visual beauty, the rarity of the round barn makes it even more mysterious and appealing. Far less than one percent of barns were round. At most, perhaps only 700 round barns remain today, and the majority of them are in the Midwestern states, which stands to reason that most Americans have yet to lay their eyes on one. I feel fortunate to have visited over 350 round barns in 21 states over the past 25 years. I enjoy posting them and their stories on my Facebook page and Facebook group for all to enjoy.

—Vincent Loveall
Founder, Facebook sites: *Round Barns of America* and *Round Barns of the US*
Jeffersonville, Indiana

Having taken over as the director of the Pump House Center for the Arts in the fall of 2020, I came across an email from Dr. Robert Kroeger inquiring as to our interest in showing him some barns in the area, as he was an artist in search of vintage barns to paint. He was working on a project to document historic barns in all of Ohio's 88 counties. And so our relationship began.

The Pump House ended up sponsoring a very successful show of Dr. Kroeger's work in August of 2021 and I was able to scout barns to tour with him for future projects. One of the most unique barns near our town in Ross County is a round barn known as the Maxwell barn. Long a favorite subject of photographers and painters alike, it is a well-maintained barn still in use today! I am pleased that Dr. Kroeger has included it in his new book.

Round barns were popular at the turn of the 19th century since they were considered a labor-saving tool for the farmer as well as requiring less material to build. As the farming industry became more mechanized, however, the design lost its favor and more traditional designs became the norm. Today, thanks to historical preservation efforts of Dr. Kroeger, future generations can learn about these barns and their stories through the pages of this book. I hope you enjoy the work of this author, a gifted writer as well as painter.

—John Payne, Director
Pump House Center for the Arts
Chillicothe, Ohio

Ohio barns — of one kind or another — stretch back to the days when the forest gave way to the rise of agriculture as the base of the economy. Barns, it's been said, were early forms of saving accounts where wealth, surplus crops from rich harvests, could be stowed for sale some other day. Of course, not all barns took the same form or function. And while so many of Ohio's remaining barns are treasured features of our landscape, round barns pop out and command our attention. Bob Kroeger's passion for historic barns is exceptional. So too are his vibrant impasto oil paintings. Here, Bob's artist's eye and skilled painter's hand showcase the country's extraordinary collection of round barns. Taken together, they form a keepsake for all — and there are many of us — who prize these survivors that dot and complement the quiet panorama of rural roads across America.

—Stephen George, Senior Advisor to the CEO
Ohio History Connection
Columbus, Ohio

ACKNOWLEDGEMENTS

I owe much gratitude to many who contributed to this book. First, I thank the round barn owners for taking time to show me their barns, for allowing me to paint their barn, for telling me its story, and for occasionally supplying me with old barn siding to frame the painting, one more touch of nostalgia. I also appreciate the many local and state historical societies and barn foundations for giving me images, connecting me with owners, and sending me newspaper and magazine articles.

My barn scouts helped enormously, too, in directing me to round barns. They include: Leianne Heppner of the Summit County Historical Society, Jenny Clark of the Garst Museum in Darke County, Nate Stitzlein and Tammy Drobina of the Fairfield County Heritage Association, Rheuben Gibson of Allen County, Dave Keller of the Perry History Club, Carl Feather and Jeff Scribben of Ashtabula County, and Ron Myer of the Whitley County (Indiana) Agricultural Museum. These wonderful scouts not only provided leads but drove me around their counties, allowing me to take notes, make compositions, and see several barns in relatively short time.

Without Dale Travis and his website on Ohio barns, which I discovered in 2014, I would never have found the eight round barns that are featured in *Historic Barns of Ohio*. And then, a little later and thanks to Dale again, I stumbled upon his national round barn site, which prompted me to write this book. Travis, from western Illinois, started his site in 2000, a few years after he began a quest to document covered bridges, another magical part of Americana. Other photographers with similar interests began to share photos of round barns with him, which enabled him to compile a user-friendly, commercial-free list of round barns and covered bridges. Dale spent many years on this project, often driving far from his home to photograph the barns. He deserves credit for making round barns accessible to all — via his site, http://www.dalejtravis.com.

Another individual, Vincent Loveall, taught me that Facebook is full of round barn lovers, evidenced by his two sites, *Round Barns of America* and *Round Barns of the U.S.* He continues to post images of round barns and their interesting stories. I'd like to thank him for his part in the foreword, along with John Payne and Steve George.

John and others (artists and concerned citizens of Chillicothe) rescued an extraordinary 19th-century pump house, when it was scheduled for demolition. Thanks to their efforts, this stunning Victorian brick building has been converted into an art center, which John now directs and continues to restore. Historic barns abound in this county, including the iconic Maxwell round barn, also saved when it became endangered.

Steve George has been kind to me by convincing Burt Logan, the CEO of Ohio's state historical society, to agree to contribute to the foreword in my book, *Historic Barns of Ohio*. Steve knows barns well. Prior to 2003, our state's bicentennial, Steve directed a state-wide program, which commissioned artist Scott Hagan to paint Ohio's bicentennial message on a highly visible barn in each of Ohio's 88 counties. Scott, who learned this trade from the Mail Pouch barn painter Harley Warrick, continues to paint historical themes on barns, thanks to Steve and the Ohio History Connection, where Steve acts as senior advisor to the CEO.

The National Register of Historic Places, which, for brevity's sake, I'll refer to as simply the National Register, holds an enormous amount of information on barns, which helped me write their stories as did the many newspaper articles and books on round barns. John Hanou, author of two books on Indiana's round barns, expertly detailed the early round barn builders of that state, who were probably the most significant group of such builders in a single state, ones who built round barns not only in Indiana but also throughout the Midwest and West. Another vital book was *Without Right Angles: The Round Barns of Iowa*, written by Lowell Soike, a historian for 30 years with the State Historical Society of Iowa. The many barn books by Professor Allen Noble, who's probably written more university-published books on old barns than anyone, provided more help and references.

If I have omitted anyone who helped, I apologize deeply. Traveling many miles to see these barns and meet their owners, spending countless hours in researching their history, and capturing them in a painting and essay became a labor of love. It's my hope that if, 50 years from now, someone sees one of these paintings and reads its essay, he or she will understand a little bit about the early pioneers, who sculpted our country into America, the land of the free and the home of the brave.

INTRODUCTION

Round barns — circular, hexagonal, octagonal, or any polygonal shape without right angles — provide a fascinating look into not only early America but also its architectural and agricultural heritage, though they represent far less than one percent of all barns. Many of their stories are compelling and need to be shared before they, like other old barns, disappear into the ruins of time.

Just like the traditional timber framed barns of 18th- and 19th-century America, round barns were the "money makers," providing storage for livestock and crops. Without them, farmers wouldn't have survived. That said, most round barns built in their "golden age" (1870-1930) were designed for dairy farming and usually did not exhibit hand-hewn timbering, mortise and tenon joints, and wooden pegs, typical of rectangular barns built in the 1800s.

Most suburbanites and urban dwellers have never heard of a round barn, much less have seen one, and, if you asked them, they'd probably not believe such a barn would have ever been built. But, in fact, some round barn lovers are building them today. And, though mostly unknown and located in a remote region, the oldest existing round barn is now over 200 years old. President George Washington built the first recorded round barn in America in 1794, which, though long gone, is remembered in a replica in Mt. Vernon.

Many experts believe that only affluent farmers could afford to take a chance on building such a nontraditional barn, which is largely true. However, many round barns were built by average farmers, working on modest acreage, who wanted to try something different. And round barn builders wrote articles in the agricultural press and promoted this design, based on various attributes, including a lesser construction cost, which simply was not accurate. Despite such positive publicity, the average farmer was not sold on this idea and stuck with the traditional rectangular design, which made round barns, especially the few that exist today, even more of an oddity.

I grew up in the suburbs of Youngstown, Ohio, which is noted for its steel mills, especially in the northern part of Mahoning County, though its southern region, as I've discovered in the past several years, is full of old timber-framed barns. But no round ones.

After I lost my first wife to cancer, I remarried. Laura decided that we should have a tradition of an annual surprise trip on our wedding anniversary. And so, in 2012, she chose a rural B&B in Licking County, about an hour east of Columbus. As we turned down the country road, I noticed a small gray barn, perched on a small hillside, its roof sagging, boards missing, tilted about 10 degrees. As I looked up, it sent a message to me, almost like a thunderbolt: *You're going to do a painting of me, write an essay about my story, and preserve Ohio history.* Wow. It was startlingly real.

That night at dinner Laura and I talked about this supernatural epiphany and decided to try to meet the barn owner. The next morning, Saturday, I knocked on the door of the circa 1830 farmhouse and met Mr. Herbert Hall, who at first was skeptical of my unannounced visit. After I explained his barn's message, he

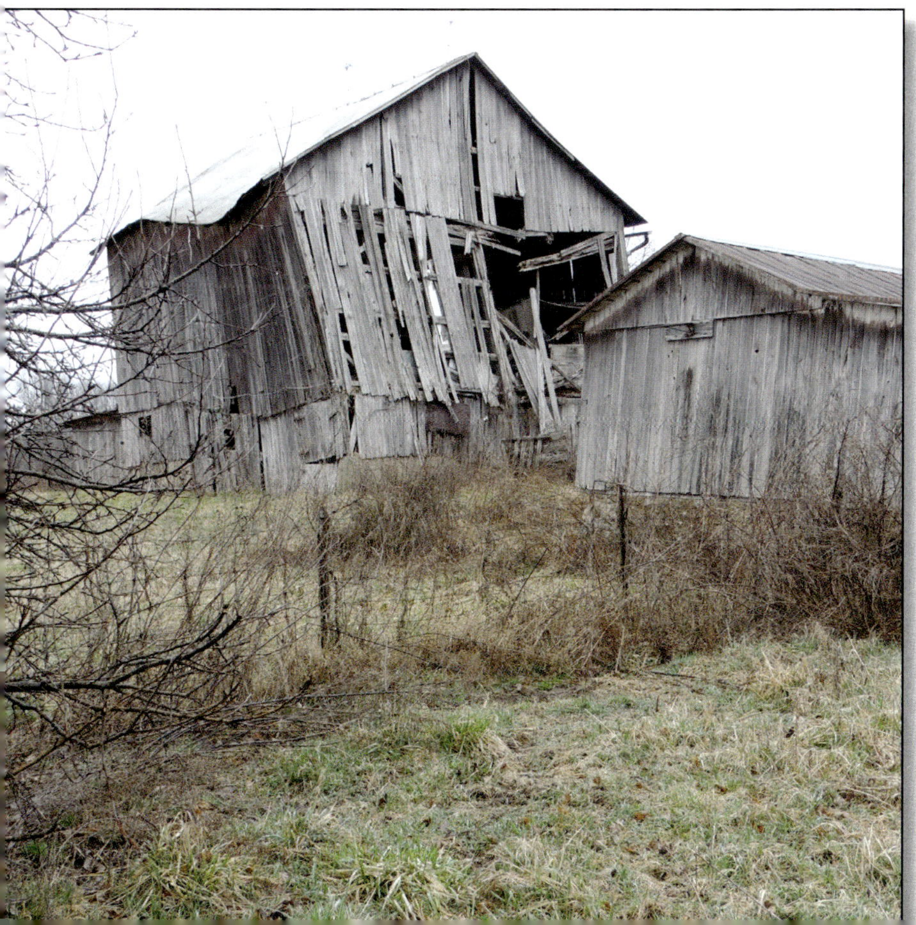

Granville Gray, 2020

lightened up and told me how Welsh farmers moved here from the east coast, about the land grants for Civil War soldiers, and about the old gun shop across the street. His barn, one I call "Granville Gray," was full of hand-hewn timbers, some with bark still attached, joined in mortise and tenon fashion and connected with wooden nails. My Ohio Barn Project had begun.

Although my father had a fine art degree from Notre Dame and worked as a commercial artist for Truscon Steel, he didn't mentor me in art. So, I had to head back to the basics, studying, reading, practicing, taking workshops and learning much from an accomplished Cincinnati artist, all of which took time. Along the way, I fell in love with impasto (thick) oil painting with a palette knife, which gives a three-dimensional, rustic look, fitting for an old barn. I learned how to make frames out of old barn siding, which seemed appropriate — a rustic barn, thick paint, a frame of weathered wood.

I began my quest for barns on my own, which, luckily for me, didn't involve getting attacked by a vicious guard dog. However, after finding some barns, one day I faced a rifle held by an irate expert marksman. That's when I decided that searching on my own was not a good idea. That led to finding barn scouts throughout Ohio, who guided me through their counties safely and who often knew the barn owners. Without these barn scouts, my project would have died.

Now, armed with paintings and essays, I decided to put the paintings in fundraisers, at first for 4-H groups, but eventually — and now — in events for historical societies and museums throughout Ohio. I also was fortunate to meet a trustee of an agricultural museum in northern Indiana, who became a wonderful barn scout and whose museum has benefited from my fundraisers.

As I began to cross off counties from the list of 88 in Ohio, I wondered if I had enough years left in me to get to all of them. In the early going, around 2014, I found a website on Ohio barns, run by Dale Travis, and discovered my first round barn, an old octagonal in Ashtabula County. Intrigued by the odd shape, I visited others on the Travis site and finally decided, after an adventurous, yet successful journey through Ohio's Appalachian southeastern counties — where a straight road is the exception — that I could find an old barn in each county.

In time, I accidentally stumbled upon the Dale Travis site of round barns throughout the country, which dumbfounded me. Over 30 states had them at one time or another. So, even though continuing my Ohio Barn Project, I began to read as much as I could about round barns and collected data, thinking that this, too, might merit a book someday. So I started this round barn project, which unearthed stories from coast to coast. I kept on reading and researching, though my immediate goal was to finish the Ohio project.

In the summer of 2019 an editor from the History Press contacted me about doing a book, which made me hesitate at first since I had envisioned a coffee-table sized book with plenty of exposure to the paintings. But, when I realized that an inexpensive paperback would be the best way to spread the "gospel" of the old barn, I agreed to the editor's request. The press did an excellent job in producing *Historic Barns of Ohio* — both in editing and design. I was just as happy as its readers. But, after the copy was finished, when more incredible barns and their stories had surfaced, I knew I should write a second Ohio book, which must wait for now.

I wondered if a book on round barns would be feasible but the History Press does not publish nationally-focused topics. So, without a publisher to push me, I plodded along, reading, researching, painting, and writing about round barns. Finally, thanks to John Roscoe, author of *Minnesota's Round Barns*, I met Vincent Loveall in November of 2020 for a tour of one of Indiana's round barns. Vinnie explained that he had launched two Facebook sites on round barns in 2019, which had attracted over 14,000 followers. Initially, since I knew little about the demographics of Facebook, this surprised me, but, after Vinnie educated me, I began to understand that many older adults use this social media, not the younger crowd. They've moved on to Instagram, Twitter and maybe something else by the time this book is published. Older adults like old barns. So I began posting my barn paintings and essays — @historicbarnproject.

After the History Press released my book in March, 2021, I did many fundraisers for historical societies and museums throughout Ohio, which culminated in an event in September, held in the famous Muhlhauser barn in West Chester, a suburb of Cincinnati. The event raised funds for 10 local nonprofits and featured about 100 of my barn paintings, including those of the 88 counties in the book. And even though, this exhibit signaled the completion of my Ohio Barn Project, I decided to set a new goal of capturing 5,000 old barns — in paintings and essays — while continuing to do fundraisers.

With my second Ohio historic barn book on hold, I started organizing this book on round barns. First, I had to decide on how many barns to include. Early on, I thought 125 would be a good number, but, as the years evolved, I realized that this number was unrealistic since some of the stories were lengthy and I wanted to include chapters on the evolution of the circular and octagonal architectural forms. I wondered, *How about 75?* That number was less than the 88 in my Ohio barn book, more substantial than 50, and allowed me to share stories in 32 states. *Now*, I asked myself, *which ones should I include?*

I based my selections on three criteria: esthetics, history, and the human-interest factor. A listing on the National Register of Historic Places was a plus. From the standpoint of a round barn lover or historical expert, there are probably some barns that should have been included instead of the ones I chose. Perhaps their exclusion will prompt another author to someday write about them in another book on round barns.

Others may grumble that my home state of Ohio has the most barns in the book and that's a fair criticism. My answer is that I had the opportunity to visit each of them, connect with the owners, and inspect their insides. And although Ohio has only about two dozen still standing, some of them rank with the best in the country.

Another question that might arise is why I included round barns that are gone. And my response is that their stories were too valuable to ignore and shouldn't slip into obscurity. For example, the round barn that burned down in Sonoma County, California, with its essay titled "Fountain Grove … Utopia?," illustrates several fascinating pieces of American history. Other round barns, now gone, have captivating regional stories, such as the octagonal in Dickey County, North Dakota, the Bootlegger barn in Montana, and West Virginia's Kuykendall's 15-sided barn, whose story traces back to the French and Indian War and to, more recently, a lady's love of her "royal" Hampshire hogs.

One last question. Did I visit each barn? No. As it was, the project started in 2014 and ended with two final visits in the spring of 2022. To have visited each of the 75 barns would have taken me many more years, which, at my age, might not have happened. As you age into your 70s, the specter of death flickers every now and then, making you wonder about longevity. So many old barns, so little time. Fortunately, I did make contact with most of the historical societies or owners, who provided information.

The barns are arranged geographically, beginning in the northeast and ending with the far western states. About half of the states have only one barn represented and others have multiple barns, which are listed in the order of the date of their construction. This book must acknowledge that round barns may have existed in even more states than the 32 included. Some, victims of fire, tornadoes, and strong winds, have eluded the best of historians.

Of the 75 barns in the book, though most have a true circular shape, there's an interesting variety of other configurations: one hexagonal, one seven-sided, 19 eight-sided, two nine-sided, four 12-sided, one 13-sided, two 14-sided, one 15-sided, and five 16-sided. Two barns have unusual shapes — an oval and a donut — and three are rare stone octagonal barns.

Most of the round barns in this book were built between the 1870s and 1930, the start of the Great Depression. Two were built in 1939 and the last one came in 1949, though two significant classics were built more recently: a replica of the Shaker barn in Cape Cod was built in 1969 by the Lilly family and George Washington's 16-sided threshing barn was reconstructed in 1996, over 200 years after our first president built his original round barn.

After this book is published, I'll continue to spread the "gospel" of old historic barns, including all types — polygonal, circular, or rectangular — in fundraisers for historical societies, whose goal is the same as mine — historical preservation. And RFD-TV, a cable station in 50 million rural homes, may help in this effort. In the autumn of 2021, Rock Mann contacted me to see if I would allow him to post my barn paintings and stories on the RFD-TV Facebook page, which has about half a million followers. After I agreed — since this, too, spreads "the gospel" — he referred Joe Mischka, who stopped to film me for a segment on his show, *Rural Heritage*, which airs twice weekly on this cable channel. More of my barn stories have continued to be featured on his show.

I hesitate to say exactly how many of the 75 barns in this book have been lost, but, as of early 2022, that figure would stand at just below 20, a testament to the ravages of nature, changes in ownership, and attitudes away from historical preservation.

Though I've tried to make sure the information about each barn is correct, there's always the possibility that it's not. I relied on books, newspaper articles, nomination forms for listings on the National Register of Historic Places, interviews with the barn owners, historical societies, and museums. As most know, not everything on the Internet is accurate, though often the worldwide web did point me in the right direction. And, I've tried to hedge my bets with the use of words such as "maybe," "presumably," "possibly," and the like. Let's face it; facts can become distorted over a century.

Regardless, as long as this book remains in print, these memories will be preserved in paintings and essays. And, despite many claims to the contrary, round barns were more difficult and expensive to construct than traditional ones, which, in retrospect, might have been a blessing. It meant that only a relative handful of farmers were willing to take a chance on one — making round barns rare birds in the barn world. The few still standing represent charming curiosities, even for those living in rural areas.

— **Robert Kroeger**
Cincinnati

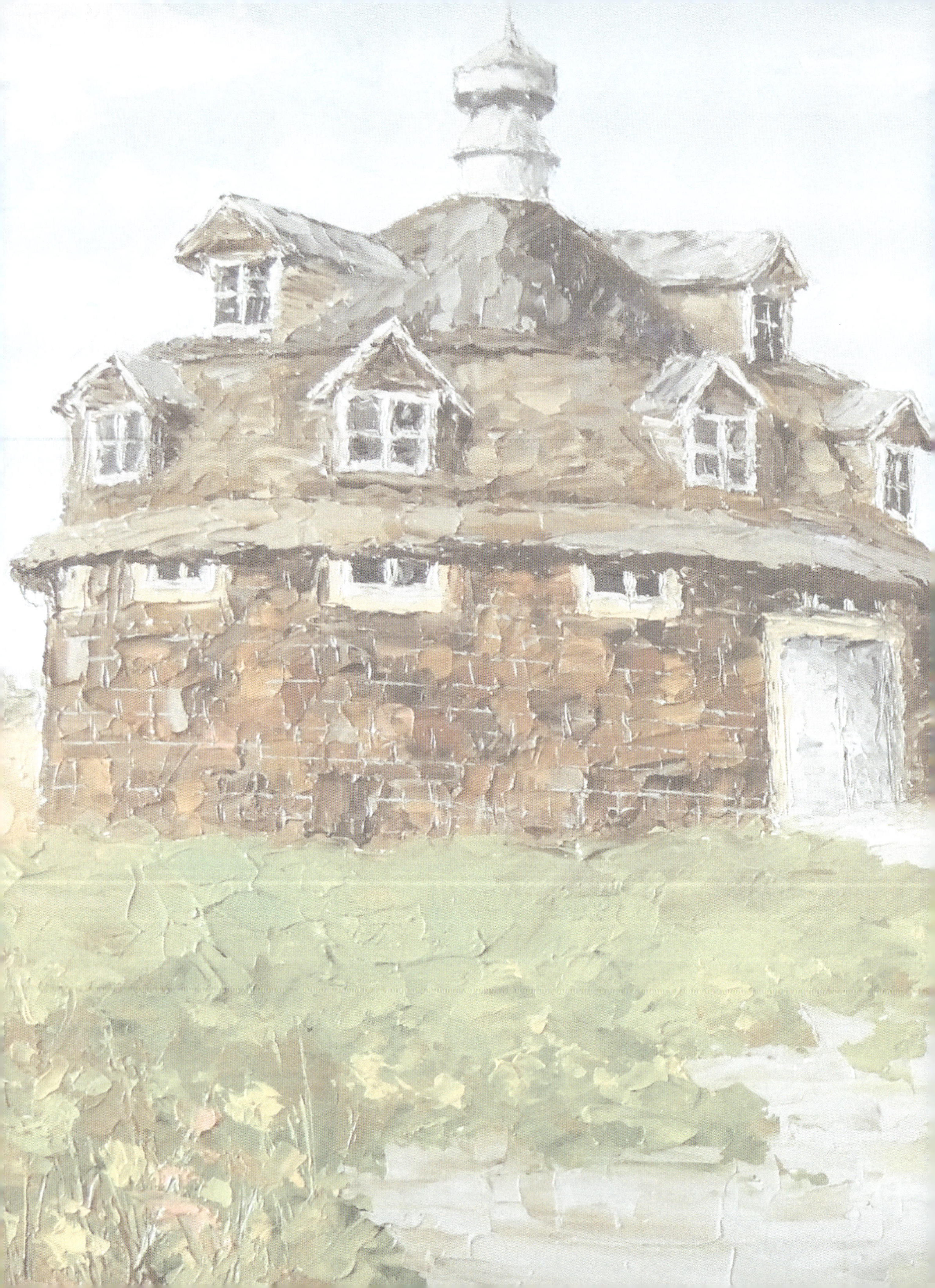

PART I
BEGINNINGS

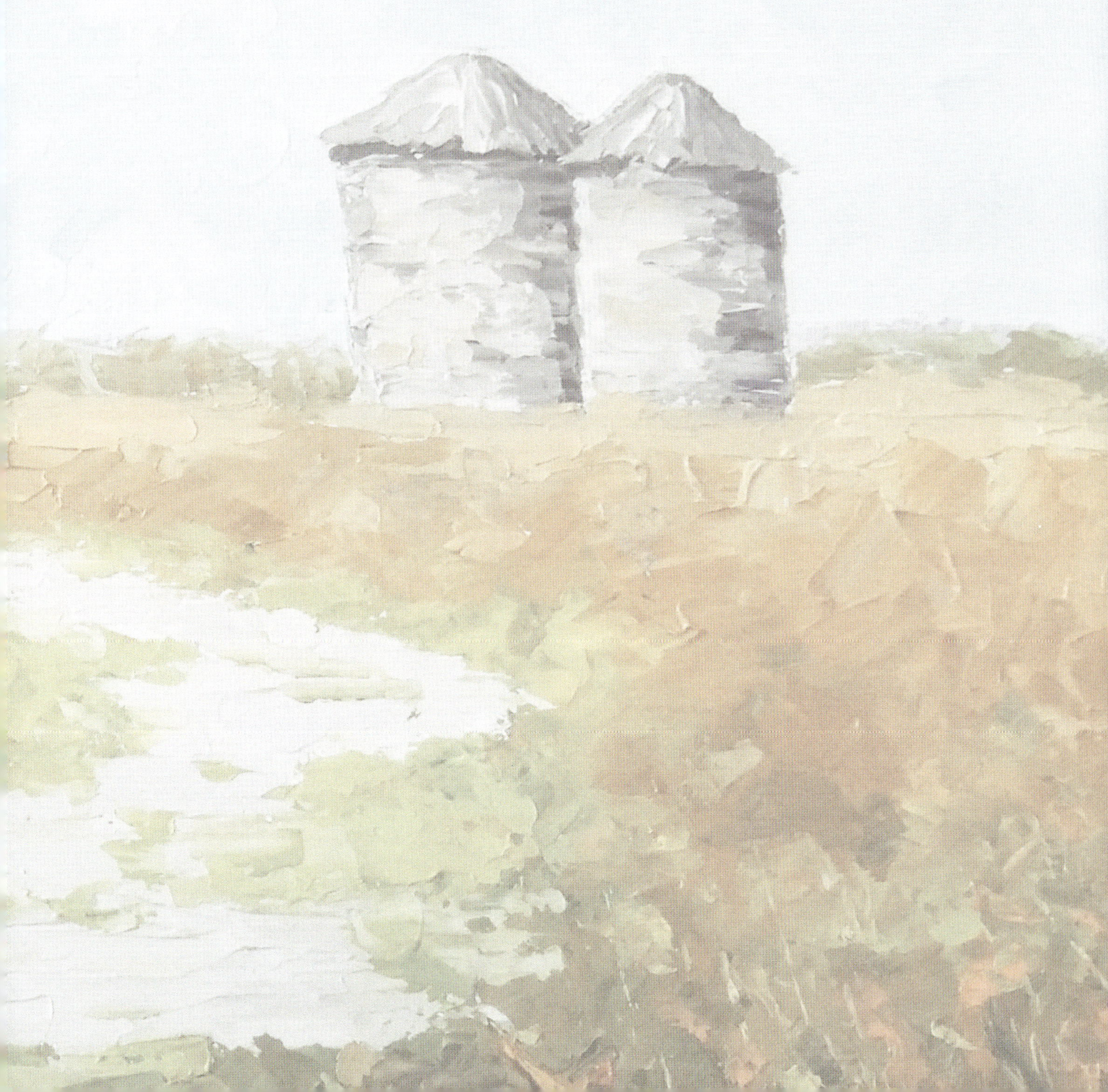

1. THE EVOLUTION OF BARNS

The Merriam-Webster Dictionary, 2022, defines the word, barn, as an "usually large building for the storage of farm products or feed and usually for the housing of farm animals or farm equipment." The barn's definition was more detailed in *Webster's American Dictionary of the English Language, 1860*: "Barn, a covered building for securing grain, hay, flax, and other productions of the earth. In the Northern States of America, the farmers generally use barns also for stabling their horses and cattle; so that, among them, a barn is both a corn-house, or grange, and a stable."

In that light, barns began thousands of years ago, even before the times of the Romans and their far-flung empires, when storage of grain to feed the growing population became important. To gain favor in Rome, in 5 B.C. Emperor Augustus Caesar distributed grain to 320,000 male citizens and he recorded this feat in a great public inscription. Food for all Romans was as important as military victories.

As Christianity, adopted by Rome as its official religion in the early fourth century, spread along well-developed Roman roads, monasteries sprang up, often serving as temporary quarters for travelers. In the early sixth century, St. Benedict, considered the father of western monasticism, wrote a set of rules, which included welcoming guests, many of whom were making pilgrimages. The Benedictine, Cistercian, and Trappist monasteries follow his rule and, even today, most continue farming traditions of centuries ago.

By the 16th century there were over 600 monastic communities in England and Wales and many had barns, often timber-framed initially and later covered with stone. Glastonbury Abbey, in Somerset on England's southwestern

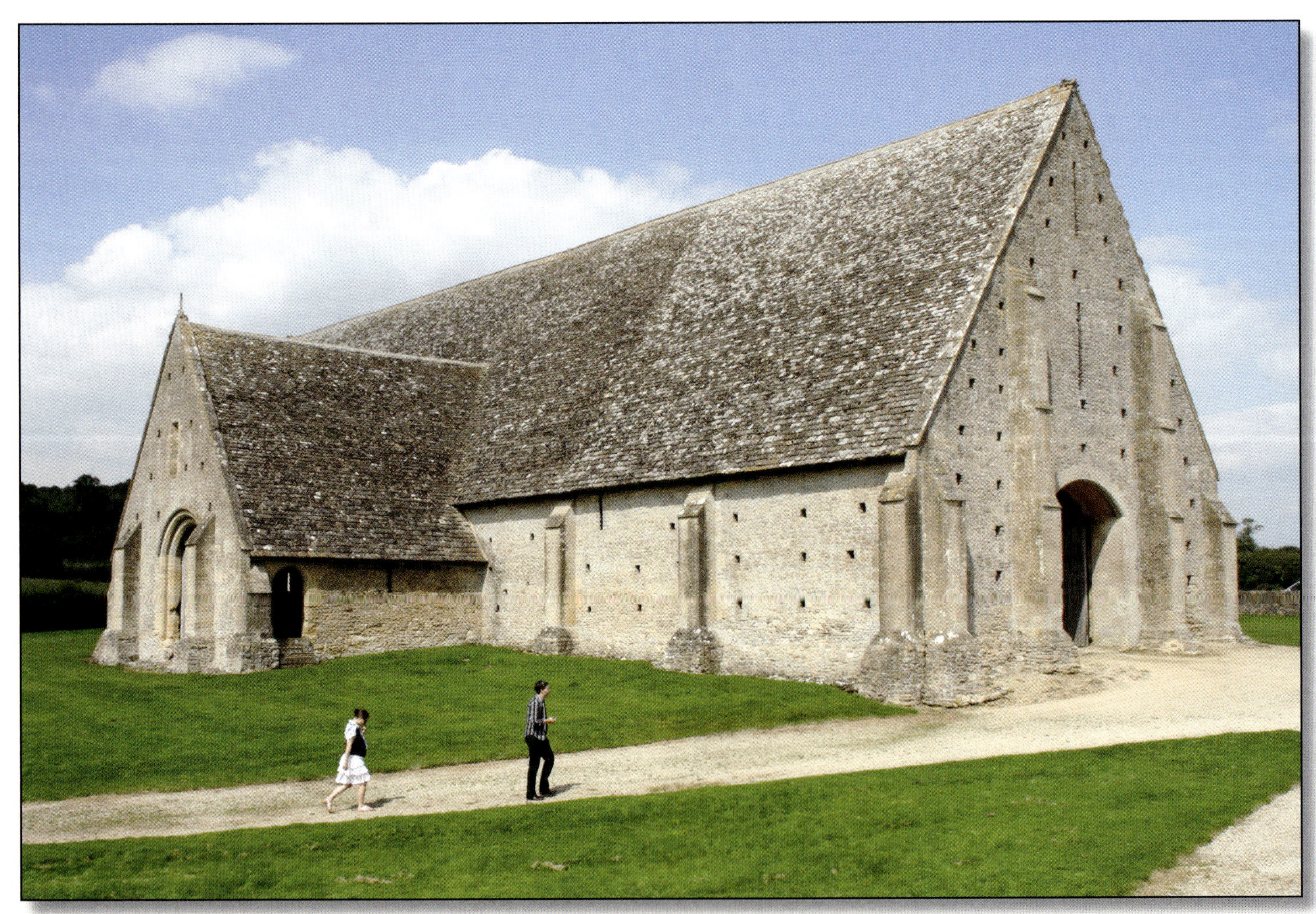

England's Great Coxwell stone barn. Courtesy, Ken Bonham, greatbarns.org.uk

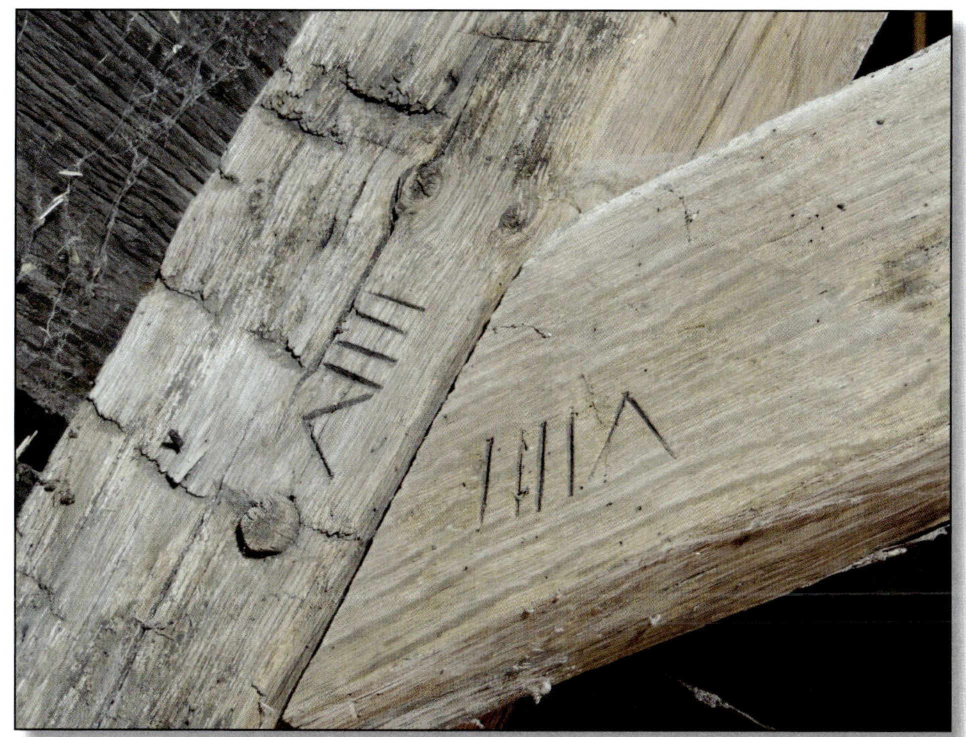

Hand-hewn beams, mortise and tenon joint, marriage marks

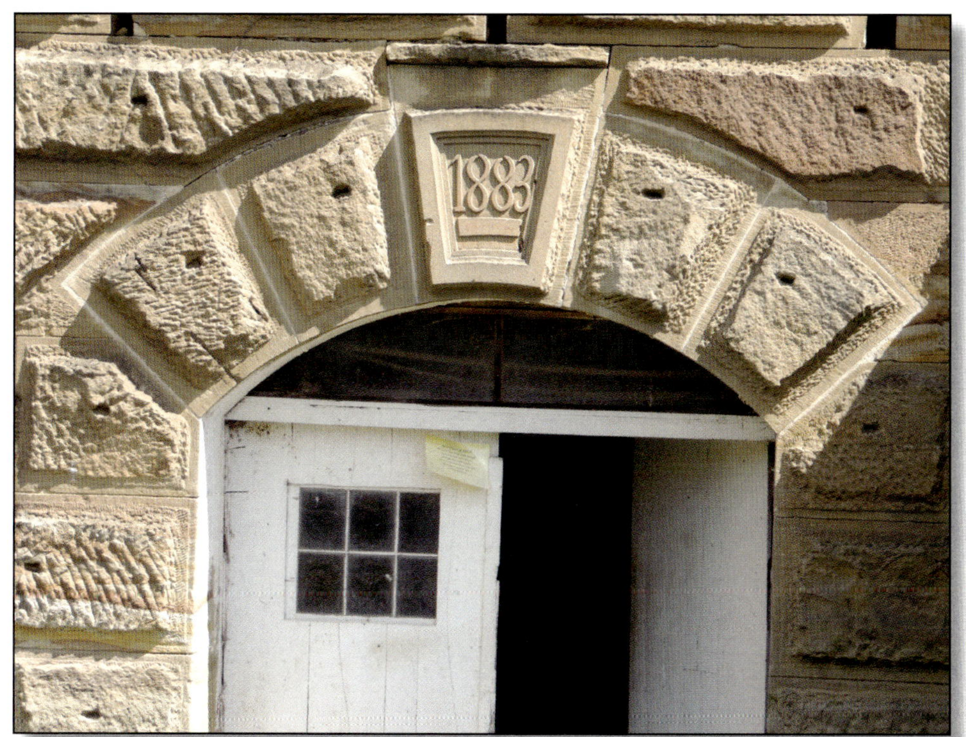

Kindelberger stone barn, Monroe County, Ohio

coast, had 25 manors with stone barns, stretching for miles. An English medieval proverb hypothesized that if Glastonbury's abbot married the abbess of Shaftesbury, the union would have more land than the king of England. Unfortunately, Henry VIII dissolved the monasteries from 1536 to 1541, destroying many, leaving only ruined skeletons. However, some of these monastic barns survive today and are managed by the National Trust, such as England's Great Coxwell, a 152-foot long stone barn built by Cistercian monks in the mid-13th century. In fact, when the Royal Institute of British Architects awarded their gold medal to Frank Lloyd Wright, they asked him which building he would most like to see. He chose the Great Coxwell barn.

Most, if not all, of these barns were used for grain storage and were rectangular. With mild temperatures in the British Isles and Europe, livestock remained outside year-round and did not need protection from the elements. Further north — in cold Scandinavia — barns did house farm animals. Throughout Europe in the 15th and 16th centuries and notably in Ireland, farmers and their livestock lived in a byre — under one roof, which often was thatched or sod-covered. In time, farmsteads included other buildings, depending on the farmer's or monastery's prosperity: stables, piggeries, chicken houses, hop stores, and granaries.

The Protestant Reformation, both in 16th-century England and in Europe, led to the dissolution of most monasteries, shifting agriculture into estates and small farms. And, the loss of forests — in Britain especially — meant that timber-framing barns was difficult and might have become obsolete if North America had not become colonized.

Along America's eastern coast, the simple three-bay English barn was the most common, used principally for threshing, grain storage, and, especially in the northern regions, livestock protection. Most were built of logs or were timber-framed with mortise and tenon joints and the occasional marriage marks, thanks to skills learned in the old countries.

In a few regions, notably eastern Pennsylvania and Gasconade County, Missouri, stone was used both for homes and barns. Many of these survive — from the 18th and 19th centuries.

After the American Revolution — and motivated by land grants to veterans — settlers headed west, desiring more land and a fresh start. At that time the Ohio Country, officially labeled as part of the Northwest Territory in the Northwest Ordinances of 1785 and 1787, was a giant hardwood forest — as was the rest of this region, stretching to the Mississippi River. Some claimed a squirrel could hop from one tree to another, starting in Ohio's eastern boundary and ending in the western flank, without ever touching the ground. Trees were plentiful and provided logs for the first homes, sometimes a byre — which the family shared with a horse, cow, and a few chickens. After clearing land for a farm field, pioneers would start with a tiny log barn, sized typically about 20 by 20 feet, and, if they prospered, they would eventually build a timber-framed barn that provided more storage space. As decades passed, barns grew larger and more sophisticated. But they were rectangular. Prior to the Civil War, only a handful of round or polygonal barns existed in America.

Timeline — Round Barns in the United States

1680–1750
Octagonal Dutch churches in Hudson Valley, New York.

1715
Octagonal brick magazine, Williamsburg, Virginia.

1761
Gentlemen's Pool House — an octagonal spa, Bath County, Virginia.

1782–1787
Thomas Jefferson spends five years in France. His love for the octagon increases.

1794
George Washington builds a 16-sided threshing barn, Dogue Run Farm, Fairfax County, Virginia.

1804–1805
Belvidere estate nine-sided barn, Angelica, New York (earliest extant round barn).

1806
Jefferson begins building Poplar Forest, his octagonal retreat home.

1826
Shakers build a stone circular barn, Pittsfield, Massachusetts.

1832
Bronck 13-sided dairy barn, Greene County, New York.

1846–1857
Patchin seven-sided barn, Westport, Connecticut.

1848
Orson Squire Fowler publishes *The Octagon House: A Home for All*. Later editions recommend octagonal shapes for barns.

Calvert octagonal barn, Prince George's County, Maryland.

1858
Nutwood circular brick barn, Urbana, Champaign County, Ohio.

1875
Cornell University Professor Elliot W. Stewart builds an octagonal barn, Erie County, New York and publishes his plans in "Practical Work Upon The Laws Of Animal Growth" in the *Buffalo Livestock Journal*.

1890
University of Wisconsin Professor Franklin King builds a circular barn and publishes "Barn for a Dairy Farm" in agricultural journals.

1875–1930
The height of round barn building in America.

1930
After two decades of articles critical of round barns and a decade of depressed farm prices, the Great Depression spells the end of round barn building.

2. ORIGINS: THE CIRCLE AND THE POLYGON

There's something pleasing about a rounded shape. Author Manuel Lima explains this emotional connection in *The Book of Circles,* his effort to show why love of this form has been a product of evolution. And perhaps it transcends into barns, as well.

Although the round shape came at the dawn of civilization — in the form of the wheel, coinage, and buildings — the most influential circular design in western architecture started with the Greeks. The first was the Doric order and an early example was the temple to Athena, built in the 7th century B.C., which not only featured rounded Doric columns but a circular form. Destroyed in the next century, it was rebuilt and became known as the Tholos of Delphi — tholos meaning a circular temple. Perhaps the best example of Doric architecture is the famous Parthenon of Athens, dating to 44-32 B.C.

The Ionic order followed, a bit fancier with scroll work at the top, though its columns retained a rounded, not square, shape. Then came the Corinthian order, with an even more elaborate design at the top — volutes, rosettes, and the graceful leaves of the acanthus plant. The curves and arched ceiling of the Temple of Apollo Epicurius at Bassae, Greece, a UNESCO World Heritage site, illustrate the Corinthian flare, along with the Doric and Ionic orders.

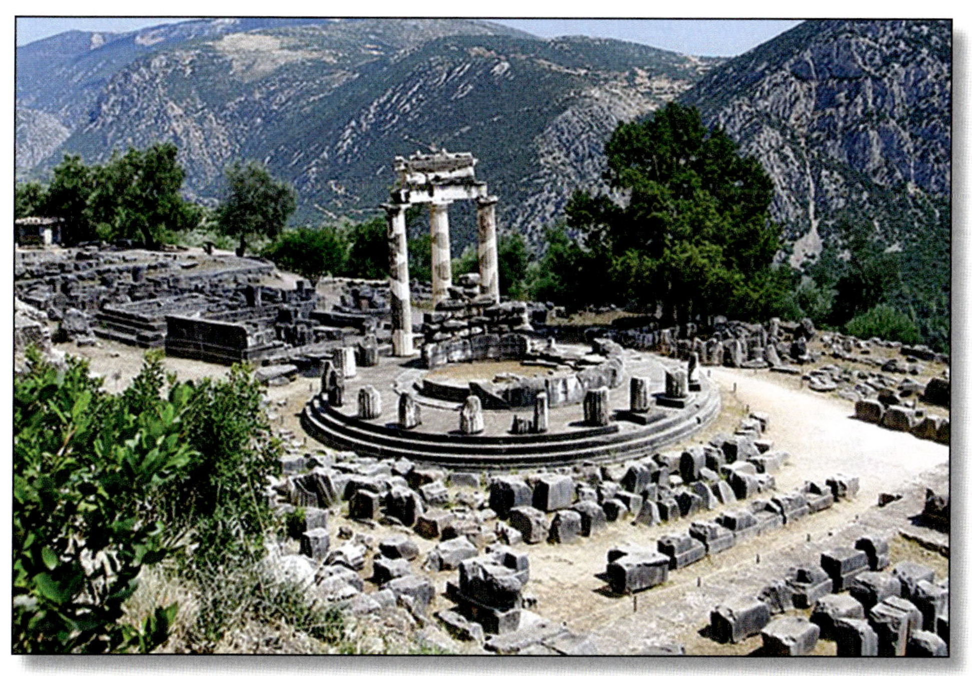

Tholos of Delphi, Wikimedia Commons, Michael Nicht

Greek architecture influenced the Romans, who continued the use of the circular design in their buildings, many of which still show the skill of their builders. From the Latin, rotundus, comes the rotunda, a building with a circular ground plan, often covered by a dome. Probably the most famous is Rome's Pantheon, whose rotunda stretches 142 feet. The curved architecture continues in its domed ceiling, where light shines through.

Another of Rome's buildings, its Colosseum, the largest ancient amphitheater ever built, still stands today and dates to the reigns of emperors Vespasian and Titus in 70-80 A.D., another testament to Roman engineers. As they expanded their empire, the Romans built more amphitheaters, about 230 in total, each featuring a circular or oval design. Many could accommodate 20,000 to 100,000 spectators, all eager to watch one spectacle after another. Many of our college and professional football stadiums, though filled with football players instead of gladiators, feature the rounded, oval shape.

In eastern England approximately 185 round tower churches still survive, left over from the time of the Vikings. The towers, a defensive measure against attacks, were attached to rectangular churches. Norfolk has the majority, 124 of them.

Later, during the eight major Crusades (between 1096 and 1291), when soldiers reached Jerusalem, most wanted to complete their pilgrimage in the Church of the Holy Sepulchre, built by Emperor Constantine in the fourth century. When they returned to their homes in Europe and England, they took the design of the chapel's circular rotunda back with them. Soon afterwards, Romanesque architecture spread through medieval Europe, including semi-circular arches and rounded turrets that highlighted buildings, churches, and monasteries. Even the Vikings, after they converted to Christianity, built round churches. Some, located in Denmark, Sweden, and Norway and dating to the 12th and 13th centuries, still exist today.

As time passed, most churches, abbeys, and buildings became square or rectangular, presumably because they were easier to build. Yet, round churches didn't disappear. In London, the Temple Church, a round one and still extant, was built in the 12th century by Knights Templar, who based the round design on what they had seen in Jerusalem — the Church of the Holy Sepulchre. Other more recent examples in Britain and Ireland often manifest round turrets and round towers. St. Chad's Church, built in 1792 (shortly before George Washington completed his 16-sided barn), stands out prominently with its distinctive round shape and high tower. In 1796 All Saints Church, in New Castle Upon Tyne, was completed — after replacing a 13th-century church — and it remains the only elliptical church building in England.

Eventually legends crept in, suggesting that one of the benefits of a round church was that the devil wouldn't enter since he couldn't find a corner to hide in. Such is the folklore behind the church sitting high on a hill in the village of Bowmore on Scotland's remote island of Islay, a round one built in 1769 — with its circular shape still attracting tourists. The island's laird, Daniel Campbell, traveled to Italy, where the round architecture might have inspired him towards this design.

Since many of America's early barn builders came from Britain, Germany, and Switzerland, it's reasonable to assume that they were familiar with circular buildings, even though early European barns had mostly rectangular configurations. However, round and polygonal barns were present in Europe and Scandinavia as early as the 18th century.

Three round barns still exist in Mecklenburg-Vorpommern, a state in northern Germany. One, a true

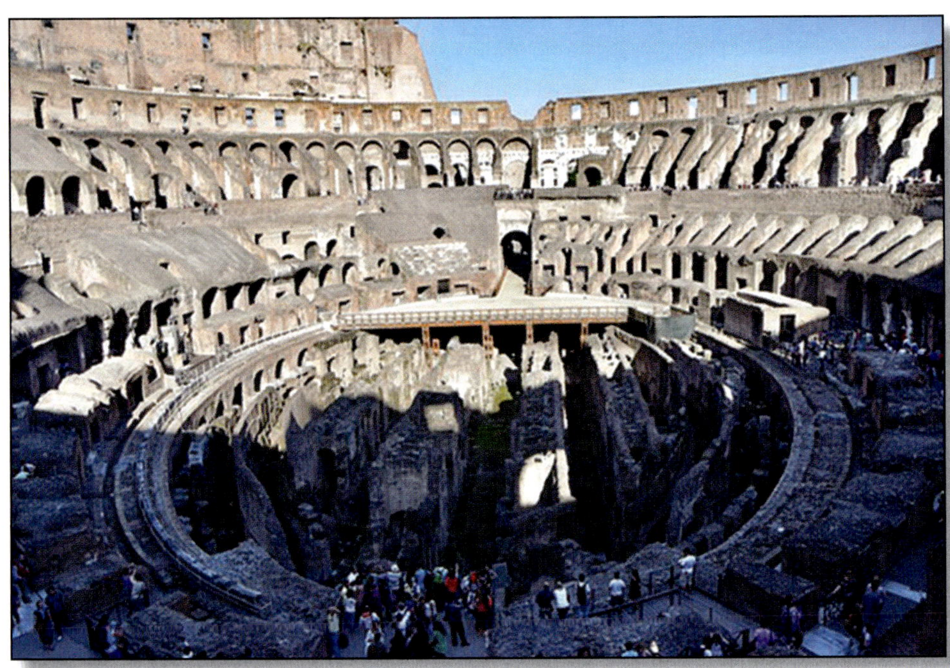

Roman Colosseum, Rome, Italy, Wikimedia Commons, Ank Kumar

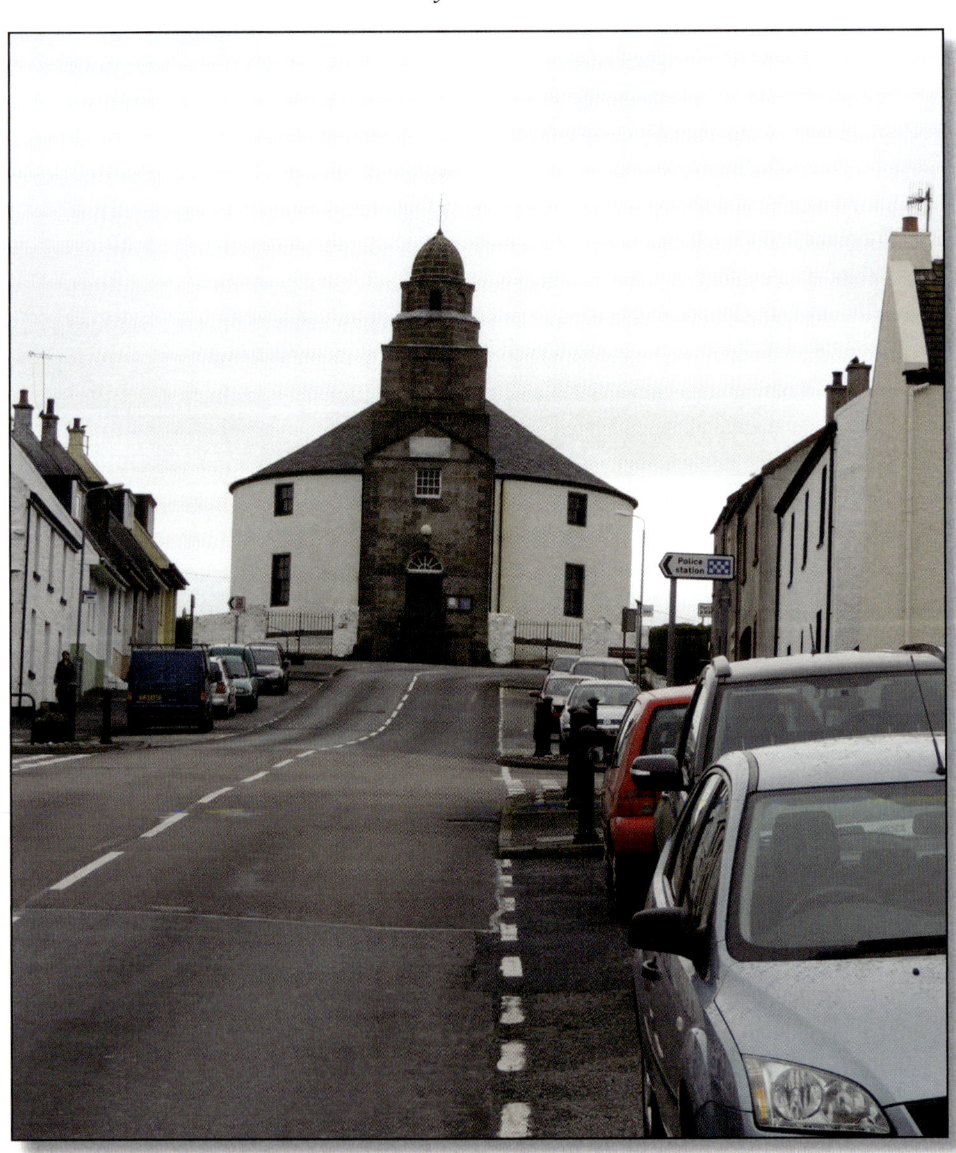

Round church, Bowmore, Isle of Islay, Scotland

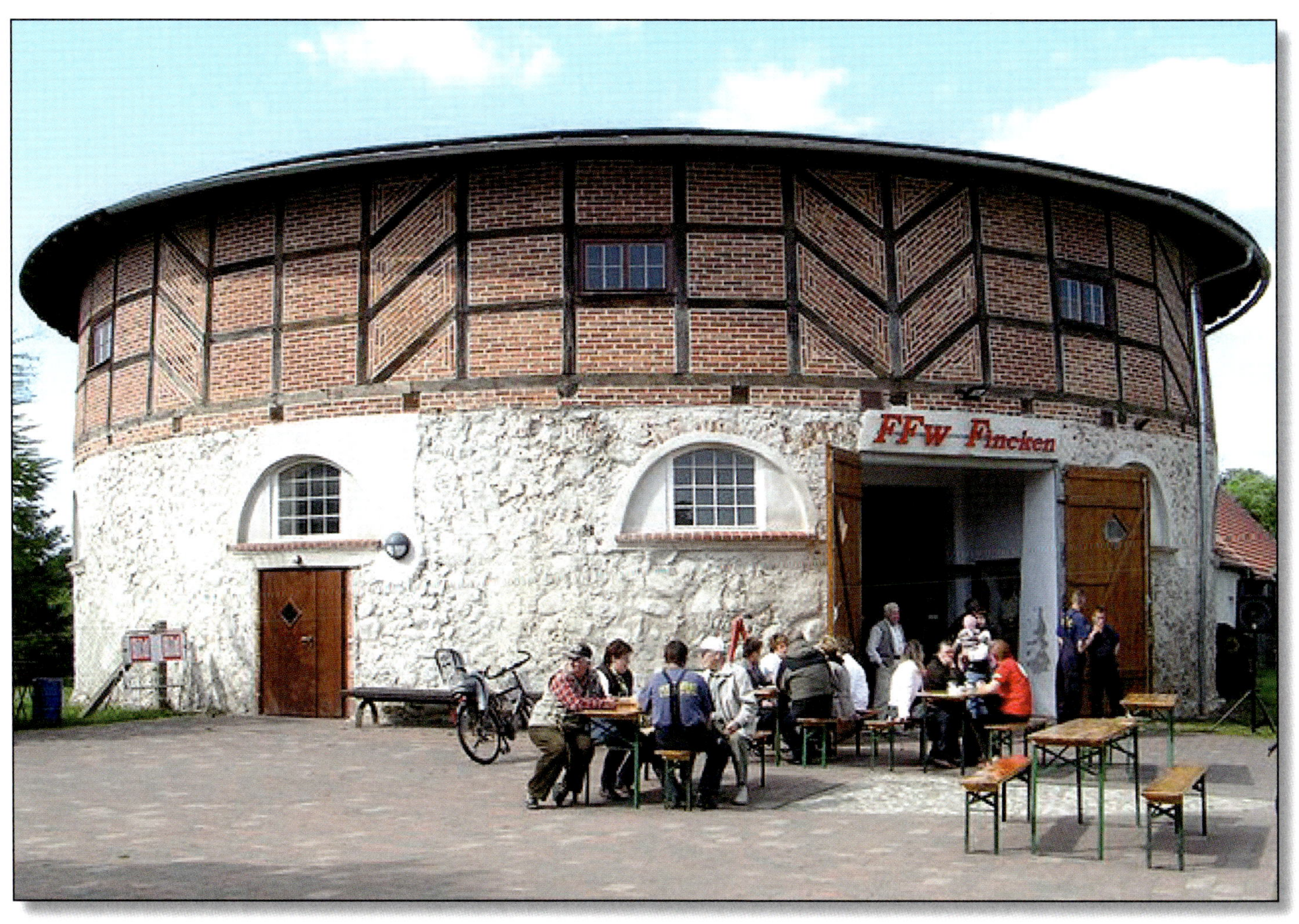

Fincken barn, Germany, Wikimedia Commons, Kopist

round barn in Fincken, dates to the 1700s and was used as a stable for horses. It's been converted into a community center. Another round barn, in Bakendorf, also built in the 18th century, has become a residence. And a third, the Ländliche Rundbauten, was built in 1815 and used for rapeseed threshing. Though it burned in 1917, its brick walls survived, and a new flat roof preserves the barn, which appears to be either octagonal or 10-sided.

And, finally, after the American Revolution, round barns began to appear, slowly but surely, in the United States.

3. EARLY AMERICA AND ITS ROUND BARNS

Thanks to the American Revolution, land ownership became possible for the common man, although most early American farmers were poor. Regardless, they owned their land, unlike the tenant farmers of the U.K. and Europe — called crofters in Scotland.

These American farmers raised enough crops and livestock to sustain their families and little else and their barns reflected such minimalism. Most barns of the late 18th century and early 19th century were small three-bay English threshing barns. Exceptions were the barns of wealthy landowners, whose ownership preceded the Revolution — such as Thomas Jefferson and George Washington, whose 16-sided barn remains the earliest example of a round barn in America.

Let's begin with the English explorer Henry Hudson, who sailed his ship, the Half Moon, up the Hudson River in 1609, leading to colonization of this valley, an attempt by the Dutch West India Company to capitalize on the North American fur trade. By 1650 the colony had become a major port for the fur trade and, according to the work of Russell Sturgis, an architect and editor-in-chief of *A Dictionary of Architecture and Building* (published 1901-1902), there were at least 20 octagonal churches in the Hudson River Valley, built between 1680 and 1750. However, this design faded and surviving churches in this region are rectangular.

A few buildings stood out from the norm — a powder magazine and a gentleman's spa. In 1715 in Williamsburg, Virginia, colonial governor Spotswood built an octagonal brick magazine, dubbed "The Powder Horn," which has been reconstructed as part of this historic village. A half-century later, in 1761, the octagonal Gentlemen's Pool House, the oldest spa structure in the United States, was built in Bath County, Virginia. Inside, the octagonal wooden pool measured 120 feet in circumference, held 40,000 gallons of constantly flowing mineral spring water, and maintained temperature, regardless of outside weather. Legend suggests that Native Americans discovered these natural hot springs in the mid-1700s, around the time of the French and Indian War, which ended in 1763.

Though there is no evidence that Thomas Jefferson spent time there in the 1760s, he did spend three weeks in the spa in 1819. In 1761, Jefferson was 18 years old and nine years later he began building his dream, Monticello, which embellished his love for the octagonal design.

Did George Washington visit this octagonal spa house? And, if so, would he have been influenced by its unusual shape? Why not a square spa house? Why not a rectangular one? These questions may never be answered.

By 1765 Jefferson — whose estate was about 90 miles from Warm Springs — was 22 years old and had recently inherited his father's large farm. Washington, on the other hand, had been a surveyor in Culpeper County in the colony of Virginia — ever since he was 17 in 1749. He continued this work for three years. He also fought in this vicinity during the French and Indian War. When his father died in 1757, he inherited his plantation, and, after being denied a commission in the British Army, he returned to farming in 1758. The next year Washington was elected to the Virginia House of Burgesses, where he served until 1774. Jefferson was elected to this house in 1768. It's reasonable to assume that they both knew each other at this time. And, since both were wealthy plantation owners, they likely socialized with other owners, some of whom probably were aware of the gentlemen's retreat in Warm Springs. In those days, mineral springs were considered to have healing powers as well as providing recreation. And, though the spa house was a striking example of an octagon, it wasn't the primary influence that spurred Jefferson to incorporate this design into his buildings.

Thus, in the early 1770s these two affluent "gentlemen farmers" probably talked about their agricultural ideas and may have corresponded frequently. Did Jefferson share his love for the octagonal design, although there's no mention of such a barn on his farm in those years?

After the war, Washington reluctantly returned to serve the young country as its first president, though, like the Roman general Cincinnatus, he preferred to farm. In 1792 — while president — he began constructing a 16-sided barn, which he finished in 1794, possibly influenced by Jefferson or by reading farm journals from England, still considered to be the leader in agriculture.

The next evidence of a non-rectangular barn, a nine-sided horse barn, still existing in western New York, traces back to circa 1804. Built on a huge tract of land, a vast wilderness in those years and still remote today, the barn sat next to the Genesee River. Its story involves Alexander

Hamilton, Thomas Jefferson, Angelica Church, and, to a degree, possibly George Washington's barn. Two years later in 1806 Jefferson started to build his retreat, Poplar Forest, an octagonal-shaped home with four octagonal rooms. Yet, despite these two polygonal barns and Jefferson's octagonal home and his famous Monticello, farmers continued to build rectangular barns and most of them were the basic three-bay English barns, functional and relatively simple to construct.

In 1826 a religious group, the Shakers, built an impressive stone round barn in western Massachusetts. Were they influenced by the work of Washington and Jefferson? Did they know about the octagonal Dutch churches along the nearby Hudson River? Coming from England, were they aware of the round buildings there? And, although the original round barn burned in 1864, church members reconstructed it. Today it hosts thousands of visitors annually.

For the next two decades there were a handful of round barns and buildings in this region, including an octagonal fieldstone schoolhouse in 1827 in Essex, New York, an octagonal cobblestone blacksmith shop in Alloway, New York, two cobblestone round school houses built between 1830 and 1850 in Yates and Ontario counties in New York, the Bronck 13-sided barn in Coxsackie, New York, and a seven-sided cobblestone barn in Westport, Connecticut.

Another influence might have come from railroads. The nation's first railroad began in 1827 in Baltimore — with a goal of reaching the Ohio River — and, as time progressed, roundhouses were built along the lines. These were large round buildings, where maintenance was performed on railway cars and whose round self-supporting roofs may have fueled the imagination of round barn builders. Many lines featured these roundhouses. The one in Martinsburg, West Virginia, has been restored and is available for rentals.

Finally, in 1848 Orson Squire Fowler, a writer in New York state, published a book on the octagonal home, a design he claimed was ideal. Although his writings did spur many into building such homes, barns remained rectangular.

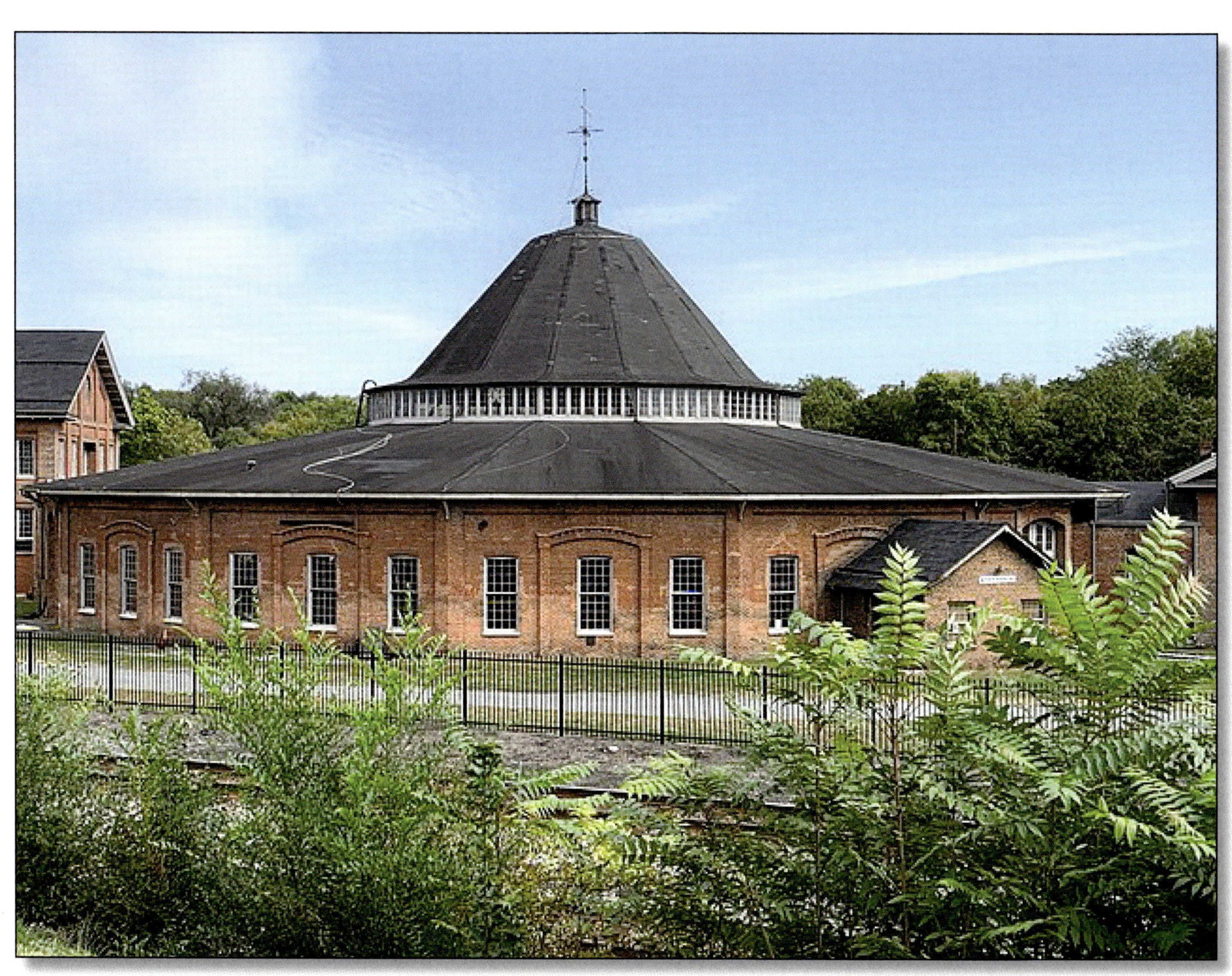

Railroad roundhouse, Martinsburg, West Virginia, Wikimedia Commons, Willingham 88

4. THE OCTAGONAL BARN

Of all "round" barns, the octagon was probably the easiest to construct and many examples still exist today, some having been repurposed into event centers, museums, and even wineries. Thomas Jefferson was a strong, early proponent of the octagon.

Jefferson, author of the 1776 Declaration of Independence and President for two terms from 1801 to 1809, was a renaissance man, one with an unquenchable thirst for knowledge. His interests were so varied — architecture, writing, politics, violin playing, practicing law, and reading — that he sold his 6,700-volume library to the Library of Congress in 1815 to replace books lost when the British burned the Capitol building in the War of 1812. Outside of his national leadership — which, of course, included purchase of the port of New Orleans and lands west of the Mississippi River, leading to the expedition of Lewis and Clark — his most beloved interest was architecture. And that involved the octagon.

As a young man, Jefferson was a voracious reader and was well educated in English, Latin, and Greek in several schools, thanks to his wealthy parents. At 17, he enrolled in the College of William and Mary in Williamsburg, where he often spent 15 hours a day in his studies over a period of two years, finishing in 1762. His professor and friend, Dr. William Small, arranged for Jefferson to begin studying law under George Wythe, a prominent Virginia attorney, who taught him for five years, becoming, as Jefferson later referred to him, "my faithful and beloved Mentor in youth, and my most affectionate friend through life." In 1767 he was admitted to practice law though his path took him elsewhere.

The next year, aside from beginning his political career when he was elected to Virginia's House of Burgesses, he had other plans and, now the owner of a 5,000-acre plantation, he began clearing land for his dream home, Monticello. Having inherited the family estate when he turned 21 (his father died when Jefferson was 14) and still single in 1770, he began building his home, beginning with the south portion. Although there is no octagonal room in this part of the home (that came later in when he added the octagonal north bedroom), each room has a slanted wall — instead of having perfect right angles. In 1772 he married Martha Wayles Skelton, who inherited a large plantation when her father died in 1773. However, significant debt came with that land, which Jefferson worked to pay off.

Changing, adding to, and remodeling Monticello became a major part of his life, a passion he continued well into the early 1820s — including the expensive re-covering of the roof with tin shingles. Unfortunately, Jefferson's spending on Monticello caught up with him, although other factors were involved — such as his benevolent co-signing of notes — and, upon his death in 1826, his debt had mushroomed to more than $100,000, forcing his daughter to sell Monticello, the plantation and its slaves, and all furnishings. Sadly, now penniless, she had to accept charity from others to feed her 12 children. One aspect missing from Jefferson's many qualities was the ability to become financially independent. Regardless of such misfortune, he left a legacy of architecture to America, which began with his voluminous reading of books, grew during his time with the lawyer George Whyte, whose father-in-law was a "gentleman architect," and blossomed during his years in France.

In late 1782, a year after England lost the American war and after a difficult childbirth of their third daughter, Jefferson's beloved Martha died, crushing his spirit. Possibly hoping for a change of scenery, he accepted an appointment to France and spent five years as ambassador there, returning in late 1789, just before the outbreak of mob violence in the French Revolution.

During his time overseas, he brought his elder daughter, Martha, and later sent for his other daughter, Maria, as he resolved never again to be apart from his family. And while he lived in Paris, he saw in person what he had read about in his youth — the art and architecture of Europe.

One of his favorite Parisian buildings, the Hotel de Salm, finished in 1788, featured a circular round dome and elaborate Corinthian columns. Jefferson wrote that he was "violently smitten" with its design and would view it daily. He saw in person what he learned from *The Four Books of Architecture*, written by the Italian Andrea Palladio, a father of the architecture of the Renaissance. Though Palladio never used the octagon, Jefferson employed it widely, halving it, elongating it, and using it in domes.

In 1787 he made a three-month journey — solo and at his own expense — to the south of France and northern Italy, though he never visited Rome — a curious omission

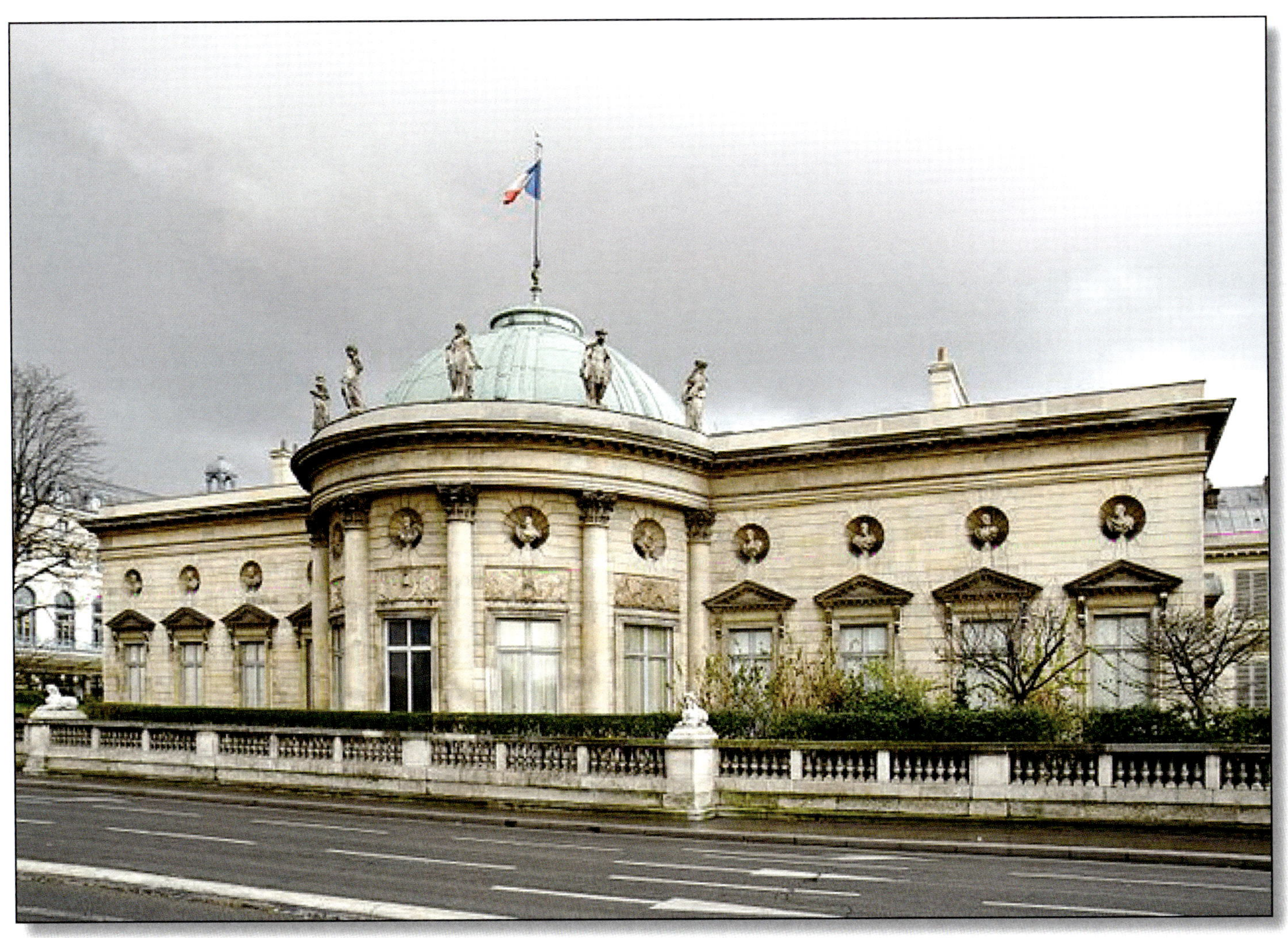

Hotel de Salm, Paris, France, Wikimedia Commons, Jebulon

since he mirrored the domed Pantheon in his architecture. However, while traveling, he fell in love with a neoclassical Roman building, the Maison Carrée, in Nîmes, a small village in the south of France. The square building with its elaborate Corinthian pillars, the best-preserved Roman temple outside of Rome, was built during the reign of Augustus. It captivated Jefferson so much that he sent plans across the sea to his beloved Virginia — with instructions to use this design in the statehouse in Richmond, which was finished in 1788, a replica of this ancient temple.

Upon his return to America, Jefferson learned that he had been appointed the first secretary of state under the nation's first president, a position he accepted reluctantly since he wanted to retire from politics to work on Monticello, continue farming, and do other projects. Despite his civic duties — being president for two terms — he managed to begin additions, including Monticello's classic octagonal dome, which he modeled after a drawing of the Temple of Vesta. He also added the north bedroom, a perfect octagon, where President James Madison and his wife spent many nights.

As secretary of state, Jefferson staged a competition in 1792 to design the Capitol building. William Thornton's design, which won the contest, was influenced by the Louvre and the Pantheon in Paris, which, no doubt, pleased Jefferson. He also hired Major Pierre Charles L'Enfant to design the plan of the city of Washington, which had only a few buildings at the time.

At Washington's urgings and probably suggested by Jefferson, Colonel John Taylor, III, a fellow wealthy Virginia planter, bought a lot in 1797 and began construction two years later on the first private residence in the city. It's probably no coincidence that Capitol architect William Thornton designed this house, also shaped octagonally. In 1898 the American Institute of Architects located its national headquarters in this building, which briefly served as the official home of President Madison after the British burned the White House in the War of 1812. Today the Architects' Foundation operates The Octagon as a museum.

In 1806, while still president, Jefferson began building another home, this one at Poplar Forest, a 5,000-acre tobacco plantation in Virginia that he and Martha inherited when her father died in 1773. For this design, he chose a perfect octagon, but one without a dome. Four ionic columns added to the classical form and four octagonal rooms connected to the central rotunda. After he finished his presidency, Jefferson often retreated here for privacy, a comfortable 80 miles from the always hectic life at Monticello.

Next came Jefferson's role in education. In 1814 Jefferson, anxious to provide public education for all — not just the privileged few — made drawings for a college, which consisted of a large, U-shaped field bordered by pavilions for the teachers and rooms for students in between. Eventually this concept of an academy changed names, later becoming the

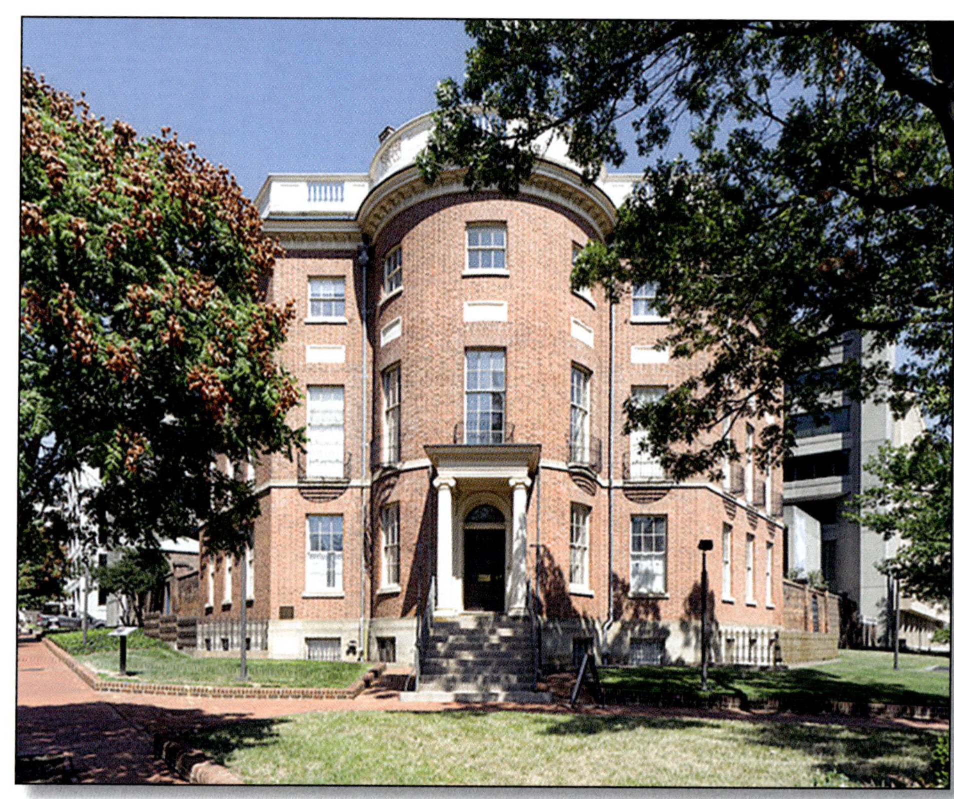

Octagonal house, 1799, Washington, D.C., Wikimedia Commons, Steveturphotg

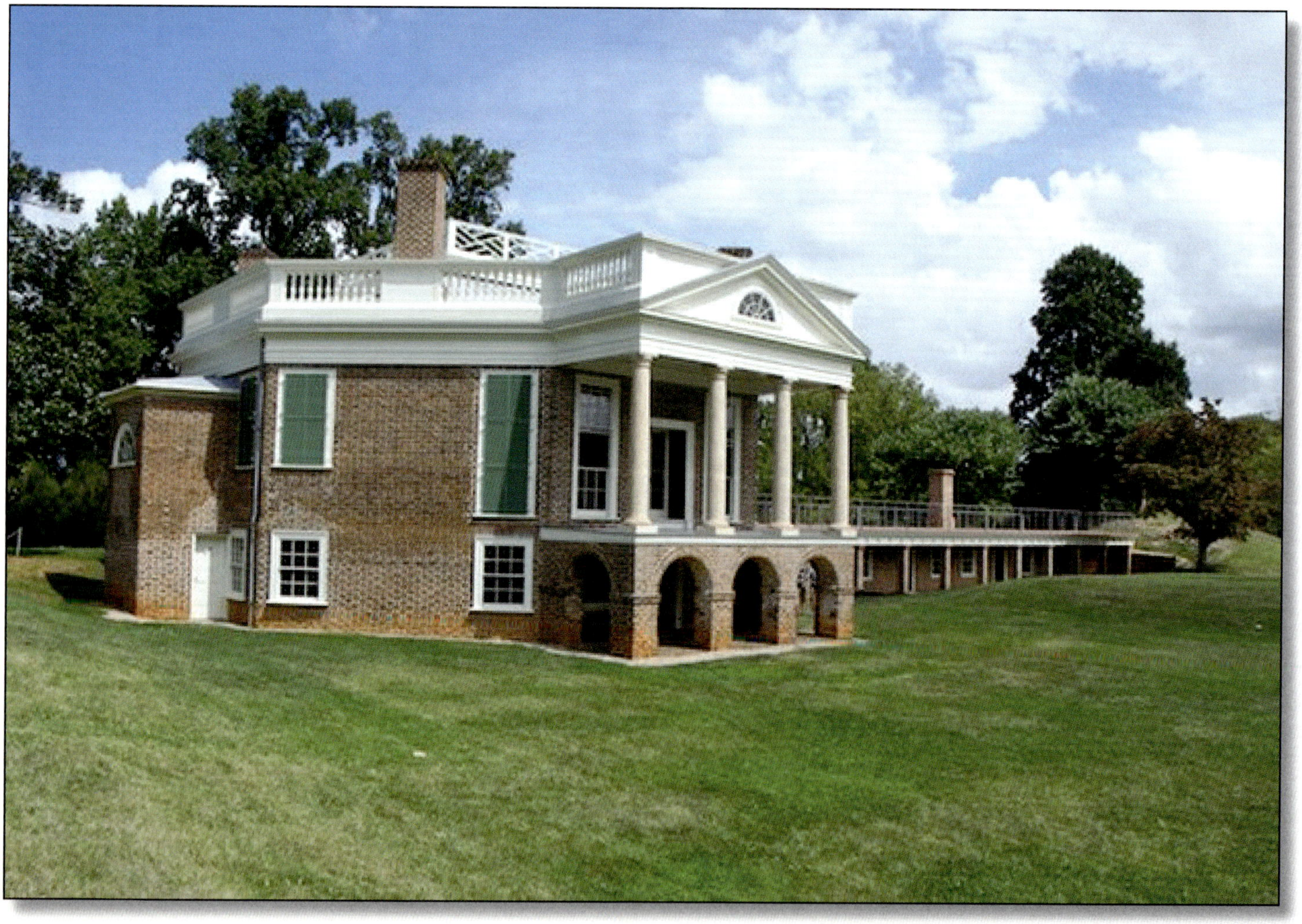

Poplar Forest, Forest, Virginia, Wikimedia Commons, Warfieldian

University of Virginia, which was built on land outside of Charlottesville. Jefferson collaborated on its design with William Thornton and Benjamin Latrobe, both his friends and architects of the Capitol building, who agreed to yet another of Jefferson's classic designs. This one featured a central rotunda, based on Rome's Pantheon, and a front that mimics Jefferson's beloved Maison Carrée. Now in his early 80s, he was once more committed to installing classic architecture into this young country. In 1976 the American Institute of Architects voted it "the proudest achievement of American architecture in the past 200 years." The rotunda was completed in 1826, the year that Jefferson died.

Fittingly, when the Jefferson Memorial was built during the early years of World War II, the architect styled the building after the circular Roman Pantheon, added Greek columns, and placed a rounded dome on top. Though the front resembles Jefferson's favorite Roman temple, the addition of an octagon somewhere would have brought another smile to Jefferson … if John Russell Pope would have included it.

Despite his political presence, Jefferson's love of the octagonal did not spread into the farmlands of young America. Most buildings and barns remained rectangular. Orson Squire Fowler ushered in the next phase of round architecture when he published a book, *The Octagon House: A Home for All*, in 1848.

Born in 1809 in Cohocton, New York, Fowler graduated from Amherst College in 1834. He and his brother Lorenzo became interested in phrenology, which spread from Britain to America in the 1830s. This pseudo-science was based on the unscientific study of the skull, which promoters used to predict mental and behavioral characteristics. Fowler and his family traveled widely, giving lectures and conducting exams on individuals. They even established a publishing house to spread their ideas. This "science" was used frequently to infer that African-Americans were suited for menial work and that people of Jewish descent were deceitful. With slavery and anti-Semitism prevalent in the mid-19th century, these beliefs were common. What would this phrenologist have thought about Wisconsin's Algie Shivers, an African-American who not only served in WWI but also built dozens of round barns in Wisconsin?

Fowler and his brother published articles in the *American Phrenological Journal* from 1838 to 1842 and, with his book on the octagonal house, he broadened his scope to include buildings, claiming that the circle was the most perfect shape, though more difficult to construct than the octagon.

He argued — accurately — that the octagon could enclose 20 percent more space than a square could, based on the same perimeter. And, since builders of that era were installing bay windows, which were usually at 135 degrees, he asserted that they could easily adapt an entire building into an octagonal shape. According to his book,

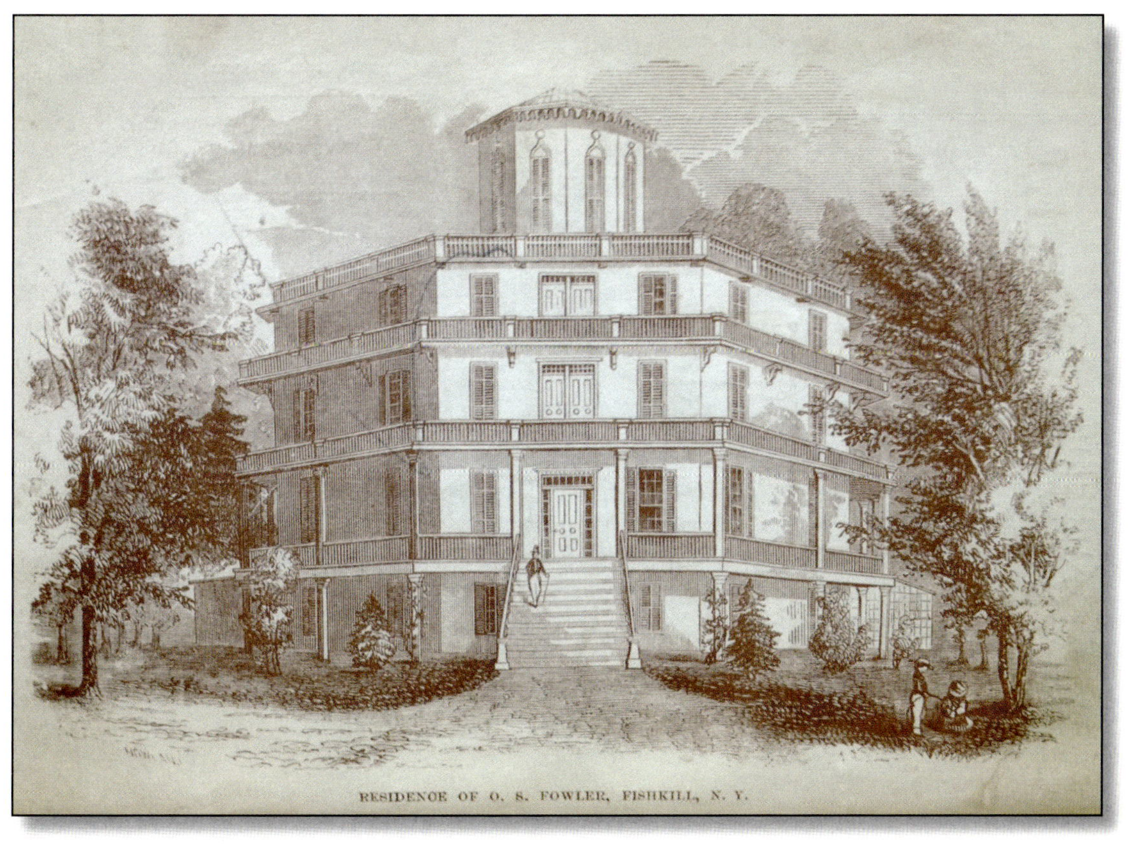

Fowler's Folly, Fishkill, New York, Wikipedia, artist unknown

such houses were less expensive to build, were easier to heat in winter, easier to cool in summer, and enclosed more living space when compared to a square or rectangular home. This book went through nine printings — into the 1850s — and within a decade over a thousand octagonal homes sprang up, mostly in the eastern United States. To back up his claims Fowler began constructing such a home in 1850 — eventually called "Fowler's Folly" — and moved into it three years later. At the time he lived in Fishkill, a small village about 70 miles north of New York City.

His house was a large mansion, high on a hill overlooking the Hudson River, and took years to complete: each side of the house was 42 feet wide, it had 60 rooms, and a cupola sat atop the 90-foot-tall building. He used gravel and lime for a mix of concrete for the walls, layering one on top of the other, a method that became popular throughout the years. However financial troubles, in the panic of 1857, forced Fowler to leave his house and rent it. Over the decades, after a series of owners, it deteriorated and, declared a hazard, was demolished in 1897.

Though Fowler also wrote about the octagonal barn, he had few takers. He reasoned that a farm did not need outbuildings and could be completely served by an efficient octagonal barn partitioned wisely. He considered the perfect farmstead to have an octagonal farmhouse and octagonal barns. However, his ideas rarely motivated farmers. One exception was Charles Benedict Calvert, an influential and important part of American agriculture, who built an octagonal barn with a diameter of 100 feet.

Calvert was born in 1808 at his family's estate at Riversdale, a farm in Maryland managed by his father George, a wealthy planter. Educated well in his early life, he decided farming was his main interest and adopted ideas from agricultural journals and newspapers. After his father died in 1838, Charles inherited the family farm and continued to learn as much as he could to improve his farming. Possibly influenced either by Fowler's book or Jeffersonian buildings, he built a large octagonal barn. In 1854 a leading agricultural journal, the *Cultivator and Country Gentleman*, illustrated this barn.

An old drawing in the 1998 National Landmark nomination shows the octagonal barn, surrounded by a massive octagonal outer ring, with a notation of circa 1848. Another drawing of the Riversdale "ground plan of farm buildings" notes that the outer ring had several sections — one for hogs, a sheep house, calving stalls, and another for calves. The interior of the octagonal barn contained approximately 90 stalls, arranged in two octagons, one inside of the other. Four other smaller octagonal buildings — two horse stables, one carriage house, and one corn house — were attached to either side of the outer ring. If Fowler's book did influence this design, he would have been pleased. Unfortunately, Calvert's barn burned in 1910.

Calvert became president of the Prince George's County Agricultural Society and also the Maryland State Agricultural Society. He founded the Maryland Agricultural College, chartered in 1856, which evolved into the University of Maryland. More importantly, he lobbied for the establishment of the United States Department of Agriculture, which, thanks to his efforts, President Lincoln signed into law in 1862. However, his octagonal barn didn't attract a following.

Although there were two polygonal barns built in New York around this time — an octagonal built circa 1860 in Livonia and a 12-sided barn in Chautauqua County in 1866 — the next significant round barn, another anomaly in its circular design, was built in 1858. Nutwood Place was listed in the National Register in 1976 and still exists in Ohio.

This curious part of the evolution of round barns took place in Urbana, the seat of Champaign County, Ohio, where Absalom Jennings built an incredible round brick barn to house his racehorses. Today this barn would cost millions of dollars to build and, since most Ohio farmers had modest incomes in the 1860s, none followed Jenning's lead in the circular design.

It would take two influential college professors — New York's Elliot Stewart and Wisconsin's Franklin King — to advance the cause of the round barn. Stewart's journey began in western New York. The town of Hamburg, named after Hamburg, Germany, lies in the western part of Erie County, directly south of Buffalo, and was established in 1812. Early settlers arrived in 1803. According to the *History of Hamburg, NY,* published by the Boston History Company in 1898, one of its prominent citizens was a Professor Elliot W. Stewart. By the late 1800s several summer resorts had sprung up along the nearby shores of Lake Erie.

Stewart, born in 1817 in Madison County in upstate New York, became a lawyer, married in 1845 and moved the next year to Erie County. After practicing law for several years, he apparently got tired of this occupation, according to his own words in *Feeding Animals: A Practical Work Upon The Laws Of Animal Growth,* a book he self-published in 1883. He wrote, "Thirty years ago, to recruit his health, the author removed from professional labor in the city to a farm in the country." In 1853 he began farming in Erie County and his choice of changing jobs proved to be a good one; he thrived on being a farmer, though it's likely that he supplemented his farming income with legal work.

A student at heart, he loved to read whatever he could on farming, citing the relative lack of agricultural journalism as the reason for his research and his books. He began sharing his ideas in journals and briefly was a non-resident professor of agriculture at Cornell University, a land-grant institution, established in 1865, three years after President Lincoln signed the Morrill Act, which encouraged education in farming. Ithaca was a long journey from Stewart's farm — 160 miles — which might have contributed to his short stay at Cornell.

From 1872 to 1876 he was editor of the *Buffalo Live-stock Journal*, which later became the *National Live-Stock Journal*, where he penned many pieces on agriculture. And possibly having studied Fowler's plans for an octagonal barn — published in 1854 — he built an octagonal dairy barn in 1875 — to replace four rectangular barns that had burned down on his farm a year earlier. In January, 1876, he wrote an article about his new barn, published in the *Buffalo Livestock Journal*. He continued writing and his publications extolled round barn building for many years. However, most farmers were skeptical and stuck with the conventional rectangular shape for their barns.

In his book on feeding animals, Stewart devoted over 40 pages to barn construction, including details on his own octagonal: 80 feet in diameter, an outside wall space of 265 feet, and a total of 5,340 square feet of internal room. He claimed that this single barn easily replaced his four rectangular ones and had 25 percent more storage space than all of them had — with their aggregate of 716 feet, a total that required almost five hundred more feet of wall.

The two-floors of his barn featured a self-supporting roof, which meant that there were no vertical posts, thus providing more room, a break-through in barn design. Hay and feed were stored in the top floor and livestock were housed on the main level — cows, calves, and horses, arranged in two circular rings. His design allowed a wagon to enter the barn and unload hay. The barn's size was sufficient to handle the activity on his 210-acre farm, a typical mid-sized one of the 1870s.

Stewart argued that a 90-foot-diameter octagonal barn could house 114 head of cattle and that it was more efficient and less expensive than a comparable rectangular one. Still, he explained, larger barns would be better suited to a 12- or 16-sided design. In his book he also commented on square and rectangular barns, explaining that a long, parallel barn was ideal for raising sheep. However, even though he was surely aware of the Shaker barn and might have been familiar with Jeffersonian buildings, he did not recommend a circular design — because such construction was more difficult and, accordingly, more expensive.

By 1884 Stewart wrote that he was aware of 30 to 40 octagonal barns, many in New York state but some as far away as Mississippi. In fact, several barns built in the 1880s in Iowa and some in Kansas, still existing, bear the stamp of Stewart's octagonal design. One Iowa farmer, who didn't take his inspiration from Stewart was Lorenzo Coffin, who built an octagonal barn in 1867.

Born in New Hampshire and educated in Ohio, Coffin moved to Fort Dodge, Iowa, in 1854 and began farming. Why he built an octagonal barn in 1867 is anyone's guess, but he did. Even though lumber was scarce in western states, Coffin, having been exposed to the many timber-framed barns in Ohio, cut trees on his farm, hewed the timbers, and split wood shingles for the roof. He moved extra lumber from 40 miles away to complete his 68-foot-wide octagonal barn, perfect, in his opinion, for raising livestock.

However, despite pleas from his farming colleagues, he kept his octagonal design under wraps. Though he was the farm editor for the Fort Dodge *Messenger*, Coffin did not publicize his design until 1882 — after Stewart's plans were well known in the farming community. Benjamin Gue, editor of the *Iowa Homestead*, the state's best-read agricultural journal, published excerpts of Coffin's farm column, extolling his octagonal barn in the October, 1882, issue. In the January, 1883, edition of the journal, the editor put Coffin's design on the front page. Several Iowa farmers followed his lead and built octagonal barns, though most, unconvinced, continued to build traditional barns.

Stewart's articles most likely were read by a Wisconsin carpenter, Ernst Clausing, who built 14 octagonal barns in southern Ozaukee County in the late 1890s, according to the Ozaukee County Historical Society. Many were built within a mile of Lake Michigan, known for its vicious winds, a test for Clausing's octagonal barn. Some still exist.

Additionally, the round and octagonal shape attracted attention in farming communities and these shapes appeared in exposition buildings and in county fairgrounds, beginning with New York's Crystal Palace, the country's first and most famous exposition building, built in 1853. The St. Louis Fair Association featured an octagonal building in the 1850s and other states followed, continuing into the Great Depression, when Wyoming's round octagonal stone barn was built in 1939 on its fairgrounds. About 15 years after Stewart's octagonal barn, the round barn phenomenon evolved once again, this time into a true circular form.

5. THE CIRCULAR BARN

Born in 1848 near Whitewater, Wisconsin, Franklin Hiram King took Stewart's octagonal design one step further. Was he aware of the 1826 round stone Shaker barn in Massachusetts and the 1858 Nutwood round brick barn in Ohio? Maybe. Since he read widely, he might have seen the round barn chapter in John W. McArthur's book, *New Developments*, published in 1886. McArthur built a 16-sided barn — nearly circular — in 1883 in Delaware County, New York. Strongly influenced by the Shaker barn, McArthur designed a 60-foot-wide haymow, centrally located and rising to all three levels of the barn. His book featured diagrams of this plan. However, at that time the octagonal design was still the most popular in New York.

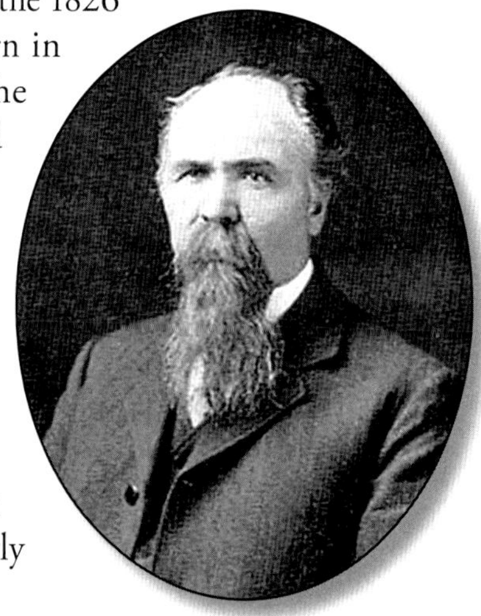

Franklin Hiram King

In his first job King taught science for three years in high school in Berlin and during the summers he experimented with agriculture. He worked for the Wisconsin Geological Survey from 1873 to 1876 and in the fall of 1876 he spent two years at Ithaca's Cornell University, where he may have either met Elliot Stewart or learned about his octagonal barn. At Cornell he studied entomology, perhaps motivated by Wisconsin's changing from wheat farming to dairy, a shift caused in part by harmful insects.

According to research by author John Hanou, King's interest in agriculture, combined with his aptitude in science, continued and in 1887 he visited 58 farms with silos, which were mostly wooden squares or rectangles (Franklin H. King personal notebook located in Steenbok Library Archives, Madison, Wisconsin). However, King's ideas for silos revolved around the circle. Finally, he had his chance to experiment.

His brother Charles, who farmed near their boyhood home in Whitewater, sent King a letter, asking him to design a barn that would house 80 cows and 10 horses with cleaning and feeding alleys — all under one roof and as economically as possible. Charles also wanted a granary and a silo. So, Professor King, who taught from 1888 to 1901 at what is now the University of Wisconsin in Madison, responded with a circular barn design with the silo in the center. This barn featured an entrance on the ground level — for livestock — and a built-up ramp to the upper level — for loading hay. It was finished in 1889.

King's barn had a diameter of 92 feet, a balloon-framed roof, supported by a silo — the first time a silo had been built in the barn's center. Unlike Stewart, King published his novel design right away in the 1890 *Annual Report* of the Wisconsin Agricultural Experiment Station, where he worked. He enthusiastically wrote that he thought the design "to be worthy of general imitation."

However, he was also interested in a self-supporting roof and so in 1892 he did another experiment: a 28-foot diameter barn on his own farm in Madison, the first design to employ a circular purlin plate, a series of laminated rings, to support the roof, making it truly self-supporting.

King's *Barn for a Dairy Farm*, first published in 1890, spread through agricultural journals, including New York's influential, *Hoard's Dairyman*, which reprinted King's plan in 1895. Gradually a small percentage of farmers began to build round barns, based on the greater volume-to-surface ratio and less lumber required, compared to building a traditional barn. Advocates also claimed that round barns withstood wind better, which was a constant threat in prairie states.

In his article, *Construction of Silos*, published by his university in 1891, King also promoted his modification of the silo from square to round, a concept that would prevent spoilage. Also, placement of the silo in the center of the barn protected silage against cold temperatures, a constant in northern winters. The central feeding and waste removal appealed to dairy farmers, especially in Wisconsin, which had become a dairying state by 1900. Professor King also invented an effective gravity system of ventilation for barns, that he called the "King System of Ventilation," still used today.

In his later years and as his work gained national attention, King became head of the U.S. Bureau of Soils, Division of Soil Management, from 1901 to 1904. He died in 1911, a time when articles critical of the round barn had begun appearing in agricultural journals. In fact, after

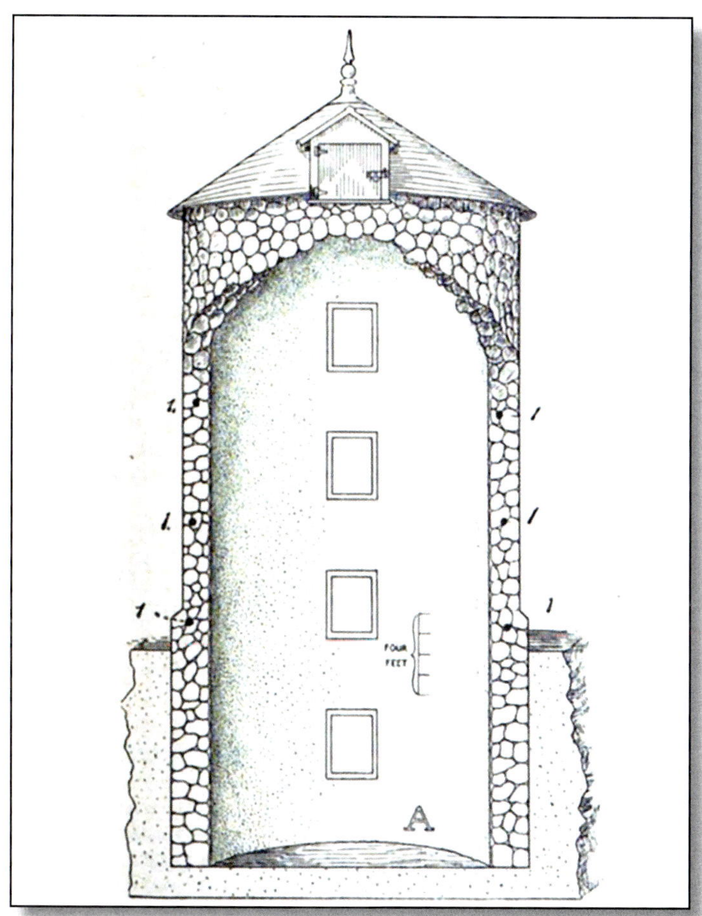

This figure shows an all-stone silo with a conical roof and openings for feeding doors. The heavy black dots show where iron rods could be imbedded in the wall to prevent cracking from the pressure of the silage. From: King, Franklin Hiram, "Silage, and the Construction of Modern Silos," U. of Wisconsin, Agriculture Experiment Station, Bulletin No. 83, Madison, WI, 1900.

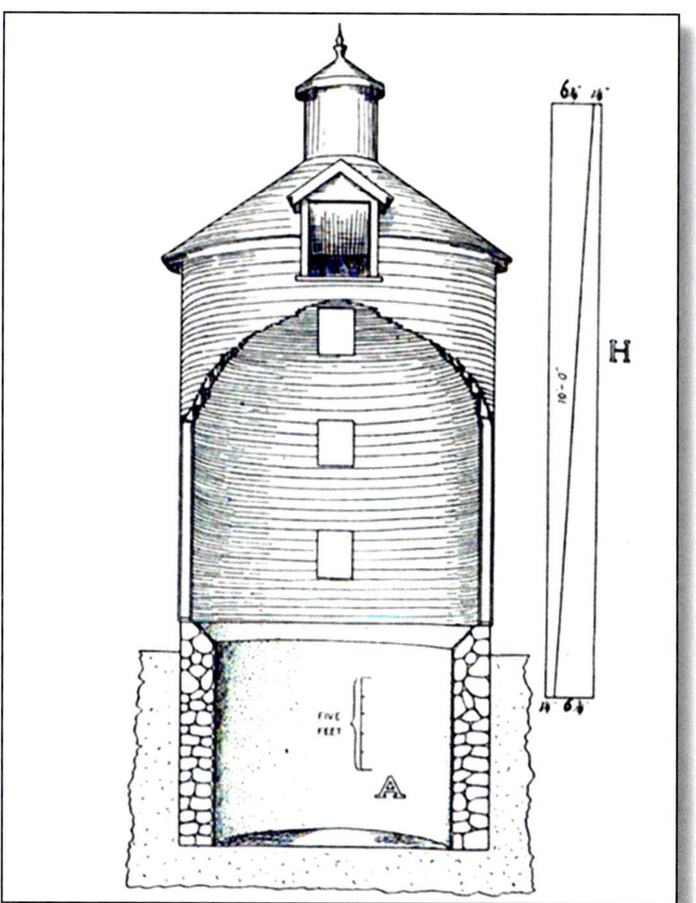

Figure for an all-wood round silo on a stone foundation. The letter H (at right) represents a method of sawing boards for the conical roof. From: King, Franklin Hiram, "Silage, and the Construction of Modern Silos," U. of Wisconsin, Agriculture Experiment Station, Bulletin No. 83, Madison, WI, 1900.

1916 the Wisconsin state agricultural extension service stopped promoting round barns.

Despite this criticism, the University of Illinois became interested in King's round barns and between 1908 and 1910 the university built three round barns at their agricultural campus in Champaign, all designed by Indiana's Benton Steele. After the university published a bulletin, *Economy of the Round Dairy Barn*, in 1911, the round barn builders got a shot in the arm, and continued building their unusual barns throughout the country, though farmers in eastern states failed to be impressed.

Over the next three decades, leading up to the 1930s and the Great Depression, King's round design flourished — especially in the Midwest and western states — thanks to the many innovative and entrepreneurial barn builders, who not only had to be able to build a round barn but had to be proficient at selling the idea to the farmer.

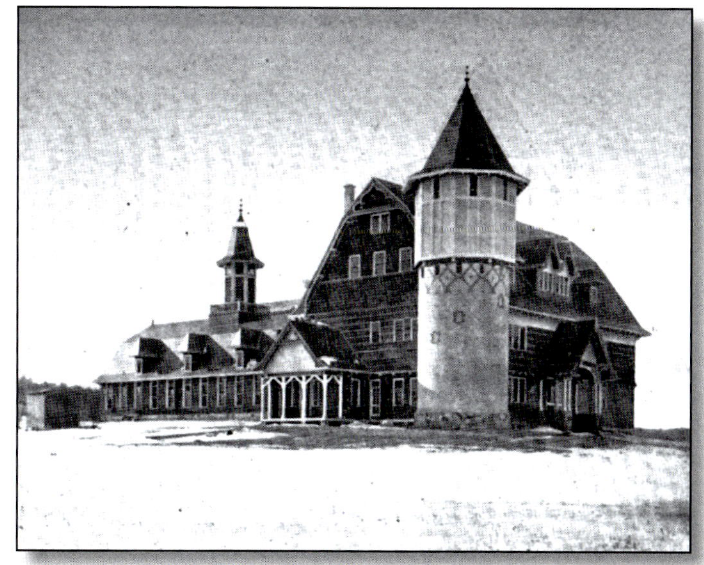

Photo of a brick lined and brick veneered silo with water reservoir for stock above it. From: King, Franklin Hiram, "Silage, and the Construction of Modern Silos," U. of Wisconsin, Agriculture Experiment Station, Bulletin No. 83, Madison, WI, 1900.

6. THE ROUND BARN BUILDERS

After the Revolutionary War, when America transitioned from British colonies to the United States, the young Congress labeled its lands west of Pennsylvania and east of the Mississippi River as the Northwest Territory. Encouraged by land grants, soldiers and other settlers began a western migration, beginning with the Ohio Country, which had relatively easy access via flatboats on the Ohio River and ports along the Lake Erie coastline. General Rufus Putnam and his company founded Marietta in 1788 and other villages came soon after that.

At the time, the Ohio area and lands west of the Great Miami River were vast forests of hardwood trees, which had to be cleared for agriculture, the principal occupation in those days. Thanks to the College of Wooster in Wayne County, Ohio, dendrochronology, the science of dating wood by examining tree ring growth, has shown a date of 1622 (when the tree began growing) in a barn in northeastern Ohio. Another analysis revealed a date of 1683 in a barn in southwestern Ohio. Forests were so thick that many claimed a squirrel could hop from one tree to another and make the journey from eastern to western Ohio without ever touching ground, a far cry from Great Britain, whose forests had been depleted.

Usually, upon arrival, the settler would build a small log house, sometimes to house both the family and livestock, and begin clearing lands for farming. Next came a barn, typically small and made of logs. Later, if successful at farming, the settler would build a timber-framed barn, using skills he learned from prior generations in the old countries.

For most of the 19th century in Ohio and the other midwestern states — especially in the pre-Civil War era — barns were built the old-fashioned way — with broad axes and adzes to hew the trees into beams, T-augers and hand-boring devices to drill holes for wooden peg nails, bow saws and one- or two-man crosscut saws to make barn siding. The builders at first used the difficult scribe rule method to connect the beams, used earlier in Europe, but American ingenuity replaced this with the much easier square rule process which is present in most still existing timber-framed barns.

Often the farmer or a friend or relative would construct the barn, using the age-old mortise and tenon joints, connected with wooden pegs, thanks to knowledge passed down from one generation to the next. When the framework was ready to assemble, the entire community would participate, raising the walls and the roof. Shake shingles were cut from wood, which was another challenge, testifying to the knowledge of these early settlers. Eric Sloane, in his book *Reverence for Wood*, describes not only the tools used by the early settlers but also the many American trees and their uses. These pioneers had to know which wood to use for beams, which ones to use for tools, which ones for shingles, and which ones for barn siding. Hardwoods were plentiful: the oaks, chestnut, yellow poplar, beech, hickory, black walnut, ash, and elm — to name a few.

Occasionally, crews of builders, often Amish or Mennonite, would travel from one village to the next, offering their services. Their barns, many over 150 to 200 years old in the Midwest, have stood the test of time. If, by luck or by design, the builder chose a site on bedrock, not much, except a leaky roof or lightning, would spell the barn's demise. Outside of a detailed family history, these builders are largely forgotten and few before the 1890s are documented.

Today there are timber framing guilds, schools — both in person and online — and books to teach this ancient art. In some regions, notably in Amish or Mennonite communities, barn raising remains a group endeavor. However, power tools have replaced ancient ones, making construction more efficient.

One reason why round barns were not popular is because builders and farm owners were comfortable with the traditional rectangular barn and many felt construction of round barn was more difficult … and accordingly more expensive in terms of man hours. They were correct: round barns required new knowledge. If framed horizontally — instead of vertically — the barn siding had to be flexible and boards were usually soaked in water for days or weeks. Interior wood that had to be curved also had to be flexible. Building a round barn — especially a circular one — ushered in a new era.

The typical round barn builder of 1900 did not have a college degree in architecture nor engineering, though many had backgrounds in carpentry and had become essentially self-taught architects, since unlike the heritage of the timber-framer, their ancestors didn't build round barns. And, though volumes could be written about these often-forgotten men — who deserve a book in their own right — this chapter will give a brief description of only some of them.

In his book, *Barns of the Midwest,* Allen Noble acknowledged that these round barn builders were indeed a new breed and could be divided into four categories. First, there were some who would travel from state to state; secondly, there were some who would build only in their home area; thirdly, some would build only their own barn and perhaps a few others; and lastly, some would buy mail-order kits, which often included plans and materials, even for round barns.

In discussing the individual round barn builders, I've grouped them by states since relying on dates of construction is never foolproof. And, since Professor King was the earliest proponent of circular barns in 1890, his state comes first.

WISCONSIN

Prior to Franklin King's having a round barn built on his brother's farm in 1889, publicizing it in 1890, and building a small experimental barn on his own farm, Wisconsin had polygonal barns. In 1850 the octagonal home proponent and phrenologist Orson Fowler visited this state as he spread his teachings around the country. Some octagonal homes, built in Wisconsin the 1850s, a testament to Fowler's influence, still remain — such as the octagonal house in Watertown, now headquarters of a local historical society and listed on the National Register. And, since Fowler's writings also recommended the octagonal barns — as did Stewart's 25 years later, it's reasonable to assume that's why polygonal barns were built in this region.

One family, the German-American Clausings, built octagonal barns along the shores of Lake Michigan. According to the Ozaukee County Historical Society, they built 10 such barns during the 1880s and into the1890s. In light of the ferocious winds coming off the lake, for these barns to survive for over a century testifies to the builders' skill.

One of the octagonal barns, built by William Clausing in 1890, was threatened by proposed construction of a shopping center in 1978. So rather than let it disappear, the Wisconsin Historical Society dismantled it and moved it to their rural heritage site in Eagle, where the round barn serves as its restaurant and conference site.

Another Clausing, Ernst, together with his brother, also built many octagonal barns in Mequon and Grafton in Ozaukee County. One of them, built in 1891, the Frank Vocke octagonal barn, has been listed on the National Register.

Carl L. Ott, born in Prussia in 1833, immigrated to Leland in 1867 and worked as a blacksmith in his uncle Gottlieb's farm. Carl and his son farmed and, apparently good carpenters, built over 50 barns in the Leland area, including a photogenic octagonal barn that they assembled in 1895 in Honey Creek, Sauk County. Although they might have felt the octagonal design easier to construct, they did follow King's plan in installing a central wooden stave silo. The barn was dismantled in 2012.

One of Wisconsin's most fascinating round barn builders was an African American, Alga Shivers, whose enslaved ancestors moved here from Tennessee after the Civil War. Born in 1889, Algie, as he was known, learned farming and, at only 17 in 1906, he helped build a round barn in Vernon County, located just south of La Crosse. In this county, part of Wisconsin's rugged Driftless Area — not particularly suited to farmland — somewhere between 30 and 40 round barns were built in the early 1900s. Algie Shivers built a lot of them, some of which still stand.

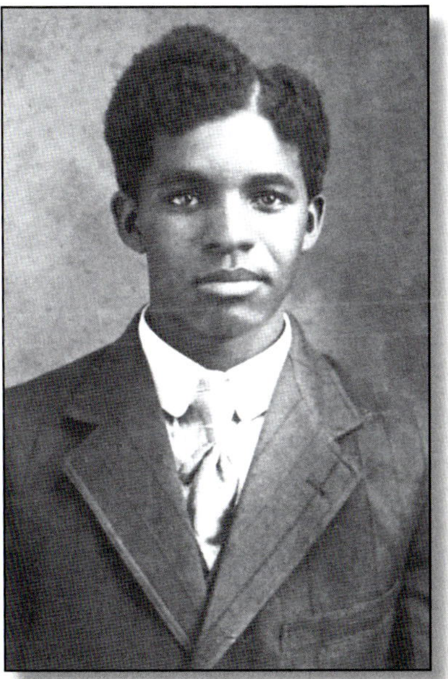
Algie Shivers, courtesy of Town of Forest, Wisconsin

Shivers studied carpentry and engineering at George R. Smith College in Missouri, an all-black institution, served in WWI, survived, and returned to farming in Vernon County. Fifteen round barns in Vernon and Monroe counties are attributed to him and most have vertical siding, which meant he didn't have to soak the lumber. Like other Wisconsin barn builders, Algie would construct a fieldstone foundation, often gathering stones from the farm. He also built conventional barns and other buildings.

However, he seldom worked outside of his county, even though he had offers, since, as a black man in the early 20th century, he wanted to avoid racial incidents. He died, just shy of his 90th birthday in 1978. Two years later his own round barn burned.

ILLINOIS

Since most farmers at the turn of the century had small acreage, they had to be frugal and often were skeptical of round barns, assuming that only wealthy farmers with large holdings could afford them. This meant that the round barn builder had to be a good salesman.

One such person was Jeremiah Shaffer, who, seven years before the University of Illinois built its experimental three round barns, decided to enter the round barn building business, even though he was a schoolteacher. One wouldn't consider an ordinary schoolteacher to be a proficient salesman, but this one was.

With his five brothers-in-law, the Haases, Shaffer began to build round barns in 1901 in the northwestern corner of Illinois — in Ogle and Stephenson counties. This area bordered Wisconsin, which had made the transition from a wheat-producing state to dairying. And round barns, as touted by Professor King, were perfect for dairy farming. In a 1984 multiple submission to the National Register, Stephenson County had 24 round barns at one time, at least 14 built by Shaffer and the Haas brothers. So, although a schoolteacher by occupation, Jeremiah was a convincing salesman.

According to the authors of *Barns of the Midwest*, Shaffer used a clever sales pitch that worked. While sitting at the farmer's kitchen table, he'd show the farmer, the prospective buyer, the advantage of a round barn by using a simple cardboard box. After cutting a rectangle out of it, he'd fill it with oats. Then, he'd shape the same cardboard into a circle, fill it with oats, and, of course, the circle would hold more oats than the rectangle. Simple, easy to understand, and effective.

The agricultural experts at the University of Illinois, a land grant college founded in 1867, probably were aware of Professor King's round barn design in 1890 but failed to act immediately. Even though located in rich farming land, the university needed a prod from one of Indiana's round barn builders, Benton Steele, to enter the round barn craze. By the middle of 1902 Indiana's fledgling assortment of builders had erected at least eight round barns in that state and in early 1902 Steele began advertising his services, which caught the attention of C.B. Dorsey, an agricultural professor at the University of Illinois. Intrigued, he traveled to inspect Steele's barns in Indiana and eventually hired him — and his partner Frank Detraz — to build a round barn on his personal farm. With that success, the University built three experimental barns on their farm between 1908 and 1912 and the head of the department, Wilber Fraser, published bulletin number 143 in 1910. *The Economy of the Round Dairy Barn* provided the kind of publicity Steele and his colleagues had hoped for. In his 44-paged, well-documented essay, Fraser offered several reasons why round barns weren't being built, including, "Another reason for the scarcity of round barns is the difficulty in getting them built. Most carpenters hesitate to undertake the work …" Regardless, his bulletin significantly helped the round barn builders to get work and hundreds, if not thousands were built in the Midwest and western states.

INDIANA

Though Purdue University, a land grant college established in 1869, had advocated round barns as economical in the early 1900s, Indiana's builders of these barns — arguably the best documented of all the barn builders — didn't get a lot of university support. However, thanks to author John Hanou and his books on Indiana's round barns, this state's round barn builders will be remembered.

Credit for Indiana's first circular barn goes to Isaac McNamee, born in 1832 in Ohio, who, with his son Emery, born in 1858 in Indiana, built a barn for William Hill in 1900. A professor of agricultural at the University of Chicago, Hill was willing to experiment with the round design and, perhaps like other well-to-do farmers, he wanted to be different and daring. Though this barn is now gone, it inspired another, built by the McNamees for John Whisler, who lived near Warrington, the home turf of Benton Steele. The three carpenters formed a business relationship that took off when the Whisler barn survived a tornado, prompting its builders to claim that a round barn was essentially immune to high winds.

Although Isaac McNamee built the first circular barn in Indiana (even though polygonal barns preceded his work), Indiana's most deserving round barn builder was Benton Steele. Born near Warrington in 1867 and, like many other children of that era, he had only a third-grade education. Though his family moved to Kansas, he remained in Indiana and worked, as most teenagers did in the early 1870s. Being on his own helped Steele grow up quickly and, working for A.B. Thomas, a wealthy businessman, he likely learned the art of sales.

Through his jobs with contractors, he learned carpentry and found that he had a natural artistic side, being able to draw well enough to make blueprints. He would use both his self-taught drafting skills and salesmanship throughout his career.

It's possible that his love for round buildings started when, at 13, he witnessed the beauty of an octagonal house built around 1880 for his great aunt. Fowler, who had traveled throughout the Midwest, might have been the influence. Regardless of what lit his fire, Steele became interested in construction and, after meeting the McNamees, who built their second round barn near Steele's home in Warrington, he became enamored with this design.

In early 1901 Steele formed a partnership, though perhaps not legally binding, with Samuel "Frank" Detraz, a woodworker, and, together, they presented a plan for a round barn to influential types in Indianapolis. Two of them, Freemont Goodwine, a state senator, and Wymond Beckett, a lawyer and eventual state senator, were impressed. Both hired Steele and his crew to build round barns on their farms. Buoyed by this success, Steele published many articles on building round barns in *Indiana Farmer* between 1903 and 1909 — as well as advertising in agricultural journals throughout the Midwest. For these self-taught architect-builders, business was good in the early 1900s and, thanks to articles written by Steele in agricultural journals and newspapers, orders came in, one of which prompted Steele to assign one of his carpenters, 25-year-old Horace Duncan, to supervise Steele's round barn design in South Dakota.

Later, in the summer of 1902, storms and tornadoes ripped through the towns of Warrington and Pendleton, causing much destruction, though the Whisler round barn, built by the McNamees in 1901, survived. This prompted Steele and the McNamees to call their round barns "cyclone proof," which became an effective part of their advertising since most farmers feared three things: lightning strikes, high winds, and tornadoes. By the end of 1904, these builders — the McNamees, Steele, Detraz, and one of their carpenters-turned-builders, Horace Duncan — had constructed over a dozen round barns.

Demand for round barns in the early 1900s, especially in Indiana, was strong, thanks to these builders, despite criticisms in such journals as the *Breeder's Gazette*. Rather than striking back at these attacks, Steele and Detraz used them to their advantage by publishing a list of solutions in a 1903 issue of *Indiana Farmer*. Orders for round barns continued.

That same year the crew of Steele, Detraz, the McNamees, and Duncan built the largest round barn in Indiana for an Indianapolis attorney, Frank Littleton, who apparently wanted to outdo his friend Wymond Beckett, who hired Steele to build a 100-foot-diameter barn in 1901. Littleton's eclipsed that one by two feet. More importantly, it led to a patent and, later, some fractured relationships.

Since Horace Duncan had made valuable suggestions when building this Steele-designed round barn, some of which may have involved methods for constructing a self-supporting roof, he asked Littleton to submit an application for a patent, which included only Duncan, Littleton, and Isaac McNamee. For some reason, Duncan did not include Steele and Detraz in the patent for this roof, which was approved in 1904. After this, Duncan insisted on financial compensation from other builders of round barns — if they used his patented roof system. His monetary demands did not exclude his mentor Benton Steele.

In years following, Steele and Detraz continued their work not only in Indiana but also in Iowa and Illinois, where they convinced the university's extension to build three round barns, which fueled more positive support, this time coming from an agricultural college. Round barn building continued to flourish in Illinois and adjacent states. However, when Duncan's fellow patent holder Isaac McNamee died in early 1909, Detraz and Steele split up and Steele left Indiana to relocate to Kansas.

In his new location, Steele continued advertising, but only in Kansas agricultural newspapers. He had no intention of returning to deal with Duncan's harassment in Indiana. Steele also worked for Iowa's Louden Company, a major producer of farm equipment, and did round barn designs for mail order kits, sold by the Gordon-Van Tine Company. James R. Shortridge, author of *The Round Barns of Kansas,* reports that, according to two of his granddaughters, Steele helped with buildings other than round barns. These included a high school in Wichita, the Pawnee County courthouse at Larned (official architect, William Hulse), and a dormitory at the state women's prison in Lansing. Though round barn popularity plummeted in the 1920s — as did crop prices — little is known about Steele's last years. Regardless, he deserves the title of "Father of Indiana's Round Barns." He died in 1946.

By 1901 these builders were busy with other round barns, a business that continued through the decade. Emery McNamee moved from town to town, building barns with his crew, though his 70-year-old father Isaac stayed home. According to John Hanou in *A Round Indiana*, Emery and his crew traveled to Canada for work, eventually settling in Montana, where he built round barns, including the Kent barn in 1939.

Duncan, who apparently was a quick learner, absorbed Steele's ideas and plans, yet was innovative enough to provide suggestions, especially regarding a self-supporting roof. Four years after gaining a patent for this roof in 1904, Duncan built his masterpiece, the Manchester round barn in Auglaize County, Ohio, although he might have borrowed Steele's design.

Regardless, this barn, though on private property, is probably the most photographed barn in Ohio. In fact, Duncan was so proud of it, he put its photo on his business envelope in 1911, which also carried the inscription, "Infringers promptly prosecuted. Beware of unscrupulous architects." Above the address side and under his name, Duncan included, "Designer and Builder of the Original Circular Barn with Latest Improvements." Well, even though that statement ignored the work of Professor King and the mentorship of Benton Steele, Duncan liked to refer to himself as "The Round Barn Man." At 33, this promoter extraordinaire was in his prime, though his endless quest to collect payments from barn owners for his patented roof may have been his undoing. With lawsuits and legal threats, there is fear, not conducive to sales, which may have played a role in Indiana's round barn decline.

Further north in Indiana, another round barn builder and his sons continued the round barn phenomenon. Charles V. Kindig, born in 1863 in Fulton County, Indiana, grew up in a family of carpenters. His father Daniel, born in Pennsylvania, married an Ohio lady, moved to Wisconsin and then eventually to Fulton County, where he purchased 80 acres and began farming. In 1910 his son Charles and his sons built their first circular barn in Fulton County for their relatives. Eventually they built 22 more in Indiana.

Today one of their round barns — the Leedy-Partridge-Paxton barn, built in 1924, the last round barn to be built in this county — serves as the Fulton County Round Barn Museum, where the historical society holds annual events. Nearby, the 1910 Wideman-Gerig round barn serves as the pro shop for the Round Barn Golf Club at Mill Creek, owned and operated by the city of Rochester. This county, thanks to the Kindigs and other builders, once had 17 round barns, giving it claim to the title of "Round Barn Capital of the World," to which Wisconsin's Vernon County graciously acquiesced. According to the website, *Driftless Wisconsin*, Vernon County once had nearly twice as many as the 17 round barns still existing there.

However, Indiana is still a hot bed of existing round barns, often sharing them with the rest of the country. In 2008 the Kindig's first round barn, built in 1910 for Elmer and Lola Wideman, was disassembled and shipped for reconstruction to Martha's Vineyard. The Huffman round barn, built in 1912, was also sold and was shipped to Baroda, Michigan, where the Moersch family has turned it into the centerpiece of their Round Barn Winery.

IOWA

Another state, though known more for corn than dairy, played a role in the story of round barns. One of its strongest disciples was Lorenzo Coffin, who built an octagonal barn in 1867 but didn't publicize it until 1882, well before Professor King's round barn epiphany.

Today, Iowa has many entries of round barns on the National Register, including a handsome circular barn with walls built with vitrified clay tile, located in Dubuque

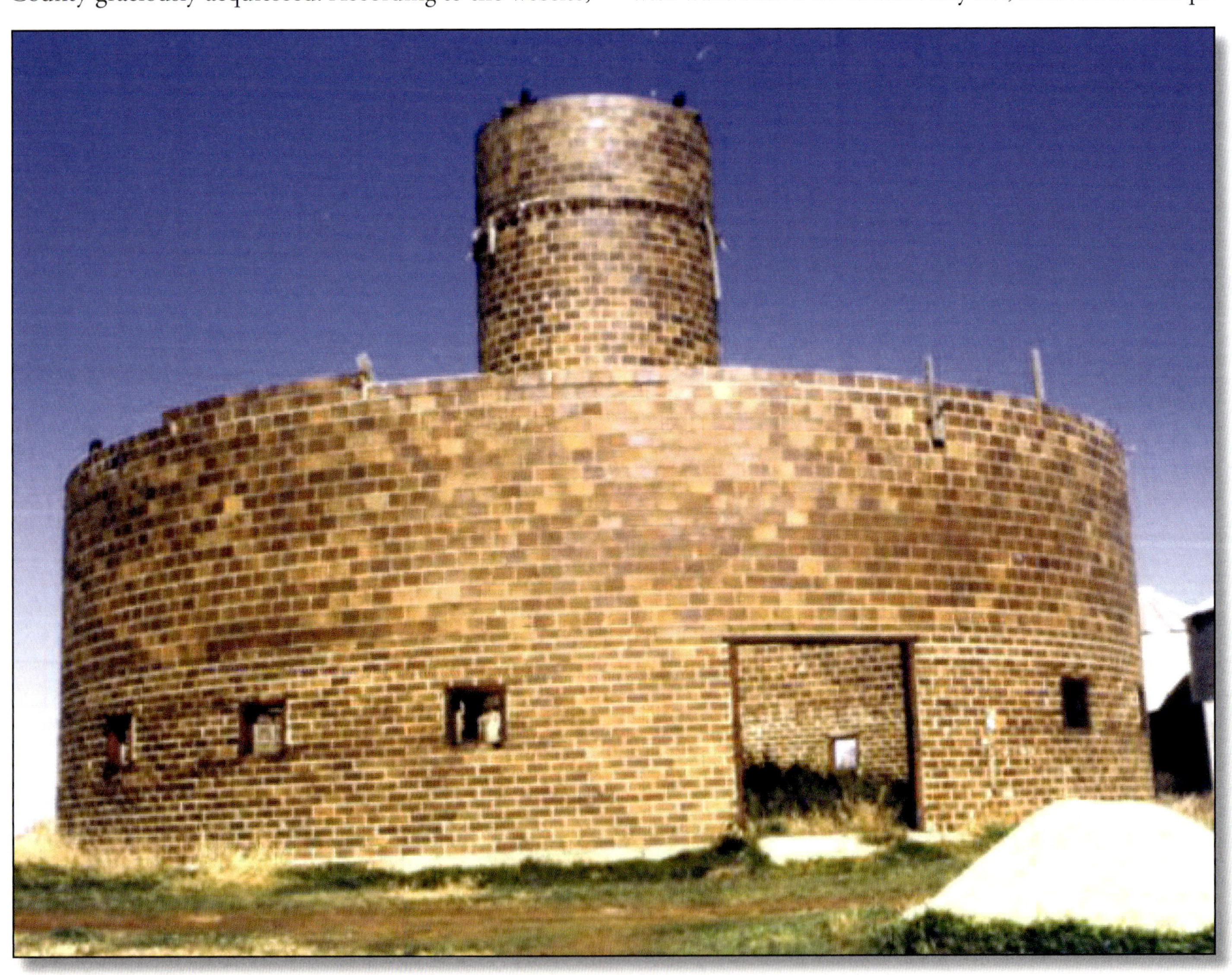

Iowa round barn, tile skeleton, Hancock County. Dale Travis website, Don Burnell

County. In fact, the use of tile may have originated in Iowa, an innovation that proved successful, even when the round barn roof failed, leaving a skeleton framework of tile walls and central silo behind, as in the case of this circular barn, built in 1915 in Hancock County.

Although rectangular barns dominated Iowa farms, at one time there were about 160 circular and polygonal barns in the state. When Iowa's historical society submitted its multiple nomination for inclusion into the National Register in 1986, 106 round barns existed. Since then many have disappeared. Some of those still standing are marvelous pieces of architecture

OHIO

A diverse farming state in the 19th century, Ohio never caught the round barn fever and today only about two dozen round barns remain. One reason for this could have been an article in a 1906 edition of the *Ohio Farmer*, written by a farmer unhappy with his round barn. He claimed that building it cost six times what a rectangular barn would have cost and that, after it was finished, he was left with a "large two-horse wagonload of small blocks." Other writers were just as critical.

Joseph E. Wing, editor of *The Breeder's Gazette*, began publishing negative comments about round barns from the early 1900s. Over the next 10 years more agricultural experts denounced the so-called advantages of the round barns, which kept their numbers low.

However, even though Ohio has relatively few rounds when compared to its fellow midwestern states, some of its barns are majestic. The eye-catching Manchester barn in Auglaize County is a photographer's dream and, a bit further to the south, Nutwood Place, a circular barn built in 1858, is a national treasure — with an equally compelling story. Ohio's only 16-sided barn is one of its most beautiful, though hidden in the hills of Harrison County, and the rare stone octagonal barn in Clark County is one of only three such barns in the country.

One spot where the round barn craze found success was in Perry County, where four circular barns were built, all within five miles of one another. Three still exist. In nearby Fairfield County the impressive round barn in the fairgrounds has delighted visitors for over a century. Elsewhere in the state are a other examples, though the names of their builders may never be known.

MAIL ORDER ROUND BARNS

Montgomery Ward sold pre-cut lumber kits for barns as did Sears, Roebuck and Company, which offered a round barn design in their catalog of barn kits in 1911. Others followed, including Iowa's Louden Machinery and the Gordon—Van Tine Company. The former began by offering only round barn blueprints but eventually sold pre-cut kits to keep up with its competition. Another Iowa company, Permanent Buildings Society of Des Moines, designed round barns but sold the plans only.

One of the more interesting companies, The Chicago House Wrecking Company, despite its ominous title, did very well, especially in selling homes. However, in time it changed its name to Harris Brothers. One of their round barns still stands in Nuckolls County, Nebraska.

Though it's unknown how many round barns were built from such kits and are still standing, it's reasonable to say that buying a kit of lumber and blueprints was easier, faster, and less expensive than hiring a round builder architect, such as Benton Steele, Horace Duncan, or C.V. Kindig. Many farmers simply hired local carpenters or built the barn with relatives. Some still survive.

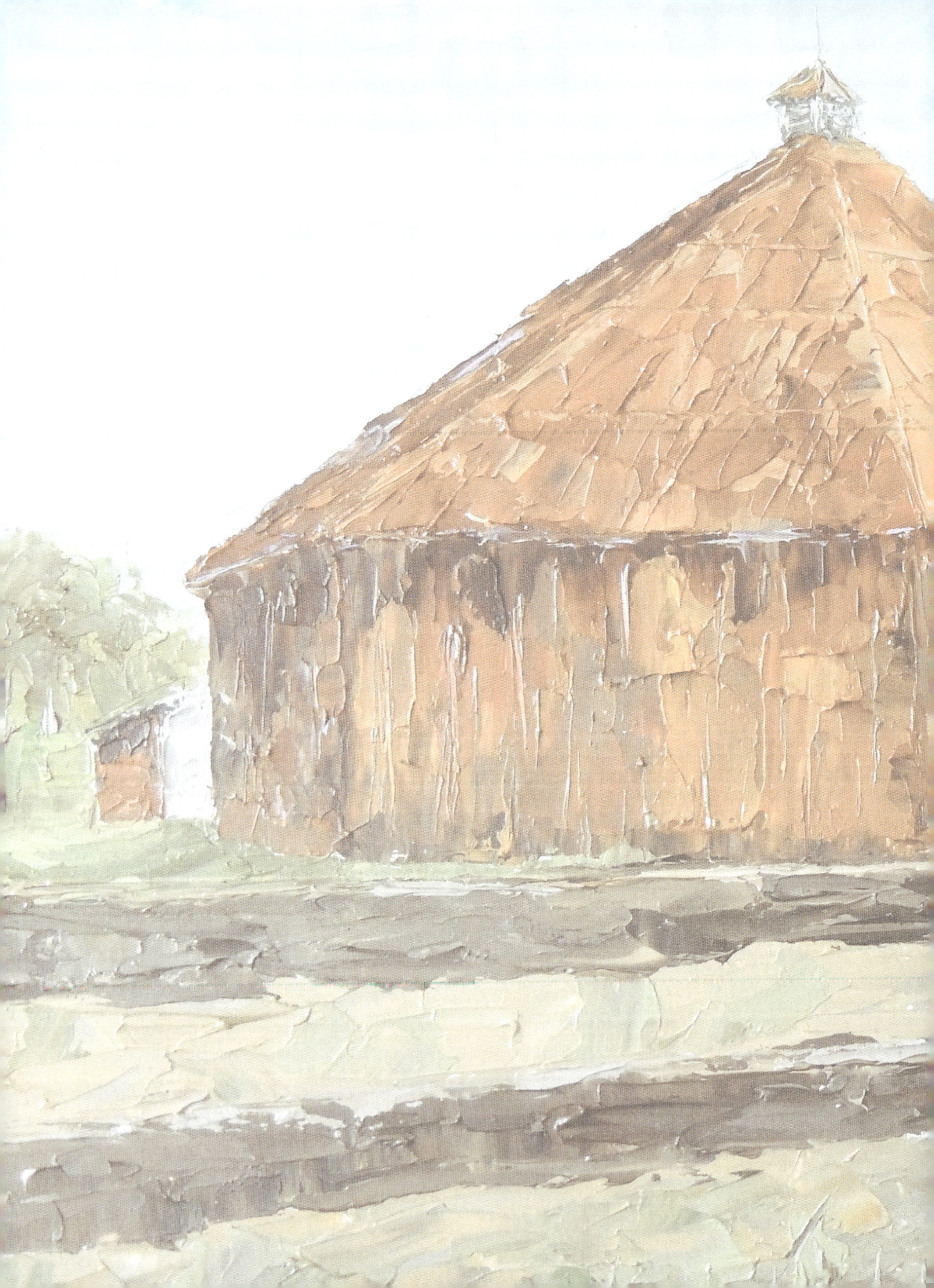

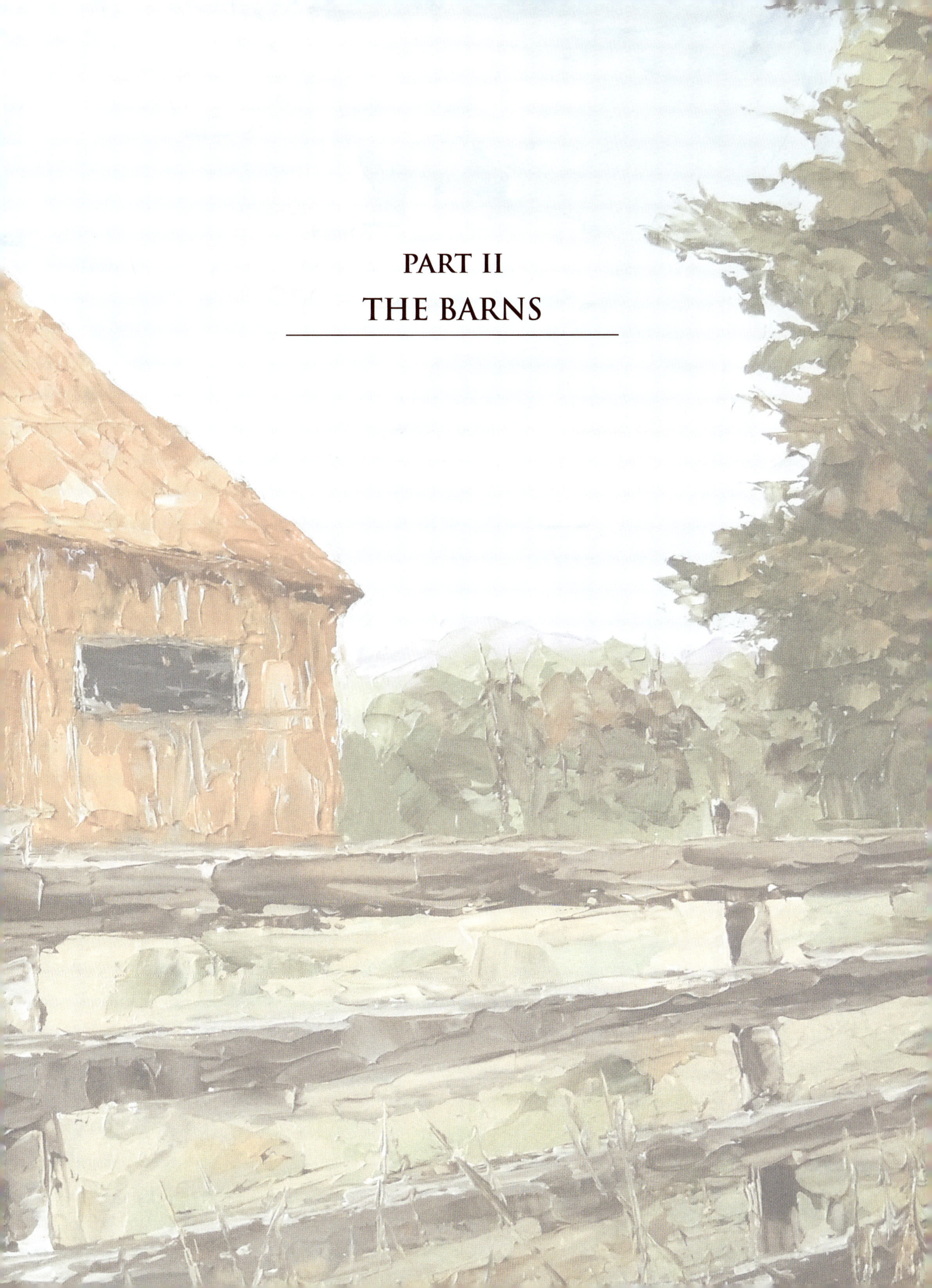

PART II
THE BARNS

REGIONAL MAP

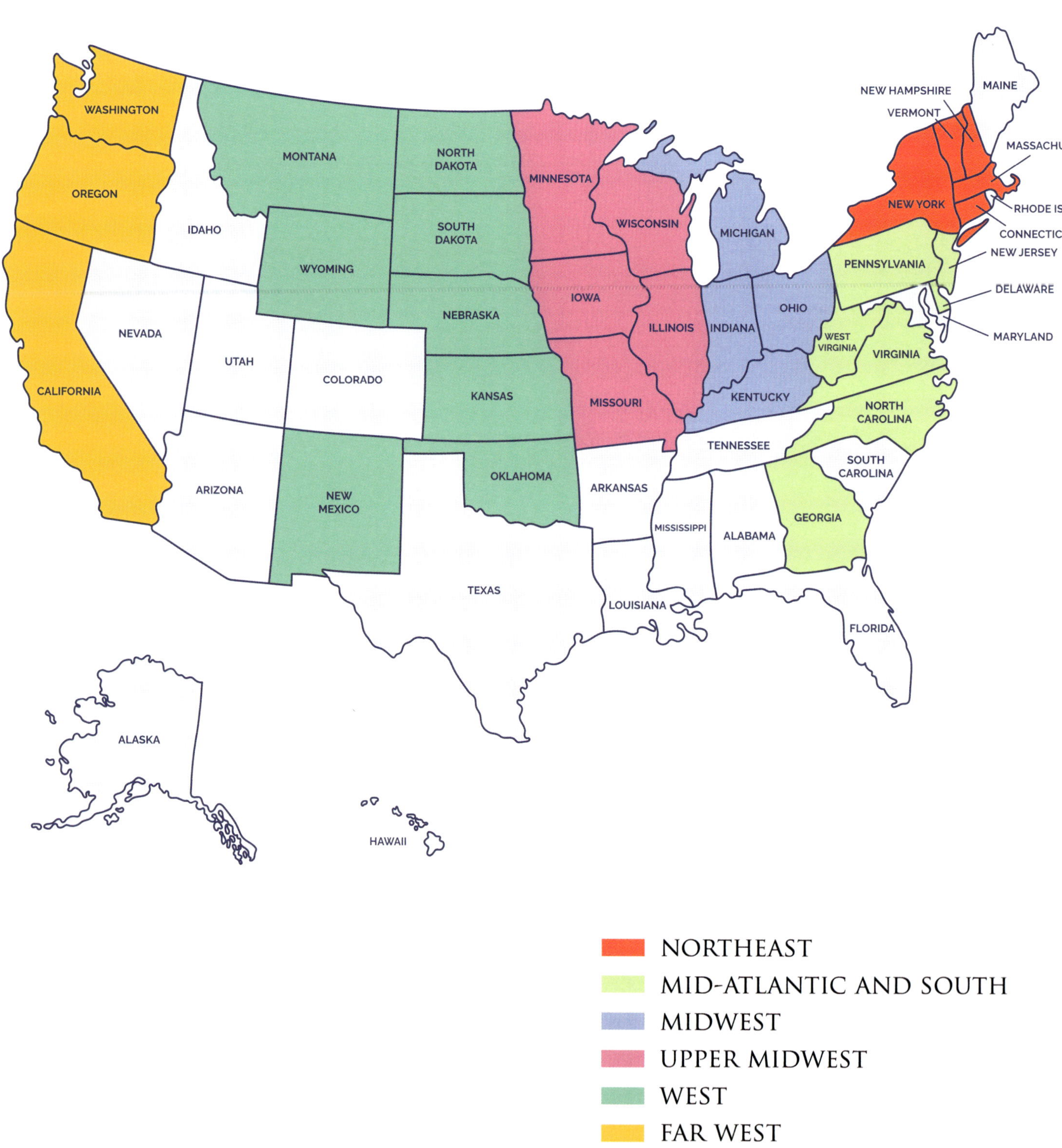

Opposite: *Belvidere's Bounty*

7. NORTHEAST

With the exceptions of Virginia's early 16-sided barn, built by George Washington in 1794, and the famous circular stone barn, built in 1826 by the Shakers in Massachusetts, the round barns of New York took the lead in developing this unique design. In fact, the earliest round barn still existing in America was built there; so, it's a good place to begin.

NEW YORK

ALLEGANY COUNTY

Belvidere's Bounty

Belvedere, a town in the southeastern section of London, may have been the source of the name of this estate in western New York — since the farmstead was established by an Englishman who, for a few years, was a member of Parliament — after the Revolutionary War. The term comes from the Italian, meaning an architectural structure that takes advantage of a beautiful view. Indeed, it's a tranquil setting — the Genesee River winds through the expansive valley behind the house.

This remote region was wilderness in 1788, when Jared Broughton and his brother Enos purchased the town of Victor (present Ontario County), which was formerly a 17th-century Seneca Village (*History of the Pioneer Settlement of Phelps and Gorham's Purchase, and Morris' Reserve*, by Orsamus Turner, published in 1850). It was raw country, one that land speculators, often from Great Britain and Europe, hoped to take advantage of: in 1789 Oliver Phelps and Nathaniel Gorham opened one of the first regular land offices in the young United States. By comparison, a year earlier, the Ohio Company of Associates, also land speculators and led by General Rufus Putnam, established the town of Marietta and built the first land office in the Northwest Territory. Of

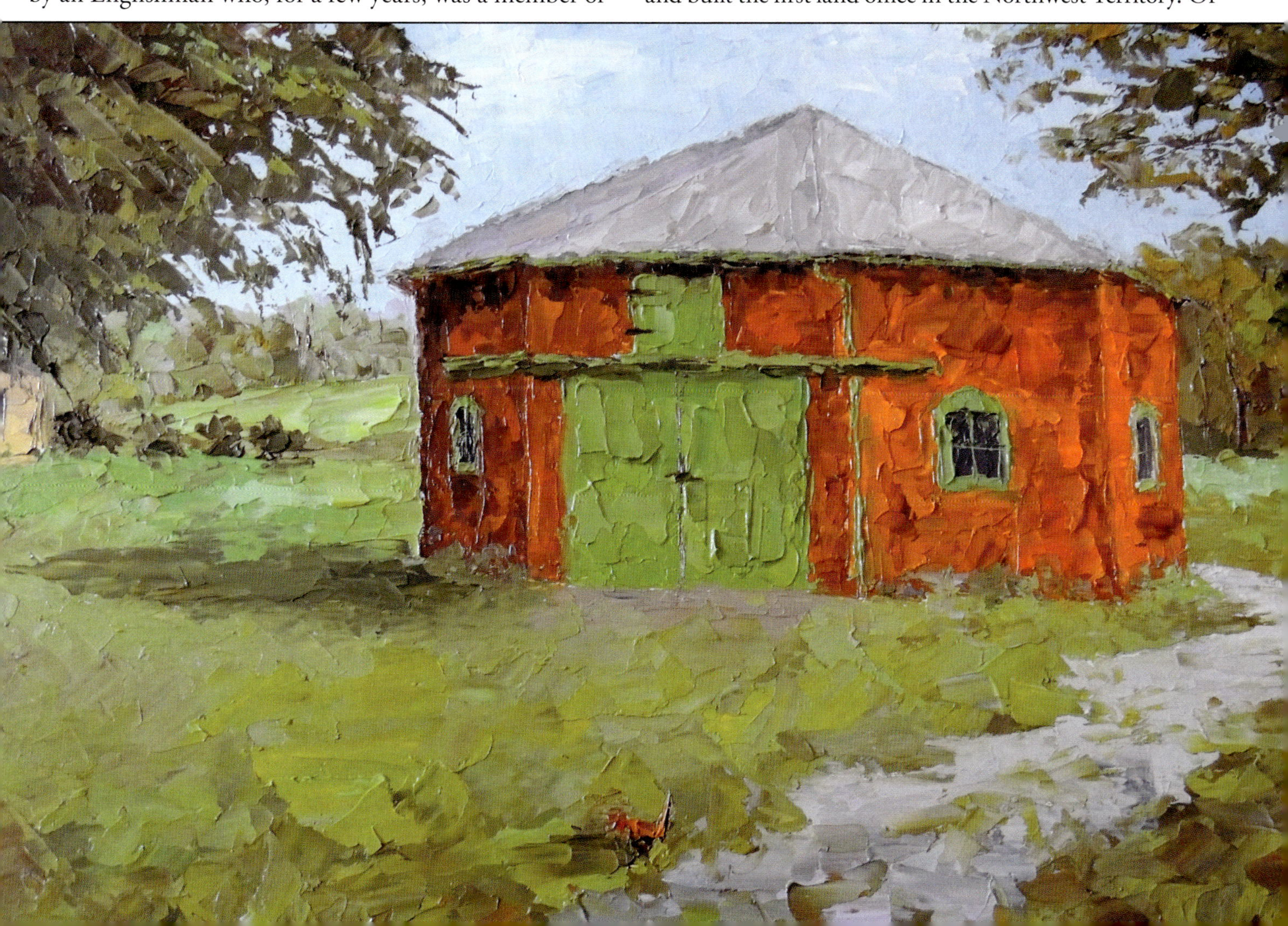

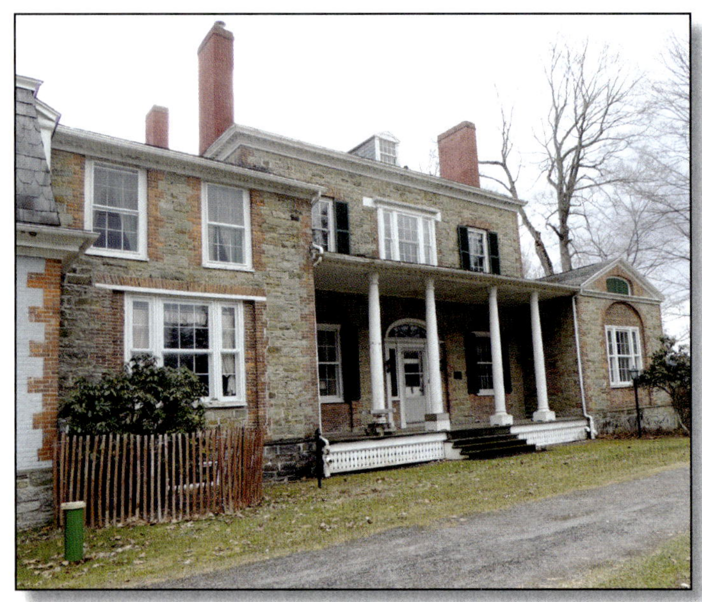

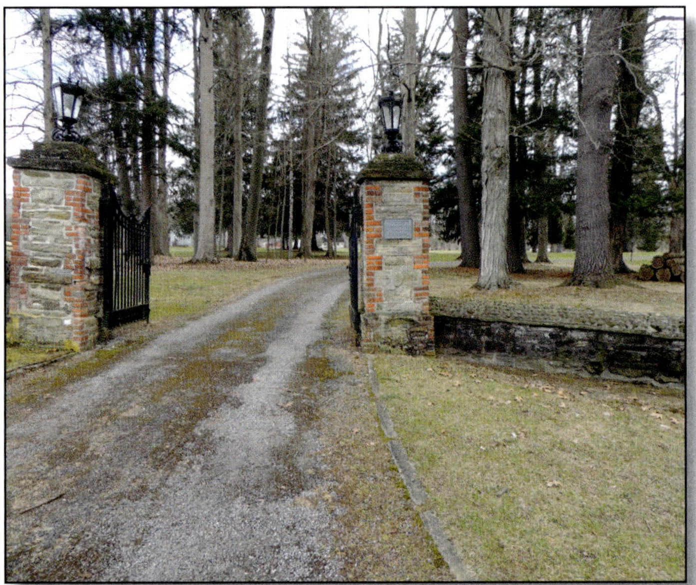

Villa Belvidere, Angelica, New York, 2022. The entrance is shown at right.

course, travel to Marietta by flatboat on the Ohio River, was much easier than reaching Victor or Angelica, New York, where this round barn was built in 1804.

Though Phelps and Gorham purchased millions of acres east and west of the Genesee River after the Revolutionary War, hard times forced them to sell hundreds of thousands of acres in 1791 to Robert Morris, signer of the Declaration of Independence and financial genius of the Revolutionary War. However, Morris, another land speculator, also ran into financial problems, and sold much of his land. Profits from this sale allowed him to buy land west of the Genesee River, which is where this round barn was built and still stands today.

Sir William Pulteney and partners purchased land east of the river from Robert Morris and hired fellow Englishman Charles Williamson to manage their lands. Innovative, he established a sales office in Bath, New York, and, in 1792, he began advertising land for a dollar per acre, provided the purchaser would settle there. The next year, again showing his creative marketing, Williamson held a number of fairs and horse races, once offering a first-place prize of £1,000, a small fortune in 1793. However, his efforts over the next decade failed to attract enough settlers who were hardy enough to persevere in this wild country. According to Daniel Fink in his voluminous *Barns of the Genesee Country*, Williamson died of yellow fever on a trip to England. His village was empty and only a cemetery remains today. On the other hand, in nearby Allegany County, Philip Church, builder of this round barn, was determined to make his father's land gamble work.

This nine-sided barn, a nonagonal curiosity, lies near the tiny town of Angelica in this rural county, about 70 miles south of Buffalo and 130 miles east of Erie, Pennsylvania. After Washington's 16-sided barn of 1794, this one, built 10 years later circa 1804, is the next documented round barn. It tells a fascinating tale of early Americans.

The 1,350-acre farmstead — with its showpiece, Villa Belvidere, a mansion built on plans of an architect name Probst — was listed on the National Register in 1972, submitted by then owners Robert and Marian Bromeley. However, although several sources intimate that Latrobe designed the mansion, this is not true. In fact, a historian and author of a book on Latrobe visited the estate and explained that this was not Latrobe's work, according to Don Fredeen.

The National Register listing also included a hexagonal tea house, built in 1806. I discovered this marvelous treasure in *Round Barns of New York*, a book written by Richard Triumpho and published in 2004 by Syracuse University Press. Though the author called the barn an anomaly, he agreed with another researcher that the barn was built soon after construction was begun on the villa in 1804. This predates the round Shaker barn in Massachusetts by two decades and New York's Bronck 13-sided barn by almost three decades. These three are the oldest existing round barns in America.

After nearly three years of research, I was rewarded with a visit in late March, 2022, and met Don Fredeen and his wife Pam, a granddaughter of the Bromeleys, who purchased the estate in 1947. My visit began with a drive through the gated entrance, flanked by two pillars, constructed with sandstone and brick, matching the stonemasonry in the manor house and the barn. The long stone fence, though not tall, was elegantly capped with cobblestones.

The story began with John Barker Church, born into an affluent aristocratic family in 1748 in England, son of Richard Church and Elizabeth Barker. A wealthy uncle on his mother's side, John Barker, director of the London Assurance Company, established John in the business world. But, alas, gambling and stock market speculation forced him into bankruptcy in August, 1774. So, with cash and strong political connections, he fled his creditors in England and came to the colonies, changing his name to John Carter and apparently relying on the Church-Barker pedigree to endear him into British society.

And, being in the right place at the right time and on the right side, in July, 1776, he became one of three commissioners appointed by the Continental Congress — to audit accounts of the fledgling army. His transition in only two years from bankruptcy in England to this important job in a revolutionary government, while lost in history, was astounding. However, a year later he resigned his commission and moved to Boston, where apparently John Carter was safe from his English creditors and flush with money. With a knack for business, he established a number of companies in banking and shipping. He also speculated in currency and land, as many wealthy folks did in that era.

According to Pam, Carter initially did business with the Livingstons, cousins of Angelica Schuyler, but later teamed up with Colonel Jeremiah Wadsworth of Connecticut, yet another land speculator with interests in the Genesee River valley. During the Revolutionary War, Church and Wadsworth made a fortune by first supplying French troops (who paid in gold and silver) and then the entire American army.

In 1776, Carter first met the attractive 20-year-old Angelica, a prominent socialite and daughter of the American general Philip Schuyler, during a visit to their mansion. After falling in love, the couple decided to elope in 1777 since General Schuyler was suspicious of Carter's past and would not bless the marriage. "Carter and my eldest daughter ran off and married ... the match was exceedingly disagreeable to me." However, their marriage succeeded in producing eight children, including a son, Philip Schuyler Church, born in 1778. (Much of this story comes from three large notebooks of letters from Angelica, Alexander Hamilton, Thomas Jefferson, and others, which Pam painstakingly found in many historical libraries.)

After the war ended, according to a letter written by Wadsworth, John had repaired relations with the Schuylers — presumably with his English creditors, too — since he now was wealthy. John Barker Church also changed his business name to Wadsworth and Church and in 1783 he took his family to Paris, where he served as U.S. Envoy to the French government. At the time, Thomas Jefferson, having lost his cherished wife a year earlier, had accepted ambassadorship to France, where his love of neoclassical design, specifically the octagon, could flourish. Thanks to Pam's diligent research, copies of many letters show that Angelica, who was friends with Jefferson, shared someone in common with him — Maria Cosway, a socially prominent Italian-English artist. Since these three spent two years together in Paris, chances are good that Jefferson shared his penchant for octagonal buildings with them. Other letters — to and from Alexander Hamilton — show his affection for Angelica, proving that she was one of the few people who was friends with both Hamilton and Jefferson, according to Pam.

Why Church left the young United States, after helping the war effort and making considerable income from it, is anyone's guess. Perhaps he felt that life in London or Paris was far more civilized than living in England's former colonies. Regardless, in 1788 Church bought a home in England so that he could run for Parliament, another strange twist in this entrepreneur's life. The investment in the house turned out to be worth it when he was elected a member of England's governing body in 1790, which is also puzzling. Why would Englishmen elect someone who not only served on the American side during the war but also profited handsomely from it? Now, with power and money, he sent his son Philip to Eton, where he studied for six years. Having named him after Angelica's famous father, the parents wanted him to succeed. Meanwhile, John Church continued to speculate in stocks and land.

In 1796 he loaned a large amount of money to financier Robert Morris, Jr., and accepted a mortgage on 100,000 acres of land that today lies in the counties of Allegany and Genesee in western New York, which, in those days was sheer wilderness. Morris was a signer of both the Declaration of Independence and the United States Constitution (and one whom many consider to have been the financial genius of the Revolution). At the end of the war Washington selected Morris to be the first Secretary of the Treasury but Morris declined, instead suggesting Alexander Hamilton for the role, which he accepted. Instead, Morris, at this time, one of the wealthiest Americans, had grander ambitions. After he left his government position, he helped found a national bank, set up a tobacco company, and started other businesses. But his major passion — as well as his Achilles heel — was land speculation. At one point, he owned millions of acres from Pennsylvania to the Kentucky region and into the rural South, more land than any other American has ever owned. Unfortunately, his land sales didn't keep up with his purchases, a business partner caused problems, and eventually Morris, land rich but cash poor and unable to pay his many creditors, went to debtors' prison, where he remained for over three years. He died, penniless, in 1806. His death didn't merit a funeral.

When Morris couldn't make payments on this note, Church foreclosed on his "friend," despite his having been a founding father of the United States. In the spring of 1800 John Barker Church, by now one of the wealthiest men in the country, sent his son Philip to collect on the Morris tract of 100,000 acres near the Genesee River in western New York, wooded wilderness and land of the Senecas. But, since John Church was not a native-born citizen and hadn't attained land rights, his son was given the deed and half the ownership in the land. His part of the deal was to establish a village and subdivide the acreage for lot sales.

Philip, now only 22 and a major landowner in this young country, hoped to sell land to settlers moving west in the new country (especially the French elite, fleeing from France). But this land was remote and not close to a major river or road, which made transportation difficult.

Earlier, Philip had begun his career as a captain in the U.S. Army during the minor, undeclared war against France in the Caribbean islands, which lasted from 1798 to 1800. He served as aide-de-camp to Alexander Hamilton, his uncle, who had married Angelica's younger sister, Elizabeth. Hamilton, then a major general, was second in command behind George Washington, and, after Washington's death in 1799, Hamilton briefly became commander of American forces. Four years later he died in the infamous duel with Aaron Burr, a rogue that John Church had dueled previously.

Still single, Philip traveled with his surveyor, Moses Van Campen, a Revolutionary War hero, and four others to his newly acquired land in 1801 and selected a site alongside the Genesee River for a village, which he named Angelica. He designed it, based on his knowledge of the 12 avenues radiating from the Arc de Triomphe of Paris. Today in Angelica, New York, five streets radiate from a circular park, named Angelica Park Circle. Though Philip had already established it, the town was formally acknowledged in 1805, the oldest in the county. Philip built a sawmill and a grist mill in 1803 and opened the area for settlement, hoping to attract settlers by building a mansion, which would show them that the area provided a safe and prosperous lifestyle. The image below shows a map of the Church property (small dark rectangle in upper left), which the family gave to prospective buyers.

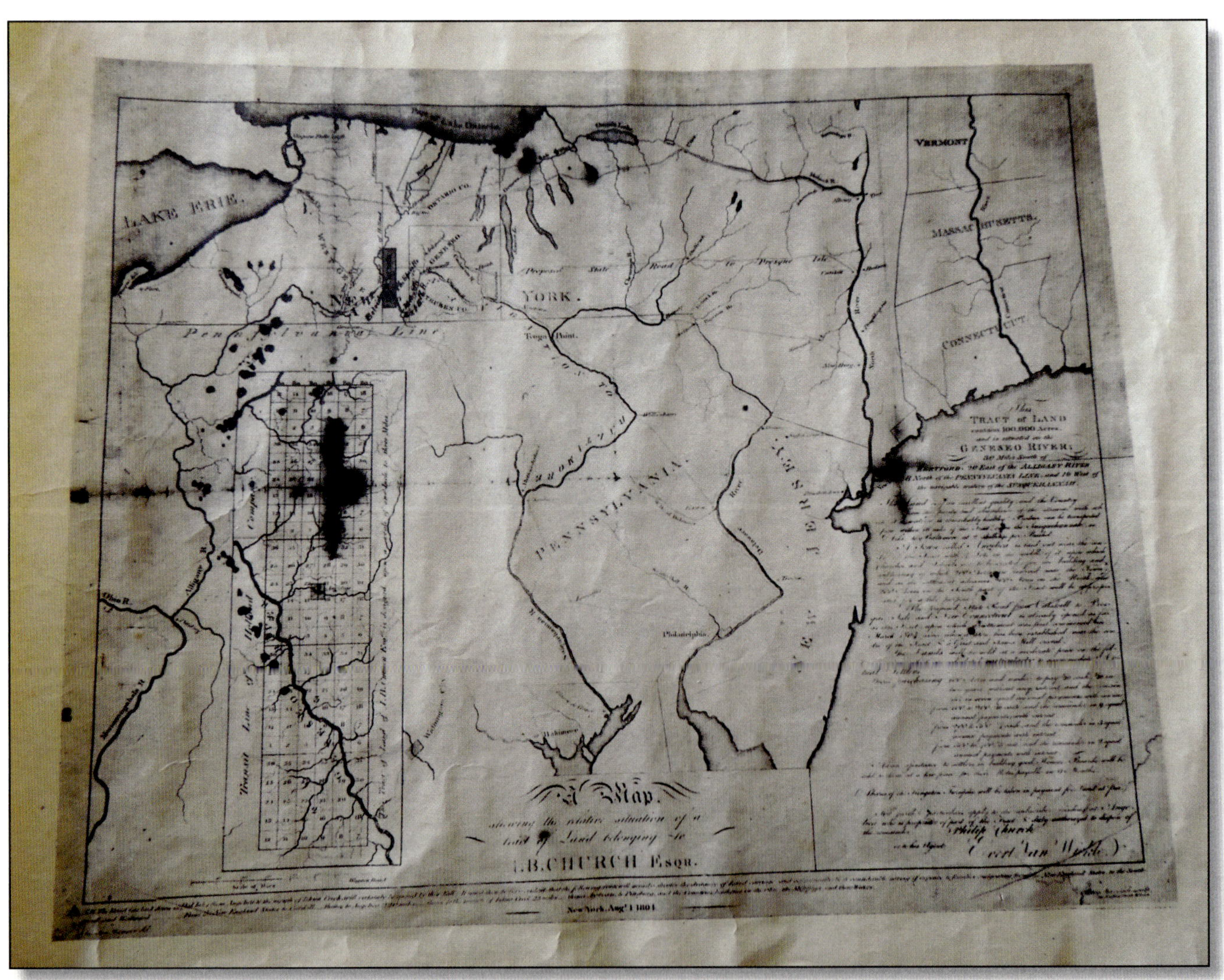

Prospectus map of Church land, August 1, 1804. Courtesy of Fredeen family.

Having decided to marry and raise a family in this new town, Philip returned to Philadelphia, where he married Anna Matilda Stewart, daughter of General Walter Stewart, a Revolutionary War veteran, who fought in the decisive Battle of Yorktown. They decided to spend their honeymoon in Angelica, traveling there first by boat, then by raft as far west as Bath, and finally on horseback. On one trip, Philip brought a flock of 24 sheep, good livestock for a cold climate, but wolves devoured 19 of them on the first night in the wilderness. Getting to this land was not as simple as taking a flatboat down the Ohio River.

To check on the progress of this real estate venture, John and Angelica visited their son and his new wife Anna, who was adapting to life in the wilderness after living in Philadelphia's high society, which must have been a dramatic change for her. However, she made friends with the Seneca Indians, who later protected her when Philip was gone on trips.

During their summer visit, the nine-sided barn was built and, according to Winifred Thornton in *A History of the Church Mansion, Belvidere,* Angelica designed the barn. Since the date of 1806 is ascribed to the six-sided tea house, which has recently been rebuilt, she probably designed the barn earlier since having a barn was far more important than having a tea house. Author Daniel Fink, in *Barns of the Genesee Country,* stated that the barn was built soon after they started working on the house in 1804. Philip, who would oversee the construction of the mansion, was likely in charge of building the barn, as well.

In spite of such logistical difficulty, settlers arrived and, by 1803, log cabin homes — including Philip's — filled the village, where Philip had built a sawmill and a gristmill, both essential components for surviving in the wilderness. And although John and Angelica had planned to make the 30-room mansion (that Philip was building) a summer home, they changed their minds and left, presumably confident that Philip would handle development of the village. Perhaps John needed to return to his businesses and perhaps they both missed the social life of the east coast.

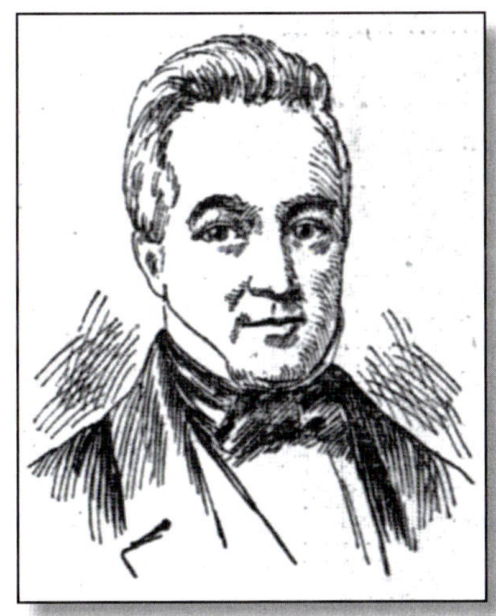

Judge Philip Schuyler, from wood engraving, circa 1895, after portrait by Giuseppe Fagnani

But why a nine-sided barn? Did her time in France with Thomas Jefferson sway her towards his fondness for the polygon? Surely Alexander Hamilton was aware of Washington's 16-sided threshing barn that he built in 1794 — during his tenure as president and during the time Hamilton was secretary of state. Did Hamilton share this unusual barn design with Philip Church, when they served together in the late 1790s? These questions may never be answered.

And why not Jefferson's favorite, the octagon, a shape that in the 1850s Fowler would proclaim to be the most ideal for homes? Since each side of the barn measures nine feet-six-inches, the Churches might have felt that they needed more room and that nine sides would give them more space than an octagon would — enough space for their horses, hay, carriages, and perhaps some vegetables, as well. Interestingly, the sides of George Washington's 16-sided barn also measured 10 feet in width. Another "coincidence" is that Thomas Jefferson, then serving as president, began building his retreat in 1806. Poplar Forest showed Jefferson's infatuation with the octagon: the main house is shaped octagonally and four octagonal rooms surround a central hall.

Meanwhile, construction on Villa Belvidere continued as Philip did most of the supervising, though John did recruit stonemasons to build the attractive sides of the mansion, sculpting stones quarried locally and making bricks from abundant clay on the farm. Presumably, they laid brick for the barn, too, since it matches both the entrance pillars and

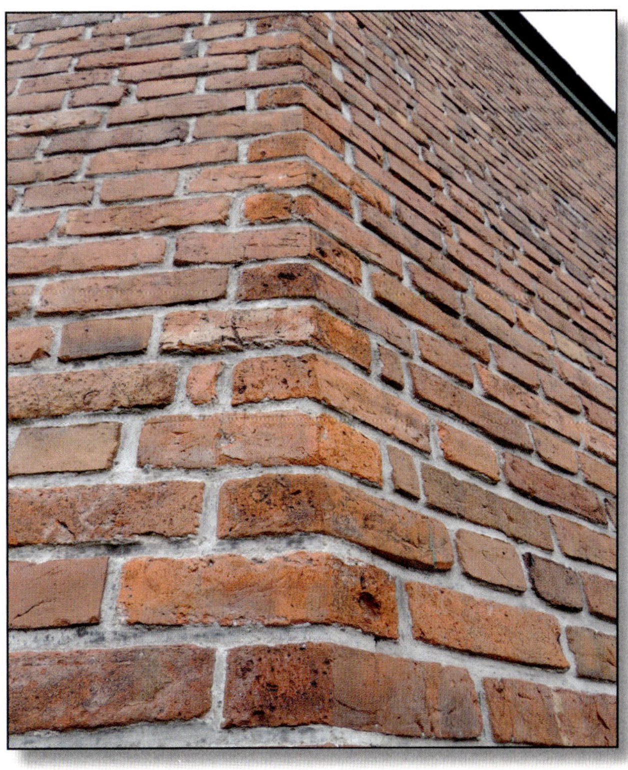

L-shaped corner brick quoins, circa 1804

the house. Interestingly, instead of placing stone quoins on the corners for support, the masons fashioned L-shaped corner bricks, which though not as strong as stone, have served well for over 200 years.

After his studies in law and since he didn't grow up in a farming family, Philip turned to another vocation and was appointed the first Judge in the Allegany County Court in 1807. In Angelica's letters to Philip, she cautioned him to pay close attention to detail while constructing the house. And Philip apparently followed her instructions well — the mansion has merited a listing on the National Register. He and Anna moved into the mansion, partially completed in 1810. Philip selected 2,000 acres for their homesite and, as years passed, they raised nine children. Daughter Elizabeth married and moved to England and another daughter, Angelica, moved to New York City. Their fourth son, Richard, took over the family estate.

While Philip was busy being a judge, working on the mansion and the farm, and selling lots, trying to encourage settlement in Angelica, John and Angelica moved away. However, John's thirst for land speculation and money lending (often loaned to those who couldn't or didn't repay him) ended up getting the best of him. After the death of Angelica in 1814 and, realizing that most settlers were more interested in cheap land in Ohio, Kentucky, and Indiana in the early 19th century, rather than in the inaccessible wilderness of western New York, John Barker Church returned to England. Why he didn't return to Belvidere is still a mystery. He died in April, 1818, with an estate of a mere £1,500.

Philip, besides being a judge, was a founding member of the Erie Canal, criticized by many as being too expensive and often called "Clinton's Folly," after Governor DeWitt Clinton, who approved it. Finished in 1825, it showed that improved transportation meant economic success. However, the Erie Canal bypassed Angelica, going instead from Albany to Rochester to Buffalo. Undeterred, Philip was instrumental in starting the Genesee Valley Canal, which opened in 1840 but had little effect in attracting settlers to Angelica.

Philip also worked hard on the creation of the Erie Railway line, which the *New York Times* praised him for, "great work to which for a number of years he devoted his time and applied his energies." However, despite his work in the railway and the canal, effective transportation to Angelica never developed. Today the population is still less than 1,000. Philip died in 1861, as the Civil War began.

His son, Richard, despite becoming a major in the state militia, went bankrupt and lost the farmstead to Rochester Savings Bank. Frederick Keeney, a farmer and early pioneer from nearby Warsaw, purchased the farm in 1892 and, perhaps to celebrate, got married in the same year. He also shipped grain and hay, along with raising a large herd of Jersey cattle. However, his tenure was short-lived. He sold the estate in 1901 to Snyder Hoxie Clark and his wife Louise.

Hoxie Clark was the only child of Silas H.H. Clark, an overachiever, who worked his way up from being a railroad conductor to company president — of both the Union Pacific and Missouri Pacific railroads. And he educated his son well. Hoxie graduated from Princeton University in 1864 and later earned a law degree before becoming a prominent attorney in St. Louis. What motivated him to purchase Belvidere as a summer home remains unknown, though, being a member of the Princeton Club might have been how he heard about the sale. He also had a home in Manhattan.

Eschewing modern conveniences, Hoxie and his wife decided to forego electric cable and live the old-fashioned way — with candlelight dinners and roaring fireplaces. They kept the long wing reserved for servants and entertained frequently. Despite its role now as a summer home, according to family photos, the farm was productive: a dairy barn, Jersey cows, poultry, oats and a threshing machine, corn, hay and potatoes. And Hoxie must have been a good farmer since his dairy butter won an award at a national dairy show in 1910.

The Clarks owned the farm for almost four decades — Hoxie passed away in 1944 — when it passed to their two daughters, who had not lived there in years. The mansion had been closed for ten years, and most of the farmland was rented. Eventually, they sold the estate, its villa, teahouse, nine-sided barn, and its 200 acres — in an auction in 1947.

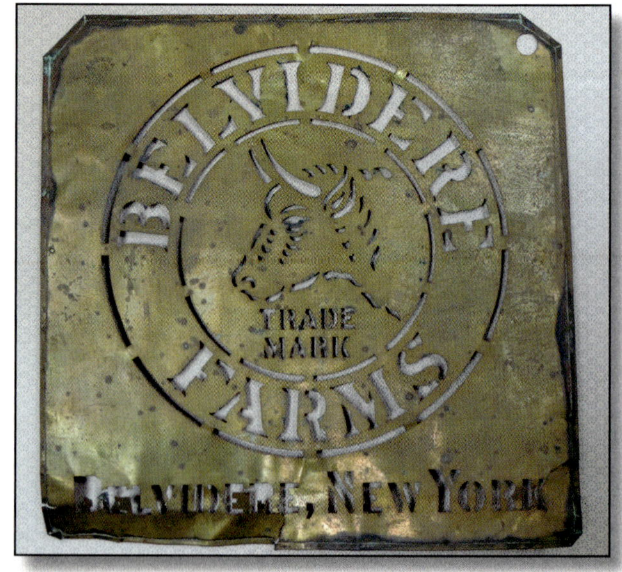

Belvidere Farms Plaque, circa 1910. Courtesy of Fredeen family.

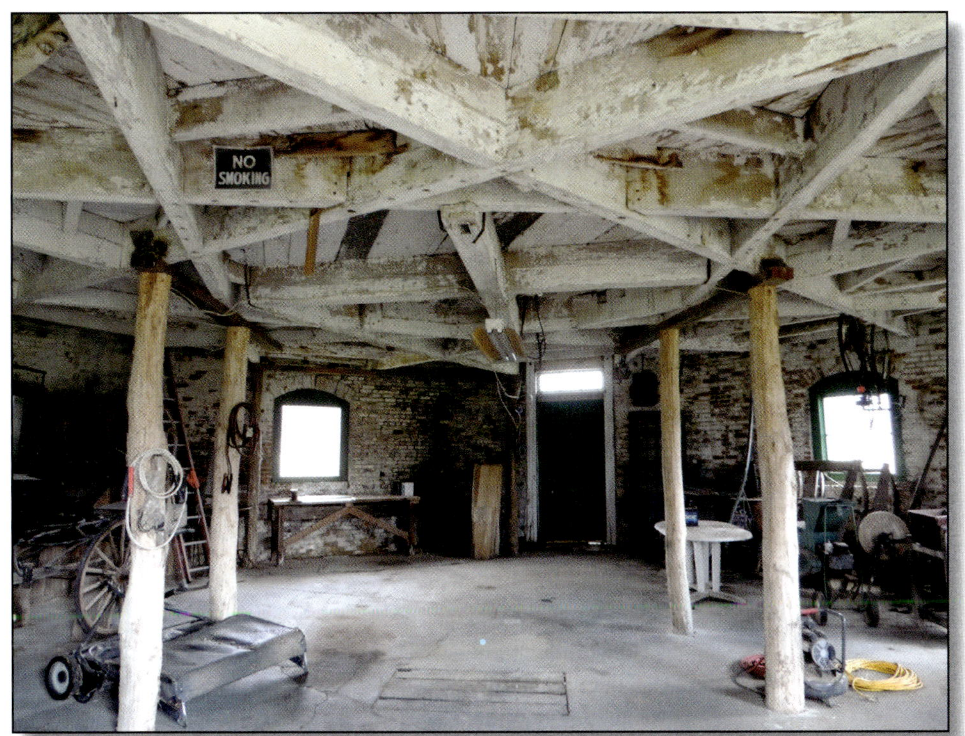

Interior of ground floor, Belvidere barn, 2022

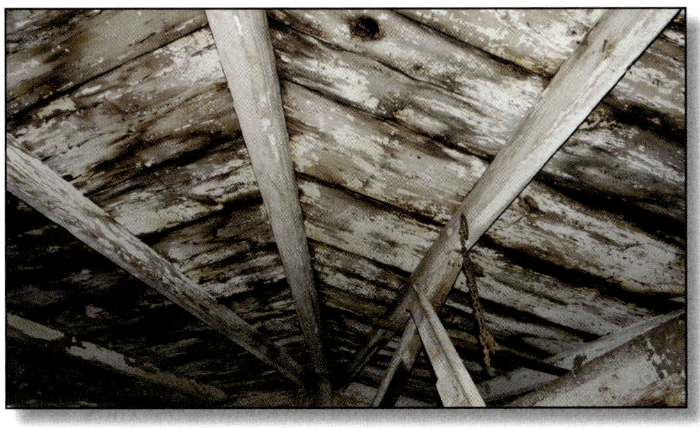

Roof interior, Belvidere barn

The next owner, Robert Bromeley, rose from a humble beginning to a wealthy businessman, which allowed him and his wife Marian to purchase Belvidere. Born in Chicago in 1910, he met his wife when they were students at Otterbein University in Westerville, Ohio. After graduation in 1929 the two married as the Great Depression started, not the best of times to begin a marriage and a career. Nonetheless, Robert landed a job selling office equipment in Chicago and a few years later moved to Bradford, Pennsylvania, where he purchased the Smith insurance agency. And, although the 1930s were dreadful times for many, Robert Bromeley's business acumen, which coupled with the expertise of two partners, Lester Edwards and Henry Satterwhite, allowed them to purchase newspapers, radio stations, hotels, a bank, and several manufacturing companies. They were involved in over 100 businesses — both local and national. While raising a family and running many companies, the Bromeleys also pursued historical preservation, which led them to Belvidere. They were busy people.

With such income and a strong sense of preserving the past, the Bromeleys purchased Belvidere and spent much of the rest of their lives bringing this historic estate back to its glory. They'd travel 50 miles every weekend — from their home in Bradford, Pennsylvania — to not only work on the estate and its grounds but also to research its rich history. Eventually they bought adjacent farms (increasing the farm to 1,350 acres) and built other homes for their two children and many grandchildren.

Despite its age — over 200 years old — the barn has been maintained in excellent condition. Inside, Philip Church made sure there was enough room for horses, hay, and carriages, which meant that the first floor had to be open, which it was. At some point after 1987 (a photo in Fink's *Barns of the Genesee Country* shows no vertical support), four posts — shaved tree trunks — were added with metal braces to hold up the ceiling. Kevin Hotchkiss, caretaker for 22 years, said that the posts were placed before he started. Other posts add support on the sides.

Though there are only a few hand-hewn marks and no mortise and tenon joints, the ceiling of the ground floor (support for the second-floor hay mow) is made of dimensional lumber, which became available around 1900. Furthermore, the planks and beams show no circular or reciprocal saw marks, suggesting that this ceiling was reconstructed (and built with common nails) circa 1900 to 1930 — during the Clark ownership. It's possible that the roof leaked (most likely wood shakes) during the late 1800s and caused the timbers to weaken. The roof planks, irregular in width, are probably original (Philip opened a sawmill in 1803) and are water-stained, hinting that this theory might be correct. Regardless, the carpenter who reconstructed the ceiling did excellent work, mitering support braces, and placing the beams to rest in the sides of the brick walls, a feature often seen in stone barns. Kevin explained that the walls are composed of a layer of rubble stone, sandwiched in between two layers of bricks, 12 inches thick and sturdy enough to support the ceiling. The barn's diameter of 40 feet was enough for the family's needs in 1804.

Outside, the roof's shingles are in good repair and, internally, beams converge to a central apex, where they insert into a central box. The boards, though weathered and water-stained, appear sound.

Belvidere Farm and its nine-sided barn stand on private property, enclosed by a gate, and are strictly not available to the public — though the family occasionally opens the grounds for fundraisers. We owe thanks to the Bromeleys and their descendants for not only preserving this historic estate but also for researching its past, a colorful page of early America. Round barn aficionados should also appreciate their efforts to take care of this nine-sided treasure, America's oldest existing round barn.

GREENE COUNTY

A Bronx Barn

Everyone who's familiar with New York City knows about one of its famous boroughs, the Bronx, and its New York Yankees, often referred to as "the Bronx Bombers." The name, Bronx, originated with the family whose descendants built this round barn, located in Greene County, about 125 miles north of the Bronx in New York City.

The family traces back to Swedish-born Jonas Bronck, who established the first settlement in what is now the Bronx and established a farm here in 1639. The area became known as "Bronck's Land," even though he lived there only four years, passing away in 1643. The name changed to the "Bronx" in 1697, a mere 300-plus years ago.

Pieter Bronck, born in 1616, probably a Swedish sailor and possibly a cousin of Jonas, moved into Bronck's Land circa 1650. But, in the early 1660s, his family moved north to Greene County and built a stone house in 1663, still existing in Coxsacki, and began farming, which, in those days, consisted mostly of feeding one's own family. The house was listed as a National Historic Landmark in 1967. Pieter and his family were likely familiar with the many octagonal Dutch churches built along the Hudson River valley.

Much later, in 1738, Pieter's grandson, Leendert, built a brick house (also still extant) next to Pieter's and continued farming, along with his son. By the 1770s, during the time of the American Revolution, the Broncks had been

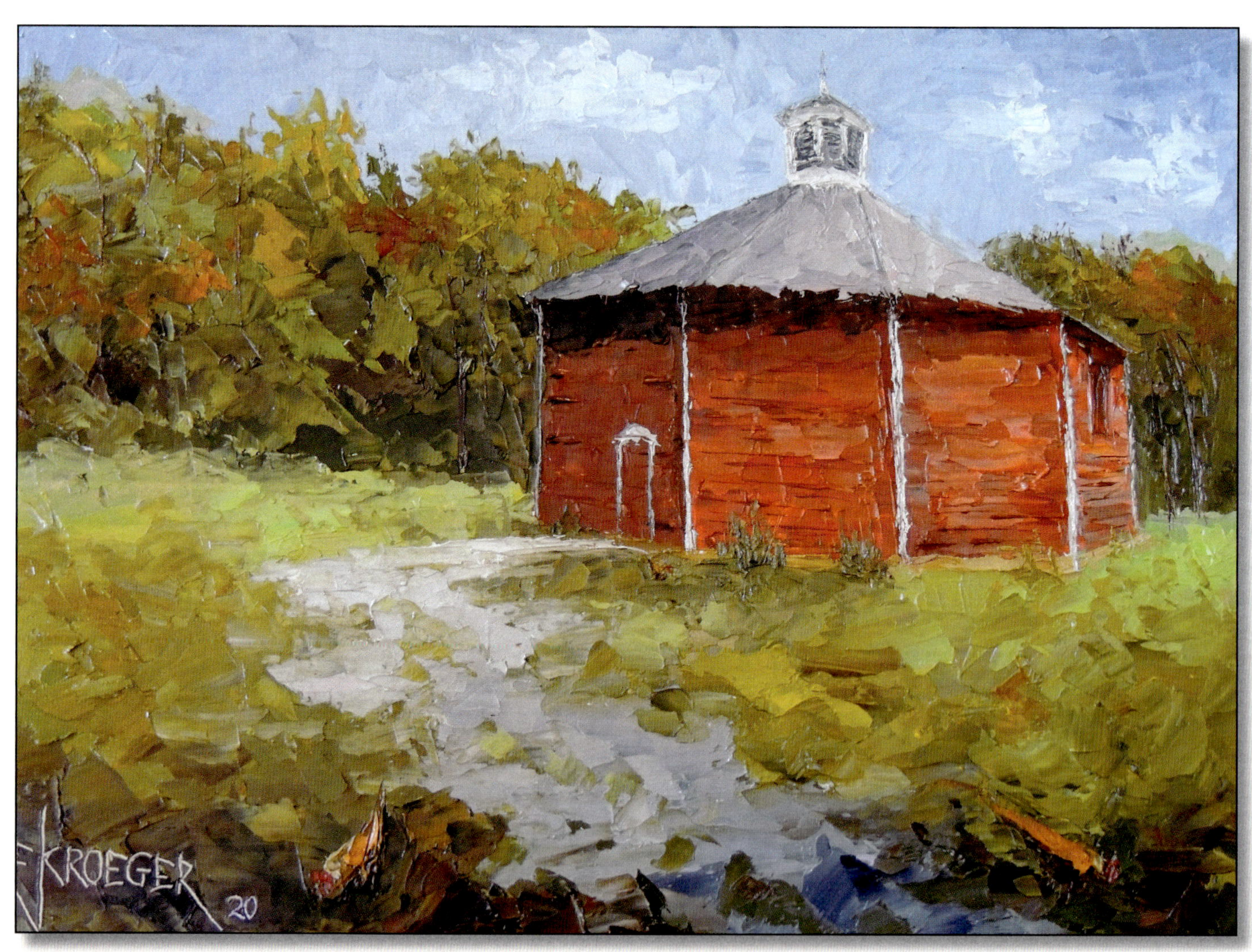

A Bronx Barn

farming in the area for over 100 years and both families pledged their wealth and support for the American cause.

Leonard Bronck, the great-great grandson of Pieter, owned the farm where this 13-sided barn was built in 1832, a barn that reflected a change in the family's farming. Previously, the family raised wheat in a New World Dutch barn with a large threshing floor and plenty of storage for grain. But, by the 1830s, when they switched to dairy farming, they needed a barn that would accommodate cows. How did they settle on the polygonal design? Perhaps they were familiar with George Washington's 16-sided barn, even though he cleverly designed that for wheat farming. Perhaps they knew about the Dutch octagonal churches. This round barn, with a diameter of 70 feet, shows evidence of mangers, though most of the cows were probably housed in a large rectangular addition, which has been dismantled.

Although Jeffersonian buildings with their octagonal shape may have influenced Bronck, the Shaker circular barn, built in 1826 and only 28 miles away in western Massachusetts, may also have been a factor. But the primary stimulus may have been religious. Turpin Bannister, in his article, "The Architecture of the Octagon in New York State," published in *New York History*, volume XXVI, wrote, "At least twenty small octagonal churches were built in the Hudson River Valley between 1680 and 1750." By 1945, when he wrote the article, all of them had disappeared. In the early years of America, many immigrants came here, yearning for religious freedom, and many attended services each week. It's possible that the Broncks were some of those churchgoers.

For nearly 300 years the farm — and barn — passed from one Bronck generation to the next until Leonard Bronck Lampman, the last family owner, willed the farm to the Greene County Historical Society in 1939. Today the Bronck Museum occupies these grounds, which hold the 1663 stone house, the 1738 brick house, an 18th century Dutch barn, and the 13-sided round barn. Though not as famous as "The Bronx Bombers," this museum and its well-preserved round barn, listed on the National Register in 1984, deserves the title of this painting, "A Bronx Barn."

WAYNE COUNTY

Hale's Heritage

Cobblestones, though a problem for farmers in clearing fields and growing crops, were plentiful in the early days of colonization of the region beneath Lake Ontario. Glacial deposits left these smooth stones behind, rounds and ovals, some no larger than a fist which, thanks to the hands of skilled stonemasons, have adorned barns and houses, many of which still stand in this region today. Like premium paint in the hands of an artist, cobblestones allowed each mason to use creativity. These cobblestone-decorated buildings set themselves apart from those built with traditional wood, brick, or stone.

Sue and Rich Freeman, authors of *Cobblestone Quest: Road Tours of New York's Historic Buildings*, estimate that over 700 cobblestone buildings were constructed in western New York State, built from the 1820s to 1860. In Wayne County alone, just east of Rochester, there are over 150 cobblestone buildings, including the circa-1824 one-room Roe schoolhouse in the town of Butler, which is probably the oldest existing cobblestone schoolhouse in North America. There's also this blacksmith's barn in Alloway, dating to 1832.

Some may question whether this octagonal structure should be labeled a barn, but, as a shop for a blacksmith in 1832, it likely housed both his horses and hay or grains to feed them, storage functions that qualify it as a barn. And, as one built with cobbles and shaped octagonally, it merits attention.

A young entrepreneur, 23-year-old Henry Towar laid claim to several hundred acres of prime land along a fast-flowing a navigable stream called Canandaigua Outlet and, in 1794, he erected the region's first grist mill and, eventually, a sawmill and two stores. Originally called Towar's Mills, the hamlet later became known as Alloway, named after Alloa, Scotland, the original home of Captain Henry Towar.

When the Erie Canal was built through Wayne County in 1820-1821, the local economy thrived and many stone masons moved to the area. After construction of the canal was finished, though many of these masons remained, few had jobs. Being survivalists, they hired out and built cobblestone structures, laboring for 50 cents to $1.25 a day. But the trend subsided and by 1845, cobblestone construction became more decorative than functional. And by the end of the Civil War, it had practically become non-existent.

During this fascinating era of cobblestone building, Henry Towar erected an impressive Greek Revival mansion in 1832, which was listed on the National Register. Not far away from Towar's home and farmstead complex in Alloway, Alfred Hale built his blacksmith barn in the same year. With many horses in the area — working in farms and pulling carriages — Hale picked an ideal spot for his line of work.

Well before advocates of octagonal buildings expounded on their advantages, which would come later in the 1850s with Fowler and in the 1870s with Stewart, both of New

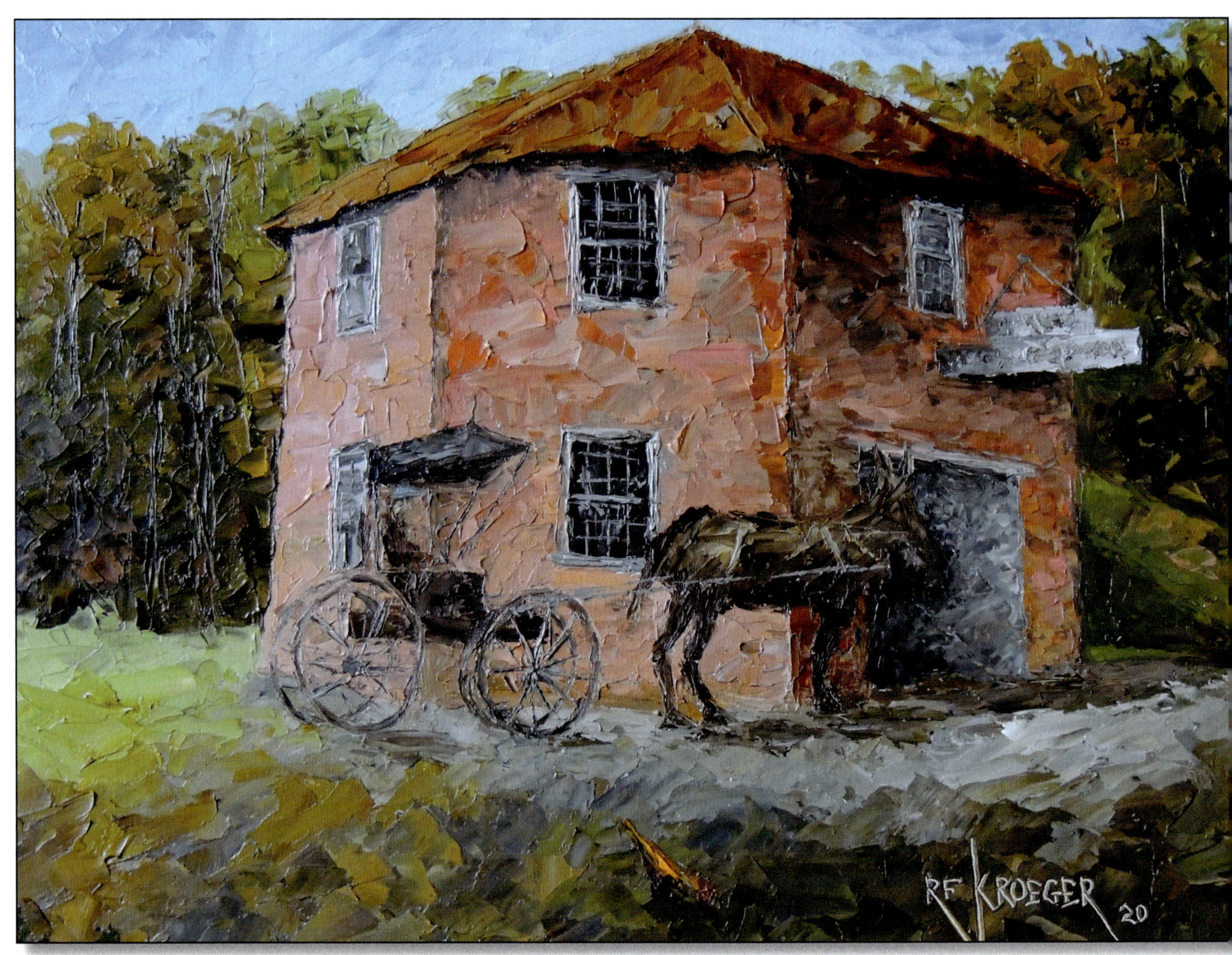

Hale's Heritage

York state, Hale chose the octagon for his barn. Interestingly, though he built his cobblestone home in a conventional rectangular shape, he may have decided the polygonal structure was better suited to the site of his barn. In fact, he built it into a bank, which leads to the second floor and he constructed it to last: each side measured 12½ feet long and had walls three feet thick, made entirely of cobblestone and mortar. Wisely, the blacksmith, who used fire to bend iron all day long, chose an essentially fire-proof structure for his barn and shop. The thick walls helped to keep the building cool in summertime and warm in winter. Now, nearly 200 years later, his choice has proven to be a good one.

In 1918 Cleveland Frind bought both the barn and Hale's cobblestone house across the street. Eventually — as the automobile replaced horses — he closed the blacksmith shop in 1936. Showing versatility, the former barn (now without horses or hay) became a machine shop, used until around 1960. Cleveland's son and daughter-in-law, Ralph and Helen Frind, occupied Hale's cobblestone house across the street for many years, selling it when Ralph died in 2008. Today, the old barn-smithy-machine shop still stands, perhaps trying to re-purpose itself, a testament to both an accomplished un-named stone mason and to the legacy of blacksmith Hale.

OTSEGO COUNTY

The Baker Barn

This county has colorful history to its credit, dating to its formation in 1791 and its name, taken from a Mohawk or Oneida word meaning "place of the rock," which fits, considering the attractive fieldstone foundation of this barn and an adjacent building. What's more interesting is that the county seat of Cooperstown, well known for its Baseball Hall of Fame, takes its name from its founder, Judge William Cooper, father of author James Fenimore Cooper. Not only did young James serve his country in the early 1800s as a naval officer, he also captured rustic

American history with his characters Chief Chingachgook and frontiersman Natty Bumppo in his series, *The Leatherstocking Tales*, which include *The Last of the Mohicans* and *The Deerslayer*, his last novel. In the 1700s this was indeed the land of the Mohicans, the Iroquois, the Seneca, and the Oneida Indian tribes. A time of adventure.

In 1806 when 17-year-old Cooper was beginning his tour in the Navy, patriarch Hamilton Baker, a blacksmith and carpenter, settled his family near Richfield Springs, about 14 miles north of Cooperstown. He acquired the farm site in 1838, where his son Norman changed paths and began dairy farming. While Cooper was writing his books about Chingachgook and Natty, Norman was increasing his herd to 40 cows, delivering milk to his neighbors, and making cheese on the farm. As the dairy operation grew, the Bakers needed another barn. They built an octagonal barn in 1882, one of seven examples of octagonal buildings in the county, still surviving in 1980.

It's always speculation to establish the reason why a farmer chose this design over a conventional one, though there were octagonal buildings in the area — one such house built in 1850 in Unadilla, only 45 miles away, still stands. New York's Orson Fowler's well publicized octagonal mode of building, beginning with an 1854 book, led to 125 octagonal houses being built from 1854 to 1860. His house in Fishkill was 130 miles south of the Baker farm.

However, a major influence might have been the writings of Elliot Stewart, who, after his fourth barn burned down, built an octagonal one and, even though being 240 miles away in Erie County, he spread the word in journals, first publicizing his plans in Buffalo's *Livestock Journal* in 1876. Two other agricultural publications reprinted it, one of them, New York City's *American Agriculturist*, presumably got a lot of distribution. By 1884 Stewart proclaimed that "30 or 40 have been built in various parts of the country."

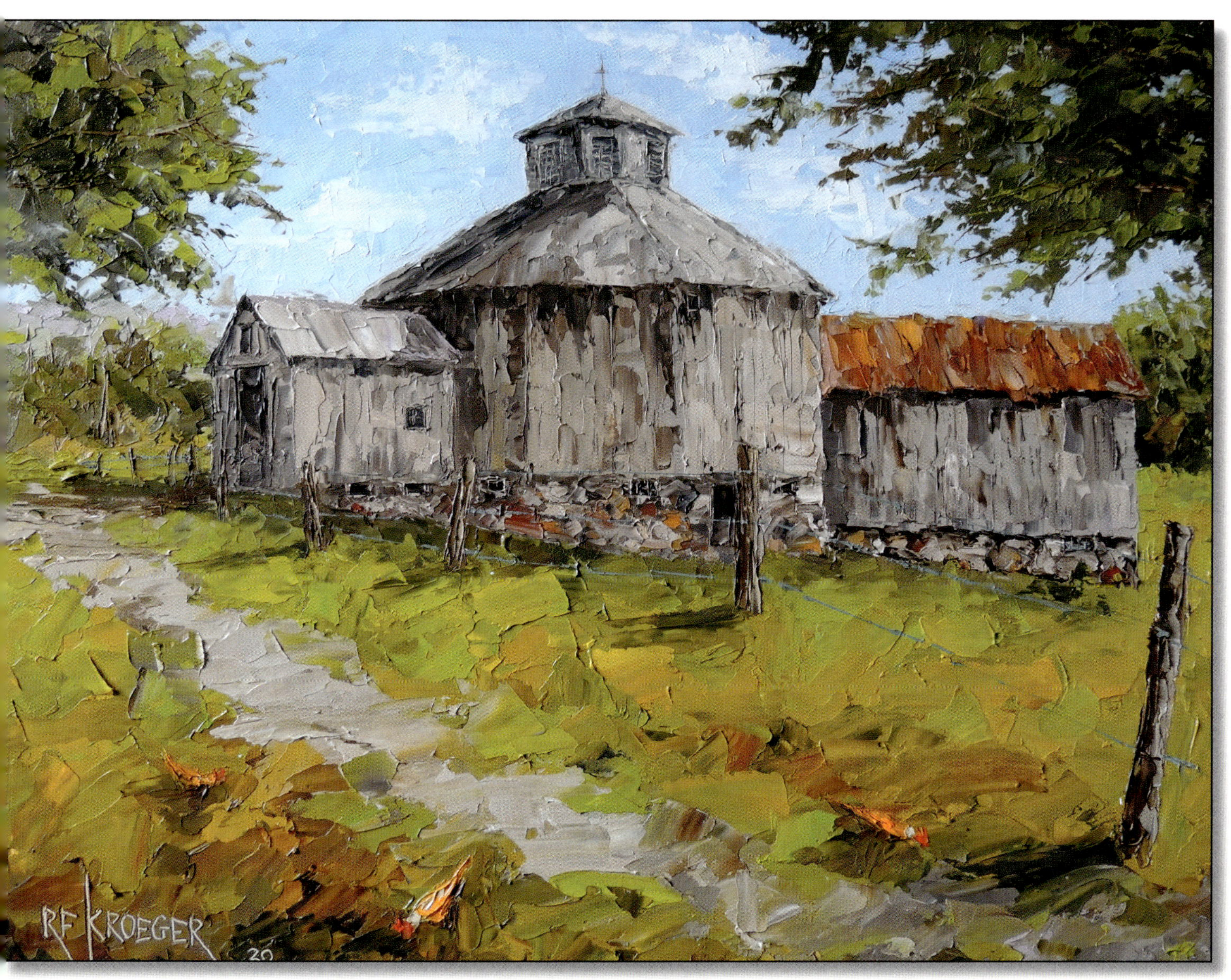

The Baker Barn

Norman Baker and his son Howard built the barn, using timber from the farm, hewing and fitting the mortise and tenon joints. According to an article in the Utica newspaper in the 1950s, a family descendant related that the builders cut down an elm tree and squared it with hand-hewing, using it as the main beam that runs the entire 60-foot length of the barn. The Bakers hired a stone mason, R. O'Brien, to lay the fieldstone foundation, which rises two levels and which matches the superb stonemasonry of two outbuildings, a corn crib with a forebay, and a cheese house. Such stonework was unusual in this region but typical of barns in southeastern Pennsylvania and in Scandinavian barns of the Upper Midwest.

Unlike the self-supporting roof of the Stewart barn, this one had four posts that extend upwards along all three stories and into the cupola, adding a margin of safety, which diagonal boards on the walls also provide. Their decision paid off: the barn has now survived over 140 years.

Another unique feature was building the barn into a hillside, rather than into a small bank, so that each level has an entrance: the bottom floor was used for cattle, the middle one was used for horses and threshing, and the top level served as a haymow. Ingeniously — and a bit ahead of their time since it was only in 1873 that a farmer in Illinois built the first silo — the Bakers constructed a silo, 18-feet square, extending from the second-floor entrance to the ground. In fact, there were only 91 silos in the entire country in 1882. The silo made it easy for the farmer to drop the corn to the lower level to feed the cows.

The barn's size wouldn't be large enough for the mega-dairy farms of today but it was adequate for a modest herd: it rose 60 feet from basement floor to cupola and, with each side measuring 25 feet, it provided four parallel rows of stanchions. Milking 40 cows twice a day was hard work. In fact, the Bakers' dairy farming business was still going strong in 1984 when the barn earned a listing on the National Register. Owners John and Jean Baker and Susan Ross were continuing the family tradition.

According to an article in the *Observer-Dispatch* newspaper, an artist, who grew up with the barn, was dismayed to see the barn in poor condition when he revisited it in 1978. He reported that it had, over a period of about 15 years, been deteriorating and so he began doing paintings on the assumption that it would soon be only a memory. Around 1999 Terry Damon, a real estate man, drove by the barn and noticed a for sale sign. A few months later he purchased it and began restoration. Fortunately, the New York State Restoration and Preservation Department issued a $25,000 grant, which Damon matched. A photograph taken in the autumn of 2020 shows matching green shingled roofs on the barn and two outbuildings. Today it still stands, just off Route 28 — the winding road connecting Richfield Springs with Cooperstown — the earliest known example of an octagonal dairy barn in the state, a testament not only to its early builders but also to the foresight of its current owner to restore and maintain it.

VERMONT

WASHINGTON COUNTY

Clem's Castle

In 1917 Vermont's final round barn was built, though there are no records of exactly how many had been built in the state by that time. A 1963 Vermont survey showed 24 round barns remaining but today only about a dozen have survived — three, thanks to creative owners who converted them into a restaurant, an apartment complex, and, in the case of this one, a cultural center.

In 1831 Cyrus Joslin purchased this land and raised 10 children with his wife. He built a large Greek revival farmhouse in 1860. After his death six years later, the family continued to farm and his grandson, David Clement "Clem," who, for some reason, changed his last name to Joslyn, took over ownership in 1901. He hired his cousin, James Joslin, who had already designed a round barn for a Bert Joslin, to plan this 12-sided barn, which was built in 1910 — specifically for his herd of Guernsey cows. Another 12-sided barn still stands near Andover.

This barn, 80 feet in diameter, was large enough for 36 stanchions, and had a central silo, which did not support the roof, as was typical of the early plans of Wisconsin's Professor King, who is credited with the design of the round silo. Its 12-sided cupola, sitting 61 feet high, provided light and, thanks to a roof of cedar shingles, the barn kept dry. Built into a hillside, the barn had three levels, allowing hay wagons to have access via a ramp to the loft before exiting around the silo. A trap door in each stanchion allowed manure to be deposited into wagons below. The clapboard siding, originally white, has now been painted a soft yellow. The barn was well designed.

The Joslyns continued dairy farming until 1969 when Marge Joslyn informed her husband Ralph, that "either the cows go, or I go." He chose the cows, sold the herd, and stopped using the round barn, which, with little upkeep, deteriorated. Enter the Simko family.

Florists from New Jersey, Jack and Doreen Simko brought their five children to the Mad River Valley for ski trips in the 1970s and stayed nearby. In those days, the Joslyns also operated a ski hostel, offering four bedrooms — with

10 bunk beds in each room — along with breakfast and dinner. So, once the Simkos sold their business and home, they decided to retire in Vermont and chose Waitfield. After having driven past the round barn in the early 1980s, Jack Simko, fascinated by the iconic barn, talked with the owners and, after a four-hour interview, agreed to buy the farm. Unfortunately, the barn was almost gone. It was 1986, the end of seven generations of Joslyn ownership and nearly 20 years after the last dairy cow had been milked.

Instead of giving the barn attention right way, these entrepreneurs decided to rehab the 1860-farmhouse and convert it to a seven-room country inn, which took 18 months. Next, they began to restore the barn in 1988. It was finished a year later — to the tune of $300,000, more than they paid for the entire farm. The restoration involved raising the barn, building a new foundation, adding a new insulated roof, reinforcing the hand-hewn beams, replacing the clapboard siding, and adding a fresh coat of paint. Part of the foundation's demise was the presence of underground springs, which the owners cleverly used to make a swimming pool for guests as well as an attractive pond, featured in the painting. Doreen, an arts enthusiast, wanted to convert the second floor into artists' studios, but, when zoning denied the request, she settled on founding the nonprofit Green Mountain Cultural Center.

Their daughter, Anne Marie, took over the inn in 1994, added guest rooms, and expanded the staff to 45 employees. However, health issues forced her to consider selling and, after several offers — which didn't suit her concept of maintaining the inn and the round barn — she found a couple that agreed to continue the legacy of the Joslyns and the Simkos.

Today the Inn at the Round Barn offers not only weekend retreats — in summer and winter — for individuals but also can handle weddings and other events, which include both a hearty New England breakfast as well as a choice of 12 luxurious rooms and a chance to see one of Vermont's few round barns. I'm sure Clem would be proud to see how well his former "castle" is faring these days.

Below: *Clem's Castle*

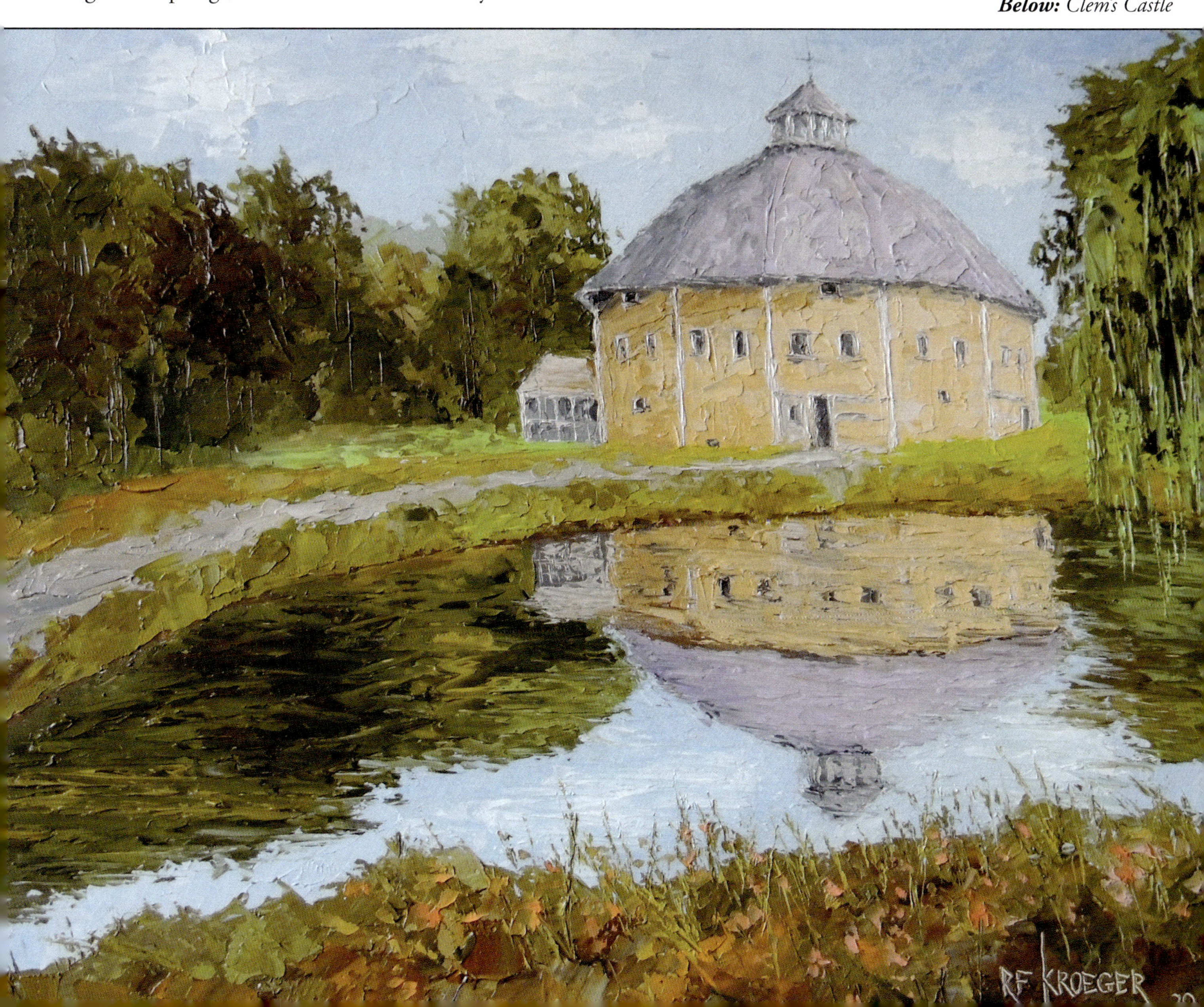

NEW HAMPSHIRE

GRAFTON COUNTY

The Round Barn Shoppe

It's not often that a round barn inspires an entrepreneur sufficiently to build a replica of it, one with three levels, including an octagonal cupola with decorative weathervane, an elaborate clerestory, metal roofs, matching burgundy siding, and a main floor with ample windows. The Round Barn Shoppe, located directly across from this old 16-sided barn, is still listed in the pages of whitemountainbiz.com, though it is no longer open. The owners advertised products such as New England crafts and gifts, cheese, jellies and jams, homemade fudge, mums, and smoked products and they represented over 300 New England craftspeople. The last comment on Trip Advisor came in 2014, possibly signaling the end of the gift shop, "Do stop and check out this shop. It is huge inside and is full of all kinds of goodies." Today it serves only for storage. The round barn across the street is a different story.

Current owner, Peter Trapp, explained that the farmstead goes back to 1842 when the founder built two small barns. In 1906 the owner, Ernest L. Stevens, replaced the two barns with this round one, something that round barn promoters often emphasized: a round barn would provide more space than a rectangular one with the same cost. The date is prominently displayed above the entry passageway which leads up the bank through an enclosed corridor to the second story. George Schmid, who built the round barn replica-turned-gift-shop, owned the farm in 1975 and leased the land and barn to Peter, who after 17 years of renting, purchased it outright in 2020. He raises beef cattle, housing them in a lateral extension off the left side of the barn.

Known as the "Round Barn of Piermont," the hexadecagon must have been a colorful legend in the early 20th

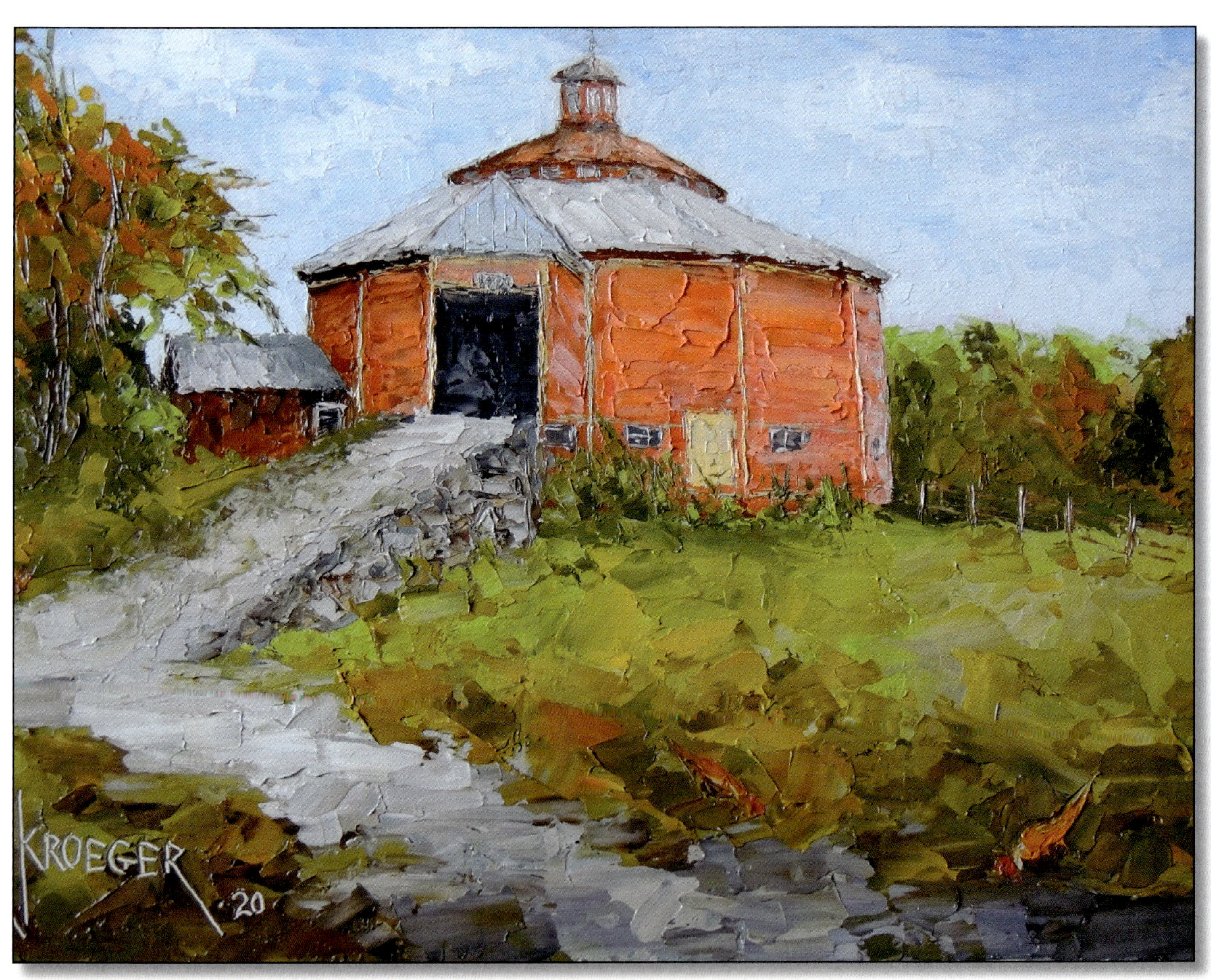

The Round Barn Shoppe

century in this little town, established in 1768. In 1790, the year of the first census, it had 426 residents; these days it has about twice that number. However, despite the barn's peculiarity, nothing is known about the builder or why the farmer chose a polygonal design, especially one of 16 sides. Elliot Stewart's plans, well publicized in the late 1800s, probably played a part in this choice, considering that Stewart's location in New York, was also in the northeast.

The basement level was used for manure storage and, according to Peter, eventually had calving pens and a milking parlor. When used for dairy farming, the barn's second floor housed the cows and hay was stored on the third floor. It was a well-built little barn, sufficient for a modest farming operation, which continues today on the 76 acres. And, although the round barn gift shop is used only for storage, its presence pays tribute to the work of Mr. Stevens, who chose this unusual shape over a century ago.

MASSACHUSETTS

BERKSHIRE COUNTY

Hands to Work … Hearts to God

This slogan identifies the builders of this round barn, the Shakers, and it summarizes their philosophy, similar to that of the Trappist monks — ora et labora. The Shakers, perhaps unfairly called this name because they incorporated animated whirling and swirling dancing, trembling, and fainting into their religious services, originated in England and came to America in 1774. Led by a woman, Mother Ann Lee, who suffered the loss of her four children and left an unhappy marriage in Manchester, the group of eight founded a colony in Watervliet, New York, in 1776. Their pacifist religion upheld equality of gender and race and it stressed the importance of confession of sin, communal life, and celibacy, which meant that any children would have to come from outside the group. Converts had to give all their worldly goods to the commune, where they were shared by all. Despite these stringent rules, the Shakers grew.

By the 1830s there were about 300 members in the Hancock community in Berkshire County, the third of 19 Shaker villages throughout the United States. They had accumulated 3,000 acres of land and built a handsome red brick dormitory, which housed more than 100. They also erected the round barn in 1826, farmed, and, using precise workmanship, built furniture, which became popular, evoking high quality and yet simplicity. Yet, although the Shakers spread throughout New England, New York, Ohio, Indiana, and Kentucky, this round barn was the only one they ever built. Furniture was a common thread but round barns weren't.

However, a report from a reader in *The American Farmer* (Volume 9, Number 3, 1827) expressed incredulity, "I hand you for the amusement and information of the practical farmer … of a large barn, built the last season, in the town of Hancock … by the family of Shakers located in that town." The writer continued, "Both the size and form are probably unfit for any common purpose; very few farmers would wish to collect so much forage and manure, or have so much stock at one place …" His comments reflect the fact that in 1826 most farmers had small acreage and would neither have been able to afford such a large barn nor would they have use for it. Yet, he admired this unusual round barn, "there is much ingenuity and convenience in the design, for a large establishment." Still, none followed until Jennings built his impressive brick circular barn in Ohio in 1858.

After an earlier barn burned on their farm, elders William Deming and Daniel Goodrich chose the circular design, which they considered as the most perfect shape. Since they originated in Manchester, they may have been aware of several round stone churches in England, which date to the 12th century and were probably inspired by Crusaders, who were impressed by the round rotunda in the Church of the Holy Sepulchre in Jerusalem. The Hancock leaders also thought on a large scale when they built this barn, choosing a circumference of 270 feet and a diameter of 95 feet. They also wanted it to last and had enough funds to construct stone walls 30 inches thick. The original design provided stanchions for 52 dairy cows and a central tower 55 feet wide and 30 feet high. Its wooden section burned down in 1864 but, thanks to its sound stone foundation, it was not lost.

Undaunted, members rebuilt the barn, finishing the reconstruction by 1883, this time making improvements by adding trapdoors behind the stalls so that manure could be scraped and dropped below to wagons. To prevent combustion of hay — which may have been the cause of the fire — they built a central octagonal ventilation shaft that rises above the roof in a cupola with windows. Just below the cupola, another addition, a 12-sided clerestory, provided much needed light to the interior.

By 1850 the American Shaker population had reached an estimated 4,000 to 5,000 members but it began to decline after the Civil War. Young people (the celibate community adopted orphans) left for the world outside. Fueled by the industrial revolution of the late 19th century, jobs became more plentiful, contributing to this urban migration, and in 1874 only 98 members were left at Hancock and by the early 1900s only 50 members

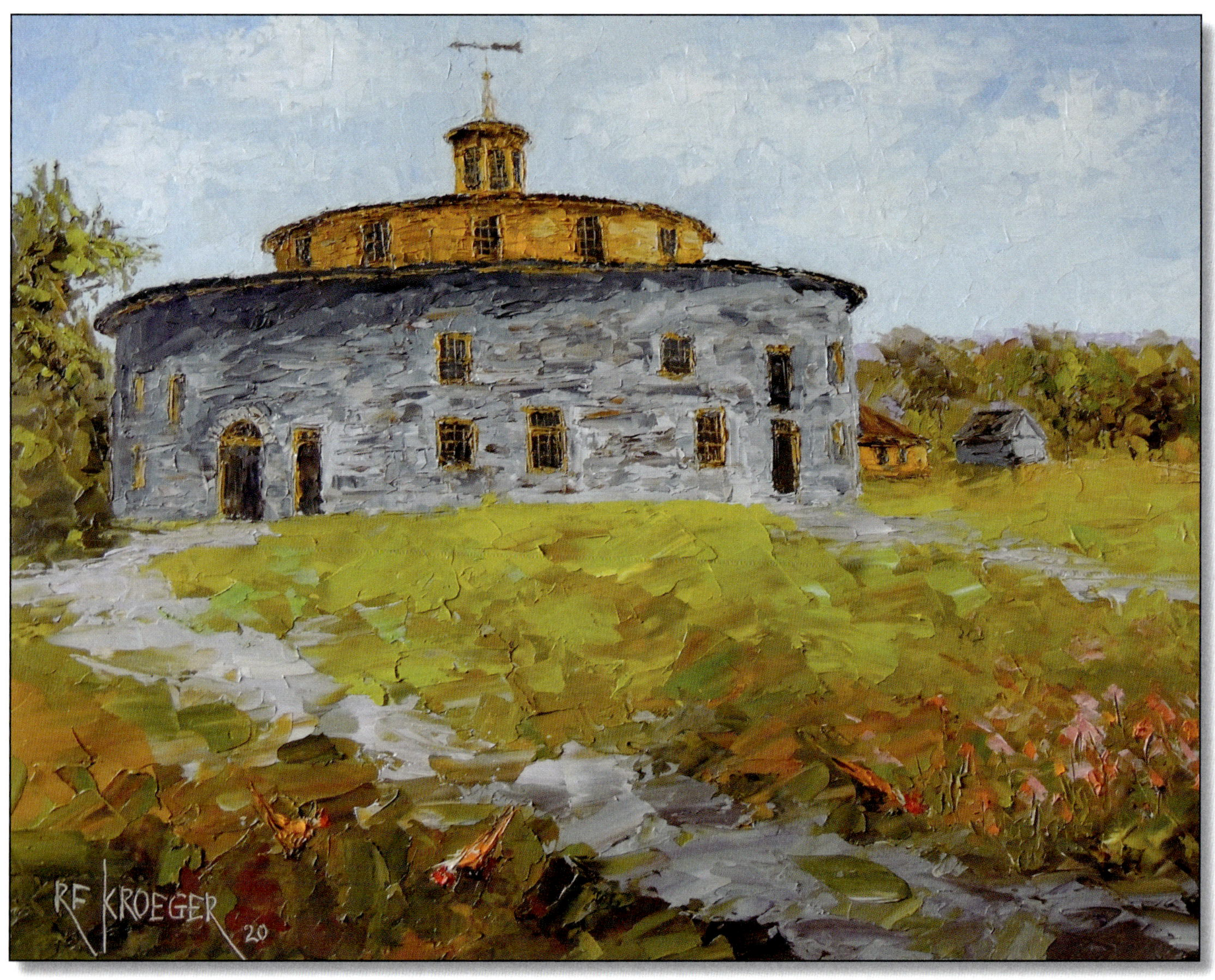

Hands to Work … Hearts to God

remained. As their numbers declined, they began selling land and dismantling excess buildings until they stopped farming completely in 1959.

A group of local citizens, realizing the historical importance of this commune, formed a nonprofit, Shaker Community, Inc., located in Pittsfield, purchased the site, and began restoring buildings. They rebuilt the barn in 1968 and got it listed in the National Register.

The group now operates the 750-acre property as a museum and a working farm. Again, in 1986 the barn got a facelift, which, as the highlight of the farm, continues to draw visitors all year round. Today there are four rings inside the barn: the innermost provides ventilation, the next ring stores hay, the third allows workers to distribute the hay to the cows, and the outermost ring is where the cows stand in their stanchions.

The Hancock Shaker Village functions as a living history museum with an extensive collection of Shaker furniture, rotating exhibits, a mile-long hiking trail, and a full schedule of events, which are held in many of the 20 restored buildings, including this iconic round barn. Oddly, though it was probably the first truly circular barn in America, it didn't stimulate other farmers to follow suit. Circular barns didn't catch farmers' attention until Wisconsin's Professor King's barn plans were published in farm journals in the early 1890s.

Undoubtedly the Shaker round barn attracted visitors from the early 1800s but farmers may have felt — and rightly so — that such a barn was beyond their means. Regardless, for the past 60 years, today's Shaker nonprofit organization has wisely undertaken a formidable task to preserve a memorial to a most unique religious sect. In a much smaller way, this painting and essay will remember this round barn, which served the commune for many years and, in a sense, symbolized its proverb, "Hands to Work … Hearts to God."

BARNSTAPLE COUNTY

The Replica

Although this project focuses on round barns built before 1930, occasionally one, built in contemporary times, merits inclusion — such as this one, a replica of the early Massachusetts Shaker barn. Located in Sandwich, a village on Cape Cod, named after the historic 10th-century town in Kent, England, the barn serves as a museum to display the incredible antique car collection of Josiah K. Lilly, Jr., a principal in the pharmaceutical giant Eli Lilly, builder of this round barn, and founder of the museum, which opened in 1969. The story goes back much further.

In 1677 Lydia Abbott was the first resident on this land, residing with her two sons — in poverty despite a second marriage. After her death, Lydia's brother, Daniel Wing, Jr., took over her house and began farming — continuing through the Revolutionary War. In the 1920s, when Charles Dexter bought the farm, it was known as the Shawme Farm. A prosperous textile merchant, Dexter and his wife began spending summers here as he developed gardens. In 1935, after he hired a landscape architect to turn the farm into a country estate, he moved here full-time.

The next part of the story reverts to the Midwest and the family of Eli Lilly, who, a chemist, opened a drug store in Greencastle, Indiana, in January of 1861 but quickly enlisted in the Civil War in April. In 1864, Major Lilly, wounded in battle, was forced to surrender with his troops. After spending time in prison camp (he was held until 1865), he was promoted to colonel upon release in a prisoner exchange. Returning to Indiana, he eventually founded the Indianapolis-based company in 1876. A pharmaceutical chemist, Lilly set a goal to produce effective medicines, contrasting to what hucksters touted as miraculous elixirs in medicine shows, and he hired a full-time scientist in 1886. Over the centuries this Indiana company has saved millions of lives through its medicines, including the first commercial production of insulin in 1923.

Below: *The Replica*

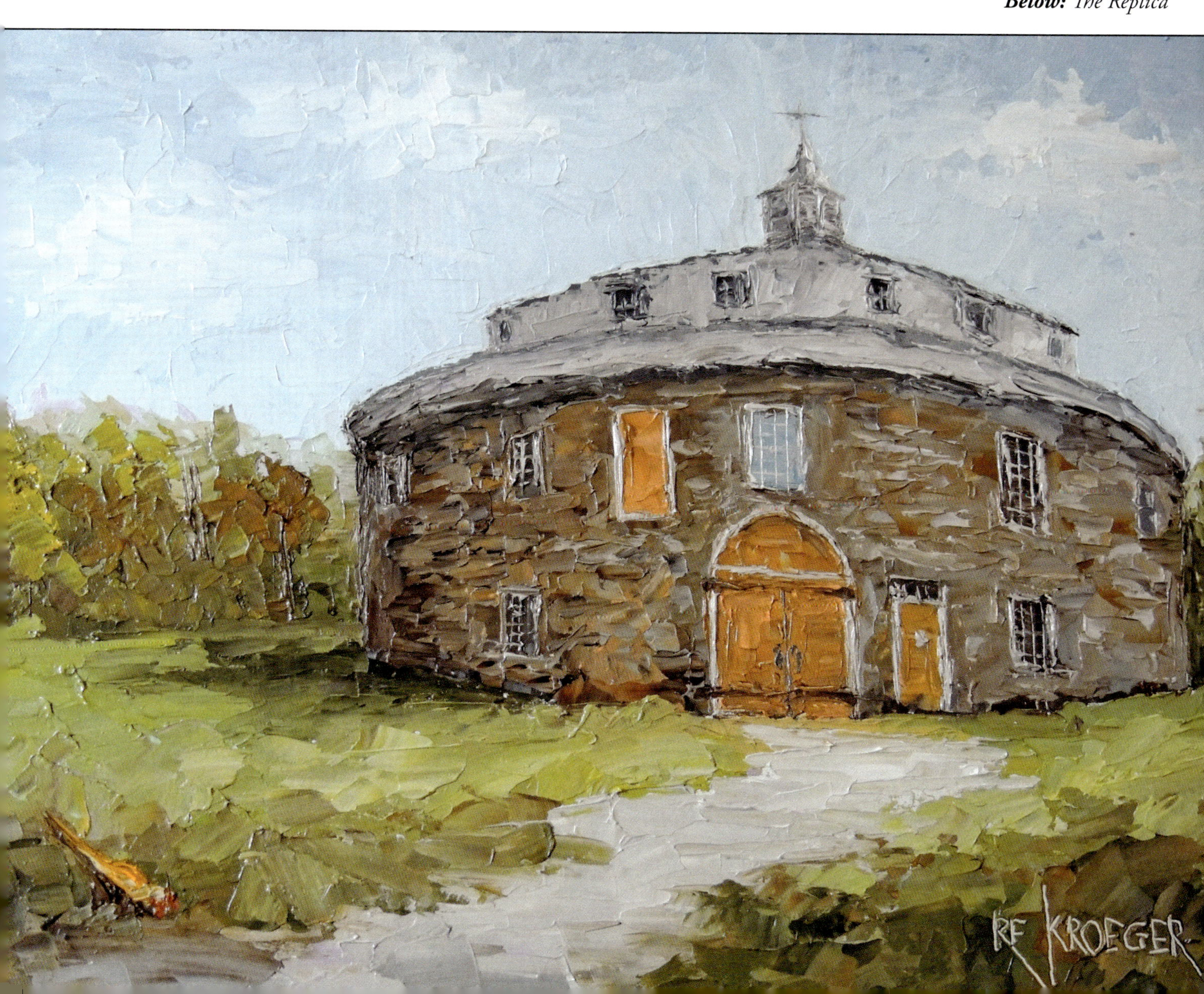

One of the sons, Josiah K. Lilly, Jr., born in 1893, loved collecting from the time of his youth, beginning with his movie ticket stubs. After college and serving in France in World War I, he continued his hobby and joined the family business, becoming president in 1948 and, later, chairman of the board, a position he held until he died. His collections mushroomed. A generous man and passionate history buff, he donated 20,000 books and 17,000 manuscripts to Indiana University and gave over 6,000 gold coins to the Smithsonian. And, as time passed, the Lilly family spent summer vacations in Falmouth, a village on Cape Cod about 20 miles from Sandwich.

After Josiah died in 1966, his son, J.K. Lilly, III, bought his antique firearms and military miniature collections from the estate and, wanting to honor his father, he brainstormed with architect Merton Stuart Barrows and landscape architect Philip Ansell for ideas on buildings and grounds. Mr. Lilly decided this estate in Sandwich would be ideal, purchased it, and, to honor the Shakers and their round stone barn, he built a replica of it in 1969 to house Josiah's collection of antique cars, one of the most impressive in the country. The other collections, including one of 1908 Charles Looff hand-carved wooden carousel figures and another of American art paintings, are displayed elsewhere.

Each year over 144,00 tourists visit these gardens and this museum — to see pages from America's past, to enjoy the philanthropy of the Lilly family, and to witness a memorial to one of the earliest of America's round barns.

CONNECTICUT

FAIRFIELD COUNTY

Cobblestones

Cobblestone streets and buildings in Connecticut were common in the 18th-century. Click-clack, click-clack went the hoofs of horse-drawn buggies, reminiscent of the pages of

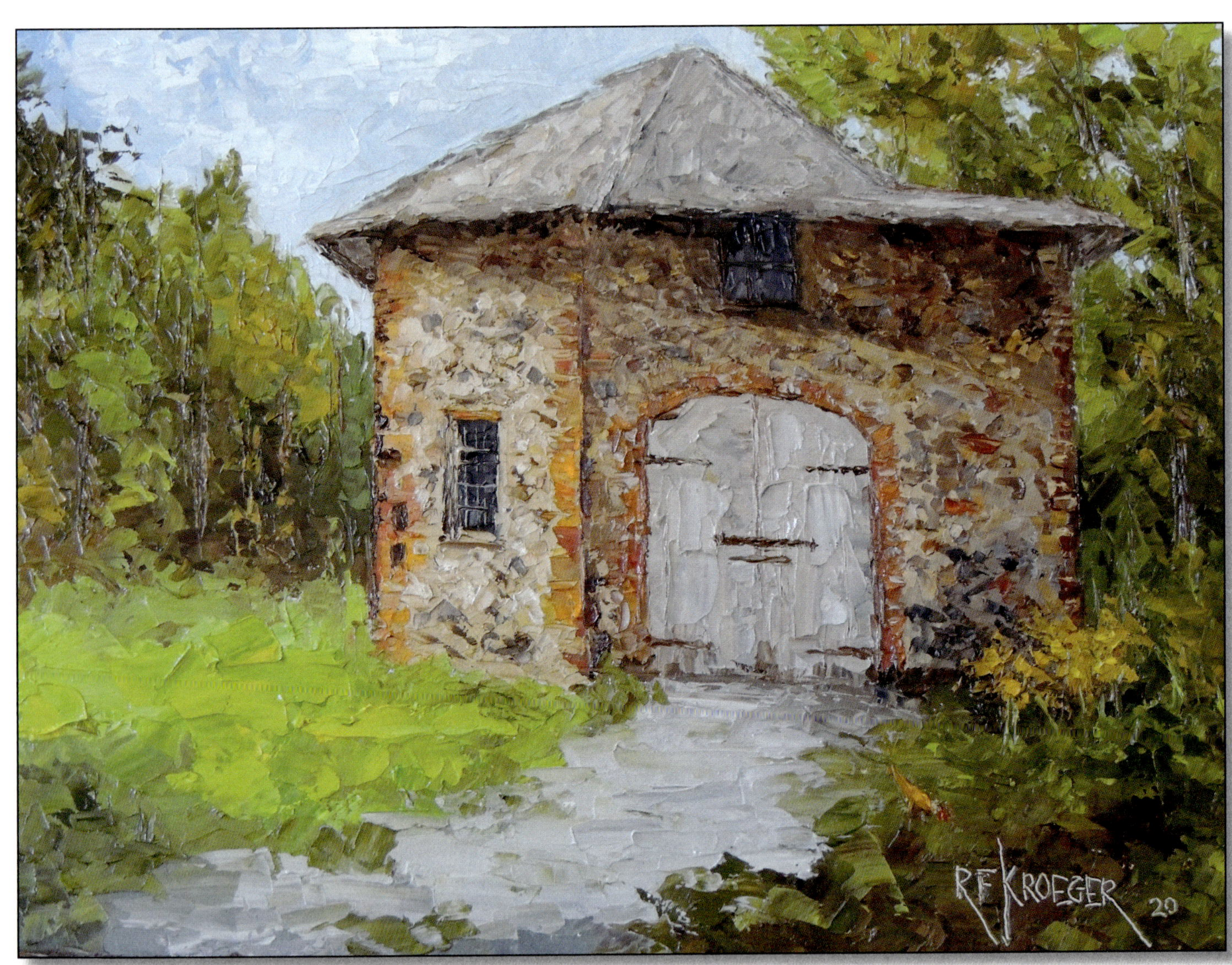

Cobblestones

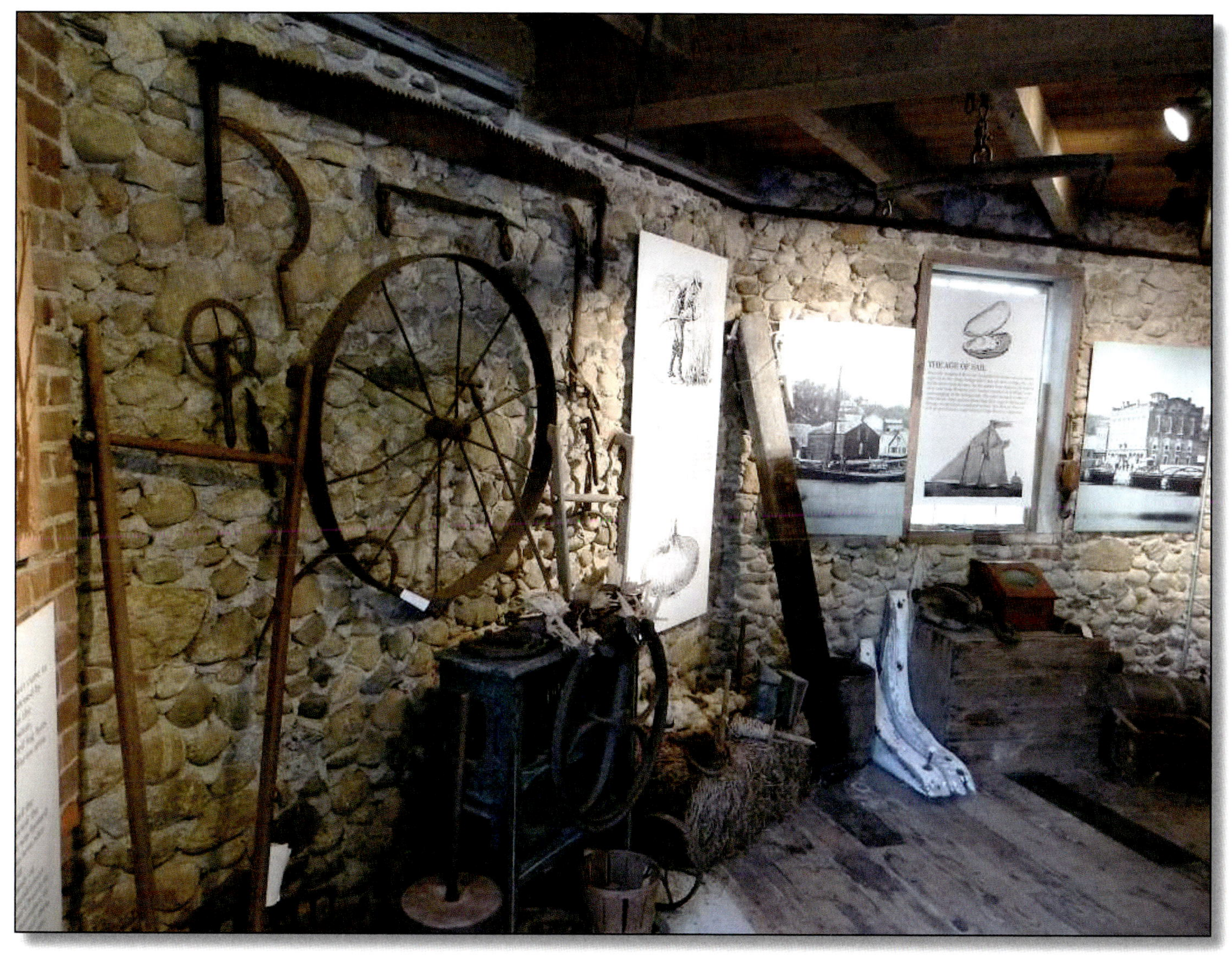

Interior of cobblestone barn. Courtesy of Westport Museum. Mike Lauterborn

a Charles Dickens novel. But such streets weren't compatible with the automobile. In fact, in 2016 the last cobblestone street in Derby — about 20 miles from Westport — was finally removed for safety reasons, after serving residents for over 200 years.

Located in downtown Westport, this seven-sided cobblestone barn, with its unusual octagonal roof, traces back to the late 18th century when Ebenezer Coley, a prosperous merchant in Westport, built a house for his son Michael and deeded the property to him in 1795. The Coleys were merchants, not farmers, and Michael, born in 1772 and married in 1793, followed his father into business. However, three years after moving into the house, Michael incurred debts and was forced to sell the house back to his father.

Ebenezer sold the house — with perhaps a wooden barn, as recorded in the National Register listing — to Mary Kent and her daughter Ann in 1799. The property — house and barn — continued in this family's hands until Paul Curtis purchased it in 1836, eventually selling to Hezekiah Allen in 1846, a resident of New York City, who may have been a real estate speculator since he sold it in the same year to Farmin Patchin.

Farmin, a stonemason and blacksmith, must have been a good businessman since he was able to afford such a house as well as another house, possibly for relatives or for rental. Sometime between 1846 and 1857 he built this cobblestone barn. Changing directions, he sold his smithy and blacksmithing equipment in 1850, which suggests that his masonry work was profitable, especially since his property value nearly doubled from 1851 to 1854. However, Farmin apparently overextended himself since, in 1857, he had to mortgage his property, eventually selling it to the Sagatuck Bank, which kept it for seven years.

Why did Farmin choose such a shape? Well, according to Turpin Bannister in "The Architecture of the Octagon in New York State," (*New York History*, Vol. XXVI), there were at least 20 octagonal churches built in New York's

Hudson Valley, about 100 miles away, between 1680 and 1750, which may have influenced not only Thomas Jefferson but this blacksmith as well. And, apparently affluent, Farmin wanted to show his good fortune to all, selecting cobblestones as his vehicle.

One corner of Patchin's barn was squared off, probably to fit against an attached wooden addition, which no longer exists, resulting in a combination of seven walls and an eight-sided roof. What the barn held may remain unknown, though the wooden addition suggests livestock, probably dairy cows, and the barn's loft suggests hay storage. And, since Farmin sold his smithy in 1850, he may have operated as a blacksmith in the barn for only four years. The Alloway, New York, seven-sided blacksmith shop-barn looks remarkably similar to this one, even though it, like many barns, was built into a hillside. Patchin's barn sits on level ground.

A nine-foot double arched door graces the entrance of the barn and twelve-over-eight windows are located irregularly on three sides. Distinctive reddish-orange brick quoins support the corners and multi-colored cobbles dot both the outside and inside of the walls. A ladder presumably gave access to the loft, where hay may have been stored, and, in the lower level, the root cellar likely provided cooling for vegetables and milk — if there were dairy cows here — as well as storing ice for those who lived in Farmin's two houses. The original stonework and subsequent restoration are a tribute both to the historical society and to Mr. Farmin's exceptional masonry.

The next owner, Morris Bradley, another blacksmith — apparently a lucrative trade in those years — purchased the house and barn in 1857 and, having made a fortune in 1849 in the California Gold Rush, made extensive improvements to the main house, converting the exterior to an Italianate design, an upgrade reflected in increased taxes in 1871. Morris transferred the buildings to his two daughters, one of whom, Julia, married a Wheeler. Eventually William B. Wheeler, a local dentist, owned the house and barn and willed it to his children, who, in turn, willed it to William's younger brother Lewis, a physician, who lived in the house until he died in 1958.

With no children, Lewis left the house and barn to his housekeeper, Charlotte Darby, who lived in the house until her death in 1979. Unfortunately, she didn't maintain the barn, which had deteriorated: the roof was caving in and parts of the cobblestone walls were crumbling. Mrs. Darby's estate stipulated that the property be donated to Christ and Holy Trinity Church, which sold it to the Westport Historical Society in 1981, creating a dilemma on what to do with the dilapidated barn — save it or scrap it. Fortunately, thanks to grants and contributions by individuals, including residents Paul Newman and his wife Joanne Woodward, the society was able to masterfully restore the unique building, the only cobblestone barn in Connecticut. They successfully submitted the house and barn to the National Register in 1984.

Today the house serves as the headquarters of the historical society and both the house and the seven-sided barn function as museums about the history of Westport. The cobblestones, laid by Mr. Patchin over 150 years ago, still glisten when the sun hits them, and represent a bygone era and the life of a man, both stonemason and blacksmith, who had a vision, which, thanks to the local historical society, still shines today.

8. MID-ATLANTIC AND SOUTH

PENNSYLVANIA

SOMERSET COUNTY

The Onions of Somerset County

Out of the hundreds of round barns built in this country, Simon O'Donnell's barn — stretching the term a bit — stands out boldly: it may be America's only round barn with an onion-shaped dome.

A brass plate on the barn states: *Erected by Simon O'Donnell, Aug. 1909.* Measuring only 24 feet in diameter, the barn's small size — essentially a round concrete pad with a green asphalt roof — suggests it might have been used as a carriage barn for horses and buggies on this homestead, named Highland Farms, established in 1866. Why an Irishman chose a Russian dome for his barn will remain a mystery.

The barn's dome conjures up images of the colorful tops of the church buildings in Moscow, which trace back to the times of Ivan the Terrible. Moscow's Saint Basil's Cathedral, a Russian Orthodox church, officially known as the Cathedral of Vasily the Blessed, was built from 1555 to 1561 under orders from Ivan the Terrible. It commemorates the capture of Kazan and Astrakhan. The domes have not been altered, except for painting, since the reign of Ivan's son Fyodor I, also in the 16th century. Even earlier, onion domes appeared on top of Saint Sophia Cathedral in Veliky Novgorod, circa 1045—1050.

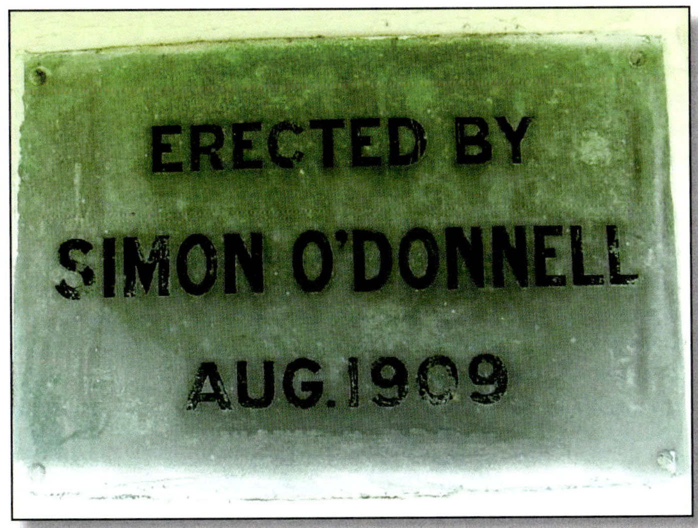

Plaque on O'Donnell barn

There have been explanations of what these domes mean. One is that they were built upwards to the sky to collect the goodness from Heaven. Another is that they show the outpouring of the Holy Spirit upon the cathedral. However, when communism and its atheism took over Russia in the early 1900s, these churches were seized from the Russian Orthodox community and no longer held religious services. Completely secularized by 1929, they became property of the Russian Federation. Yet, colorful domes still grace the top of the former cathedral in Moscow's Red Square and are regarded as cultural symbols of the country. Since 1990 it's been a UNESCO World Heritage Site.

Thanks to Jacob Miller, the curator of the local historical society, light was shed on this whimsical "barn." Peter Heffley founded this farm, and, at 17, he began working as a blacksmith and eventually a carriage maker in his hometown of Berlin, a town just south of Somerset. After several years, he decided to try his luck in the West, which, in the 1870s, was, indeed, the Wild West. And, after some years of establishing a transportation business — moving freight between Nebraska City and Helena, Montana — he made his fortune and returned with his wife to Highland Farm in 1877. A story in the *Somerset Herald* in 1905 commented on Heffley's newly found wealth and his penchant for displaying it: he brought a chest of gold bricks and gold dust into a local bank. Affluent enough to attract political attention, he entertained the prominent of his day, including President William McKinley. But he was also a farmer, one who liked to experiment. He was the first to introduce thoroughbred horses to the county and the first to use modern fertilizer. He also had a daughter, Lucy, who married an Irishman, the next part of the story.

Simon O'Donnell, according to his obituary, was born in Ireland in 1847 and was a self-made man, beginning with a humble start, at age 12, when he worked with a cattle stock dealer in Chicago. By 17, he was in charge of government purchases of livestock for the Army, which, at that time, was engaged in the Civil War. After marrying in 1867, he and his wife raised three children as he continued to grow wealthy in the livestock trade. But after his wife died in 1903, like most widowers, he married again, this time to Heffley's daughter Lucy. A newspaper report in 1904 described them as husband and wife, home-based in Pittsburgh, where Simon was a veteran stockman,

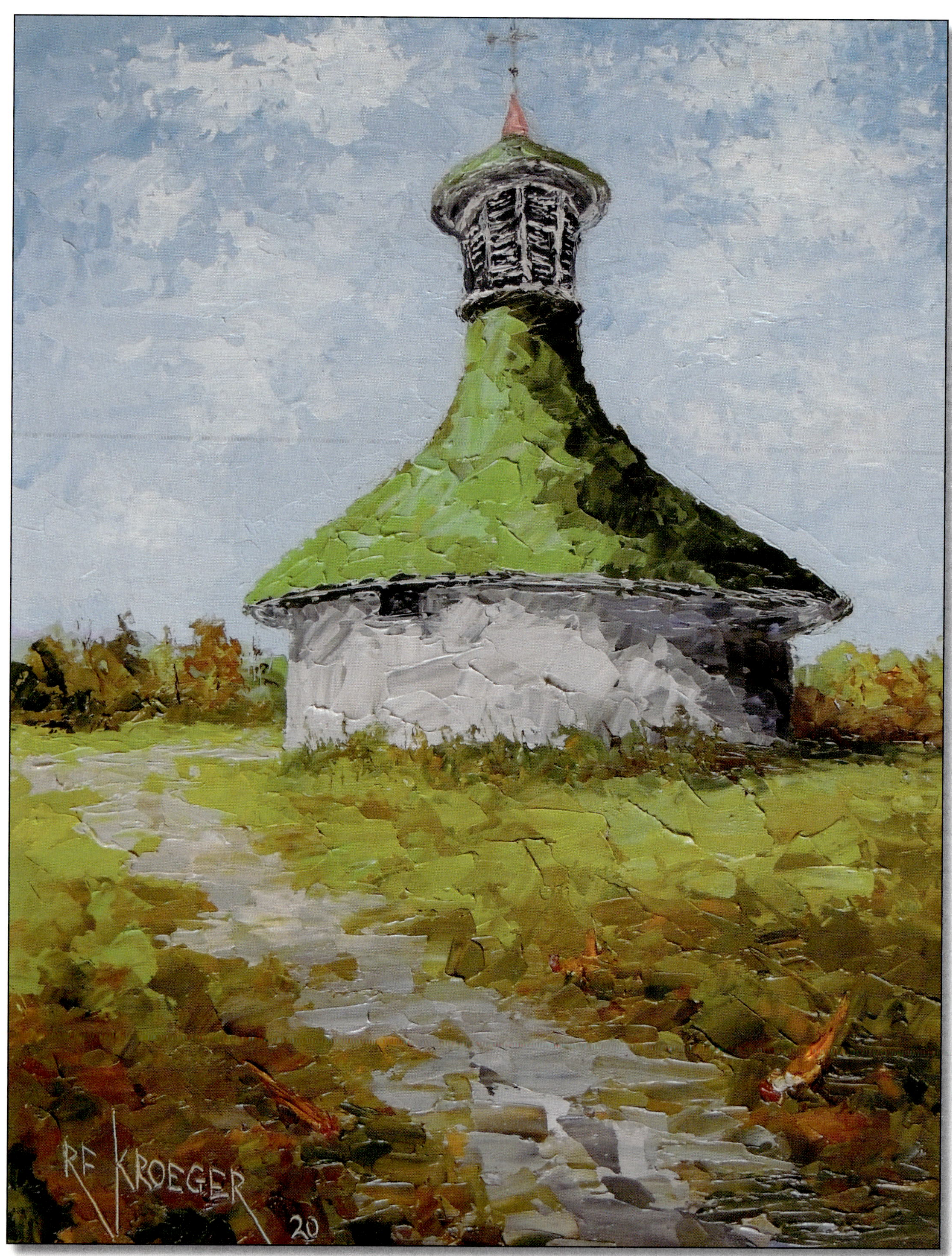

The Onions of Somerset County

apparently doing well enough to spend summers at the Highland Farm. According to his obituary, Simon and Lucy took over the farm, spent summers there, and erected the round "barn," in August, 1909. A month later Simon passed away, only 56.

Over the years, though ownership of the farm changed hands, the iconic dome-shaped structure attracted attention as it sat on a rise overlooking the busy Route 601. One historical society official thought it was a hen house since there used to be many shaped that way in the area. Hmmm. A county full of hen houses, decorated with onion-shaped domes. Now, that must have been a sight! However, the real purpose of Simon O'Donnell's building, after eluding many, was water storage. A wooden windmill, at a nearby stream, pumped water into the cistern, which the current owners, Marlin and Janet Sherbine, still use as a back-up source of water for their cattle. So, perhaps it can be labeled a "water barn."

Even though this old farm building is not a conventional barn in the truest sense of the word, it did serve a vital purpose in supplying water to the farm's livestock. Sadly, the roof caught fire and burned in June, 2019, and may not be rebuilt. Regardless, it will be remembered in this painting and essay — as a most unique piece of "round" Americana.

ADAMS COUNTY

Beauty Queen

Adams County is one of the richest historical regions in America. It's only 30 miles from York, also known as Yorktown, which witnessed battles of the American Revolution, as well as those of the Civil War. York, founded in 1741 by settlers from Philadelphia, was the headquarters of the Continental Congress from September 1777 to June 1778 and, as such, has a claim to being one of the early capitals of the fledgling United States. York also became the largest northern town that was occupied by the Confederate army when Major General Early spent three days here in June, 1863. The York U.S. Army Hospital cared

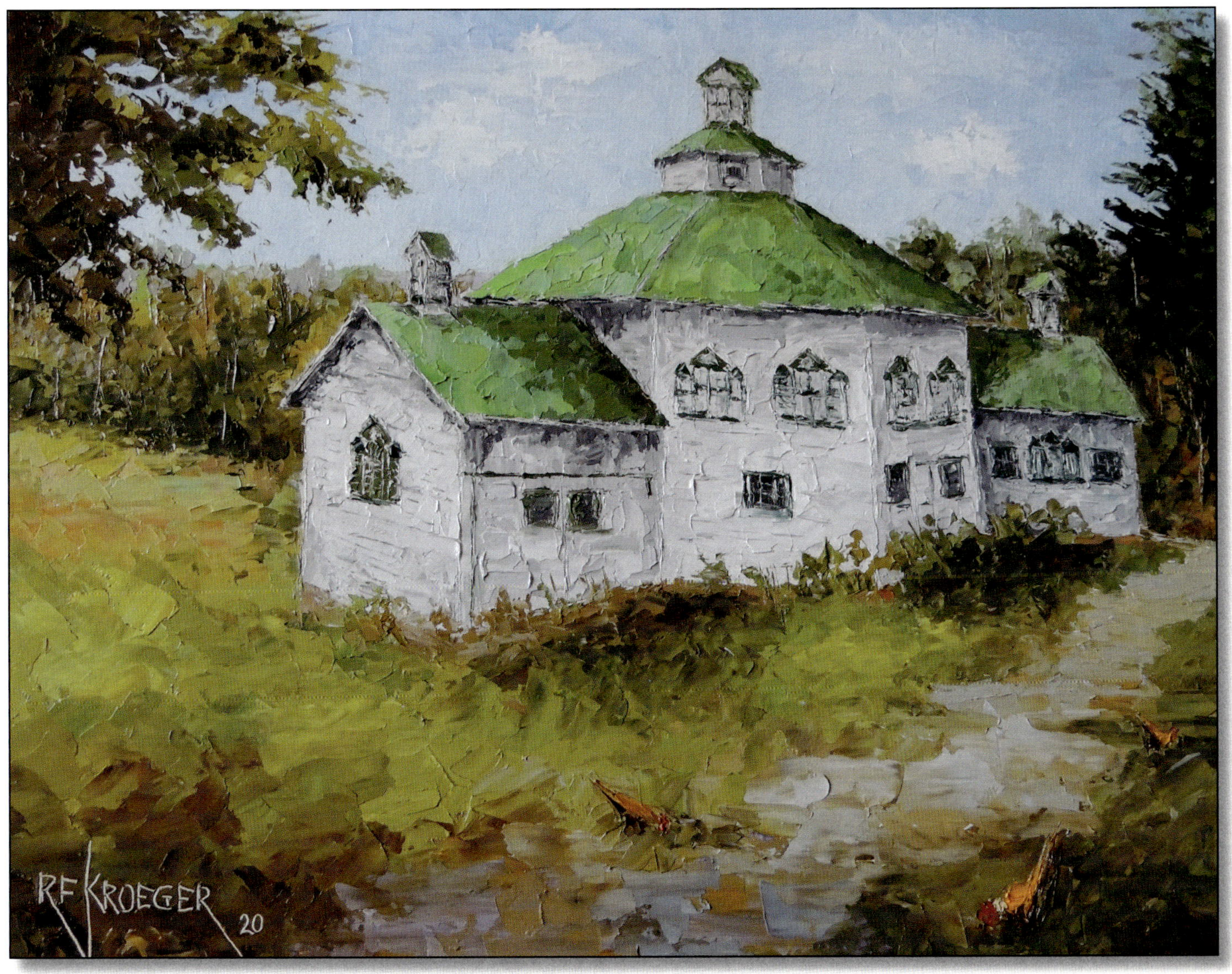

Beauty Queen

for thousands of Union soldiers wounded at the battles of Gettysburg and Antietam.

Most Americans know about the famous battle of Gettysburg, which is also the seat of Adams County. The battle, lasting three days in July, 1863, turned the tide of the war and, with approximately 50,000 casualties, ranks as the bloodiest battle in American history. On the third day, over 12,500 Confederates stormed the Union line — in the famous Pickett's Charge — only to be soundly defeated, a major blow to General Lee, though he continued the war effort for nearly two more years. Four months later — in November — President Lincoln dedicated the Soldiers' National Cemetery for the fallen Union troops and made his famous address, beginning with "Four score and seven years ago" and continuing, "that these dead shall not have died in vain—that this nation, under God, shall have a new birth of freedom." He gave his speech in Gettysburg, only 10 miles from Littlestown, where this round barn would be built 51 years later.

Littlestown, another old village, was originally laid out by Peter Klein in 1760 and was named Kleine Stedtle after this German. But, with confusion over names with a neighboring town, it changed its name to Littlestown, which is a translation from the German.

If there were a beauty contest among old octagonal barns, this one would take a prize. Not only has it been well maintained, now for over a century (it was built in 1914), but its cheery green paint covers its tall distinctive cupolas, artistically decorated louvers, many windows, doors, and roofs. The artistry is duplicated on an adjacent rectangular barn with a gambrel roof.

Two smaller buildings, each with matching design, were added, presumably later, to the octagonal barn. Thanks to the Adams County Historical Society, I was able to send a letter to the late owner, Harry C. Bentzel, who, unfortunately passed away in November, 2021. Regardless, the barn still stands in this historic region, and, if awards were given, it would surely win the title of "beauty queen."

NEW JERSEY

BURLINGTON COUNTY

Cherry and Black

Though its roof, covered in red and black semi-octagonal slate, is failing, this eight-sided barn with two lateral wings still stands, clearly one of the most distinctive pieces of barn architecture in America. Its front door and a protruding dormer, possibly the former haymow entry, lead up to a small clerestory, capped with a galloping horse-weathervane. Sitting well back from a large ornate front gate, one with Mercury, the winged Greek god of speed, at its apex, the 60-foot-long barn begs for attention. Not yet enrolled in the National Register, it someday may be.

In 1760 French immigrant Pierre Abraham Lorillard, only 18 years old, started a tobacco business by grinding snuff in a rented house in Manhattan, a venture that would eventually become the Lorillard Tobacco Company, the oldest tobacco company in the world. He cleverly created a trademark of a Native American smoking a pipe, standing beside a hogshead of tobacco, which led to trade in pipes, snuff, and cigars. Cigarettes came later. Though he died in 1776, two of his sons, George and Pierre II took over his business and became fabulously wealthy.

Pierre Lorillard IV, born into the family fortune in 1833, and his brother, George L., continued the tobacco business and became fascinated by horse racing, a favorite pastime of the upper classes in the late 19th century. In 1872 Pierre bought this 200-acre farm in Jobstown, Burlington County, New Jersey, and converted it into a racing stud farm, then known as Rancocas Stud Farm. He spared no expense, building a mile-and-a-quarter track, a half-mile ring barn, and a brick stallion barn, which was mammoth. This barn — 350 by 250 feet — had a glass roof for training in winter. He also built a barn with an elaborate cupola containing a large bell, a game preserve and kennels for hunting dogs, a bath house for rheumatic horses, and a greenhouse for fruit and vegetable raising. And, of course, this eight-sided barn.

Why the architect chose an octagonal shape for this small stable barn remains a mystery. Built in the early 1870s with saw-cut lumber, thanks to the many water-powered sawmills nearby, the barn could have been constructed less expensively with a traditional rectangular shape. Though Fowler published his octagonal house design in the 1850s, Elliot Stewart's octagonal barn didn't get recognition until a few years after this barn was built. Perhaps Lorillard wanted this distinctive shape to garner attention and, in this vein, he decorated this barn and several other buildings with a roof of striking red and black slate.

He and his brother George, who owned Westbrook Stud Farm on Long Island and helped found Monmouth Park Racetrack, loved to compete, each trying to outshine the other. They also raced their horses against D. D. Withers and his Brookdale Stud Farm. High society allowed such leisure pursuits, but Lorillard had grander ambitions.

In 1881 his horse, Iroquois, won the famous English Epsom Derby and became the first American owned and bred horse to win a European classic. His jockey, Fred, "the Tin Man," Archer, wore the farm's trademark cherry and black racing silks. Buoyed by this success, Lorillard

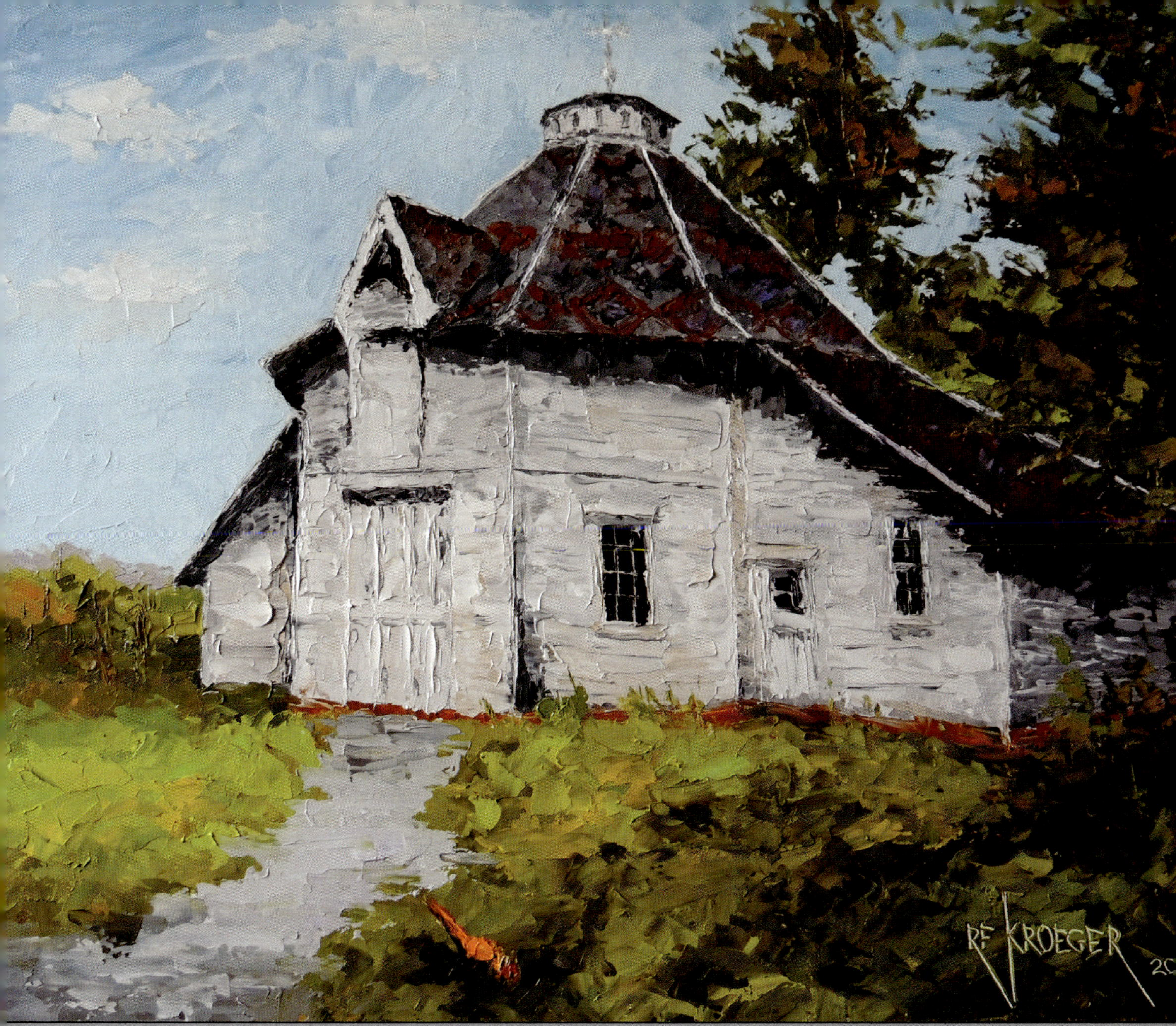

Cherry and Black

turned his sights on Newport, Rhode Island, helping to make it a fashionable yachting venue — with his schooner Vesta and his steam yacht Radha. He built the fabulous summer estate, The Breakers, which he later sold to Cornelius Vanderbilt, II.

But, after the premature death of his brother George in 1886, he lost interest in horse racing and sold his inventory. Nonetheless, a visitor in 1890 observed that the farm was doing very well: 20,000 bushels of oats each year, 7,000 bushels of carrots, 80 broodmares, eight stallions, nearly 100 other horses, cattle, sheep, and hogs. The farm also raised plenty of vegetables as well as mushrooms.

Despite this success, his marriage ended in divorce and Pierre died in 1901. Though his ex-wife Emily was still alive, he deeded the farm to his girlfriend, Lillian "Lily" Barnes-Allen-Livingston, whom he figured would be the best to run it. And she did … for awhile … until the moralist movement began to shut down horse racing. At that point, she moved with her horses to more liberal Canada, developed one of the best breeding farms in that country, and was inducted into the Canadian Horse Racing Hall of Fame in 2011.

Lily sold the farm to wealthy Kansas oil man Harry Sinclair, who continued breeding at Rancocas, turning it into one of the most dominant stables in the country during the 1920s. Their horse Zev won the Kentucky Derby in 1925 and retired with over $300,000 in earnings, enough to surpass the record of Man O' War. But Harry, founder of the Sinclair Oil Company, ran into trouble, defrauding the government in the Teapot Dome Scandal, and was convicted of attempting to bribe jurors during his trial. However, after serving six months in prison in 1929, he returned to his oil business, buying troubled oil companies during the Great Depression, and building a network of refineries, pipelines, and oil fields. His horses also won three Belmont Stakes.

Another oil man, William Helis, entered the picture when he purchased the 1,300-acre farm in 1943 and started adding more land, increasing the total to over 2,000 acres. A poor Greek immigrant in the late 1800s, Helis made his fortune in oil, earning the nickname, the "Golden Greek." As with other millionaires of his era, he became obsessed with thoroughbred racing and yearned to develop champions. He spent lavishly, often bidding against Florence Nightingale Graham, known by her business name of Elizabeth Arden, the cosmetics queen. Another rags-to riches story, she began her cosmetics empire in the early 1900s, establishing make-up as acceptable and proper for a lady.

After Helis died in 1950, his son William George, Jr., managed his father's oil empire and continued to race and breed horses, changing the name of the farm from Rancocas Stud Farm to Helis Stock Farm. When he died in 1988, his wife and children inherited the farm and chose to keep it private, hiring Ed and Linda Lovenduski to manage it.

According to local historian Dick Toone, they currently raise over 300 head of Black Angus, as well as hay, soybeans, and alfalfa. Their website promotes grain sales, corn, soybeans, hay, straw, and cattle. Sadly, the days of stud farming on this site are done but memories live on — like the one of the English jockey, who rode Iroquois to victory, wearing Lorillard's cherished colors of cherry and black.

DELAWARE

KENT COUNTY

The Round Barn of Cherbourg

The port of Cherbourg, France, served as a base for repairing French ships in WWI and, when this barn was built in 1918, it was still supporting the war effort. Some 20 years later German tanks rolled into the city, marking the beginning of four years of occupation until D-Day in June, 1944, when allied troops stormed onto Utah Beach, only 25 miles away. On a more pleasant note, a 1964 movie, *The Umbrellas of Cherbourg*, perhaps better known for its music by Michel Legrand, symbolizes the plaintive atmosphere of this historic village.

Long before the world wars of the 20th century, a farmer by the name of Cornelius Parsons Comegys owned a "mansion farm" near Little Creek in Kent County, Delaware. A veteran of the War of 1812 and a member of the Federalist Party, he also served as governor of Delaware from 1837 to 1841. After his first wife died, he married again, this time to Ruhamah Marim, a sister of Charles Marim, whose family owned a substantial farm. They had 12 children.

In the late 19th century, the farm still belonged to the Comegys family and included 376 acres and a 18th century mansion home (demolished in 1953). Family members were born on this tract of land called Cherbourg throughout the 1800s and continued ownership of the farm until Charles G. Cherbourg sold it in 1910 for $15,000, ending the legacy. The family graveyard remains on the property in perpetuity, as stipulated in the sales transaction.

The new owner, Harry McDaniel, Sr., must have been an innovative farmer since he chose a circular design for his barn, which he began building in 1912. It was finished in 1918, an usually long period of construction, possibly interrupted by wartime, and it cost $6,000, a hefty sum in those years — four times what some round barns in Wisconsin cost in the same years. A tax assessment in 1915 included a 300-acre farm, of which 30-50 acres were wooded and 20-35 acres were marsh. He listed his livestock as six mules, a bull, a calf, and one horse as well as 16 cows, which is presumably why he chose a round barn design.

And what a barn he built! Unusual in its time, the walls feature poured reinforced concrete and the gambrel roof had no interior bracing. The first-story walls, seven inches thick, were topped with a second-story concrete wall, five inches thick, resulting in a lip that supported the floor joists. The barn's diameter of 72 feet suggested it could handle a modest dairy herd of up to 80 cows. A feeding trough was located in a circular concrete platform. Twin silos, each with a grain elevator — on either side of the barn — were originally capped with 12-sided conical roofs. I decided to do the painting without some of the outbuildings and without the conical caps on the silos, thanks to a recent photo by photographer Carol Ward.

In 1935 McDaniel sold the farm to James L. Davis for $15,000, suggesting difficult times since the 1915 taxation was based on a value of over $20,000. During McDaniel's ownership in 1930 and just before the Great Depression years, he acquired more land and he added buildings: a gambrel-roofed conventional barn, stables, two milk houses, a tenant house, and granaries. Perhaps he took out loans for the new additions and couldn't make payments.

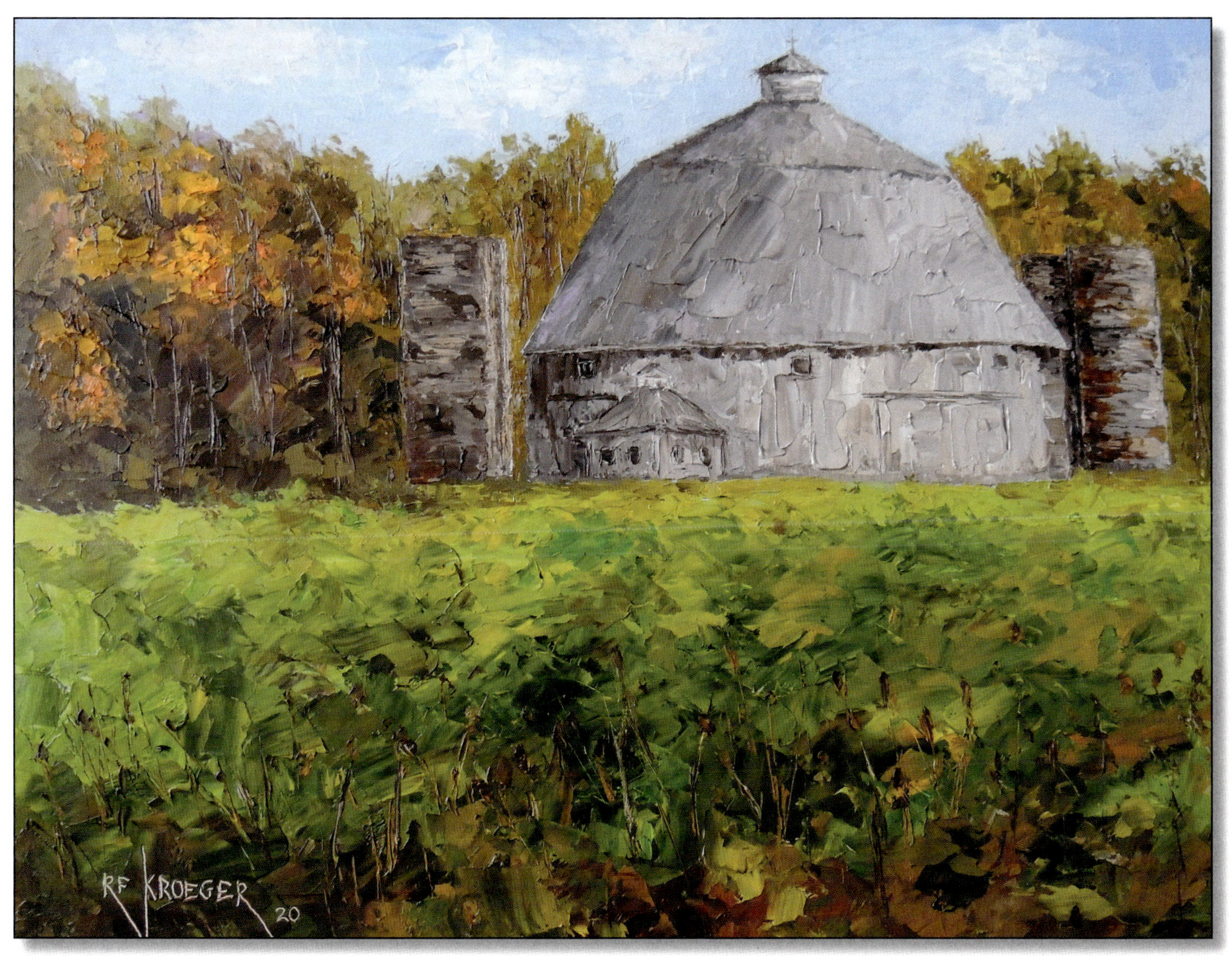

The Round Barn of Cherbourg

The next owner, Stefanie Jackewicz, took over the farm in 1954 and, five years later, passed it on to her children, Anthony and Bertha Jackewicz. Historically minded, they applied successfully for a listing on the National Register in 1978. At the time it was no longer being used for dairy farming. They sold it in 1984.

Phillip Cartanza, owner of Cartanza Farms and a Delaware farmer for decades, used the barn for storage. Being a preservationist as were the former owners, he decided to save the barn after a storm in 1999 caused the roof to capsize into the hayloft floor. He spent considerable cash in adding cedar shake shingles to the roof and restored the second story wooden floor, adhering to period drawings for round barns.

Though the barn no longer houses a booming dairy operation, it serves as Delaware's only remaining round barn, an icon of the past and a memory of a piece of farmland called Cherbourg, home to some of the state's early forefathers.

WEST VIRGINIA

HAMPSHIRE COUNTY

Hampshire Country

This 15-sided two-story barn, placed on the National Register of Historic Places in 1985, sadly collapsed in 2005, due to lack of maintenance. However, thanks to information from Mary Kuykendall-Weber, whose family owned the barn previously, its history, as rich as any, has survived.

The story begins in the early 1700s, when the region served as a hunting ground for Indian tribes and fur trappers. By 1735 six families had settled near present-day Romney, the city near where this barn once stood. Hampshire County, then the western border of the colony of Virginia, was established in 1753 — though, due to the conflict of the French and Indian War (1754-1763), the county did not become official until 1757. Lord Fairfax, who owned millions of acres, thanks to a royal grant, named it after seeing some large hogs in the colony, which had been raised in Hampshire County, England.

In fact, this English noble, officially named Thomas, Baron Cameron, sixth Lord Fairfax, born in England in 1693, was a neighbor of young George Washington, who looked upon him as a mentor. After inheriting a vast tract of land between the Rappahannock and the Potomac rivers in 1719, he eventually moved here from England, built an estate and, in 1748, hired 16-year-old Washington to survey his land. Their friendship continued even through the Revolutionary War, when Washington wrote letters to him, allowing him to be the only English titled nobleman ever to reside permanently in the American colonies. Lord Fairfax died in 1781.

The name Kuykendall, Dutch in origin, probably derives from a location in Holland, where families emigrated to the east coast of America in the 1600s. Many of these early settlers were stone masons. In 1740 one of them, Jacob Kuykendall, brought his family here, including his son, Nathaniel, who was born in the colony of New Jersey in 1728. These white settlers peacefully co-existed with native tribes in this rich, fertile valley,

A few years later in 1748 — with nearly 200 now living in the region — Lord Fairfax, visualizing an income stream, decided to sell lots to settlers or take rent if they could not afford to buy. Accordingly, he sent a team to map his land, surveyors led by James Genn. One of the apprentices was 16-year-old George Washington, who spent three summers in establishing boundaries for the Fairfax estate. In 1749, according to his diary, Washington camped near Romney.

Years later, with the French becoming a problem, the 22-year-old Washington, by then a major in the Virginia Militia, was sent in 1753 by Virginia's governor to request French cooperation, which didn't happen. Instead, the French and Indian War began and created havoc throughout these western lands, claiming many lives among the settlers of Hampshire County.

By 1754 George Washington was somewhat of a celebrity on both sides of the Atlantic after the publication of his journal about his role in this conflict. He soon rose to the rank of Lt. Colonel in the militia. Though he was promoted to full colonel a year later and, despite his heroics and achievements in this war, Great Britain denied him a commission in the British army. So, in 1759 Washington got married and returned to farming in Mt. Vernon, his family estate, only about 130 miles from Romney.

Meanwhile, Nathaniel Kuykendall was busy raising his family, farming, and using his skills as a stonemason. One of his works, Fort Van Meter (Van Meter bought the land from Lord Fairfax), was constructed of stone in 1754 and listed on the National Register in 2009. This little stone fort helped protect area families, including the Van Meters and the Kuykendalls, during Indian attacks. Even though a Kuykendall was the builder, it's called Fort Van Meter because that family lived there. A house near this fort, according to Mary, still contains a log cabin. During the revolution all the Kuykendalls supported the American cause.

Nathaniel's son, Isaac, born in 1766, continued in his father's shoes, assisting him in building turnpike roads

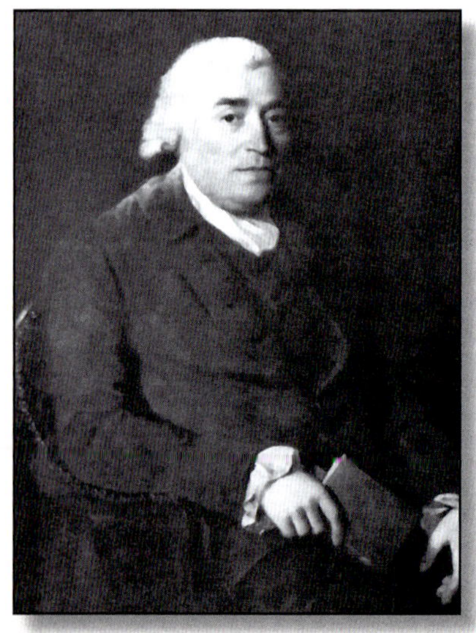

Above: *Thomas Fairfax, circa 1740. Grayscale reproduction of oil painting by unknown artist, Wikipedia*

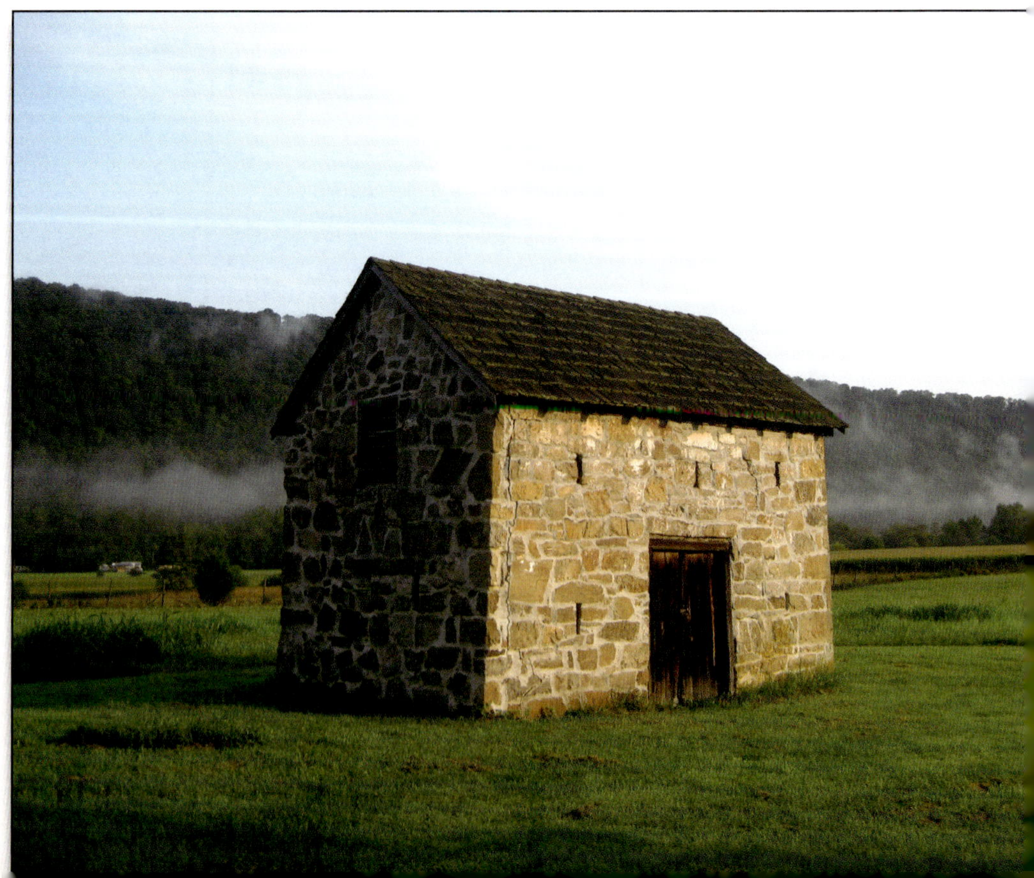

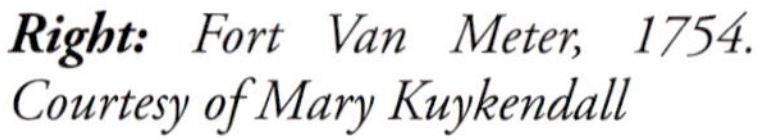

Right: *Fort Van Meter, 1754. Courtesy of Mary Kuykendall*

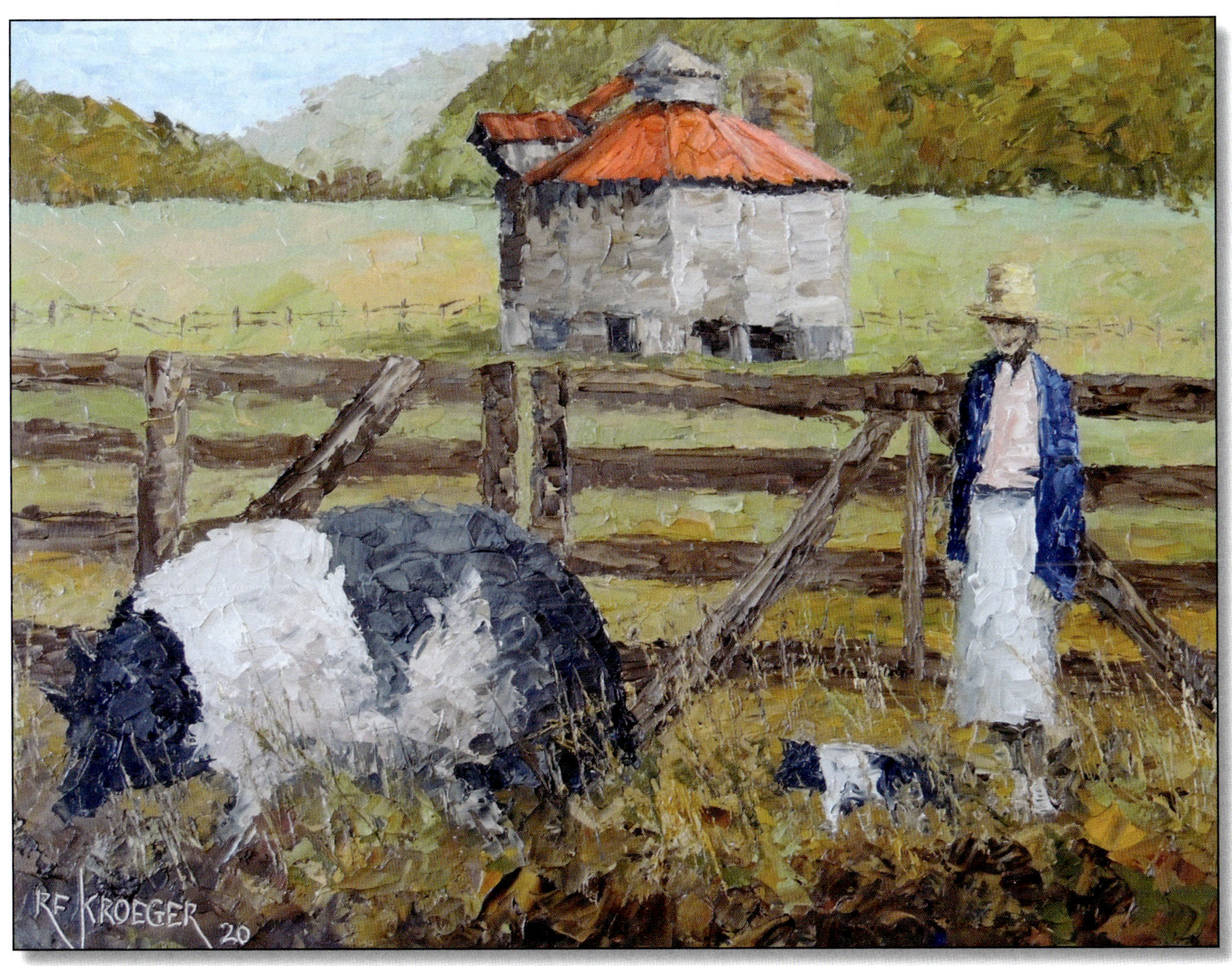

Hampshire Country

and stone houses, one of which carries the Kuykendall name and the date 1789, both etched in stone. The home is presently owned by Dan Wagoner, who, a purist at heart, has not added electricity.

By the start of the Civil War, Hampshire County was still in Virginia, but, when West Virginia became a state in the Union in 1863, the county became the oldest in this new state. Romney, the county seat and West Virginia's oldest city, changed allegiances 56 times during the Civil War, sadly illustrating this American conflict.

Decades passed and the farm left family hands. But William Kuykendall, born in 1852, got it back and passed it on to his son Michael Blue Kuykendall, who married Edith Casey Pancake, the lady featured in the painting, in 1906. That was the year he built this 15-sided barn and, though the reason for such a design may remain a mystery, Michael may have read about polygonal barns in various farm journals or he may have visited Capon Springs, a well-known mineral springs about 40 miles from Romney, where the Brill Octagonal House was built in 1890, possibly suggested by a architect there on holiday. Or perhaps he had heard of George Washington's 16-sided barn in Mt. Vernon. Nonetheless, Michael hired John Clowser, who lived about seven miles away, to build the barn.

Armed only with an eighth-grade education, Clowser surprised everyone by not only building this intricate barn but by adding internal features that belied his educational level. One feature, possibly influenced by Iowa's Louden Machinery Company, which published its patented track system in 1905, consisted of a coal car, running on a circular track, which was used to deliver feed from the central silo, a wooden one. Another track and conveyor allowed hay to be delivered to the second story for storage, initially raised by a crane. Legend has it that, after the corn ensilage had fermented over the winter, locals would sneak into the silos, drill a hole near the bottom, and drain the liquid. Voila! Instant moonshine. Later, the owners added a rectangular wing, roughly 80 feet, though it doesn't show in the painting.

William Blue Kuykendall died prematurely in 1920 but Edith, a hardy West Virginia matron, continued the family farming tradition until she died, aged 83, in 1963.

After her death there were four heirs to the farm and Mary's father William — who had been farming his own land nearby — could not afford to buy the farm outright from his siblings. So, the estate sold it to a Mr. Hood from Maryland, who hoped that his sons could take over. But, alas, that didn't happen and a corporate farmer, Renick Williams, purchased the farm, sold trees for their timber, marketed river lots (the nearby South Branch of the Potomac), and continued raising cattle. Mary and her sister wanted to buy back the barn but the farmer decided to keep it to house his cattle. Though he obtained a grant to restore the historic barn, it gradually collapsed in 2005.

In 1986 Mary and her sister revisited their roots and purchased the original family home, including a horse barn, granary, and corn cribs — along with the tiny Fort Van Meter. Unfortunately, the round barn was not for sale.

Yes, for centuries the Kuykendalls raised beef cattle and Hampshire hogs, which introduces the composition of the painting: I used a 1955 photograph of 73-year-old Edith Casey Kuykendall. She stands in the painting, admiring her hogs because they represented a major source of income for this family for over 200 years. The breed, originally bred in Scotland from wild black and white boars, was developed in Hampshire County, England, and was imported to America. Edith, according to an essay written by her daughter Mary and published in *River Roots*, a book featuring colorful stories about locals, not only prized these hogs but considered them to be nobility, just as the original laird, Lord Fairfax, was.

Mary related, "Milling around in the long skirt she always wore, she called these belted swine her tuxedo pigs." And Mary recalled her mother's words, "With their white front legs and shoulders they are as dressed up as any Victorian I have ever seen — certainly just as smart in their white shirts and black pants and shiny heeled shoes ready for a debutante's ball." Mary's father, Edith's son, who farmed with her, disagreed, insisting that the pigs were best known for the quality of their meat.

Yet Edith persisted, "Just look at their ears," she would declare, "and notice how erect they are, certainly not floppy like those on most white and red hogs. These Hampshires are very aware of themselves." She would add, pointing out that they were English in demeanor as well as culture. Accordingly, Edith named her hogs after such Brits as David Copperfield, Winston Churchill and Lady Churchill, Lord Byron, Henry VIII, and Anne Boleyn, though Jane Eyre was her favorite, to whom she always gave the best ears of corn. "Jane never failed to produce a full litter, one for each teat. Others, like Queen Victoria, were unpredictable, sometimes bearing more than they could care for, resulting in runts … which had managed to survive in spite of them being shunted aside at the teats by the stronger siblings and sometimes mashed by the mother adjusting herself for the feeding frenzy."

One such runt, Sir Walter Raleigh, so named because he appeared gracious and "okay, maybe a bit timid," was run over by a tractor when he was one. Mary and her 10-year-old sister, returning from fishing on the river, came to his rescue, pushed his entrails back in, sewed up his split belly, and helped him recover. At market he weighed over 500 pounds, though his "tuxedo" was not pretty to look at from one side. Edith, sensing his indignity from such scarring, "would go out of her way to not make him feel uncomfortable by staring at his bad side." MasterCard can buy a lot of things but it can't touch stories like this. Priceless.

VIRGINIA

FAIRFAX COUNTY

The Gentleman Farmer

Like the Roman general Lucius Quinctius Cincinnatus, George Washington was not only a military leader and a political statesman but also a farmer, an occupation he treasured above all else, including the presidency. And while it may be true, as many historians claim, that Washington's 16-sided barn was the first round barn in America, there may have been others built earlier, whose history has been lost. In fact, in 1761 an octagonal wood building was built in Virginia and was known as the Gentlemen's Pool House, which was the oldest spa structure in the United States and one of the earliest octagonal buildings, along with many octagonal churches, built as early as 1650 in the Hudson River Valley. Jefferson, a close friend and ally, may have bathed here prior to the 1790s, although his only recorded visit came in 1819.

George Washington, born into a wealthy land-owning British family, was six years old in 1738 when his father Augustine moved to the Ferry Farm in Virginia. Besides owning three plantations and an iron furnace operation, he was active in politics, but he died at an early age, leaving his 11-year-old son without a mentor on how to become a gentleman-farmer. Young George did inherit the family farm, Ferry Farm, along with 10 slaves, though his mother managed his inheritance until George turned 21.

The death of his father precluded an education in England, but George studied diligently in the local school and learned how to become not only a Virginia gentleman, a superb horseman, but also a surveyor. Beginning at age 15, George began surveying and, at 17, was appointed to his first public office as surveyor of nearby Culpeper County. Surveying made him aware of meticulous record keeping and helped him manage his estate and farms profitably throughout his life.

After serving as an officer in the Virginia Militia during the French and Indian War from 1753 to 1759, George was denied a commission in the British Army and, instead, he took over managing the family farm. By December of 1754, the Mount Vernon estate consisted of over 2,200 acres, a big job for a 22-year-old. He also realized that he would have to increase his acreage to make a profit, support his hundreds of slaves and his family, which grew in 1759 when he married Martha and took in her two children from her first marriage. At the time, Martha was arguably the wealthiest widow in Virginia.

Dogue Run Farm, one of five farms that Washington eventually owned, was the site of his polygonal barn. To develop this farm, he bought three neighboring farms: 500 acres in 1757, 1,806 acres in May of 1760, and, later that year, another 238 acres, purchases which doubled the size of his estate, bringing his holdings to over 4,800 total acres. His cash crop at that time was tobacco — the same as that of most Virginia planters.

However, tobacco raising was becoming a concern, both agriculturally and economically. Shipped primarily to England and Scotland, tobacco incurred taxes along the distribution chain and colonial farmers saw their profit margins shrinking. In addition to that, in 1764, when his tobacco crop yield was poor, indicating depleted soil, Washington realized that he needed to switch crops, which he did — into wheat and other grains. He began to rotate crops and kept precise records of this rotation in each field. His notes indicate that wheat production rose from 257 bushels in 1764 and to 6,241 bushels in 1769. He built a new gristmill in 1771, which could grind 5,000 pounds of flour a day, producing a healthy profit needed to keep his business in the black. By 1772, Washington had enlarged his estate by nearly 1,900 acres and the acreage of his five farms — Dogue Run, River Farm, Muddy Hole Farm, Union Farm, and Mansion — totaled over 6,500 acres.

During the eight years that he served in the Revolutionary War, Washington spent only 10 days at Mt. Vernon. Yet, his farm continued to run in his absence, maintained by his energetic wife. He made only one purchase during this time — 400 acres from Thomas Marshall in 1779.

When he resigned from the army in 1783, he bought more land, 118 acres, and returned to Mt. Vernon to resume business on his cherished farm, which generated no profit during the war years. While his first interest in farming was to make Mount Vernon profitable, he also realized his experiments could help all American farmers. He felt it was the duty of educated American farmers to set an example for their countrymen, now freed from the bonds of Mother England.

According to the Mount Vernon website, "Washington believed that it was the responsibility of wealthy farmers to undertake experimentation, as failures would be inevitable and losses would have to be absorbed while new techniques were perfected." He read voraciously about the latest agricultural methods and applied them, sometimes with success and sometimes with failure. He began by repairing buildings and erecting new ones and, having been born British, he enlisted the help of Arthur Young, a major figure in agriculture in England, who wrote to Washington in 1786 that he would help him by finding workers, materials, or even farm animals.

By August of that year, Washington began to reconfigure farm fields and devise a new seven-field crop rotation system at Dogue Run and Muddy Hole. He tried raising and growing nearly every vegetable and grain crop and his livestock included turkeys, chickens, dairy cows and cattle, sheep, mules, donkeys, horses, and hogs. He farmed fish on his River Farm, which bordered the Potomac River, whose fisheries brought in nearly one million fish annually, giving Washington a handsome profit. However, despite these efforts, he still needed cash.

Then came the first presidency of the new country. Despite his preference to remain a farmer — much like that of Cincinnatus in 500 BC — Washington accepted the role in 1787. But this time, unlike when he was fighting the English, he had time to attend to his farm. He began planning three major new barn complexes, one to serve the Ferry farm, a second at River Farm, and a third at Dogue Run. By 1792, he had expanded his five farms to 8,000 acres.

Originally, he intended to build three similar grain barns since wheat had become his major cash crop. And, though he could have chosen a rectangular Pennsylvania-German bank barn for threshing, instead he chose a polygonal barn for Dogue Run. But why a polygonal?

Conventionally, wheat was threshed either with a flail by hand or by having horses stomp it in a circular pattern, outside on a dirt floor, which was a slow, tedious process and was subject to the whims of Nature and its rain. Washington had a better idea, diagrammed it in his notes, which were used after the barn's demise to reconstruct a replica. He wanted to move the horse-driven method inside the protection of a barn and he wanted to make it more efficient.

So, rather than choosing a traditional barn design, he realized that a circular form would suit the horses better and so he chose an octagonal center — presumably because it was less expensive to construct when compared to a wooden circle — and, allowing for room for the horses to move, he surrounded the center with 16 outer sides, which again were easier to build than a true circle. While his choice of the octagon and the hexadecagon was unique, his creativity showed when his design called for a gap, only one and a half inches wide, between white oak planks on the top floor so that the trampled wheat kernels, once separated from the chaff, could fall below into the octagonal granary. Horses could do one load of wheat every 45 minutes, which would allow six or seven acres of wheat to be processed daily … and safely — without threat of rain — and cleanly — without dirt. From the granary, workers delivered the grain to the mill, where Washington's new process of moving both wheat and flour by means of a bucket elevator had eliminated the need for manual labor. Oddly enough, there are no records that other Virginia plantation owners followed his threshing design or his polygonal barn.

By October 28, 1792, Washington had finished his plans for this barn, drawings of which are kept in the Library of Congress and in archives maintained by the Mount Vernon Ladies' Association, the nonprofit that owns and administers Washington's estate. Plans called for a diameter of 52 feet and 16 exterior walls 10 feet wide. The steeply pitched roof of about 43 degrees, similar to that of many round barns built in Europe and in the West and Midwest towards the end of the 19th century, was designed to allow water to run off the wood shingles quickly. Inside, the octagon granary and radiating rafters provided adequate support for the roof.

Washington estimated that the lower level — with bars on the windows to discourage theft — would require 30,280 bricks, though he thought that it would be wise to make 40,000, allowing for breakage during the firing process, which was done in a kiln on the estate. Though brick was used for the lower level — since the barn was built into a bank, which meant that wetness would have rotted a wooden foundation — and though white oak

***Below:** The Gentleman Farmer*

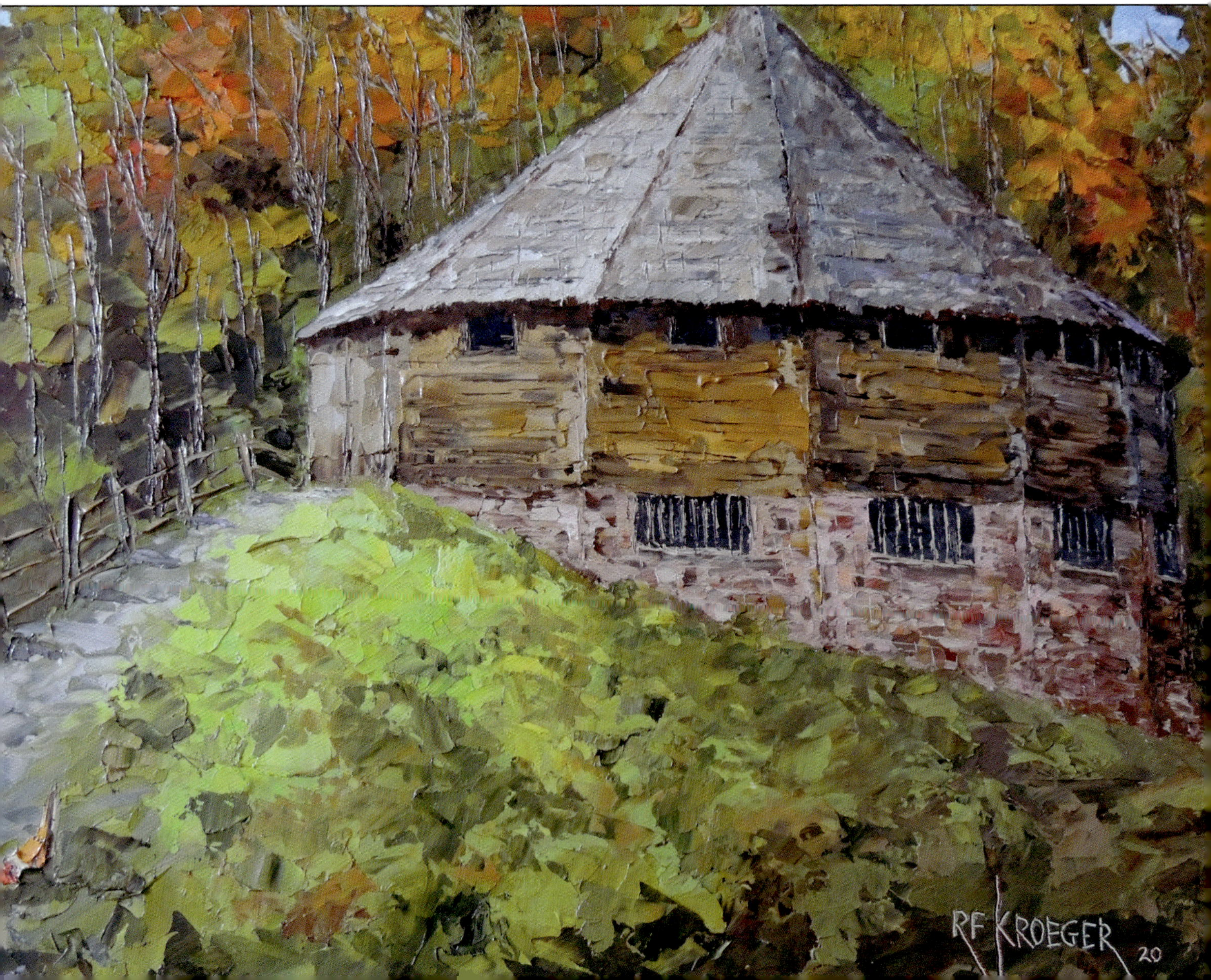

was used for the treading floor, most of the barn was constructed with southern pine, a softer but more plentiful tree in Virginia.

Thomas Green, Washington's carpenter, had probably never constructed a polygonal building but he followed orders: it took him and Washington's crew of nine slave carpenters until 1794 to finish the barn. Thomas Green worked for Washington on an annual contract.

The barn was constructed during Washington's second run as president, a term he again did not want but accepted, based on his belief that the young country needed his leadership. Though he offered to serve without pay, Congress insisted that he accept a salary, providing him $25,000 per year, which helped him considerably since his vast land ownings showed little if any profits.

Washington finally retired to Mount Vernon in March of 1797 and, at 65, probably looked forward to a lifetime of farming. But he still needed cash. Records in 1799 showed that there were 317 slaves at Mount Vernon, including 143 children, which meant that Washington had to support many who were too young or too old to work, resulting in a net operating loss for the plantation.

Another idea emerged — a whiskey distillery. Knowing that the Scots were experts in this business, Washington hired one, James Anderson, who recommended that the distillery be built next to the gristmill. Although he hesitated at first, Washington eventually agreed and, after the first production was successful, he built a larger distillery, one with five copper pot stills. This new operation produced 4,500 gallons of whiskey in 1798 and almost 11,000 gallons in 1799 — with a profit in that year of $1,858, making the distillery his most lucrative business.

He continued to work on his farm, never shirking from difficult tasks. On December 12, 1799, despite snow and sleet, Washington inspected his farms on horseback. After a full day's work, he returned home late but opted not to change out of his wet clothes, preferring to attend to his dinner guests. The next day, despite a sore throat, he again went out in freezing, snowy weather, this time to mark trees for cutting. That evening, he complained of chest congestion, but was still cheerful. On Saturday, December 13, he woke up with difficulty breathing and, sadly, on December 14 he died — after only two years of retirement on his beloved farm.

Many viewed Washington as a rich Virginian, though most of his wealth was tied up in slaves and land — 50,000 acres in various places, including 8,000 at Mt. Vernon, of which 3,000 acres were cultivated. In July of his final year he created his will, which specified that, upon the death of his wife, all slaves would be freed, old and young — and, once freed — would be taken care of indefinitely. Further, the will dictated that the younger ones would be educated and placed in occupations. One year after her husband's death, Martha freed his slaves, and, even though she died a year later in 1802, according to his wishes, funds were used to provide for the young and old slaves until the early 1830s.

Sadly, due to non-use and no maintenance, the barn, Washington's grist mill, and his whiskey distillery deteriorated over the years. Well after the distillery burned in 1814, the state of Virginia bought the land in 1932 and, thanks to a partnership with the Mount Vernon Ladies' Association, the distillery was rebuilt in 2007. Next to fall was the gristmill, dismantled in the 1850s. The state rebuilt it in 1933.

Finally, the last of these three historic buildings to vanish was the barn. A circa 1870 photograph, held in Mount Vernon's archives, shows the barn in poor condition — with the roof deteriorating, the brick foundation crumbling, and many boards missing. A note, written on the reverse of the photo, states that barn was destroyed around 1870. Eventually, thanks to a generous grant of over $2 million from the W.K. Kellogg Foundation, the threshing barn and related stables were reconstructed in 1996. However, such reconstruction — researched thoroughly and supervised by a University of Maryland historian, Dr. Dennis Pogue — would not have been possible without the copious notes, diagrams, and writings of George Washington, all stored in archives. All of America needs to thank George Washington, the general of its revolution, its first president, the overseer of its constitution, and, above all, a hardworking gentleman farmer, whose unique 16-sided barn is preserved in this painting and essay.

NORTH CAROLINA

LINCOLN COUNTY

The Commissioners

The history of this 16-sided barn began with the family patriarch, Joseph Graham, born in 1759 to Scots-Irish parents in Chester County, Pennsylvania. After his father died, his mother moved the family to North Carolina, where they became farmers and ironmongers — those artisans who fashioned implements by forging iron. During the American Revolution, Joseph served as a captain in 1781, at the age of 22, and was promoted to major a year later. After the war he returned to farming.

When called upon once again, he served in the War of 1812 and, with the rank of brigadier general, he commanded a brigade of North Carolina and South Carolina militia.

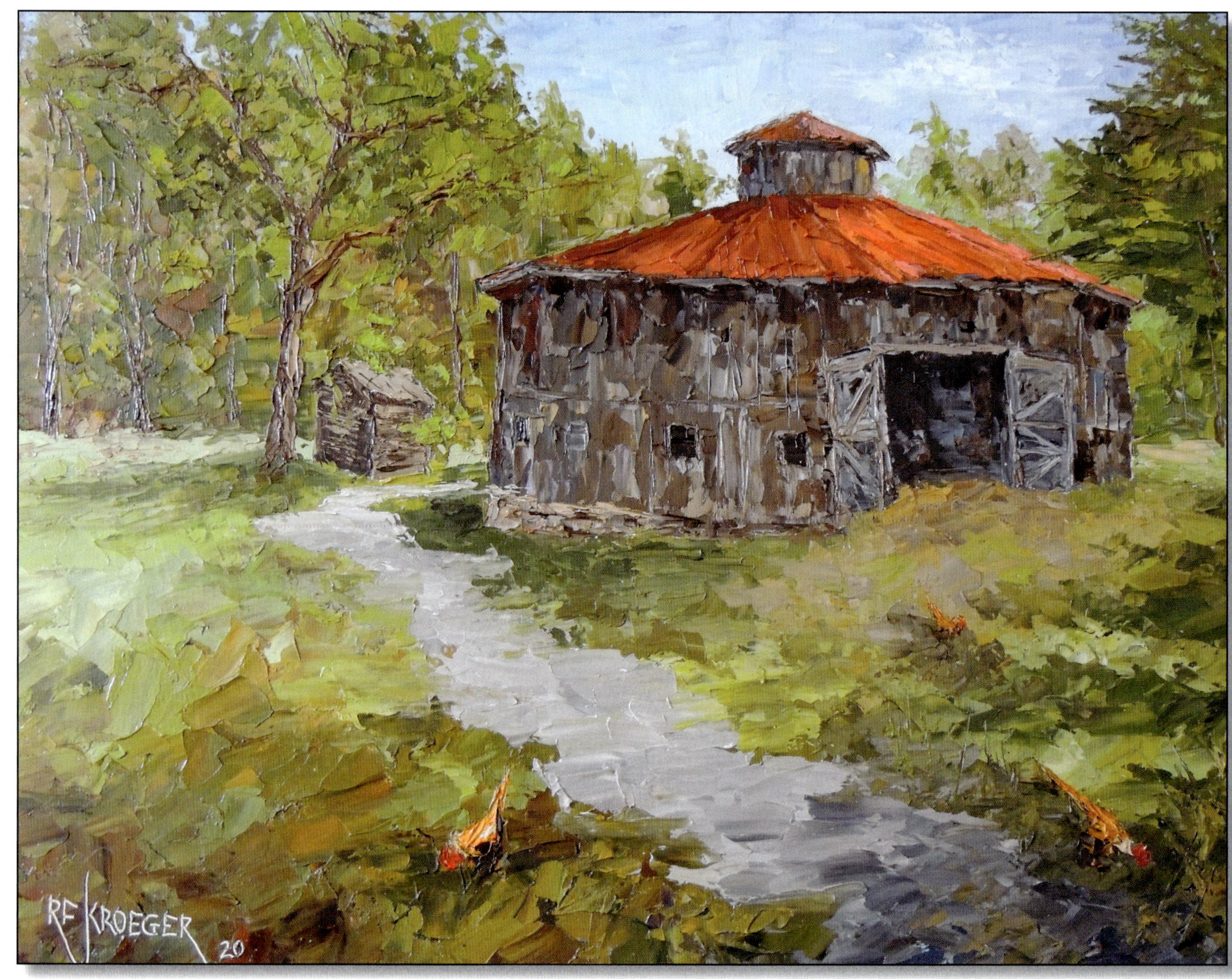

The Commissioners

When the war ended, he once again returned to farming in Lincoln County, where he is buried.

His son, William A. Graham, born in 1804, continued farming, raising hogs, cotton, and tobacco, and became involved in politics, taking after his father, who served on the state council. William not only was a United States senator (1840-1843) and the governor of North Carolina (1845-1849) but was also the Secretary of the Navy, a role that involved sending Commodore Matthew Perry, as ordered by President Fillmore, to open up trade with Japan, a story that factors in with another round barn, California's Fountain Grove. During the Civil War, he was a senator in the Confederate States Senate.

His son, William A. Graham, Jr., the architect of this barn, was born in 1839 in Lincoln County and graduated from Princeton University in 1860. He taught school for a year before the Civil War began. Like his father, he opposed secession but, coming from a patriotic family, he joined the Confederate Army and was commissioned a lieutenant, quickly rising to captain. After he was wounded at Gettysburg, William resigned his commission in 1863 and was appointed as Assistant Adjutant General of North Carolina — with the rank of major. When the war ended, he returned to the family farm, continuing to raise crops and livestock.

In the 1870s Graham earned a seat in the state senate and worked to support the state's farming interests, serving on the board of agriculture from 1899 to 1908, when he was appointed the Commissioner of Agriculture. Initially, the value of North Carolina's crops was 23rd in the country but, when he finished his term in 1923, the year he died, the value had risen to fifth, an extraordinary leap. With such a family legacy, Governor Morrison appointed his son, William A. Graham, III, as the commissioner, following the death of his father, a position he held through the Great Depression until 1936. For 28 years, the Grahams fostered farming in North Carolina.

During the Civil War, Captain Graham fell in love. But he wanted his mother's approval, which was difficult in those war years when families were separated. So he wrote a letter, hoping for her consent to marry, "I have come across a young lady over here ... She is quite pretty but does not know it (which ruins beauty of a great many) ... and would make a capital farmer's wife. I do not wish to engage myself to her without your consent." Such were the days of gentlemanly chivalry.

Agriculture also fascinated him, prompting him to experiment, not only with the design of his multi-sided barn. Possibly influenced by his family history of ironmongery, he owned the first double-footed plow, the first cotton gin with a condenser, and the first separator, weeder, and reaper in Lincoln County.

When he died in 1923, he left the farm to his son William, who, in turn, left it to his son Joseph. The next owner, David Clark, owner of the Hope Spring Farm Company, purchased the farm from Joseph. David, another American patriot, served as a bomber pilot in the Pacific during World War II. His wife, Kathryn Clark, gifted the farm to her son Allison, who continues family ownership of the farm and the barn today.

The 16-sided barn, built in 1892 by William A. Graham, Jr., features hand-hewn timber framing, a rarity since the lumber in most round barns, built mostly from the 1870s to 1930, was cut in a sawmill. William and his crew chopped down tall trees, carved them with axes and adzes into beams, and joined them with mortise and tenon joints, held together with wooden pegs. Having a great interest in farming methods, he likely read articles in farm journals that promoted the round barn design, and, since Mt. Vernon was less than 400 miles away, he might have visited — or heard about — George Washington's 16-sided threshing barn, built a century earlier.

The barn resembles a prairie barn with its low polygonal roof, designed to survive windstorms. The cupola, windowless, has also withstood the forces of nature over a century, and its horizontally louvered air slots have provided adequate ventilation for livestock and crops. Though it served originally as protection for corn and cattle, the barn now functions as storage and as well as a reminder of North Carolina history. The adjacent farmhouse, also built in the 1890s, is listed on the National Register and the iconic barn is designated as an historical property in Lincoln County, facts that would make the "commissioners" rightly proud.

GEORGIA

JACKSON COUNTY

Moos and Mattresses

Round barns, often preserved because of their unique architecture, have been changed into functional businesses such as wedding and event centers, wineries, bed and breakfasts, restaurants, and office buildings. However, the Roncadori round barn, located about 20 miles from Athens, Georgia, and one of only three round barns still existing in the state, is the only round barn in America that has been converted into a mattress store.

In 1909 the original farmer, George G. Williamson, purchased 188 acres from S.J. Nix and, four years later, hired Lee Helms, Early Barrett, and Claude Jackson to build two round barns. The smaller one, with a diameter of 30 feet, served as a barn for raising hogs but was dismantled over the years. Why round? Williamson may have seen the octagonal barns in Harris or Carroll counties, even though they're over 100 miles away, or he may have read ag journals that described Wisconsin's Professor King's round barn plans with a central silo. Regardless, he picked a round design over the conventional rectangular one and he had adequate resources to build these barns.

Williamson used the barn for his herd of 30 Jersey cows and he supplied milk and butter to surrounding stores. The cows were housed in the lower level of this bank barn in stanchions located around the central silo. Above the silo a water storage tank held liquid for the cows and a track for transporting hay made feeding easier. Over the years the work of these builders has stood the test of time, thanks, in part, to five-and-a-half-inch thick oak boards and other substantial construction.

However, when financial trouble struck, Williamson left for Florida in 1925, though he maintained ownership of the farm. During the Great Depression many farmers could not afford to make mortgage payments and lost their farms, as happened to Williamson when a life insurance company foreclosed in 1936 and put the farm on the auction block. W.H. Maley bought it and quickly sold it to his brother, Hugh Maley, who decided not to continue dairy farming. Instead, he raised beef cattle and hogs.

In the 1950s the barn began to show its age, especially in the roof, which is the Achilles heel of a barn. Mr. Maley considered tearing it down but a local builder and building supply owner, A.G. Mitchell, apparently a good salesman, convinced him to keep the barn and cover the roof's original wooden shakes with composition shingles, which he did. The barn survived.

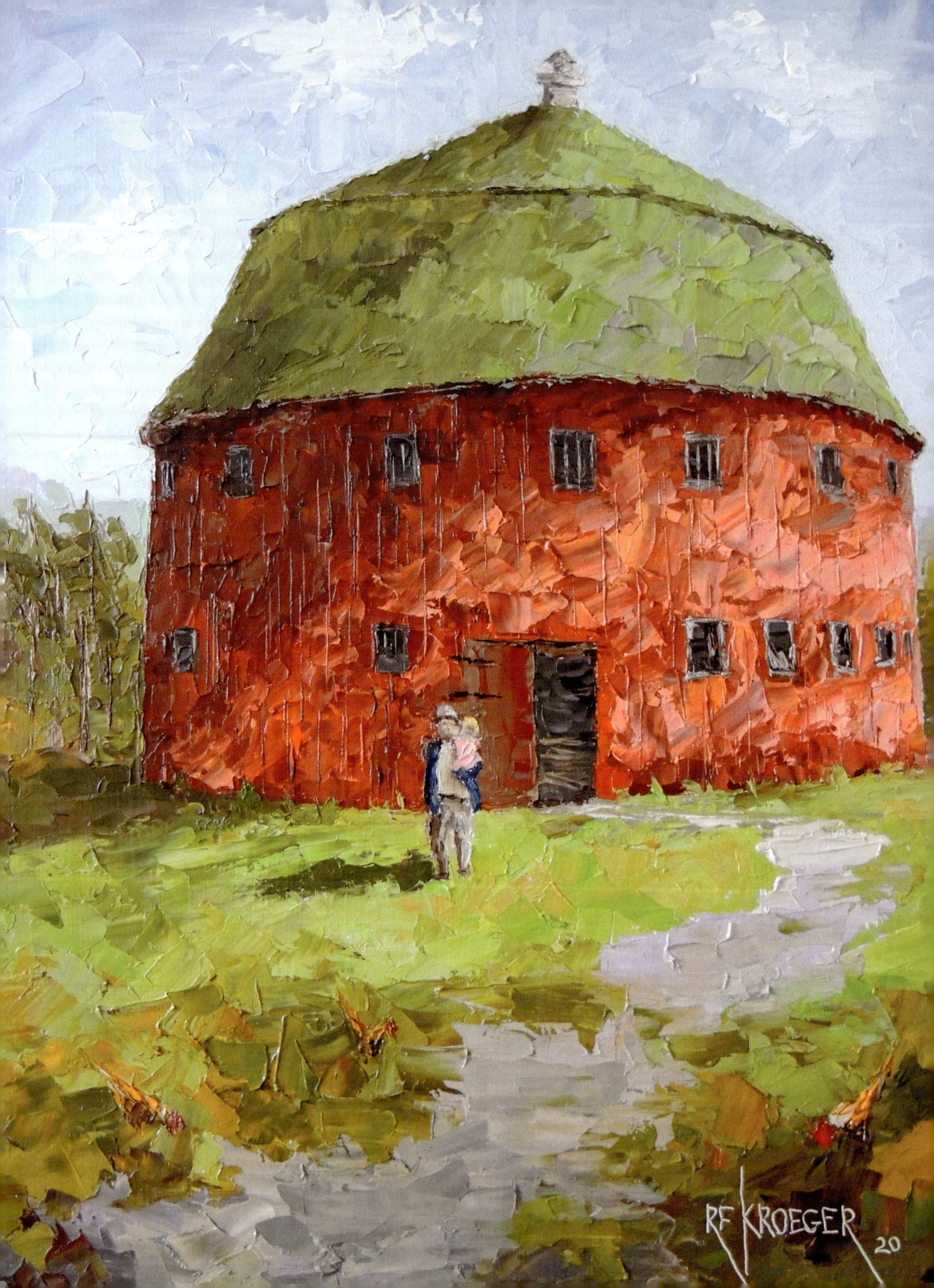
RF KROEGER
20

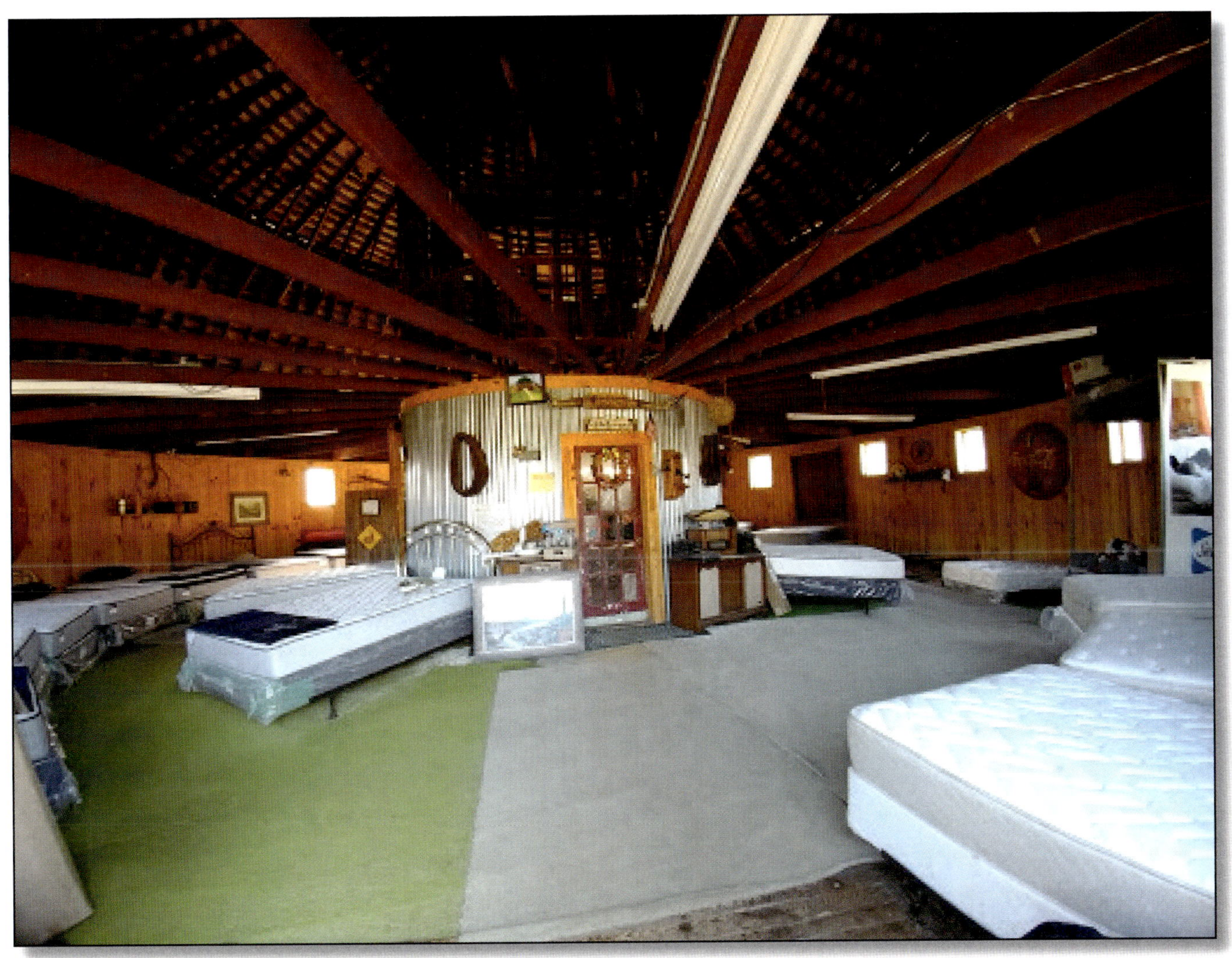

Interior, Round Barn Mattresses. Courtesy of Imogene and Mark Roncadori

Hugh Maley and his wife Jessie had one child, Dories, who married Louis Turner, who, after serving in World War II, returned to the family farm. Their daughter, Imogene, who is featured in the painting — done with the help of a 1958 photo showing her in the arms of her grandfather — currently owns the farm with her husband Mark Roncadori.

In the 1950s Louis, along with continuing to farm, also worked in a local furniture store, and, when the company eventually closed its doors, it sparked a dream for Louis. He loved the round barn, which again was deteriorating, even though it still housed cattle, and, since he knew enough about the furniture and mattress business, he thought, *Why not restore the barn and turn it into a store?* So, with a dream in arms, in 1963 he upgraded the barn, converted the silo into office space, carpeted the main floor, and gave the barn a fresh coat of red paint. The next year he began selling furniture and mattresses, though cattle still roamed in the lower level. What thoughts went through the heads of the cows? *What a nice farmer! How considerate! Maybe he figured we'd produce more milk if we had a good night's sleep. I can't wait to lie down on those comfortable mattresses. Moo, moo.* But, sorry, cows, as business picked up, the cows were asked to leave.

The farm and its many buildings — the 1913 farmhouse, the round barn, an ice house, a well, a milking barn, and a corn crib — earned a listing on the National Register in 1995, adding distinction to this iconic red barn. Today Imogene and her husband continue to raise beef cattle and run the mattress business, Round Barn Mattresses, out of the round barn, re-purposed and functional once again, thanks to their entrepreneurial spirit and to their passion for preserving a unique piece of Georgia's history.

Opposite: *Moos and Mattresses*

9. MIDWEST

OHIO

CHAMPAIGN COUNTY

Nutwood

Webster defines nutwood as any nutbearing tree or its wood. In the early 1800s when this farm's history began, plenty of nutbearing trees dotted the Ohio landscape, such as chestnut, walnut, oak, and hickory. Though William Ward founded this farm, the title of "Nutwood Place," likely named after such trees, was penned by the second owner, Absalom Jennings.

Ward, a native of Virginia, served as an officer in the Revolutionary War, and both educated and business-saavy, he made the most of his father's and his own war service land grants. After moving to Maysville, Kentucky, he used the grants to claim land that had been axe marked by Simon Kenton, the legendary frontiersman, who, unfortunately was basically illiterate and never bothered to register his claimed land. However, Ward and Kenton became business partners and, though this partnership — between an educated and refined gentleman and a rough-cut frontiersman — may have been unusual, by 1810 the two had amassed over 25,000 acres of land.

As early as 1788, Ward and Kenton began exploring the Ohio Country, still hostile territory, and made claims in the Mad River Valley. By 1799 Ward led six Virginia families to settle this area and in 1805 he traveled to Chillicothe, then the state capital, to appeal for a new county, Champaign, taking land from Greene and Franklin counties. After the county was established, area settlers might have approached Ward about making Urbana (a town he named) the county seat, which he also successfully campaigned for. He laid out Urbana and donated proceeds from the sale of every other lot to support the development of the town. Ward built a brick home on this farm, where he and his wife raised their children. He died on Christmas eve, 1822.

Decades later, another Ohioan purchased the farm. Absalom Jennings, born in 1815 on a pioneer farm in Clark County, Ohio, began work in the harness trade when he turned 15, after moving to Urbana. He eventually started his own harness and saddle company, selling goods in Marysville for four years before moving to New York in 1844. Not content again to be an employee, Jennings joined forces with a partner to launch a company that made hats, caps, straw goods, and fancy millinery. It must have been wildly successful — since Jennings began buying and racing trotters. In those days everyone wore a hat.

Despite his financial prosperity on the east coast, Jennings yearned to return to his native Ohio and, in 1856, he purchased the William Ward farm. Three years later at the age of 41, he sold his New York City business, and, according to his obituary, "brought with him a number of fine horses to put on the farm." And, though retired from his hat company, he decided to enter the horse business. Yes, he loved horses and he built a barn to house them, raise them, and watch them run.

And what a barn it was. Brimming with money — presumably from the sale of his business, possibly from investments, and perhaps from the horse trade — he commissioned a young Charles Theodore Rathbun (aged 28 in 1856) to design this brick barn. Rathbun was born in Pittsfield, Massachusetts, in 1828, two years after the Shakers built their round barn, which he must have been familiar with during his youth. After working in New York City for an established ecclesiastical architect, he returned to Pittsfield to work as an architect on his own. It's possible that Jennings might have seen his work and mentioned his idea about a horse barn in Urbana. Regardless of how he met Jennings, Rathbun went on to design many impressive buildings in the second half of the 19th century in New England, including a farm complex in 1868 for Massachusetts Agricultural College (today's University of Massachusetts).

Let's go back in time and pretend to eavesdrop when Rathbun may have shared the concept of the Shaker barn with Jennings. Maybe their conversation went like this, "Absalom, I have the perfect idea for a barn for your horses. Let's model it after the round barn I grew up near. We can put an observatory at the top for you to watch your horses run on a track around the barn." What a good sales pitch that would have been! However, though this architect did a masterful job, finding carpenters to construct it must have been a challenge.

Finished in the autumn of 1858, the barn cost $23,000, which equates to well over $700,000 today. To put that into perspective, some of Jennings's horses were valued in the thousands and their stud fees in the hundreds. Apparently, this harness apprentice had become a prosperous businessman and horse breeder. And what a barn it still is.

Nearly 100 feet in diameter and approximately 286 feet in circumference, the barn, fortified with 180,000 colorful bricks, rises to a peak of 51 feet. At the top — in a large observatory, reached by a wooden circular winding stairway — Mr. Jennings was able to watch his horses running on the one-mile track he built. According to the barn's current owner, timbers were hand-hewn, connected with mortise and tenon joints, and rested on 17-inch brick ledges along the barn's perimeter.

Another rarity was the roof — 6,700 square feet of tin — which was not only expensive but unusual in the 1860s, a time when most barn roofs were covered with wooden shakes. The 30,000 feet of oak timbers, 11,800 feet of flooring, and a cistern that had a capacity for 300 barrels of water ensured that the racehorses were well cared for. According to Rathbun's plans, six granaries were to be placed on the second floor, which was to be two-inch oak, planed.

But why a circular barn? The only existing such barn at that time, though there may have been others lost to history, was located in western Massachusetts — the Shaker stone barn. Did Rathbun or Jennings know about the round home built in Boston in 1856, the residence of the inventor Enoch Robinson? Had Jennings seen railroad roundhouses? The nation's first railroad started in Baltimore in 1827 as the Baltimore and Ohio Railroad, with a goal to head westward to reach the Ohio River. And rail lines from New York to Ohio had roundhouses, which might have inspired this round barn design. Had Jennings read Fowler's writings about octagonal homes and his love for the circular shape?

Besides training and breeding racehorses and Jersey cattle, Jennings had other business interests, eventually

***Below:** Nutwood*

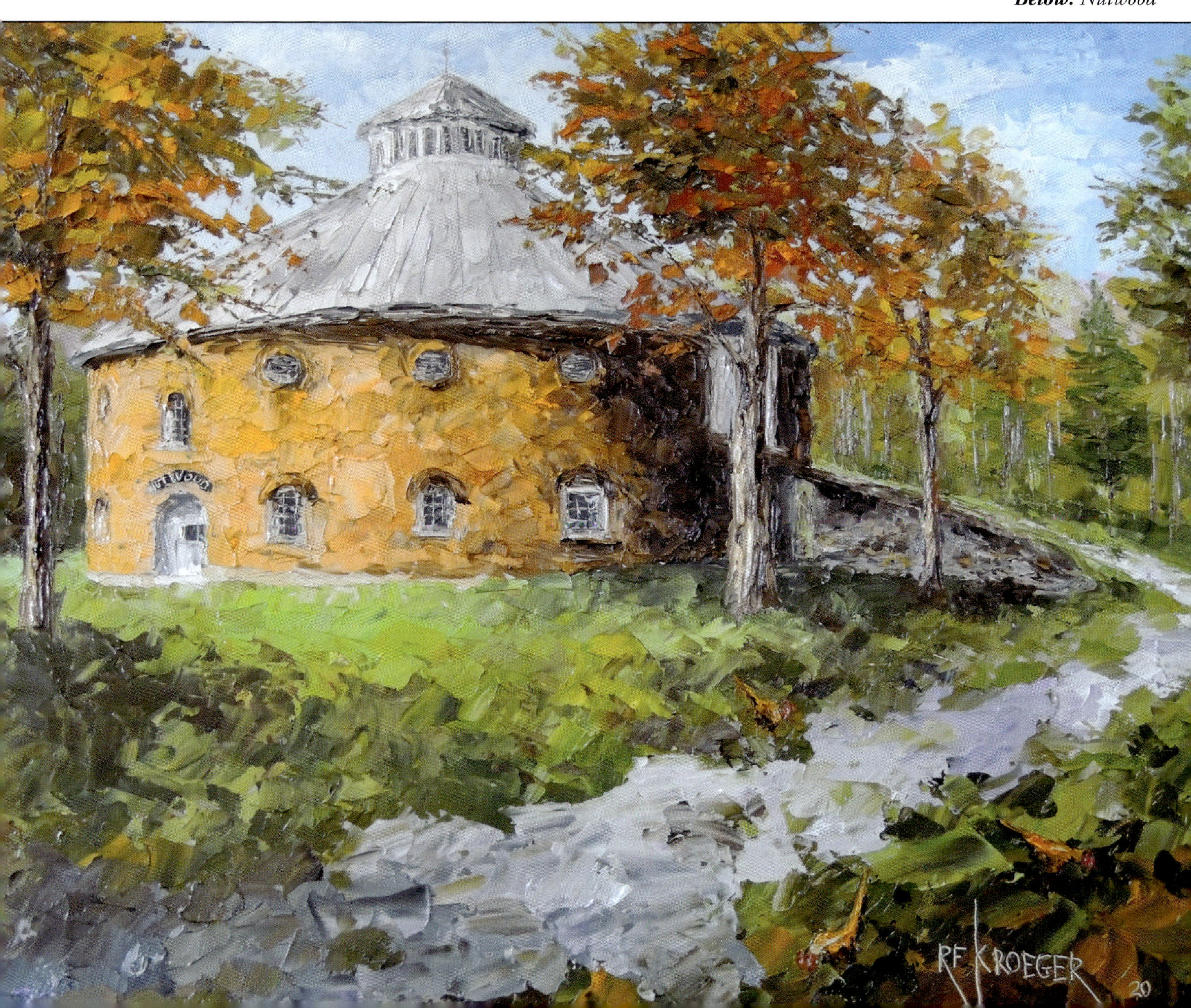

expanding the farm and testing new varieties of crops. In the late 1800s Nutwood was recognized by Ohio's state agricultural college for its "adaptability for every kind of agriculture." Though his oval racetrack, where his trotters paced as he watched from high in the barn's observatory, is gone, its memory lives on in one of the nation's most impressive round barns. Absalom Jennings died in 1895.

And even though this iconic round barn was finished before the start of the Civil War, none followed its example. Even after Stewart spread his fondness for the octagonal shape in 1875, circular barns didn't become popular until Professor King publicized them in the 1890s, 30 years after Nutwood.

The historical legacy of both William Ward in founding this county and making Urbana its seat and Absalom Jennings in building this barn is being continued by current owners, who plan to restore this national gem. They've also kept up the 1815 farmhouse, preserving yet another page in Ohio history.

ASHTABULA COUNTY

The Octagonal

Intrigued by photos I'd seen on the Travis site, I visited this beauty with barn scouts Carl Feather and Jeff Scribben in 2014, on a day when the orange day lilies in front and alongside the barn were at their best, almost begging to be in the painting. Although we didn't meet the barn owner, we talked with Julia Barton, whose husband Patrick rented the farm from his father Dennis Turner at the time. She agreed that the barn was special. In fact, it's one of only a few surviving octagonal barns in Ohio. The couple eventually purchased the barn in 2019. Three years later, when I visited Julia and Patrick on a cold day in late March, I didn't see the beautiful lilies, thanks to a sudden storm off nearby Lake Erie, which covered the ground with a few inches of snow. Brrr. Patrick pointed to a clump of green and said that it usually snows three times on the daffodils before spring truly arrives. This was number two.

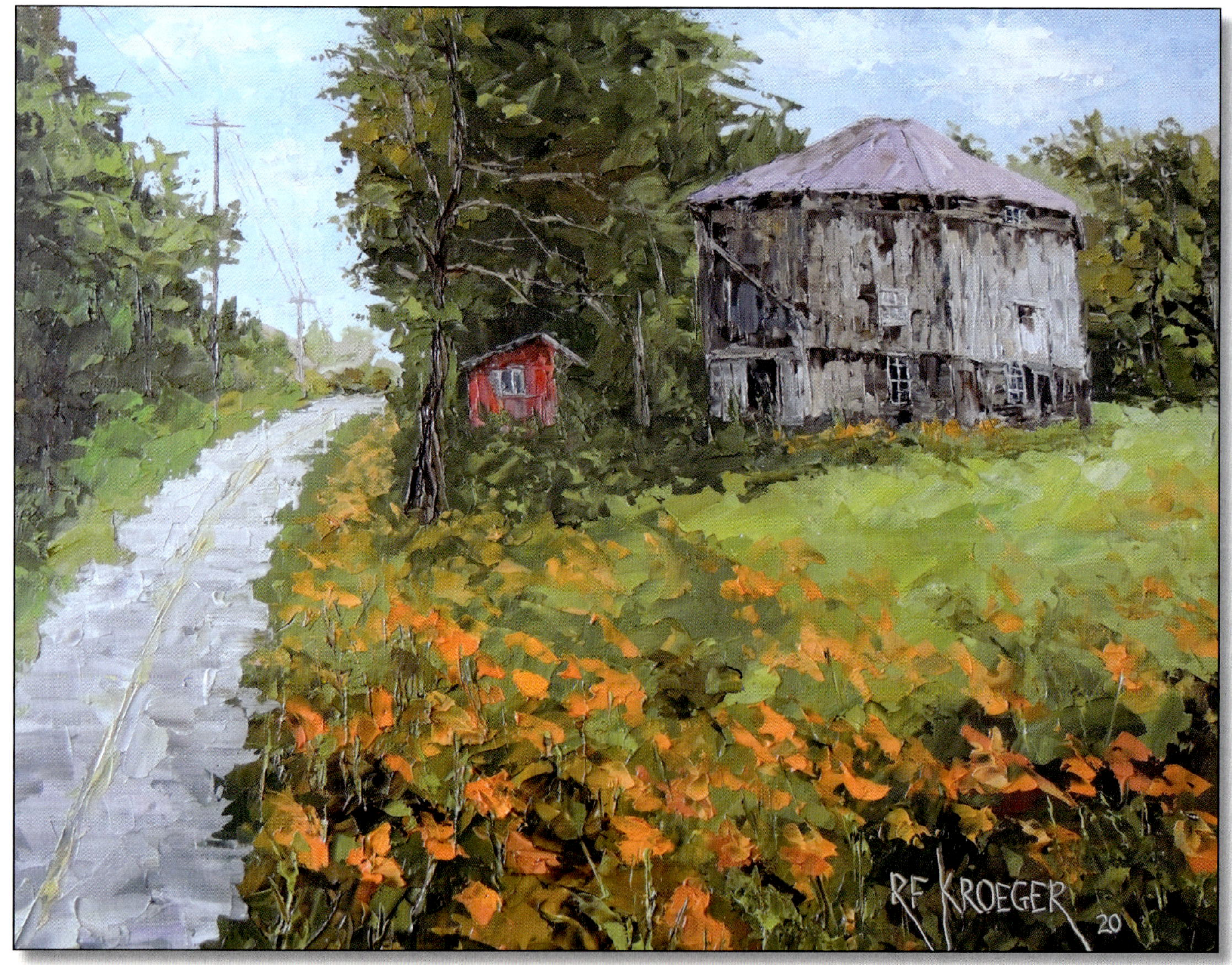

The Octagonal

Julia explained that they do use the old barn. They keep livestock in it: two goats, chickens, beef cattle, and a small herd of Soay sheep, which trace back thousands of years ago to a tiny, uninhabited island of the same name (*Soaigh* in Gaelic) in Scotland's Inner Hebrides. The island's name derives from the Old Norse word, *Seyðoy*, which means "island of sheep." The Turners also have an organic farming business and raise various vegetables on two acres. The rest of the 120 acres lies in woods, hay fields, and pasture.

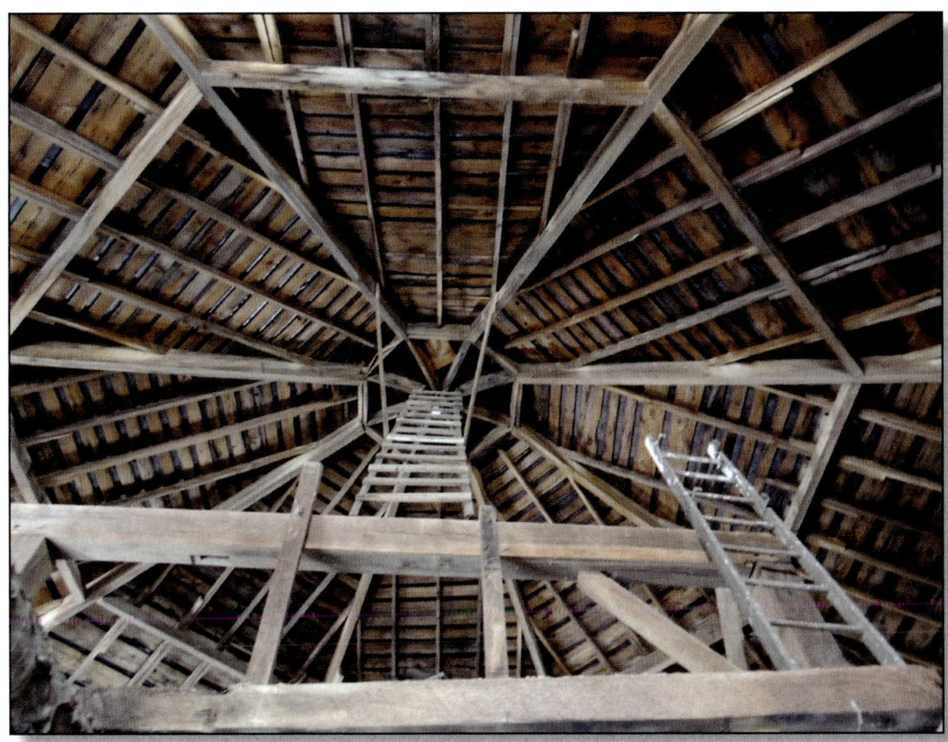

Self-supporting roof with original boards

On the barn's left side, an attractive foundation of fieldstones and cobblestones rises into a natural hillside, making this a rare example of a round barn built into a bank. Inside, though there are some mortise and tenon joints, wooden connecting pegs, and hand-hewn beams, the majority of the lumber has been cut in a sawmill, not surprising for construction in the 1870s. What is more interesting are the empty mortise slots on the long beams in the basement level, hinting that the ceiling may have been replaced. Though both long beams are sagging, they're held up by vertical posts, thanks to Dennis. Other beams connect directly into the walls, much like a stone barn.

On the second level, which is also in good condition, empty mortises suggest that they formerly held planks for the floor for the haymow. The self-supporting roof converges into an apex, where a cupola once sat, Patrick said. Despite the roof appearing intact, the new owners plan to replace it in the not-too-distant future. At one time, this three-level octagonal bank barn was a busy place! With walls 21 feet wide and a diameter of 40 feet, the barn was large enough to support a moderate farm. Formerly, Dennis advised, the farm had 600 acres.

Local legend gives credit to a Mr. Dewey for building it and, according to Dennis, he built it in 1876, not long after Elliot Stewart began publicizing octagonal barn plans. Though the name of the original owner is unknown (It may have been a Hatch, since the name of the road is Hatches Corners.), according to Carl, the farmer imported blue glass from Belgium for the windows, with the hope that the glass would make the hay look green, thereby encouraging cows to eat it. Of course, hay dries to a beige color eventually but the color doesn't seem to affect the cows' appetites. According to Dennis, another theory, perhaps a bit more plausible, is that the blue glass, placed over clear glass (which often had bubbles in it) could lessen the intensity of sunlight through such bubbles and help prevent a barn fire.

Belgian blue glass

Lue Turner, late father of Dennis, bought the farm (which had been split up from its original acreage) in 1942. He used it to store hay and for dairy; the cattle lined up around central stanchions. After his mother died in 2014, Dennis took over the farm and then passed it on to Julia and Patrick in 2019, keeping this farm and its rare barn in the same family for three generations.

Yes, this barn is old, but its siding and its shingled roof are in good repair, which is the key to longevity. Once the roof leaks, look out! The farmhouse, constructed with hand-hewn beams and less than 100 yards from the barn, dates to 1848, suggesting that this octagonal was not the first barn built here. Maybe the first one burned — as did four rectangular barns owned by New York's Elliot Stewart, convincing him to build an octagonal. However, like many other old Ohio barns, this one is showing its age and needs maintenance, a cost that the Turners view as a challenge. After all, Ohio has only a few of these unique treasures left. They're worth saving!

MIAMI COUNTY

Orrmont

Janelle and Tim Baker, who grew up in West Milton, an old Ohio village about 25 miles away from this barn, one day decided they'd move and, since they both enjoyed restoring old houses, they purchased the Orrmont Estate in 2003. Even though the 9,000-square-foot mansion, carriage house, and other buildings had once entertained the high and mighty, the grounds had not been maintained over the years. The Bakers had their work cut out for them.

They quickly filled in the pool with cement and erected a large tent which they rented for weddings and events, helping to offset the expense of restoration of the mansion. Then they started a family, which now includes four sons, who continue to learn valuable lessons about entrepreneurship from their parents. Janelle, who grew up on a farm, became concerned about the possible loss of their parking lot and visualized the old octagonal barn nearby as another commercial asset. So, in 2012 they added the barn and 15 acres to their holdings, which again meant more rehabbing.

Eventually they began hosting weddings and events in the barn — as well as in the tent — and constructed a fairytale bed and breakfast (Well, breakfast is on you.), featuring old world stucco, a Romeo and Juliet balcony, a copper spire, and wrought iron light fixtures. Janelle, a

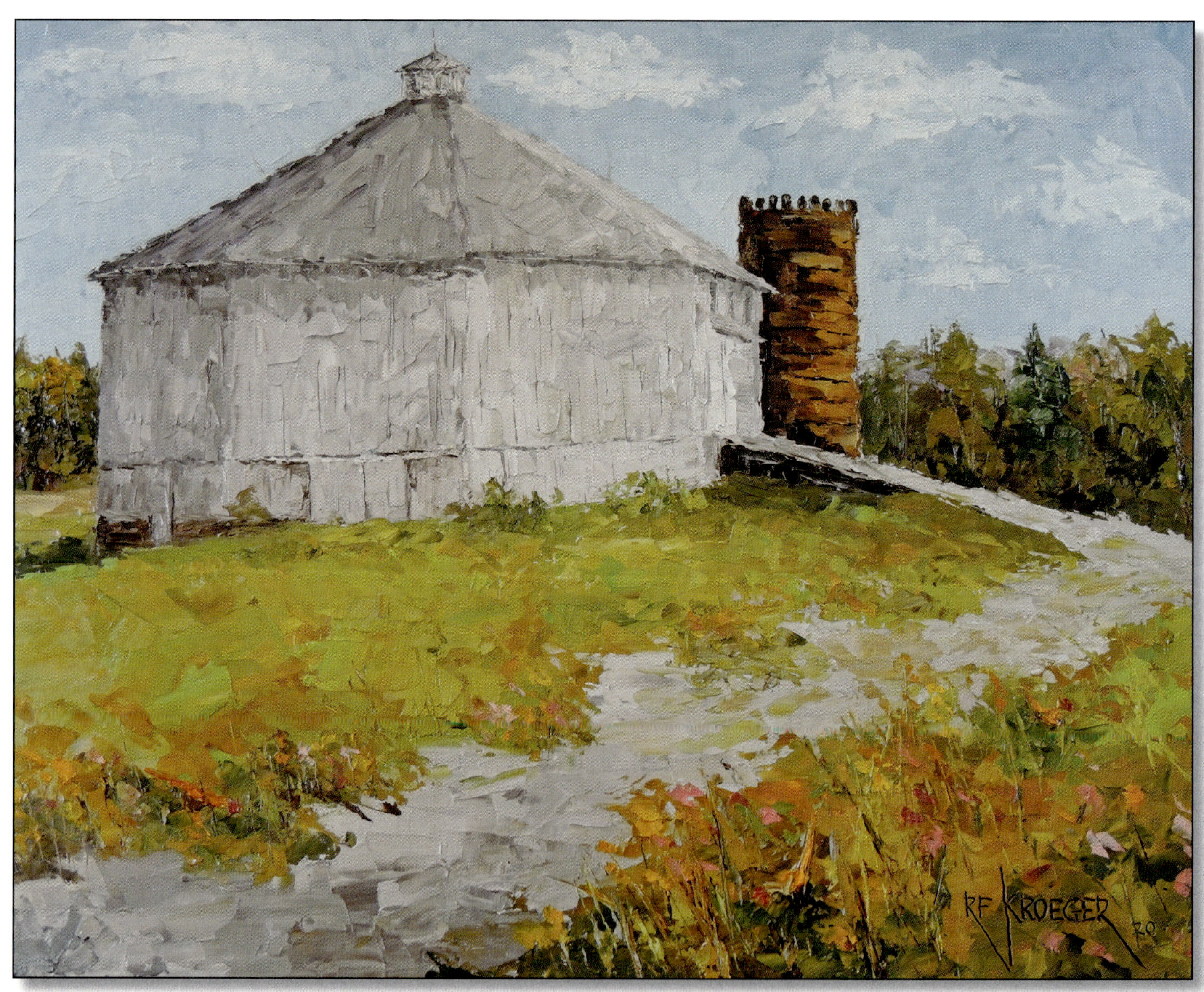

Orrmont

CPA, now works full time in booking their many events. The barn's interior is wide open, immaculate, and now features a side wing with bathrooms and a changing room. Air conditioning and heating allow the barn to function all year long. This old barn has new life.

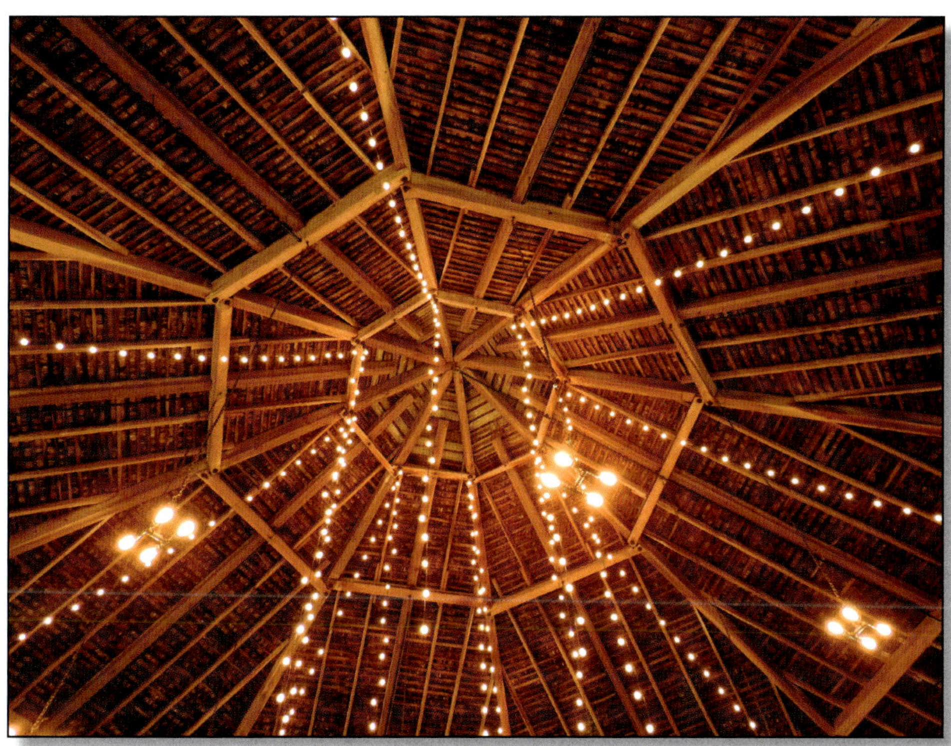

Roof, Orrmont Barn, Miami County

Though historical records show that George McCabe owned the farm in 1875, he may have used a traditional rectangular barn to begin farming. Tax documents valued a barn at $900 in 1880 but didn't specify the shape of the barn. In 1894 William P. Orr bought the farm and may have built this octagonal barn if McCabe hadn't built it earlier. Interestingly, the saw-cut lumber and iron bolting are the same as in another octagonal barn, still standing, only a mile away. The difference between the two barns is that the Orr barn has an outside silo, whereas the silo lies in the center of the other barn. It's plausible that Elliot Stewart's 1875 octagonal barn publications may have influenced McCabe or Orr to build his octagonal, keeping the silo outside, and that Professor Franklin H. King's publications in 1890 may have influenced the other barn's design. Were these builders the same person?

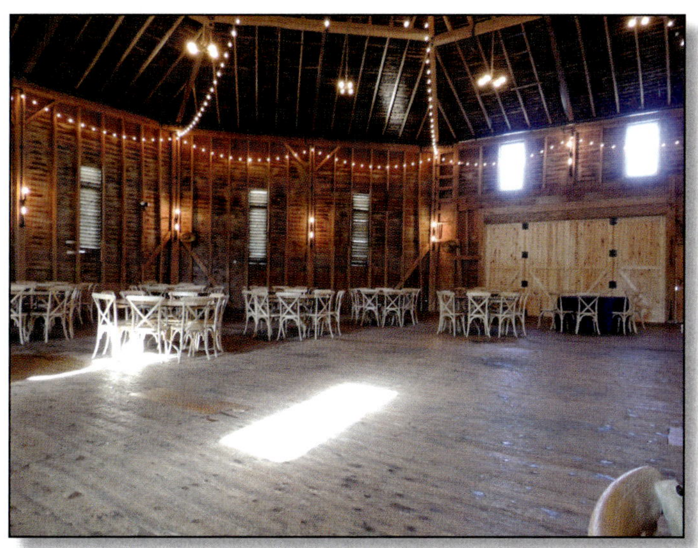

Interior, Orrmont Barn, Miami County

Regardless, W. P. Orr bought the farm in 1894 and led a life that illustrates another rags to riches tale of early Ohio. Born in the nearby village of Covington in 1833, the 17-year-old Orr learned the trade of carriage painting in Piqua but, an entrepreneur at heart, he left Ohio, as did another young Ohioan — Joseph Sharp of Fairfield County — for the gold rush in California. As Sharp did, William endured the hazardous and arduous 113-day journey through the plains of Nebraska, the Rocky Mountains of Wyoming, and the deserts of Utah and Nevada — as many did in the famous emigrant wagon train migration. Unlike Sharp, whose daily diary reminds us of the many perils he endured, Orr seldom mentioned his trip, though it must have instilled in him a strong work ethic; after two years of gold mining, he had enough cash to start a grocery and mercantile business when he returned to Covington in 1854.

When he finished service in the Civil War, rising from private to captain in four years, he returned to Piqua in 1869 and, according to his obituary in the *Lima News*, May 24, 1912, he "interested himself in many enterprises." Among them were grain businesses, boats on the Miami-Erie Canal, three strawboard mills, and Piqua's grand Hotel Plaza and other city buildings. He also purchased a textile company, which became known as the Orr Felt company, a paper manufacturer, which employed 200 at its peak, though it closed in 2016.

Along with running many companies, Orr had strong connections with the Citizen's National Bank, the Piqua Savings Bank, and the Seventh National Bank of New York. Another major industry he became involved with was linseed oil, made from flaxseed, which grew well in southwestern Ohio. Today this linseed oil company has customers from over 80 countries. His businesses and financial acumen helped build Piqua.

And he was also a patriot. After the Civil War, Orr joined the National Guard and was promoted to lieutenant colonel. In 1896, two years after he bought this farm, he was commissioned quartermaster general — with the rank of brigadier general. He served four years under Ohio's Governor Bushnell, which included wartime duties during the ultra-short Spanish-American War. During this war, General Orr lived in Columbus and equipped 12,000 soldiers, readying them for combat.

At 21, and back home with cash from his gold digging in California, he married Martha Morrison in 1854, who bore two sons. However, after Martha died, William married for a second time, this one in 1884 in a slightly different venue — Westminster Abbey. Yes, that Westminster Abbey. His second wife Frances died in 1909, three years before his death.

His son Aaron, at 43, built the Orrmont mansion in 1900 and continued the family legacy … for a while … though his death came only a year after his dad died — in 1913. And, although W.P. Orr had built a fortune, his heirs could not continue to maintain the mansion, its 11 bedrooms, five fireplaces, and four servants' quarters, along with the spacious pool, the carriage house, and the octagonal barn. Eventually the estate passed into other hands, and, fittingly perhaps, ended in the stewardship of two other entrepreneurs, Janelle and Tim Baker, who mirror Willam Orr's penchant for running businesses. In time perhaps their sons will expand Orrmont and continue to preserve this gem in Ohio history.

VINTON COUNTY

The Jewels of Vinton County

As I rounded a curve on County Road 21, also known as Shurtz Road, this large immaculate jewel of a barn appeared out of nowhere, making me hit the brakes. It stood there, close to the road, defying Father Time and resisting the advances of developers — a monument to an

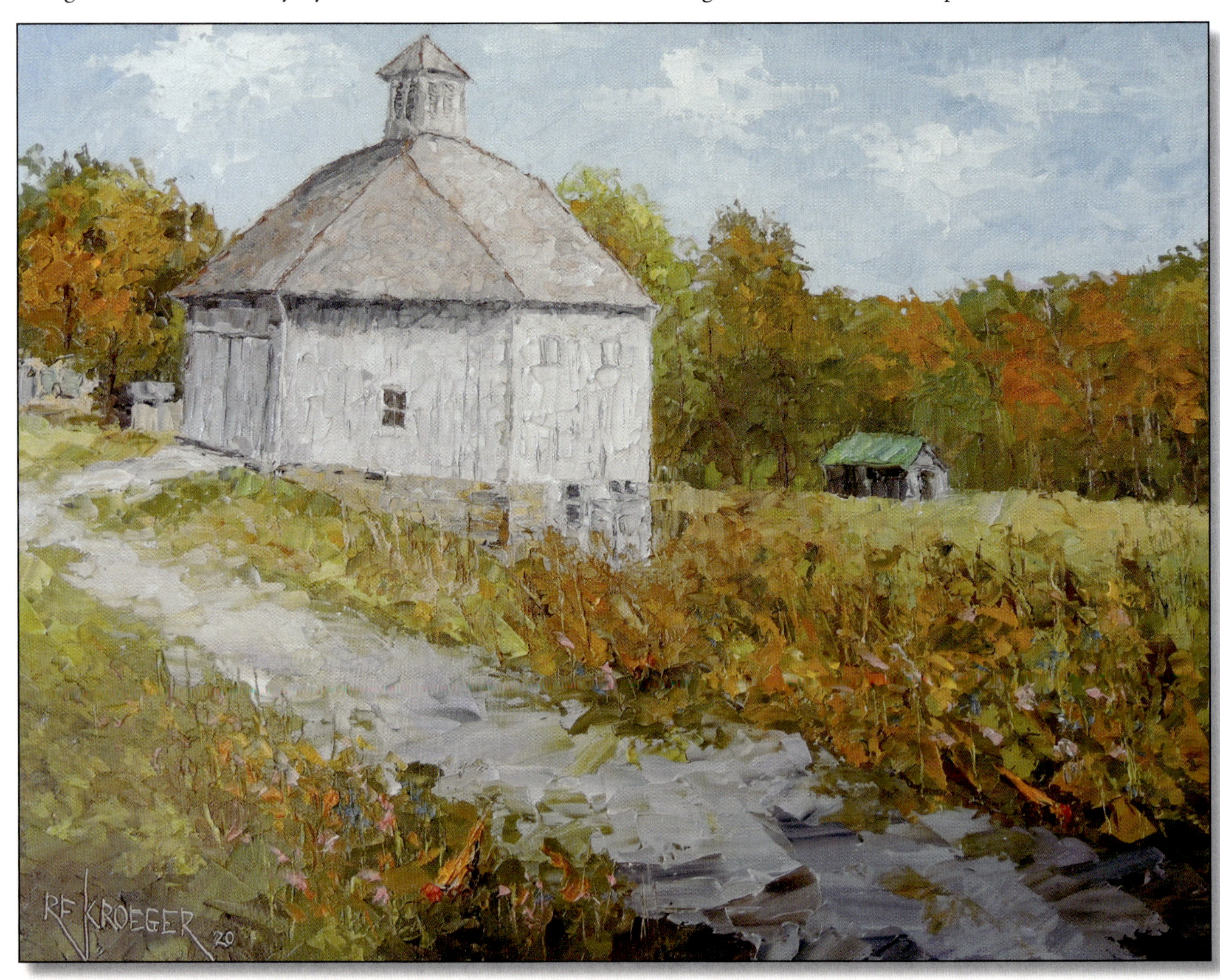

The Jewels of Vinton County

unknown barn builder, who constructed it in 1885, one of the earliest octagonal barns in Ohio.

Earlier, I had tracked down the owner, Ronald Davis, through the county auditor, and sent him a letter since he resides out of the county. He chose to respond via a hand-written letter, giving me permission to visit, paint, and enter the barn, which I did. The interior was in good shape and the saw-cut timbers — instead of hand-hewn beams, typical of barns in the late 19th century — indicated that the builder had access to a sawmill close by.

Mr. Davis wrote that George and Kate Shurtz purchased the land via a government grant in 1837, possibly a war warrant, and established the farm. They became prominent and prosperous farmers in the region and farmed 640 acres, while a relative of theirs farmed 300 acres on adjacent land. Accordingly, the Shurtz name now graces the country lane that leads directly to State Route 93, one of the main roads in this rural county, Ohio's least populated.

The family's farming success allowed them to build a delightful Hansel-and-Gretel-like sandstone block cottage, which, according to Mr. Davis, who has owned the farm since 1965, was broken into many times, once by burglars who stole all the antique furnishings. More recently, in July, 2019, the cottage was burned — most likely by arsonists. The multicolored hexagonal slate on the roof must have been costly in 1882 when the family built it — just as expensive as the white gothic roof struts, which survived the fire. Unfortunately, some of the roof has caved in, hinting that the end has neared.

The family farmed the land, though hilly and wooded, and used the barn to house dairy cows, work horses, and "buggy" horses, according to Mr. Davis. Eventually the Shurtz sisters inherited the farm and one of them, Minnie, a daughter of the original founder, was like a mother to Mr. Davis, who began working on the farm when he was 14. Since the sisters had no heirs, they gifted the farm to Mr. Davis, who told me, then 87, that he was not sure he'd be around to read about his barn in my book, *Historic Barns of Ohio*, published in March, 2021. "The Shurtz family were of the best quality people I have ever known. It was a pleasure to have known such nice people," he wrote.

Why does the title include "the jewels?" Yes, the octagonal barn is the main attraction, but it's only one of several impressive buildings that remain. The barn across the road has a slate roof, a round steel corn crib still stands, and a chicken house in the distance is well protected with a green metal roof. Sadly, the stone house, once a historic gem, is now in its final stages, a piece in this necklace of "jewels" — a memory of what was once a sparkling part of Ohio history — the Shurtz family and their farm.

STARK COUNTY

In Henry's Honor

The story of one of America's most iconic barns began in 1831 when Henry Timken was born in Germany. At seven, he came to the United States with his five siblings and recently-widowed father, who started farming in Missouri — along with many other German families. However, Henry, like Harvey Firestone (who later would become one of his good friends), was not content to stay on the family farm. Instead, he left to apprentice under carriage-builder Caspar Schurmeier. In 1855, Henry, a budding 24-year-old entrepreneur, started his own carriage company, made improvements to carriages, and got a patent for the Timken buggy spring, which jump-started his fortune. He briefly retired in 1887 but his work ethic returned him to his business. His son, Henry H., born in 1868, built this barn.

It's likely that Henry's love of horses motivated him to build this remarkable barn in 1894, which, with its four conical turrets, resembles a European castle. In fact, the elder Timken and his son Henry H., seeking to improve their roller bearings, traveled to Europe in the early 1890s to learn about different designs of bearings, which were further advanced in Europe than in the USA. The trip proved successful: in 1898 they patented an improved tapered roller bearing and a year later, Henry and his sons, Henry H. and William, established the Timken Roller Bearing and Axle Company in St. Louis, Missouri. This era was America's Second Industrial Revolution: Henry Ford was making affordable Model T cars, Edison and Westinghouse harnessed electricity, and Harvey Firestone and other Akron rubber barons were selling tires. Timken's product fit in well with the mass production of cars, trucks, and farm tractors, even though America was still predominantly an agricultural country at the turn of the century.

Timken realized his company needed to be closer to the steel and automotive companies of the Midwest — that wide swath of land between Pittsburgh, Ohio's Youngstown-Warren-Cleveland area, and Detroit. He chose to relocate in Canton, possibly because he was friends with Gordon Mather, president of the Canton Board of Trade but more likely because this city was well connected by rail to the steel producing and car manufacturing factories. In December, 1901, with forty employees, the newly renamed Timken Roller Bearing Company opened its doors. Henry's two sons, Henry H. and William ran the company and by the 1920s over ninety percent of the country's roller bearings were produced here. Today the company maintains plants in many countries and is one of Canton's top employers.

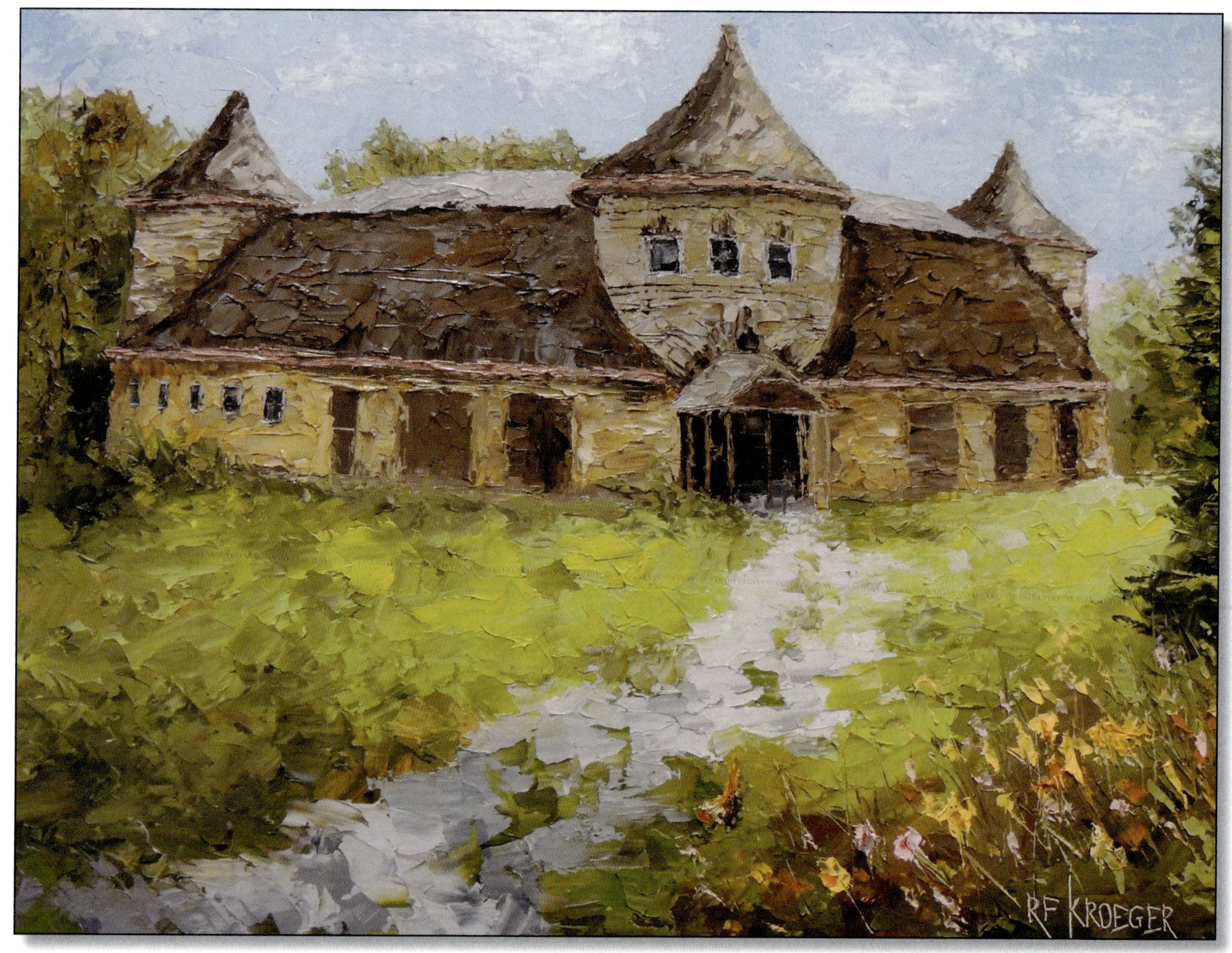

In Henry's Honor

Henry's son, Henry H., built a mansion in 1915 on about 300 acres, which were close to the roller bearing factory. The mansion, with 40,000 square feet, had over 70 rooms. Earlier, in 1894, and wanting a distinctive design, he commissioned a Pittsburgh architect to construct a stables barn and he didn't spare any expense. The 15,500 square-foot two story barn was not rectangular as most barns were, but rather was donut-shaped with an internal courtyard, 80 feet in diameter, for training horses. The barn itself was 125 feet wide. Several donut-shaped barns still exist in Illinois.

Reflecting European design, its four conical turrets, covered in decorative slate, are 26 feet in diameter, have 14-inch-thick walls, and are perfectly aligned in the four directions of a compass. The stable's caretaker lived in the east turret and other turrets served as storage for hay and grain. Brick covered all walls of the barn — in attractive, contrasting colors of yellow, brown, and orange. Its asphalt roof — a replacement — is now showing wear, allowing some of the original slate to be seen. The barn's foundation was sunk into 19 feet of bedrock and remains solid to this day: the sheer weight of the building hasn't caused any cracking or shifting in over a century. Inside, many stalls were built to house Henry's horses and carriages. After all, in 1900 automobiles were still a novelty. Horse-drawn carriages were the norm.

Henry H., who died in 1940, also founded the Timken Foundation, which generously donated his mansion and 30 acres to the Sisters of Charity of St. Augustine in 1950. Though the sisters used the mansion to accommodate 72 patients, they did not own the barn, which was not donated, ended up being abandoned, and became a target for vandalism. No one seemed to care about this old fellow.

But, in 1978 it was listed on the National Register, thanks to the Western Reserve Historical Society, who prepared the nomination for Investor's Holiday, Inc., a group that owned it at the time. Still, it continued to deteriorate. Ten years later the city planned to demolish it, hoping to add land to the adjacent Pro Football Hall of Fame, which was built in 1963.

But then a young girl had a dream. Heidi K. Hickman, then only 17, dreamt that she saw the Timken barn in a vision — with angels ascending and descending from heaven, walking up and down on a ladder in the barn's central courtyard. Without financial backing, she contacted an architect, who, in turn, referred her to his employer, an architectural firm, which did a pro-bono architectural plan for remodeling the barn. Using these plans, the teenager approached city officials, convincing them to save the barn. They listened and scrapped their plans to tear it down. But, without a suitor, the barn remained vacant and continued its downhill spiral. Enter a football star.

Former Ohio State linebacker Chris Spielman, a football star at Ohio State and the NFL Detroit Lions, came to the rescue when he purchased the barn in 1991 and renovated it into a restaurant. He covered the open part of the donut with construction materials salvaged from the demolition of the old Washington High School, where he played football decades earlier. Initially he thought the restaurant would thrive, being so close to the football hall of fame, but after ten years, Chris sold his Stables Hall of Fame Grille to Harry Potroos, who continued to operate it as a restaurant.

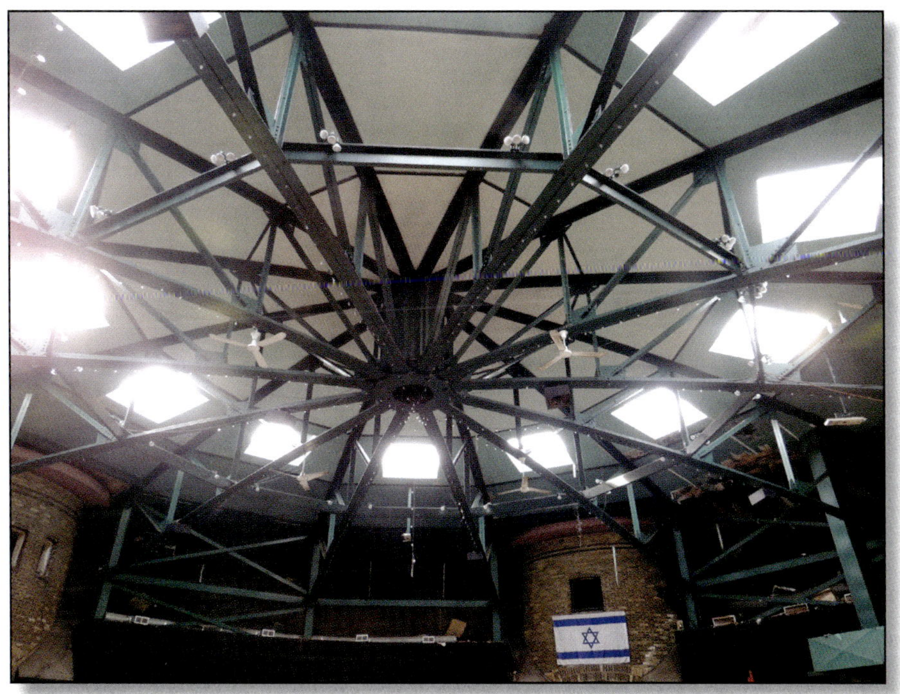

Reconstructed roof, Timken donut barn, Stark County, Ohio

However, a recession took its toll and Potroos closed the restaurant and tried to sell the business and the barn — without any luck. Heidi, now the wife of Rabbi Mark Lancaster, entered the picture again and convinced Potross to lease the barn for the synagogue's services, beginning in 2009.

Sadly but understandably, anxious to recoup their loans, PNC bank foreclosed on Potroos and put the barn up for auction a few times. Finally in 2013, the Beit HaKavod Messianic Synagogue, spurred on by the Lancasters, purchased the barn for $168,300 and made plans for restoration. In 2014 the Canton Preservation Society staged a fundraiser, a "Sneak Peek" tour, trying to garner public support. Although the synagogue still owns it, signs, posted in 2019 on the barn's front door by the city, have declared it unsafe. When barn scout Dave and I visited in the autumn of 2021, a

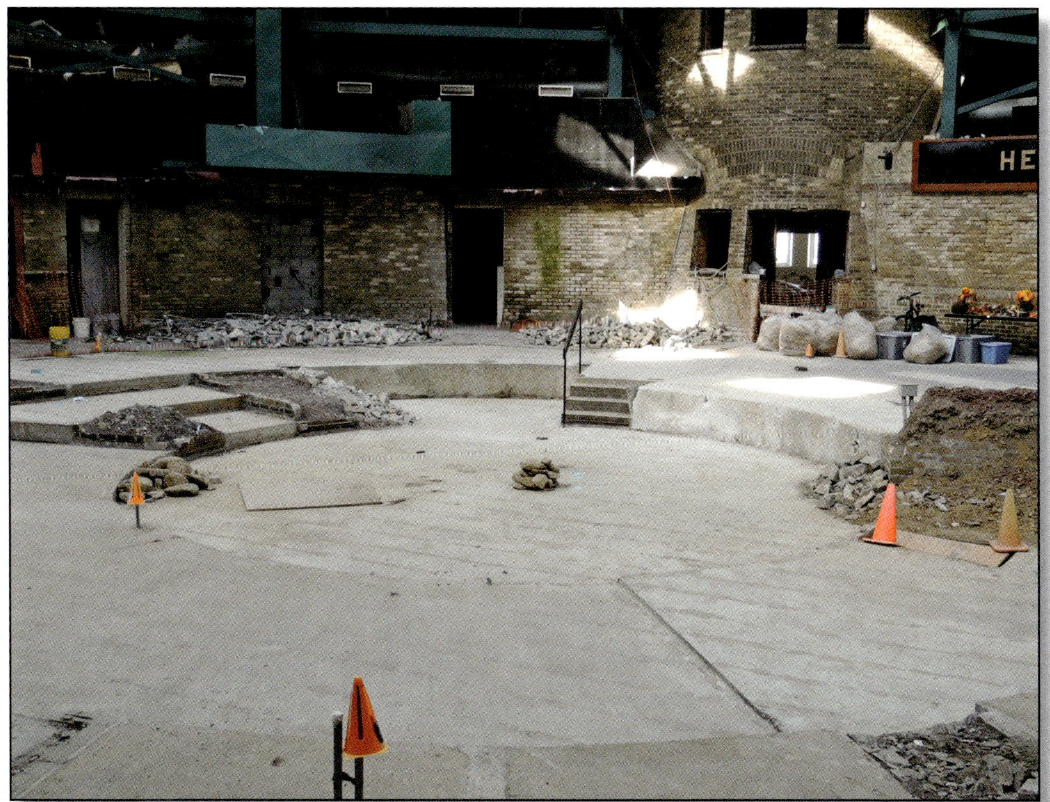

Interior courtyard, Timken donut barn, Stark County, Ohio

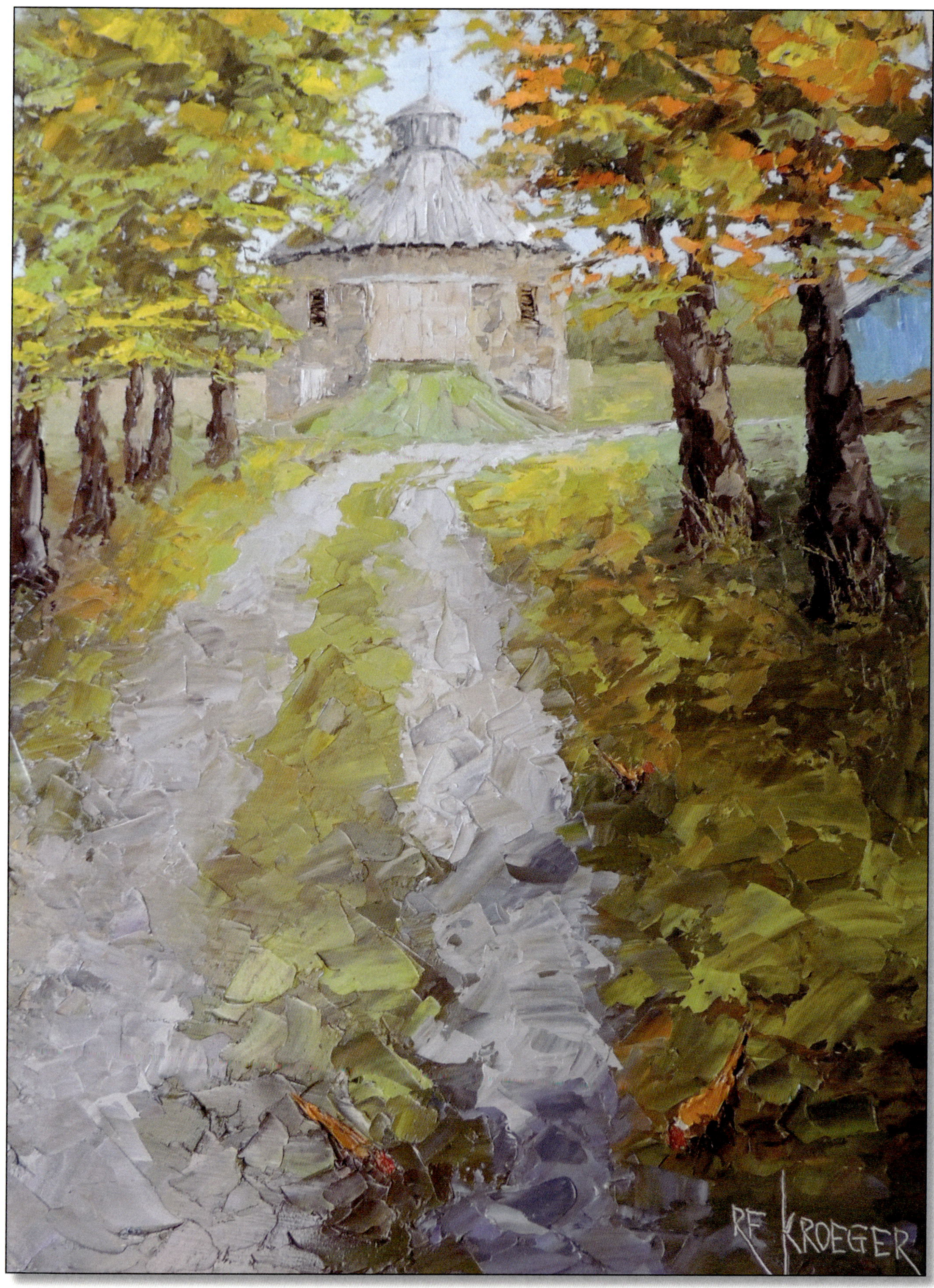

Rarest of the Rare

workman was repairing one of its many defects and told us that the congregation hoped to save it from the wrecking ball. A large sign in front, appealing to the many drivers passing by here daily, lists a goal of $4 million, with only a fraction of that being raised so far. Unfortunately, the building continues to worsen.

Though Henry Timken died in 1909, he was inducted into the Automotive Hall of Fame in 1977, a recognition he richly deserved, and in 1998 he was voted into the National Inventors Hall of Fame.

Another hall of fame, this one dedicated to America's professional football and sitting across from the barn, close to Interstate 77, recently received a two-year, $27 million renovation that was completed in 2013. Unfortunately, Timken's barn, an architectural marvel of the 1890s and a national treasure, currently sits neglected, on its way to the graveyard, getting ready to join Henry County's spectacular Pagoda barn, which burned in 1985. Perhaps some kind philanthropist will step forward to restore it to its former glory, a gesture that would please every historical preservationist and would remember its patriarchs, Henry Timken and his son Henry H., two Henrys who deserve such an honor.

CLARK COUNTY

Rarest of the Rare

This octagonal stone barn is almost one of a kind. In fact, I had to search far and wide before I found another — the Gilmore barn in Missouri, a three-story limestone octagonal bank barn, built in 1899. Restored smartly, it serves as an event center for the community. In 1994 it made the National Register. Another stone octagonal was built later — in 1939 — for the fairgrounds in Sheridan County, Wyoming. *(See painting on previous page.)*

Most of Ohio's round and polygonal barns are wooden. Exceptions are this one and Champaign County's Nutwood, which is brick. So, I was excited to visit and to meet Bob McClure, son of the owner, Marjorie McClure. Fortunately, Bob took some time out of his farming schedule to show me not only his barn but several others close by, including a nearby wooden octagonal. Ohio's wet spring had delayed planting.

Mrs. McClure bought the barn in 2010 in a farm auction from Glenn Murphy, not because of the unique barn but because of the 64 tillable acres that came with it, ideal farmland. The stone barn was a bonus, but it was a mess. Bob told me that they filled 40 dumpsters with trash from the barn and disposed of hundreds of old tires in the clean-up. He also installed new shutters and a front door.

Bob didn't know much about the history of the barn, though a local farmer, Joe Shank, at one time owned it, along with the wooden octagonal barn a few miles away. McClure's barn was probably built around 1900 in an era when many polygonal barns were built, though it came much later than another Ohio treasure, the octagonal brick one-room schoolhouse in Sinking Spring, Highland County, which was built in 1831.

Inside, most of the timber in the top level is saw-cut, but hand-hewn beams, possibly reclaimed from an earlier barn, frame the front door. On the lower level, most of the lumber is hand-hewn and stalls for sheep remain intact. The octagonal cupola was in good shape and the stonework reminded me of the craftsmanship of the Kindelberger stone barn in Monroe County. Stone masons can leave a legacy that withstands all kinds of weather.

Overall, this barn, well maintained by the McClures, is not only an Ohio gem, but a national one and deserves a listing in the National Register. After all, it's the rarest of the rare.

FAIRFIELD COUNTY

The County Affair

Signage, above several entrances to this circular barn, clearly state its history: *Round Cattle Barn — Built in 1906 — By J.E. Hedges — Dairy Cattle.* It's a rarity — a round barn built specifically for a county fair. Throughout the country, floral halls in county fairgrounds are often round or polygonal, but round cattle barns are uncommon.

Hedges, a local farmer and barn builder, could have chosen a traditional rectangular barn for this project, but this was an era when round barns were considered ideal for dairy cattle. For his labor and materials Hedges was

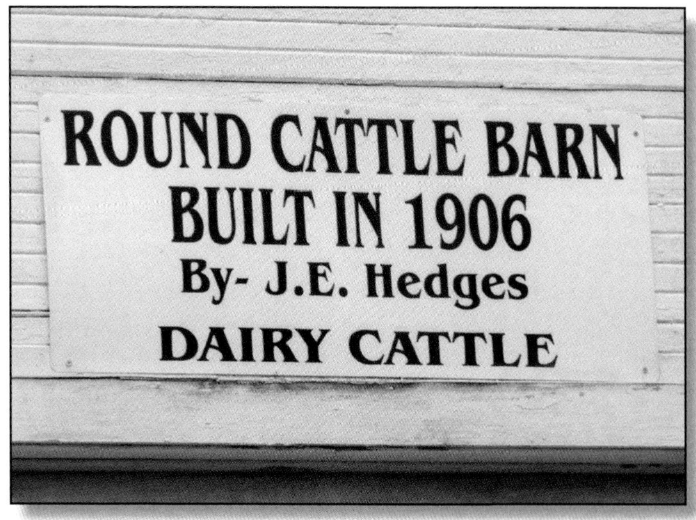

Hedges Round Barn, Fairground, Fairfield County, Ohio

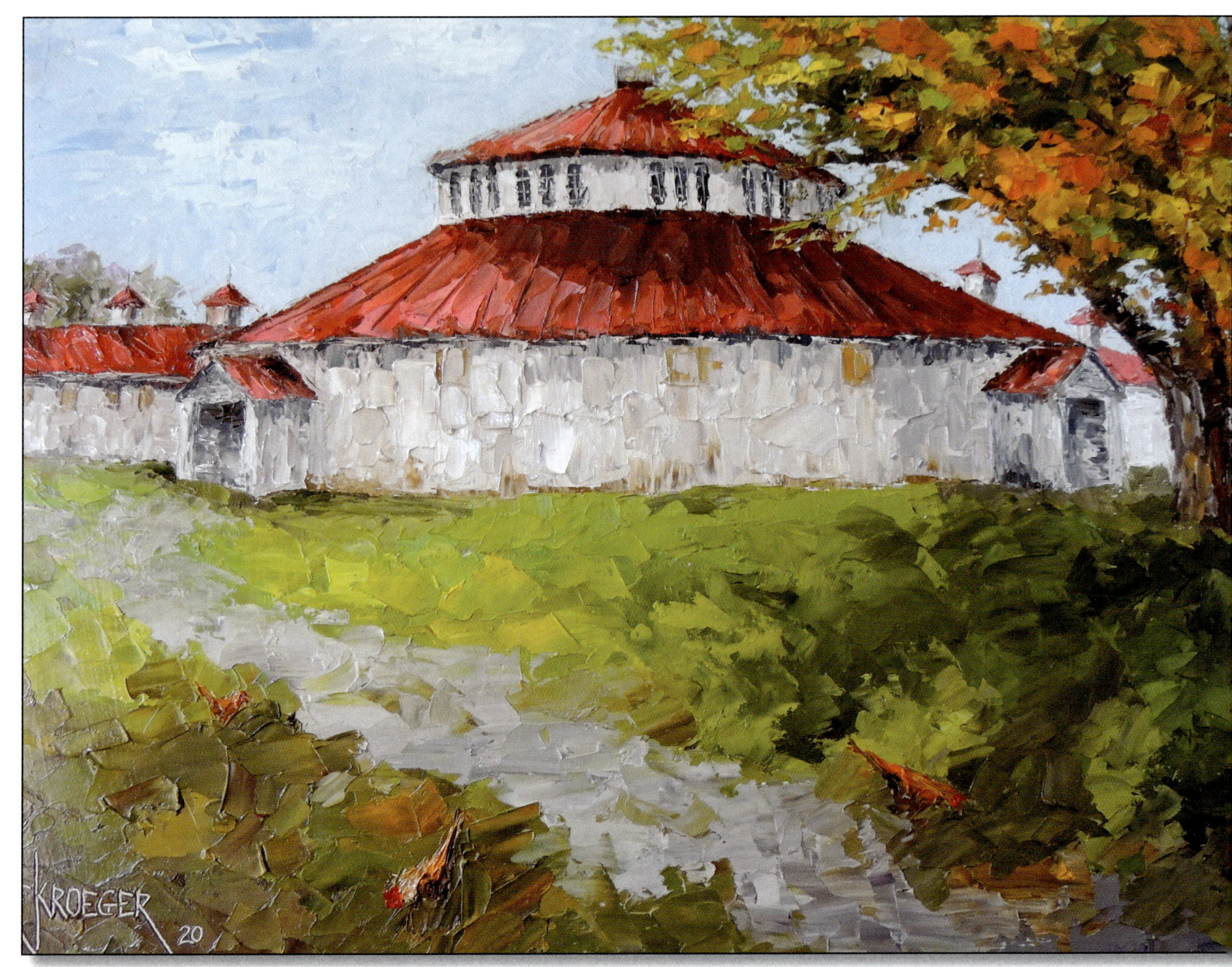

The County Affair

paid $3,022.14, a huge sum in 1906. He cleverly soaked the lumber for the curved section in a creek so that it was flexible enough to bend. The barn, built for dairy and beef cattle, also housed the junior livestock sale.

With a diameter stretching to 95 feet and a roof covered with wood shingles, the sight must have commanded attention during the county fair in 1906. Local residents began to appreciate the uniqueness of the barn and so they covered the roof with galvanized metal in 1934, assuring longevity. In 1937, with the fair's popularity growing — despite the throes of the Great Depression — they added two large wings to the round barn.

What's just as impressive as the barn is the county fair, which dates to 1851, the oldest continuously running county fair in Ohio. The Fairfield County Agricultural Society was established in 1850 and it hosted the first fair in Ohio the following year. Only 60 years earlier Lancaster, the county seat, was comprised of 100 wigwams and 500 people. The fertile fields drew immigrants and agriculture became king. Indians were moved westwards.

In 1876 the fairgrounds expanded to 22 acres and again to 36 acres in 1880, when a half-mile racetrack was added. Three years later organizers built a new amphitheater and eventually drilled for natural gas. In 1889 they found it, tapping its energy to provide light for night-time races, the only place in America that offered horse racing at night. They also piped gas to the center of a lake in the fairgrounds and ignited it as it bubbled up through perforated pipes, earning the title, "Lake of Fire." What a sight that must have been!

Another feather on this barn's cap was that it was used in filming the 1980 movie, *Brubaker*, starring Robert Redford. Chances are that the film crew didn't know much about J.E. Hedges but they liked his barn well enough to use it. I'm sure, if he were alive, Mr. Hedges would be proud.

AUGLAIZE COUNTY

Magnificent Manchester

This iconic round barn is probably Ohio's most photographed, and rightfully so. The dark roof, contrasting with burgundy siding and white trim, provides a striking composition, which many photographers have been drawn to capture, as evidenced by the hundreds of images found in a Google search.

An article, *Economy of a Round Dairy Barn*, written by Wilber Fraser and published by the University of Illinois, described the benefits of a round barn: more efficient housing for cows, time savings in feeding, a protected silo, and easier silage distribution. The article also inferred that construction of a round barn was less expensive than a rectangular one and that "progressive" farmers should consider such a barn. The opposite was true — circular barns were more expensive to construct than rectangular ones and the "progressive" farmers were mostly only the wealthy ones.

One of those farmers was Jason H. Manchester, who came with his parents from Vermont to central Ohio in 1858, when they bought 200 acres of swampland in the northern tip of Auglaize County and began farming. At first, the thought of moving from her beloved Vermont to the wilderness of Ohio depressed Mrs. Manchester … until her husband built an elaborate Italianate farmhouse, in reality a mansion, in 1877. That cheered her up. Yes, they were prosperous and by 1900 their son Jason had acquired 2,800 acres of farmland. He decided to build this barn eight years later.

I met Tim Manchester, the fifth generation of this farming family, in the fall of 2021. He graduated from Ohio State University as his wife Martha did, but decided that any business job he might land, thanks to his college degree, was not strong enough to lure him from his roots of farming.

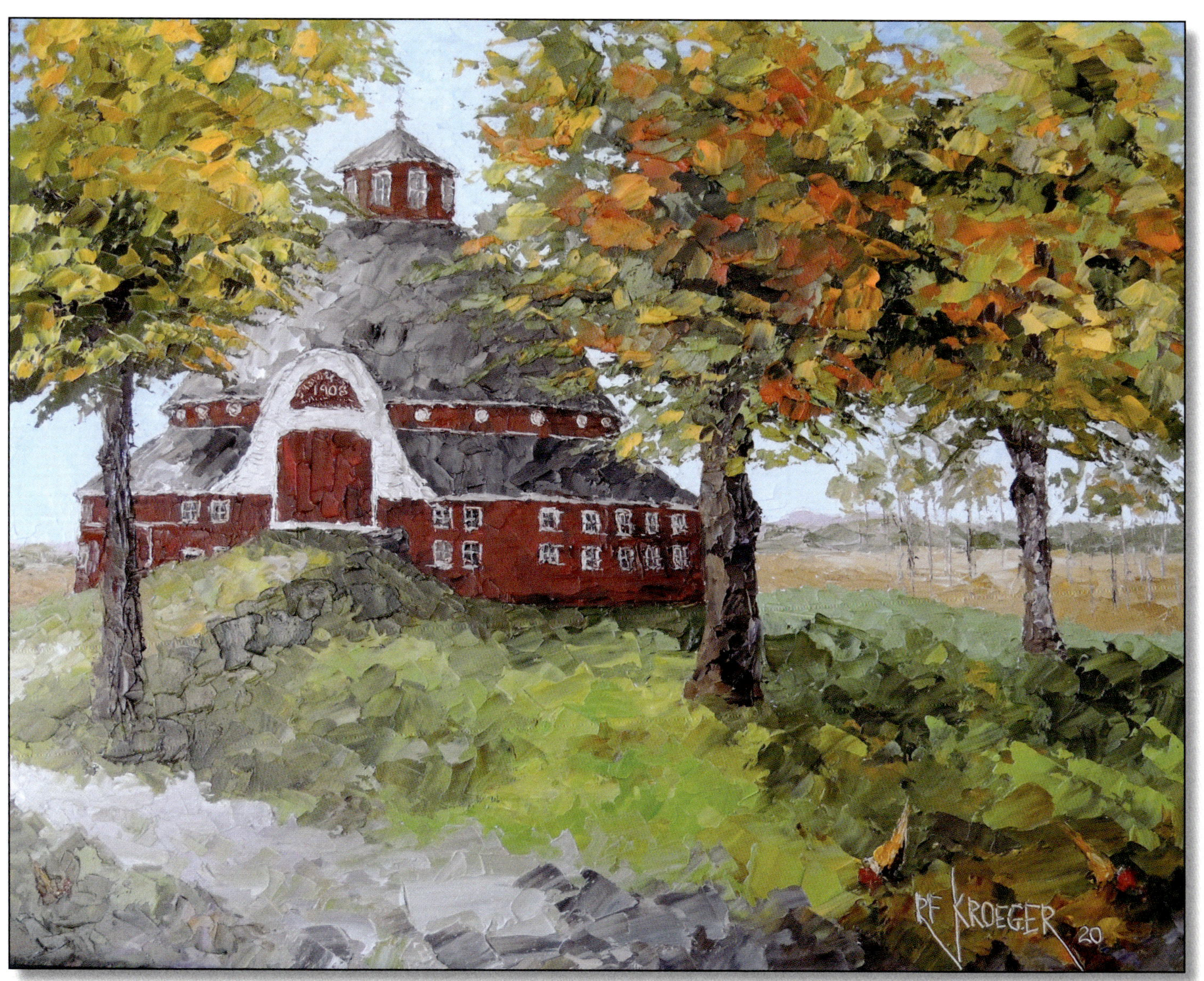

Magnificent Manchester

Carrying on the tradition of his family, Tim has expanded the farm to 5,000 acres and has maintained the barn immaculately.

With a diameter of 102 feet, it's one of the largest round barns in America and today, besides being an Ohio treasure, it serves as storage for equipment. It earned a listing on the National Register of Historic Places in 1980. White lettering above the entrance continues to preserve the legacy: *J.H. Manchester, 1908, Maple Avenue Farm, Horace Duncan Builder*. Yes, it's rare that the builders of such impressive barns are ever remembered, which makes this sign all the more special. Mr. Duncan, a native of Knightstown, Indiana, was born in 1877, and, as a young carpenter, he was mentored by experienced round barn builders, the McNamees and self-taught architect Benton Steele, who is known today as "The Father of Indiana's Round Barns." Duncan's first known exposure to round barns came in 1901 and by 1902, at the age of 25, he was skilled enough to supervise construction of one of Steele's designs — the Boettcher round barn in Artas, South Dakota. He quickly developed a reputation for building round barns.

At this young age and armed with confidence, Duncan began getting jobs. In fact, in 1911 his business letterhead carried an image of Steele's Boettcher barn and a warning to farmers to be wary of amateur barn builders. It stated, "Some unscrupulous, would-be architects, in order to obtain a few dollars for worthless plans, gotten up with no knowledge of circular construction, thus causing many disappointments and much extra and unexpected expense during construction, are endeavoring to make prospective builders believe that my barn is not patented. … I will promptly prosecute each and every infringer."

In time, his reputation spread to other states, and in 1908 Duncan built the Manchester barn — which may have been a Benton Steele design — in Auglaize County, less than 50 miles from Indiana. The barn was so spectacular that Duncan put a photo of it on his business envelope in 1911, which also carried the inscription, "Infringers promptly prosecuted. Beware of unscrupulous architects." Above the address side and under his name,

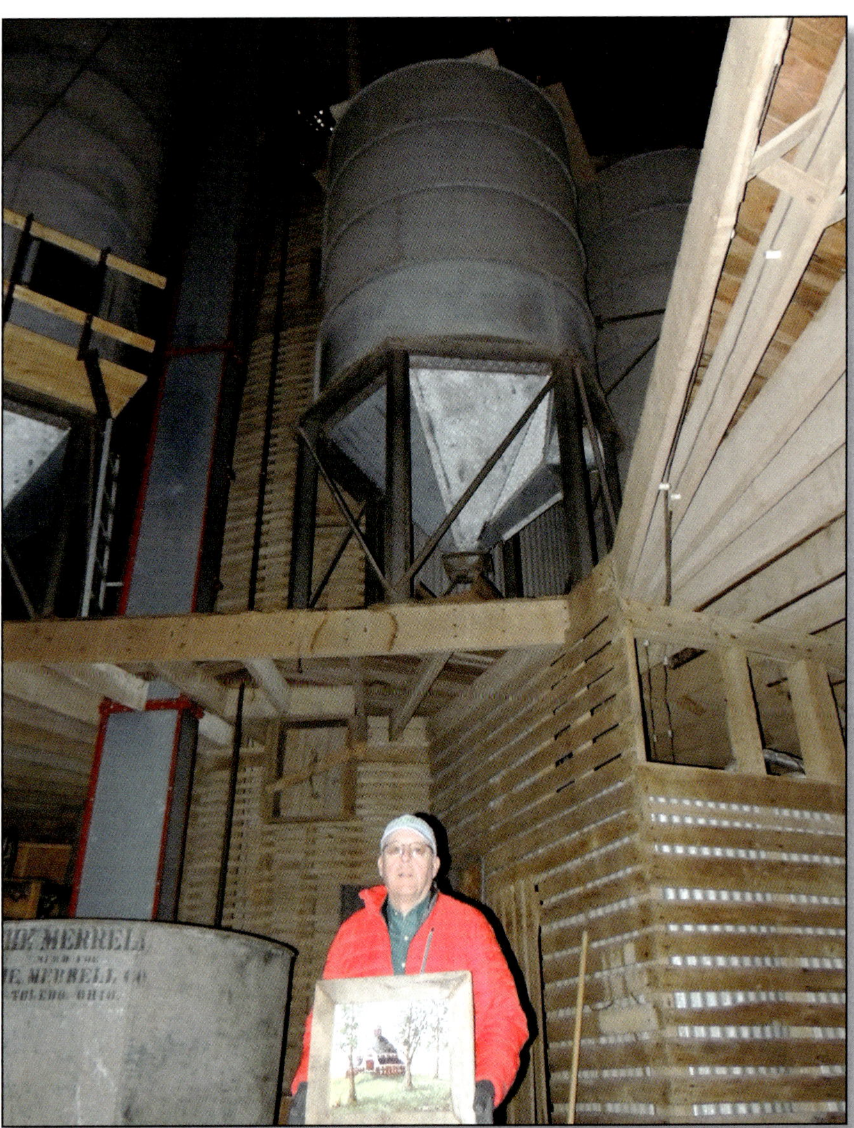

Interior, Tim Manchester in his barn, Auglaize County, Ohio

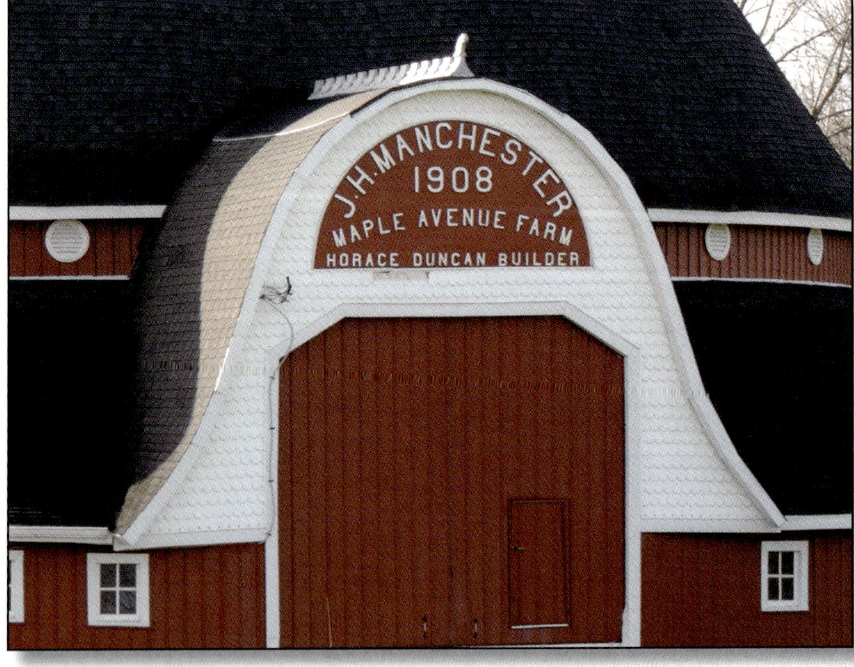

Duncan plaque, Manchester barn, Auglaize County, Ohio

Duncan included, "Designer and Builder of the Original Circular Barn with Latest Improvements," an unusual claim since Benton Steele mentored him and others built circular barns before Duncan turned 21.

At 33, this carpenter-turned-round-barn architect was in his prime, but, despite his prosperity, Duncan had a dark side. Tim recalled stories from his grandfather, explaining that Duncan didn't hesitate to insist on payments for using his roof design without his consent, even from those barn owners who were widows. Another story from his grandfather was that when Duncan built the Manchester barn, he brought with him a few carpenters from Indiana but hired about 10 locals. They stayed in a nearby abandoned schoolhouse and, after a week of work, would celebrate on Saturday, a night that included poker and drinking. The locals, who were paid that morning, would typically lose to Duncan, who often won back what he paid them.

Regardless, Duncan and his crew continued building round barns throughout the Midwest, though this may have been the only Ohio barn he built. As agricultural journals began to question the cost and efficiency of this type of barn, the round barn craze began to fizzle by 1918. Duncan died ten years later, but is remembered as the "Round Barn Man."

The original color of the barn was a reddish orange, paint which Manchester bought from a bankruptcy sale involving the Big Four Railway, which formed in 1889. Its major cities were Cleveland, Cincinnati, Chicago and St. Louis, though it had many routes throughout the Midwest. And their red-orange paint was a bargain. Later, wishing to have the barn look more prestigious, they painted it white. Today it's come full circle, having returned to dark red.

Although many of the barns that I paint and write about are now gone, this one, thanks to expert construction by Horace Duncan and careful maintenance by its current owners, may last for centuries. Tim and his son-in-law Caleb, along with four employees, continue to farm their 5,000-acre farm. Long live the mighty Manchester.

ROSS COUNTY

Marvelous Maxwell

Sunshine Hill Farm, a small 15-acre corn and soybean farmstead, isn't hard to miss on a drive along State Route 180, just out of Kingston, thanks to this barn. A brilliant beacon of red and white, it can be seen for over a mile away, after ascending a hill. Its recent coat of fiery red paint and its twenty-eight-foot double cupola attract visitors, photographers, and artists from around the state. Indeed, this circular barn is one of Ohio's treasures. Peg Hays, sister of owner Chip Maxwell, emailed me to arrange my visit.

Using trees from adjacent woods and a sawmill for cutting them, Robert P. Maxwell, the family founder and great-grandfather of Chip and Peg, built the barn in 1910. He farmed 500 acres and kept 100 head of beef cattle in the barn's lower level. Over the years the farm passed down family lines until 1978 when three families divided up the 500 acres. Chip Maxwell and his wife Cherie were the lucky ones; they got the barn and eleven acres. But as the years passed by, a century of age caught up with the barn and the silo tilted, spelling impending doom.

According to a newspaper article, Cheri said, "You cannot put a price on sentimental value." Yes, her husband Chip didn't want to be on his deathbed, according to an article in the *Chillicothe Gazette* (Ohio's oldest newspaper, founded in Cincinnati in 1793), knowing that he didn't save the barn since his great-grandfather built it and his own dad cared so much for it. So, he put his money where his sentiments were and

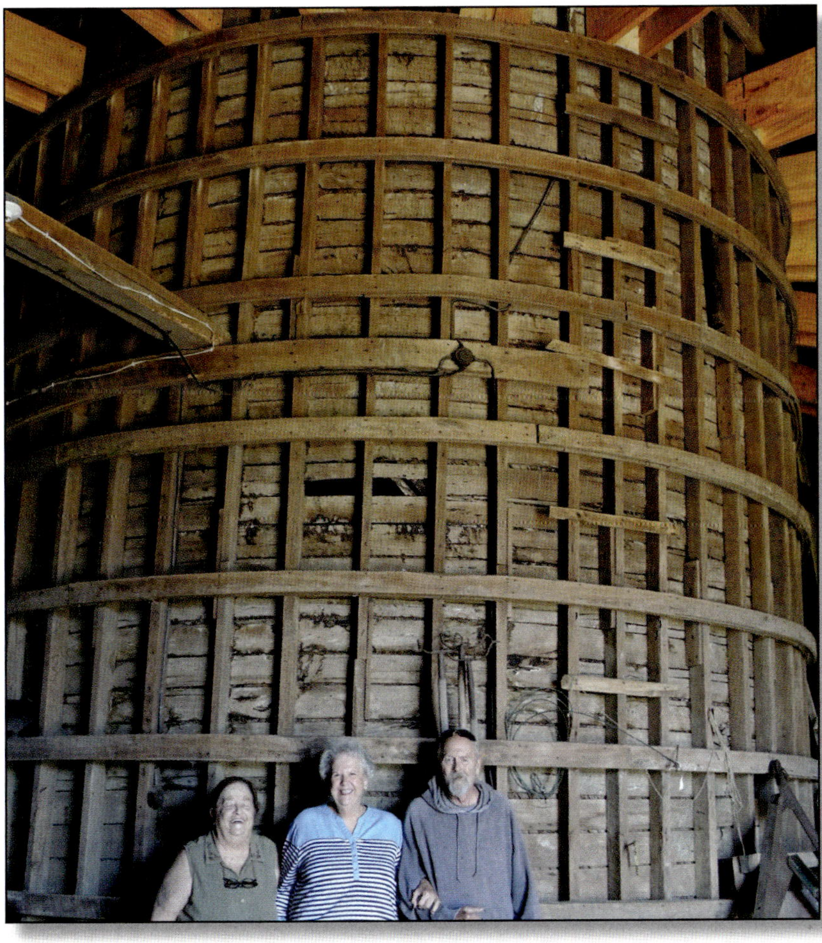

Peg, Nancy, and Chip in front of wooden stave silo, Maxwell barn. Ross County, Ohio

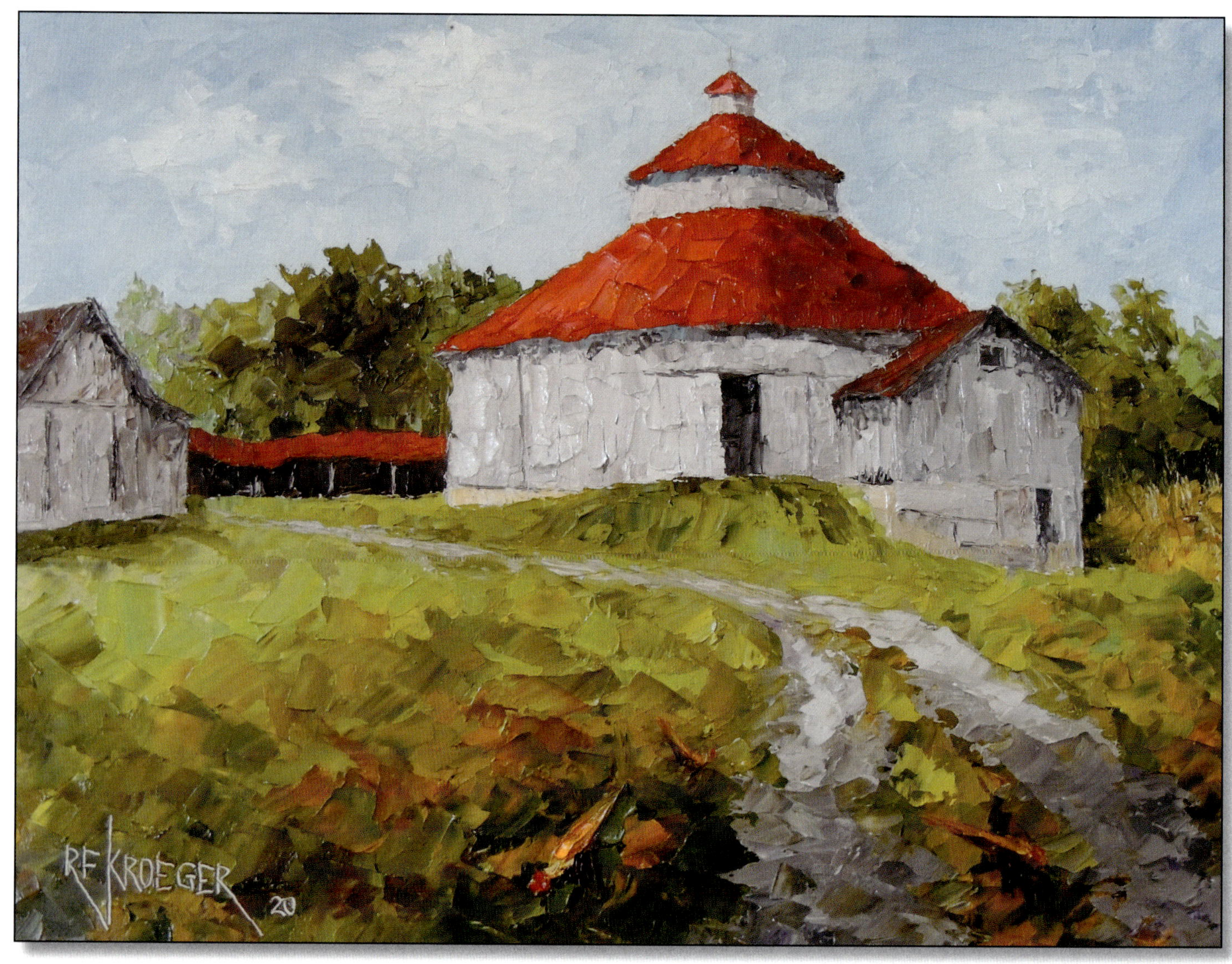

Marvelous Maxwell

paid a substantial sum to the Mt. Vernon Barn Company to repair it. They uprighted the silo with cables and then stabilized the barn with new supports — mission accomplished. But, after such a costly restoration, what good is the barn? It doesn't house crops or livestock. It's just a beautiful old non-functioning barn. However, Chip's daughter Chelsea has plans.

Her finance, Ryan Muncy, runs a well-known restaurant in Chillicothe, and his entrepreneurial spirit seems to have rubbed off, giving Chelsea ideas about transforming the barn into an event center. Across Ohio, owners are converting old barns into wineries and venues for weddings and family reunions. They're giving new life to old barns, which is a trend that Chelsea hopes to follow, putting restrooms into an adjacent small barn, running electric, and remodeling the lower level into a refreshment lounge. She even plans to be the first to have an event here — her own wedding. After all, it would be hard to pass on a barn called "Marvelous Maxwell."

HARRISON COUNTY

Workley's Wonder

Images of this striking round barn have managed to grace not only the tourist brochure of Harrison County but also those of other counties in this region. Originally, when I discovered it in the Dale Travis Ohio round barn website, I penciled a visit onto my bucket list, where it sat for years. But what the tourist brochures don't mention is that it's not easy to find. Fortunately, the historical society gave me the contact information of the barn's owners, Judy and Ollie Workley, whom I called. Judy, 78, had just celebrated 61 years of marriage to Ollie, who, she said, also made picture frames out of barn wood. They were interested in showing off their barn.

Nearer to my visit in September, 2018 — on my adventuresome barn hunting trip down the eastern Ohio Appalachian Plateau, where a straight road is rare — Judy told me not to follow my GPS, which would lead me up

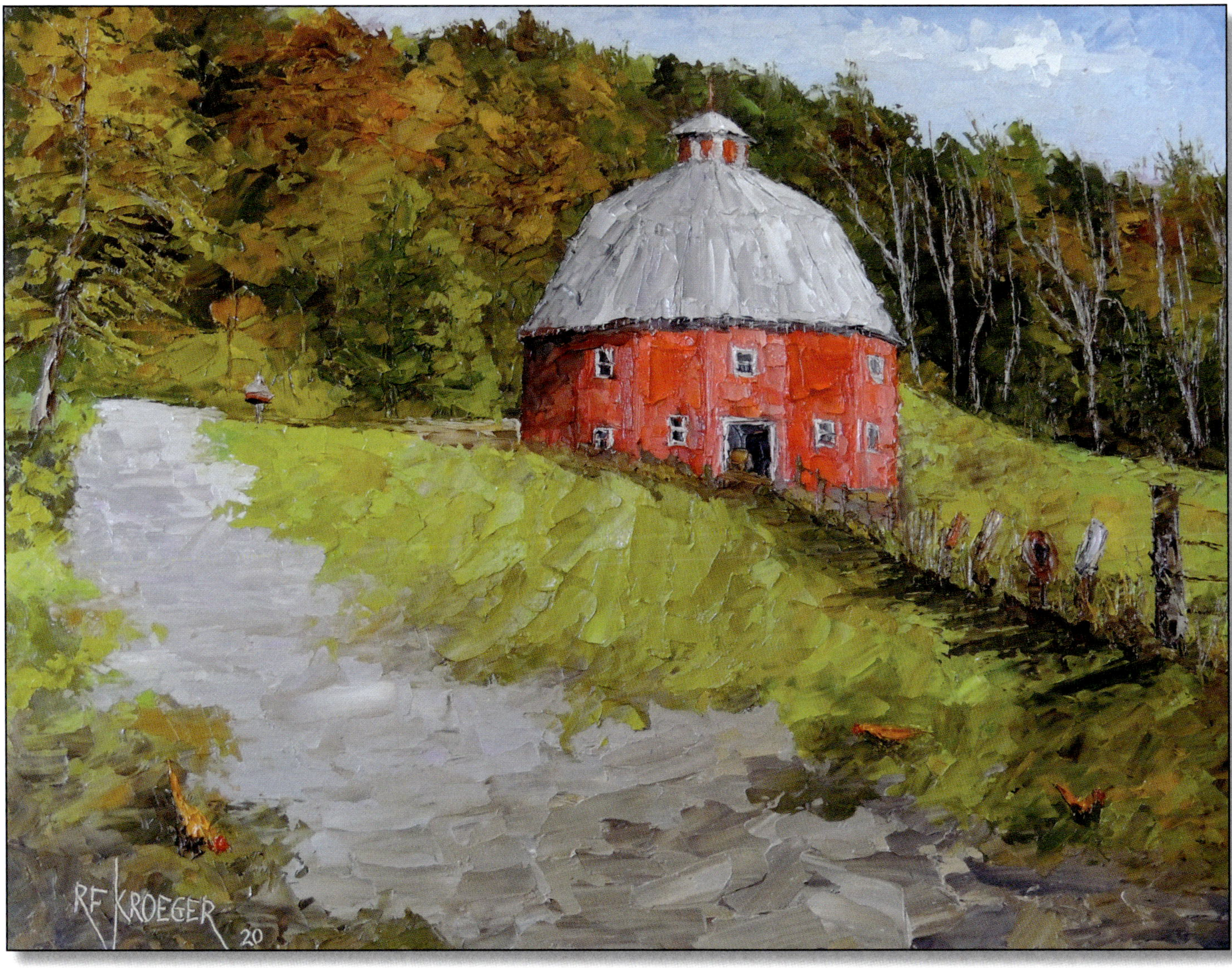

Workley's Wonder

a nasty gravel road. Thanks to her, I successfully found the eerily-named Skullfork Road, navigated the hills and forests, and arrived safely, emerging from the woods and smiling when I saw this bright red barn perched upon a hill, like a lighthouse beacon shining into the sea. It was stunning.

I met Judy, Ollie, and their daughter Tracy, who was visiting from Cleveland. Soon after my visit, they'd be going to the annual Barnesville pumpkin festival. I'm glad I got there before they left. The barn was worth it.

According to Judy, the original owner, John B. Steward, built the house and barn in 1921. His two sons fought in WWI and presumably helped their dad farm the hilly land — before and after the war. Over the years, the farm fell on hard times and had deteriorated by the time the Workleys bought it in 1971. Thankfully, they felt so strongly about preserving Ohio history that they began to restore the barn, even adding a fresh coat of red paint recently. I loved the matching mailbox.

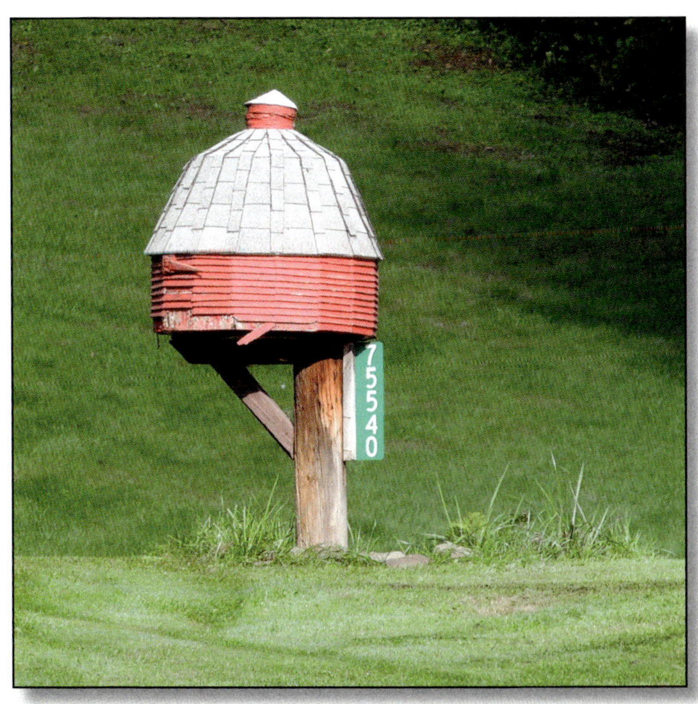

Matching mailbox, Workley barn. Harrison County, Ohio

Actually, the barn is not round, as Judy proudly proclaimed, "It's the only 16-sided barn in Ohio." Each side is 12 feet long, the barn is 60 feet high, and it stretches 60 feet wide. Its sandstone foundation, quarried on the farm, reminded me of the Kindleberger stone barn in nearby Monroe County. The attractive cupola sits on top of a round silo, which, according to Judy, was filled only once. Removing the corn took too long.

Judy and Ollie raised cattle, horses, but mostly pigs — at one time 186 of the porkers. Over the years, they've maintained the barn well, as its new roof proves. Judy also added a flair of her own by painting old car tires red, gold, and violet and attaching them to fence posts leading up to the barn. I had to include her art in my painting.

Although this barn is hard to find — virtually hidden in Appalachian woodland — it stands as a tribute not only to its builder of a century ago but also to the current owners who've been faithful stewards of history. Hopefully it will continue to survive as a reminder of Ohio's early days, something that this essay and painting — framed in the barn's own wood — also hope to accomplish.

PERRY COUNTY

The Round Barns of Perry County

Like Vernon County, Wisconsin, and its 10 round barns, three of which lie within a few miles of one another, and Fulton County, Indiana, and its eight round barns, three of which also are close together, this rural Ohio county also has a distinctive cluster of round barns. Until recently, four circular barns sat within five miles of one another. Three remain today. I visited them in the autumn of 2018.

When I arrived in Perry County, while going up a gravel road, I managed with difficulty to find the first, which belongs to Linda and Neil Cooperider. Neil's great-grandfather built the original barn in the late 1800s, but lost it to a fire. Neil's grandparents took over the farm and its 270 acres around 1920 and built this barn around 1926, which is unusual since farmers had such difficulty in those years. Today the barn stores hay, which they use for beef cattle. They also raise corn.

Linda told me that the roof used to have a golden color, but, since it was deteriorating, they replaced it, determined

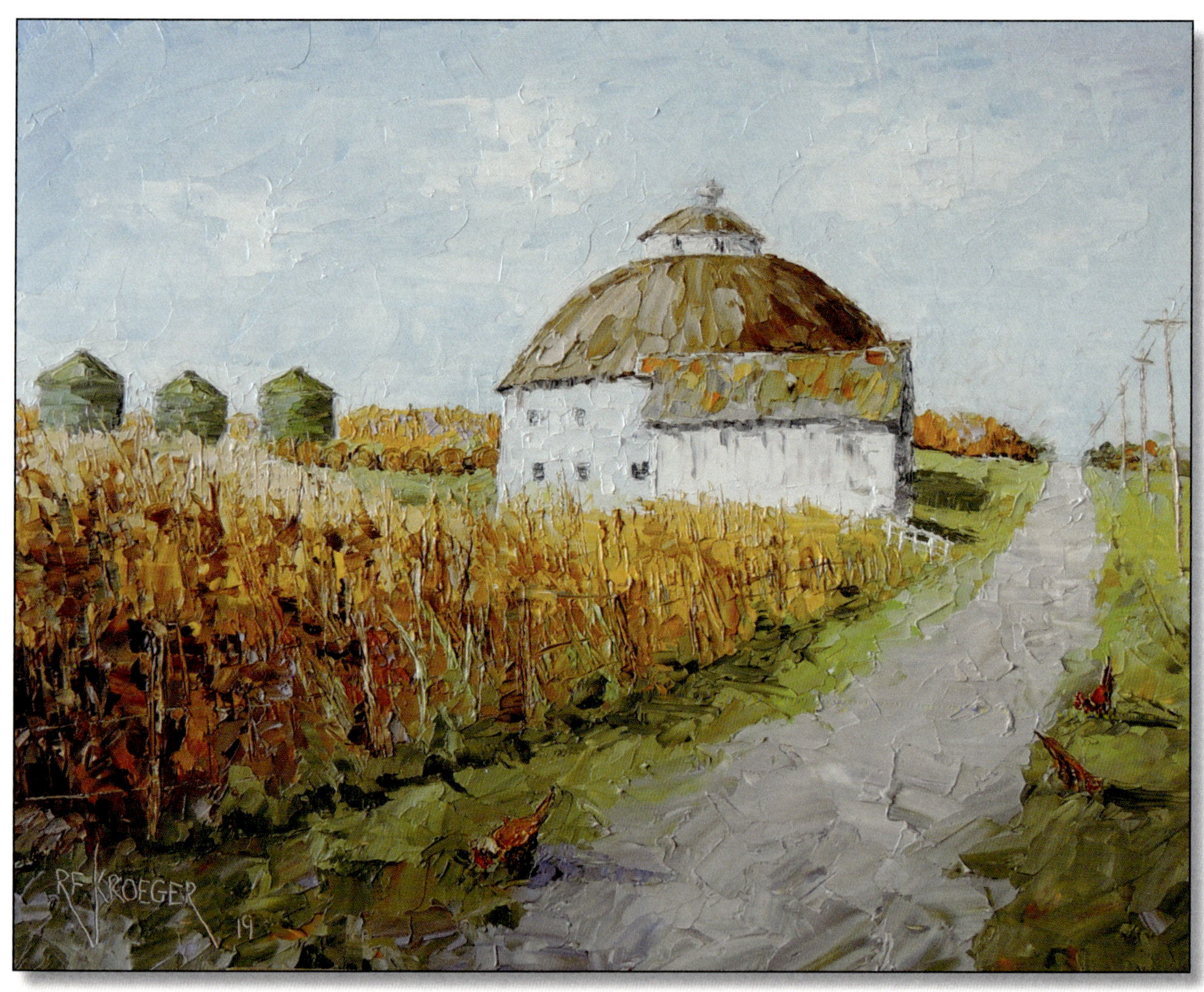

The Round Barns of Perry County

to preserve this treasure. Though she was gone when I visited, Neil was home and showed me the inside of the barn, always a treat to see since round barns are so unique. A giant metal silo rises to the top — with hatch doors every six feet or so from bottom to top. Large hay bales were stacked next to the empty silo, proving that this barn still functions, though its silo does not.

The second barn was easier to find. Owners John and Judy McGaughey explained that it was built in 1909 and they also related that they were having trouble finding a roofer to climb up the ultra-steep conical roof to repair the damaged cupola. Ah, the difficulties of maintaining an old barn.

Although locating the third round barn challenged my navigational skills — I managed to get lost a few times — the trip was worth it even though I couldn't contact its owner. This barn was nearly a duplicate of the Cooperider's — a perfectly domed roof and a double cupola, topped by a metal ventilator. Both have walls that are vertically sided, liberally sprinkled with small windows, and supported by a cement base.

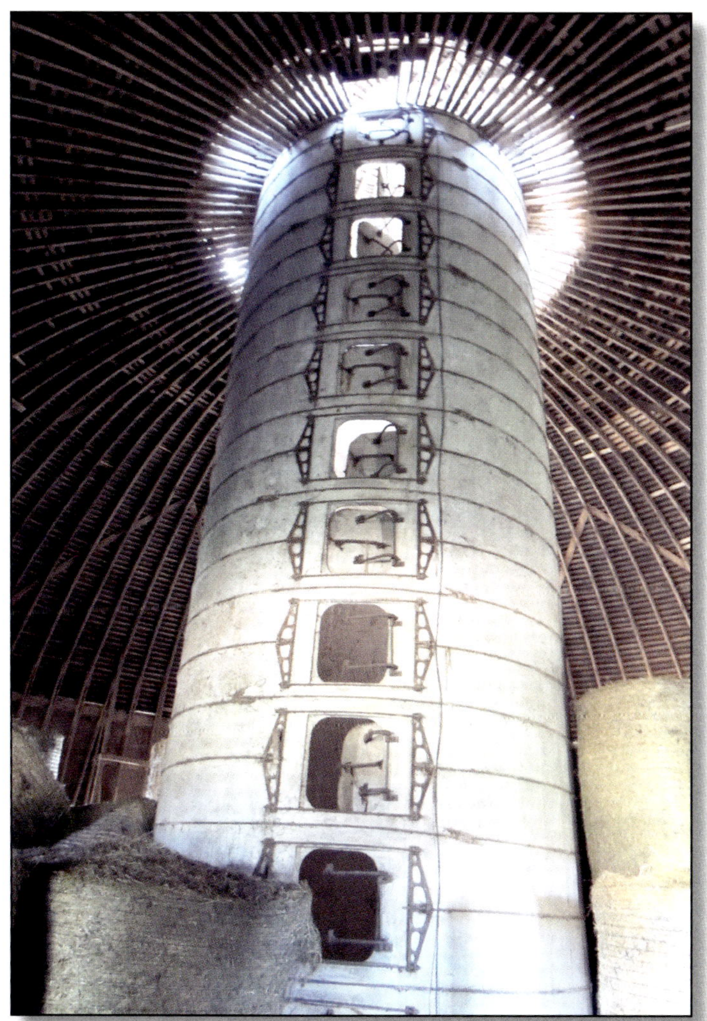

Interior, central metal silo, Cooperider barn. Perry County, Ohio

Owned initially by the Gilmores, the barn was built in 1917 but burned years later. Undeterred, the family rebuilt it in 1932, apparently prosperous enough to stick with this expensive type of barn during the somber days of the Great Depression.

Since I didn't know if the fourth barn was merely a pile of collapsed lumber or if it was completely gone, I passed on trying to find it. From old photos, the Dornbirer barn looked intriguing: circular form, a large cupola with louvers spaced about three feet apart, curved horizonal siding, and an internal wooden silo, a barn much different from its three neighbors. However, it's just one more page of history that's missing.

Why these four barns were built so close to one another will likely remain a mystery since there are no records of any other round barns in the county. Did the Gilmores know that the Cooperiders lost their first round barn, but were courageous enough to rebuild in 1926? Then, when their barn burned, did the Gilmores borrow plans from their neighbors to rebuild? Why were both farmers so prosperous during these tough times? Such are the unanswered questions about the round barns of Perry County.

KENTUCKY

BOURBON COUNTY

Kentucky's Best

Formed in 1786 as part of the state of Virginia, Bourbon County was named for France's royal family of Bourbons, who supplied troops, ships, and arms in the American Revolution. Three years later the French Revolution began, signaling the end of the Bourbons. However, the name now lives on in one of Kentucky's famous whiskeys. In 1792 statehood arrived.

The story behind this 14-sided barn, surrounded by iconic black fencing — typical of Kentucky's horse farms — began in 1879 with the birth of John Daniel Hertz. Born into a Jewish family, Schandor Herz (his name later changed to John Hertz) spent his early years in a village in present-day Slovakia until 1884, when his family immigrated to the United States and settled in Chicago. As a young man without much money, Hertz began selling newspapers and started boxing, which led to modest success when he won amateur fights.

He switched to reporting but lost that job when his newspaper, the *Chicago Record*, merged with another and trimmed its staff. But, being a scrapper, he wasn't ready to give up and, at a friend's suggestion in 1904, he began buying and selling cars. When he accumulated an inventory, he started a taxi company — with fares low enough for the common man. From a humble beginning of seven cabs in 1907, this 28-year-old entrepreneur turned his venture into the Yellow Cab Company in 1915. Buoyed by this success, he founded a bus transportation enterprise and started assembling his distinctive yellow cabs from parts he purchased, saving him manufacturing costs.

At some point he became infatuated with horses, first working as a jockey's valet at an Indiana racetrack. And, by 1920, flush with cash from several burgeoning businesses, he bought land in Cary, a town about 50 miles north of Chicago, where he eventually built Trout Valley, a palatial get-away that he'd visit during the 1920s, often landing his sea plane on the nearby Fox River where an employee — his estate employed 100 at one time — would pick him up and drive him to his 35-room mansion. To design the grounds, Hertz hired Jens Jensen, recently retired from being superintendent of Chicago's western city parks, whose work must have impressed Hertz. After finishing the magnificent landscaping at Trout Valley, Jensen's reputation grew, commanding jobs for the rich and famous, including the Fords of Michigan as well as architects such as Frank Lloyd Wright.

When finished, Trout Valley with its nearly 1,000 acres had several homes for estate employees, barns and riding stables, a Roman-style swimming pool with stone balustrades, polo grounds, trout fishing ponds, fields for pheasant hunting, riding trails, and a spectacular arched set of iron gates with stone pillars. Today the gates lead into an affluent housing subdivision. A barn that Hertz built for his Kentucky Derby champion, Reigh Count, has been converted into a sumptuous private residence, on the market for $525,000 in 2019.

In the 1920s Trout Valley represented the best of the Roaring Twenties and Hertz invited Hollywood actors and actresses as well as other famous folks — such as Walt Disney and Eleanor Roosevelt to his palace for parties reminiscent of the Great Gatsby. Hertz also bred and raised thoroughbreds. But all was not peaches and cream.

Below: *Kentucky's Best*

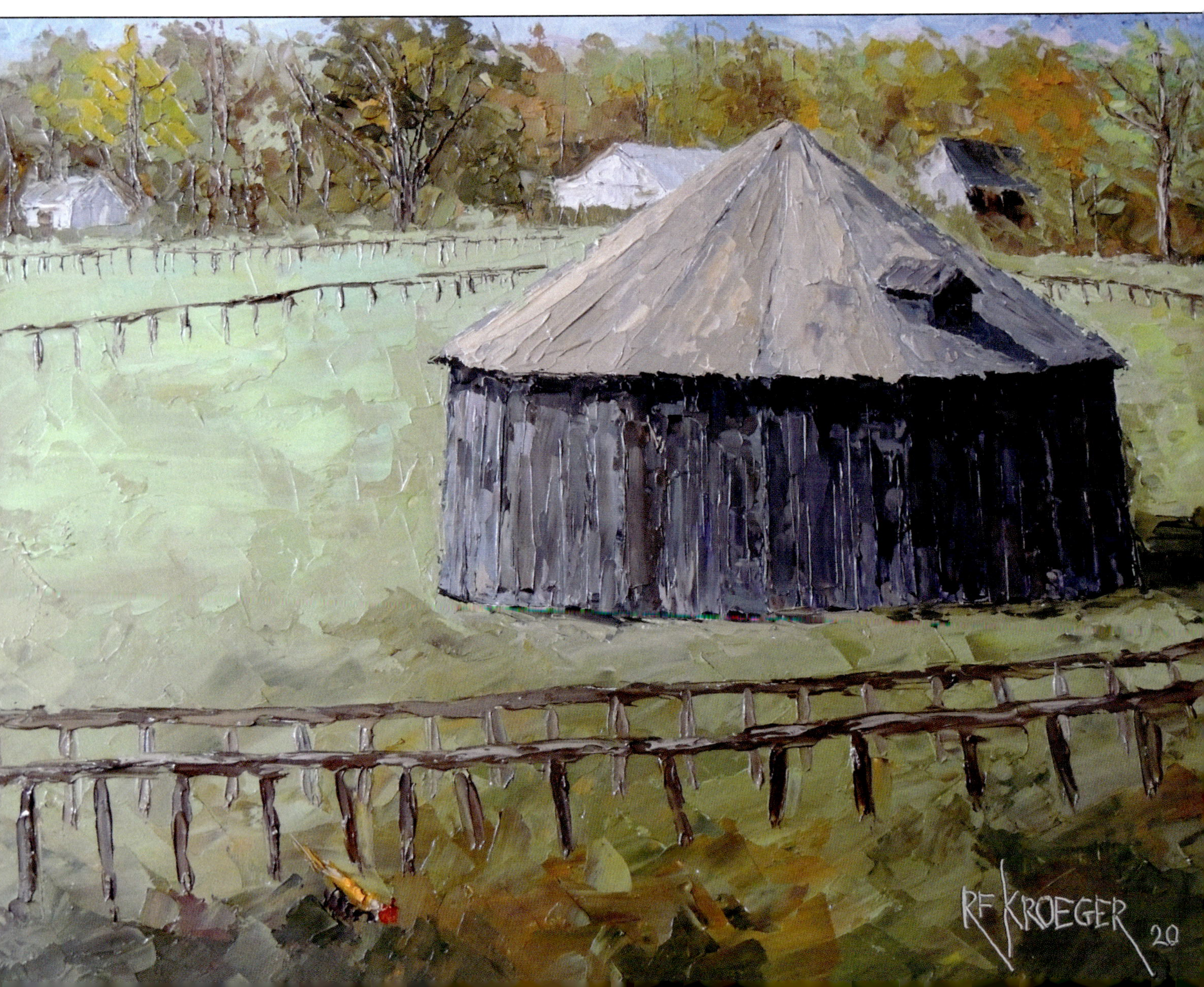

Business-wise, everything Hertz touched turned to gold. By 1925 he owned or was involved in eight companies, including a rental-car company he purchased, changing its name to Hertz Drive-Ur-Self, which eventually became Hertz Rental Car. However, choosing to employ non-union drivers in his Yellow Cab service, he often incurred ill will from the other major Chicago cab company, Checker Taxi. Violence escalated in 1920 when hundreds of shots were fired in an early morning battle and in 1921 a Yellow Cab driver was killed. Hertz gave a statement to the news media, "It has only been comic opera, warfare until tonight, but from now on it is going to be a fight to a finish." He offered a $5,000 reward for the killer, who confessed the next day.

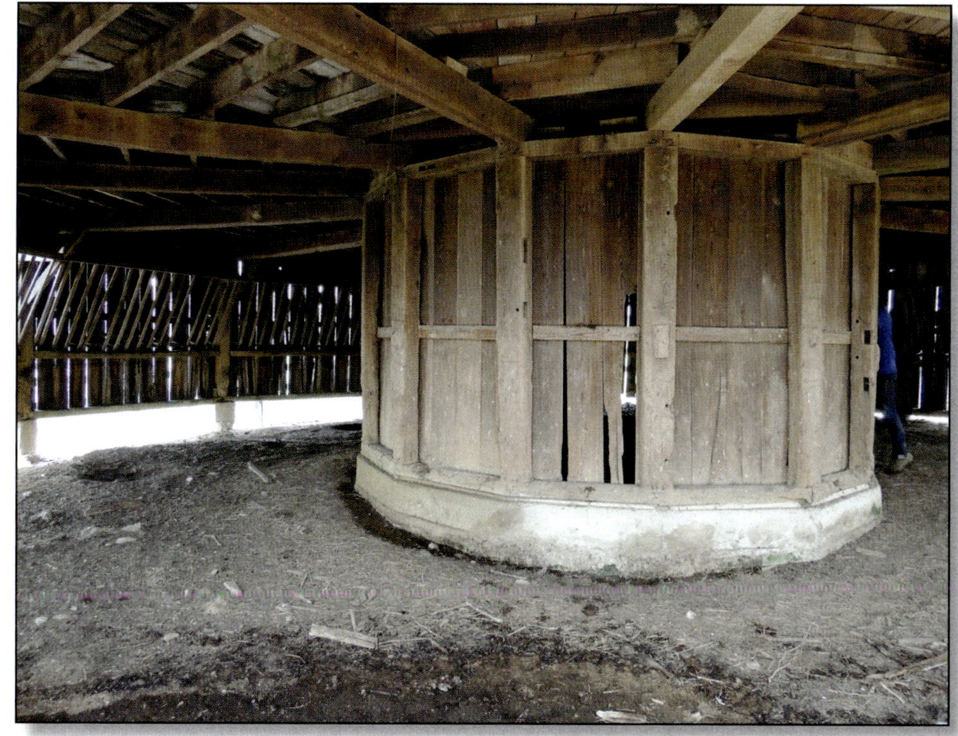

Polygonal central storage bin, Hertz barn. Bourbon County, Kentucky

However, the fighting continued, helped, no doubt, by some of Chicago's notorious criminals, such as Al Capone and Bugs Moran. Chicago mayors turned their heads as did the police force. After all, money talks, especially when Prohibition introduced a lucrative new business — bootlegging. It was the era of drive-by submachine gun terror and almost constant feuding between the Irish North Side Gang, headed by Bugs Moran, and the South Side Italians, commanded by Al Capone. The taxicab wars, although playing a minor role in Chicago crime, hit home in 1928, when a "mysterious" fire broke out in the Trout Valley stables, killing 11 Hertz racehorses, valued at $225,000. Was this the work of the rival Checker Taxi or of the more sophisticated gangs of Bugs Moran or Al Capone? Hertz didn't care; he'd had enough, his only solace coming when an alert stable boy saved Reigh Count, the horse that won the Kentucky Derby later that year. In those days Hertz attached a siren to his racing trophies on his mantle, which would sound if a piece were moved, noise loud enough to be heard for blocks. Fear and paranoia were creeping into the household.

He sold his majority share in his cab interests and rental car company to General Motors in 1929, luckily raising cash before the massive collapse of the stock market. In the 1930s, discouraged by continual crime in Chicago and heeding the advice of his friend, Arthur B. Hancock, Sr., owner of the famous Claiborne horse farm in Paris, Kentucky, Hertz decided to move. Eventually he bought land in Paris — including this round barn, which was built, according to locals, around 1913 and home to J.D. Butler, who farmed and raised mules. Hertz again hired the famous Jens Jensen, landscape architect of his former estate, to design his new farm, Stoner Creek Stud. Reigh Count's first crop as a stud included Count Fleet, who was named two-year-old champion of 1942. The next year, Hertz once again struck gold when Count Fleet won the Triple Crown, becoming the sixth winner of these prestigious races. In the same year he sold Trout Valley to another multi-millionaire, Otto Schnering, founder of the Curtiss Candy Company and inventor of such treats as Butterfingers and Baby Ruths.

He continued to raise horses on his Kentucky farm but, apparently missing the car business, Hertz re-purchased his rental car company from General Motors in 1953, which he ran for the rest of his life. At that point, money didn't matter anymore. In an address he gave in 1956 to the Thoroughbred Club of America, Hertz explained that, when Count Fleet turned four, a wealthy Texan offered to buy him for $1 million but Hertz refused to sell. "I think a fellow who would pay $1 million for a horse ought to have his head examined," Hertz said after the negotiations. "And that the fellow who turned it down must be absolutely unbalanced."

After Hertz died in 1961, his heirs decided to sell the 730-acre Stoner Creek farm, which they did in 1964 — to two gentlemen, both racehorse experts. Norman Woolworth and David Johnston continued to raise horses, more champions, but sold the farm in 1981 to a wealthy friend, a Swedish lady, who began leasing the farm in

1996 to Steve and Cindy Stewart. They merged their former horse farm, Hunterton Farm, and called their new establishment, Hunterton Farm at Stoner Creek Stud.

Steve, who grew up in Kentucky's horse-racing capital of Lexington, explained, "We've expanded to over 900 acres ... on land that used to be Stoner Creek Stud and Woodlawn Farm, another piece of racehorse history." They've turned the operation into the world's largest Standardbred farm that does not stand stallions. Each year they breed over 200 mares and sell about 150 yearlings in auctions in Lexington and Harrisburg, Pennsylvania. They're busy people.

This little round barn may seem out of place in such bucolic grounds designed by the famous Jens Jensen. (There are about 20 barns on the property to service about 500 horses.) In fact, driving down the dozens of lanes lined with giant sycamores with views of handsome horses and their young colts trotting around is as good a therapy as any psychologist can provide. Yes, the 35-room Hertz mansion and the trout ponds are missing, but a large attractive manor home that Hertz built remains — as do other barns and buildings.

Apparently, the round barn, a rare tetradecagon, wasn't the first. Interior rough-cut wooden beams surrounding the central feed bin show many wooden nails and remnants of mortise and tenon joints, suggesting that a timber framed barn existed before this one and may have dated to the 1800s. Using some reclaimed lumber from the original barn, the owner may have built this round barn, as locals claim, around 1913. But why the farmer chose a round shape is anyone's guess. The barn's 50-foot diameter, not large by any means, indicates it was used only for a handful of horses and, perhaps in its early years, by, shudder, mules. Inside, on the first floor, stanchions for the livestock still stand, though the stalls are gone. The large enclosed central corral most likely held hay, stored above in the spacious second floor. The all-important roof, well protected over the years, including a new set of shingles, is in excellent condition. Perhaps part of the reason for the roof's durability is that six vertical beams support it. The barn's not used for anything now, just surviving as an important part of round barn history.

And, although this barn does not have a specific spot in the National Register, it deserves a place there, just as much as the region, which is already listed: The Stoner Creek Rural Historic District was listed in 2001. It contains 22,000 acres, 526 buildings, 207 structures, 33 sites, and seven contributing objects. The district includes 12 historic farms, including the Stoner Creek Stud Farm. Surely this round barn fits in well with such company and, at least in this painting, merits the title, "Kentucky's Best."

INDIANA

LAPORTE COUNTY

Door on the Prairie

LaPorte County was formed in 1832 and was named by French explorers who discovered a natural opening in the forest, an old Indian trail that resembled a door and led to lands further west. To the south and westwards was the prairie and to the north and east were dense woods. It was an easy call: in French la porte means "the door." This nine-sided barn is situated southeast of the county seat, La Porte, a city of over 21,000 and about equidistant from South Bend and Chicago. Marion Ridgeway built it in 1878, though the story begins much earlier.

His grandfather, James, must have been a wealthy man when he purchased over 3,000 acres from the government in 1831 and began farming. The farm passed onto his son and eventually to Marion, who was born in 1843. By this time, the Ridgeway farm was prosperous, allowing Marion to become a well-known horse breeder since in much of the 19th century most farmers were content to feed their families and little else.

In his late 20s, he decided to expand his stable of horses and, after witnessing the disastrous Chicago fire of 1871, he saw the need for better work horses — for pulling heavy loads and for transportation down Indiana's dirt roads. Wanting to learn about proper breeding methods and to purchase stock, he traveled to England, Scotland, and France, where perhaps he saw polygonal barns, though most were the rectangular English three-bay threshing type. Back in La Porte, he began raising Clydesdales, Percherons, and Morgans, as well as short-horned cattle and, with business booming, he hired a local builder E.G. Anderson, whose trademark was the Gothic revival style. He built not only the nonagonal barn but tenant farmer homes, other smaller barns, and a track for training horses. His two-story brick farmhouse still stands.

Marion also realized the value of marketing and, since the unique barn had plenty of exposure from the main road leading into town, he painted the sides of the barn with his name and the horse breeds he was selling. In lieu of billboards, barns began to advertise; soon after this came the Mail Pouch and Visit Rock City barns — the former throughout the Midwest and the latter frequently seen in southern states. Soon La Porte became known as a center for draft and carriage horses. Today's four-lane highway that passes the barn treats motorists to a clear view of this icon.

With a diameter of 50 feet, the barn is not a large one but its construction proves that it was built to last — sawmill-cut beams are supported by triangular bracing, which

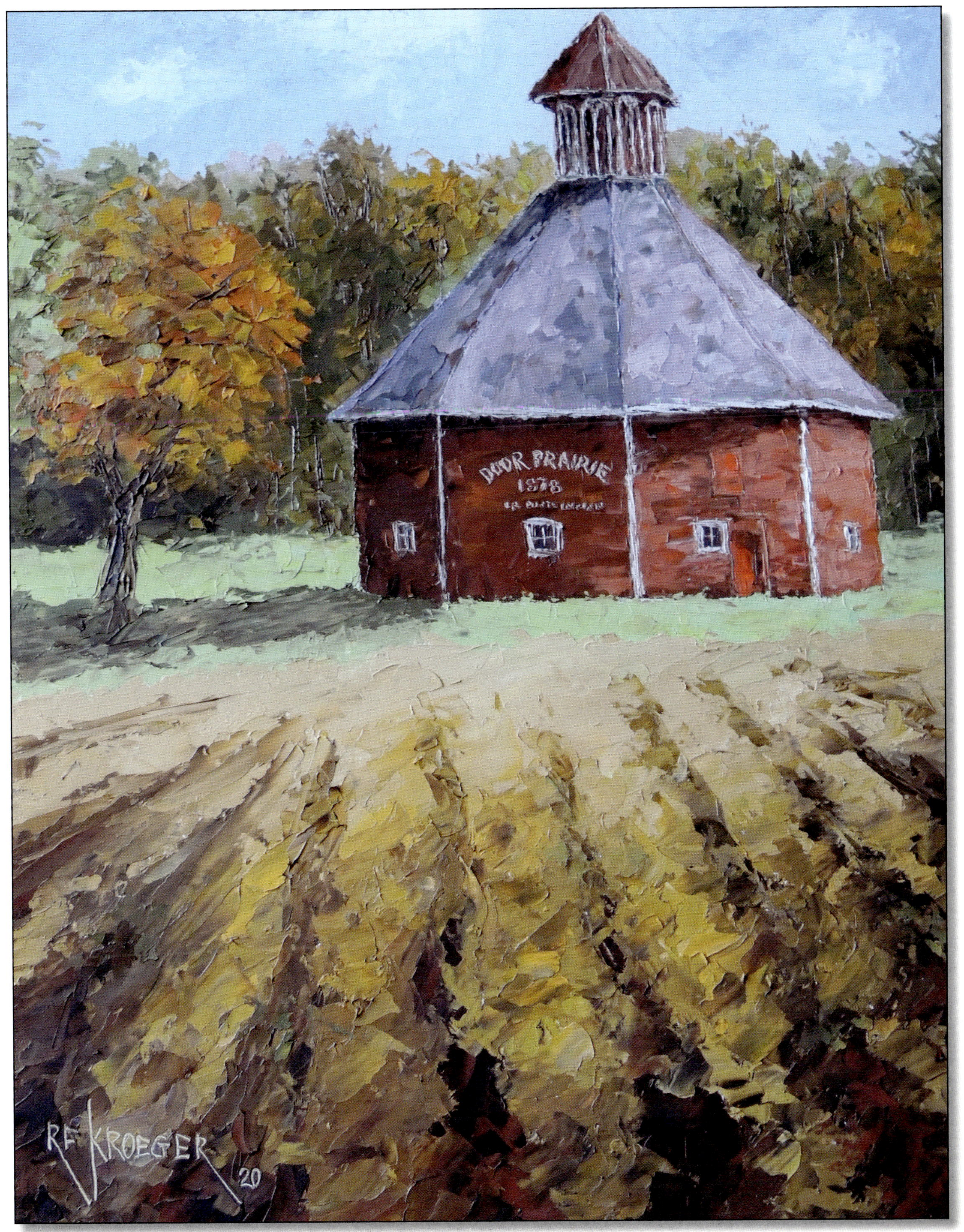

Door on the Prairie

inhibits twisting and resists high springtime winds, which often plaque the Midwest. And nearly 150 years old now, its construction has proven the test of time, especially considering its distinctive tall cupola, perched high on the steeply sloped roof. The ground level housed the livestock while the upper level provided storage for hay and grain, which could be dropped into the central feeding area.

However, despite a thriving business, Mr. Ridgeway didn't enjoy his success for long; a heart attack claimed him in 1879, dead at 46. The farm passed through one generation to the next until his granddaughter Lorena Harwood sold it in 1982. Dr. Peter Kesling, a local orthodontist who grew up on a nearby farm, had made several offers to buy the farm but the owner wasn't interested. Finally, when he saw a for sale sign, he swooped in, paid $800,000 for the large farm and turned his attention to preserving a piece of history, one that was sadly deteriorating.

Wisely, he established the Peter C. Kesling Foundation, which now owns the barn, and he listed it on the National Register. In an article in the *South Bend Tribune*, Kesling commented on his purchase, "When we bought it, the roof was gone and you could see through the boards. It was in really bad shape." But, thankfully having sufficient funds, the dentist did extensive renovations, resulting in a beautifully preserved piece of Indiana history. Only the second polygonal barn to have been built in Indiana — the first was built in Henry County in 1874 — this barn serves as a memory of Marion Ridgeway's horse breeding farm and also stands proudly as a marker for the door on the prairie. Thanks, Dr. Kesling.

FAYETTE COUNTY

A Founding Father

Nearly a spitting image of Straughter Pleak's wedding cake barn, this one was built in 1904, seven years before Pleak's. It, too, resembles the traditional cake, a slice of which is often shoved by the bride into the mouth of

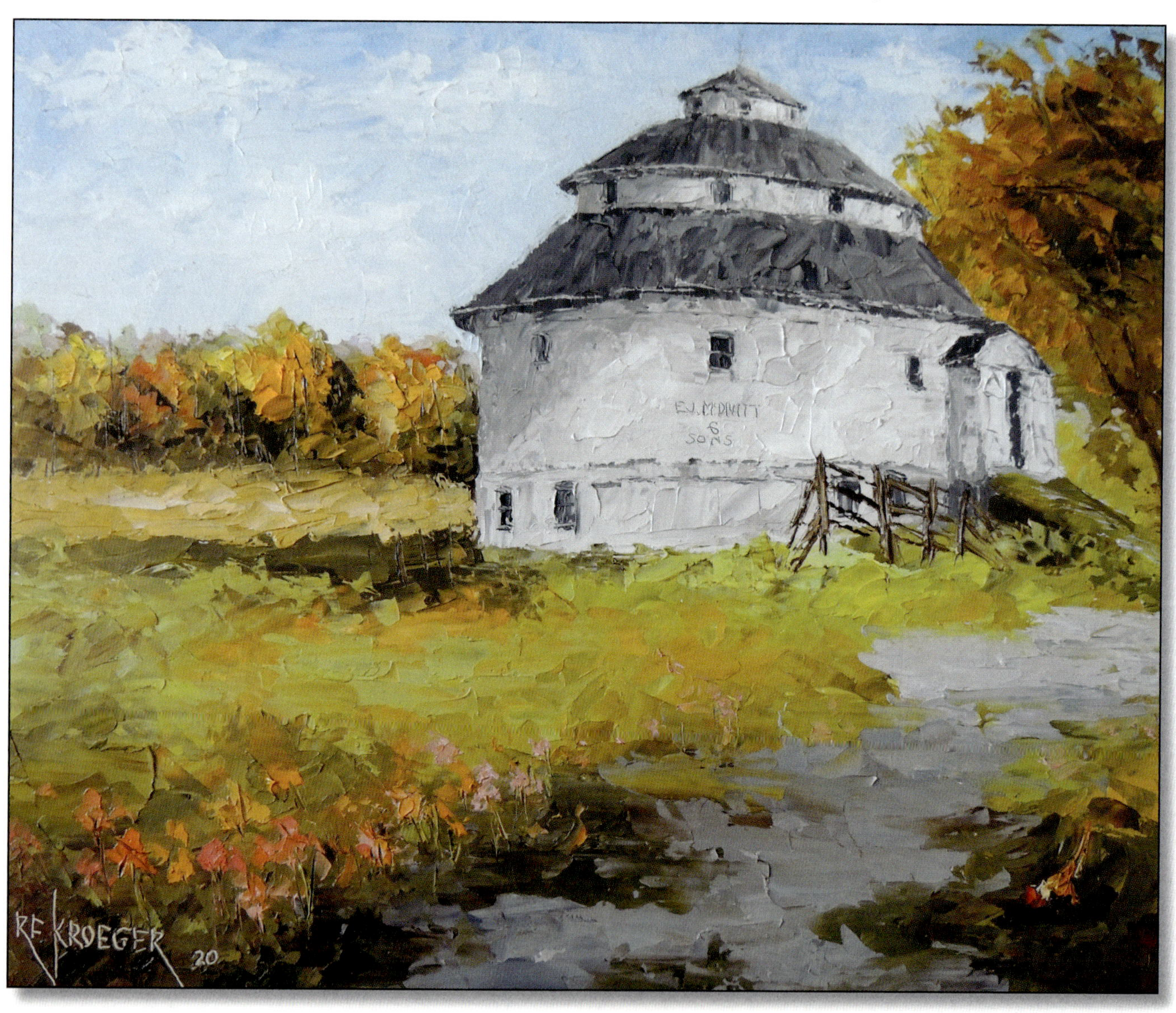

A Founding Father

her new husband, sort of a message about who will be boss in the marriage. Though Straughter is given credit for building his own barn, original owners Thomas and Nancy Ranck hired one of Indiana's famous round barn builders, Isaac McNamee. Interestingly, Fayette County is just north of Decatur County — where Pleak's barn was built — lending some credence that Straughter may have seen this one before building his.

McNamee, born in Akron, Ohio in 1832, was orphaned when his family traveled west and was taken in by an Indiana Quaker carpenter, who mentored him. In 1900 another Quaker, William Hill, hired Isaac, now nearly 70, and his son Emery to build a round barn, a circular one as advocated by Wisconsin's Professor King. Not much later, the McNamees built their second round barn near Warrington in Hancock County, just a bit further west. Their popularity — and that of the round barn design — soared when this barn survived a tornado in 1902, leading to more jobs. Soon afterwards, the McNamees formed a business arrangement with another carpenter-architect, Benton Steele, and, together, they became missionaries for round barns. In 1903 Emery McNamee declared, "Scores of the cyclone barns will be built this year," in an article in the *Anderson Morning Herald*.

True to his prediction, a year later and two years after their round barn in Warrington survived the tornado, the McNamees started construction of the Ranck barn. A large one — 70 feet in diameter and standing 70 feet tall — it differs from the Pleak barn in that it has an earthen ramp that leads to the second-floor haymow. The barn's two rows of windows in the double cupola also differ from the layers in Straughter's barn. Unlike Professor King's prototype that included a central silo, this barn stored feed in a one-story wooden corncrib and two grain bins, each 10 by 15 feet, which were located in the center. A hayloft covered about a third of the main floor and horse-drawn hayforks, with ropes and pulleys, were used to load hay, simplified by a self-supporting roof. Livestock stalls were arranged around the perimeter of the lower level. Its vertical wood siding has survived for over a century.

A year after he built this barn, McNamee got a patent for a self-supporting conical roof, along with round barn builder Horace Duncan and Frank Littleton, the Indianapolis attorney who filed the paperwork. Unfortunately, round barn architect Benton Steele and his partner Frank Detraz were excluded, leading to friction among these famous Indiana barn builders, although they continued to spread the gospel of the round barn throughout many Midwestern and Western states.

However, despite being "cyclone-proof," the roof blew off this barn in 1930 and Emery, then in his early 80s, was hired to fix it, reputedly making a handsome profit since he was the only one with such expertise. Later, in 1937, after the worst of the Great Depression, the family sold the farm to a local veterinarian, Dr. Ralph Carmack, and his wife Tena. Their tenure was short, lasting only until 1945 — near the end of World War II — when Everett and Mary McDivitt bought the barn. Historically minded, they not only maintained the barn but listed it on the National Register in 1983, a place it deserves. Today it still stands, a tribute to the Rancks as well as to septuagenarian Isaac McNamee, one of Indiana's round barn's founding fathers.

DECATUR COUNTY

The Wedding Cake

Since several writers have used the phrase, "a three-tiered wedding cake," to describe this round barn with its distinctive separate cupolas, it seemed to be a fitting title for this painting and essay. Though it was built in 1908 by Strauther Van Pleak, the barn's history traces back much further.

Strauther's great-grandfather, John Pleakenstalver, born in 1755 near Philadelphia, became a frontiersman, much like Daniel Boone and Simon Kenton. Some records indicate that he served with Boone in Fort Boonesboro, Kentucky, and later became an ensign under George Rogers Clark in his Illinois campaign in 1778. Also, during the Revolutionary War — in 1780 — John was one of the 256 signers of the Cumberland Compact, a document outlining rules of the settlers at Fort Nashborough, which later became Nashville, Tennessee.

After his marriage, he and his wife Esther moved to Morgan's Station in 1791, a time when land — at a dollar an acre — was affordable but also a time when Indian skirmishes were still prevalent, probably motivating them to move the next spring to Mt. Sterling, Kentucky. The move was timed well since the settlers at Morgan's, sensing no danger, dismantled the fort stockades, using the logs for firewood. Unfortunately, in that spring of 1792 a large band of Shawnees killed many men, women, and children in this region, according to the eyewitness account of John Wade, Jr., the son of a settler at Morgan's. Two miles away in Mt. Sterling, Pleakenstalver and his family were safe. They had 12 children.

One of them, named after many generals — Narcus Barren Steuben Isaiac Henry Fielding Lewis Pleakanstalver — moved to Decatur County, Indiana, and founded the family farm, recorded in the family land deed, dated 1827 and signed by President John Quincy Adams, a copy of which is proudly displayed inside the round barn. Despite having seven first names, the son was referred to simply as

"Fielding" as was his son, Fielding, Jr., who was the father of the barn builder, Strauther Van Pleak. The grandchildren of Narcus, including Strauther, were spared the long name when it was shortened to Pleak.

In the 19th century the family farmed the land and also raised mules, often selling them to the army, who trained them for transporting supplies. During the Civil War, Strauther was about seven years old, and, according to his grandson, related a story about selling mules. Once when an army officer was inspecting mules, he was checking the animals' mouths, which were indications of health or disease, along with age. Being a clever child, the boy spoke to his grandfather, with the army inspector close by, "Dad, is that the mule you knocked the tooth out of?" Smart kid.

However, why he chose a round design for the barn remains unknown. At the time, Indiana was fertile ground for early round barn builders — the McNamee family, Benton Steele, among many others, including the flamboyant Horace Duncan, who built his masterpiece, the J.H. Manchester barn, in Auglaize County, Ohio, in 1908, the same year as the Pleak barn was built.

Strauther built an octagonal central silo first and then constructed the barn around it, which would allow the mules and horses to surround the silo for feeding. More than 100 animals could feed at one time and, on the outer perimeter, another manger and a large watering trough provided hay and drink. The silo, originally made of stacked lumber and coated with tar, was later covered with brick and cement when it began to leak.

The barn's top cupola is covered in decorative rounded wood shingles while conventional horizontal curved wood siding covers the lower sections. Although eight single-paned windows provide some light, the barn's interior is dark. Today, thanks to interior Christmas-styled lights, placed by friends of the Reeds, current owners, for a wedding, there's plenty of light. In 1914, the Pleaks sold the farm to a Reverend I.E. Morgan.

Apparently, the mule business was so successful that the next year the Morgans built a large rectangular barn, one with a series of pens on either side of a central walkway that connected to the round barn. In 1937 Morgan's son, Ati, took over the farm, continued farming and, realizing the historic significance of the round barn, got it listed on the National Register in 1993. Three years later his heirs put the barn and farm into an auction, which begins the next part of this story.

In 1996 Richard Reed owned farmland acreage surrounding the 180 acres of the Pleak-Morgan farmstead and wanted to merge it into his farm. He related that he went to the auction, intent on buying it and that his friend, who also wanted to acquire it, was willing to let him have the property, mutually deciding not to escalate the price. Despite the auction being well attended, Richard ended up with the farm after bidding only once, as much a shock to him as it was to his friend. Currently, the Reed families farm about 1,500 acres.

Richard, also feeling a responsibility to Indiana heritage, decided to save the round barn but had to dismantle the large rectangular one, also in disrepair. In 1997 he began restoring the barn, raising it with 13 house jacks, and pouring a new foundation. When he started power washing the black siding, he couldn't believe the beautiful golden color that emerged, "So we just stopped what we were doing." The barn's white coat sparkles today. He removed the other barn later in 1999.

Richard and his family exemplify a farm family that sticks together, something common in the 19th and early 20th century but becoming rare today as young people leave home for travel, job opportunities, and eventually become nomadic, moving from house to house and state to state. Richard's father, Francis "Nick" Reed, started a fertilizer company in 1935, during the dark days of the Great Depression, an era when many farm families struggled and many lost their land to banks. His company, KOVA, has become one of the Midwest's premier agricultural enterprises, even branching into nearby Ohio, Illinois, West Memphis, and Nebraska.

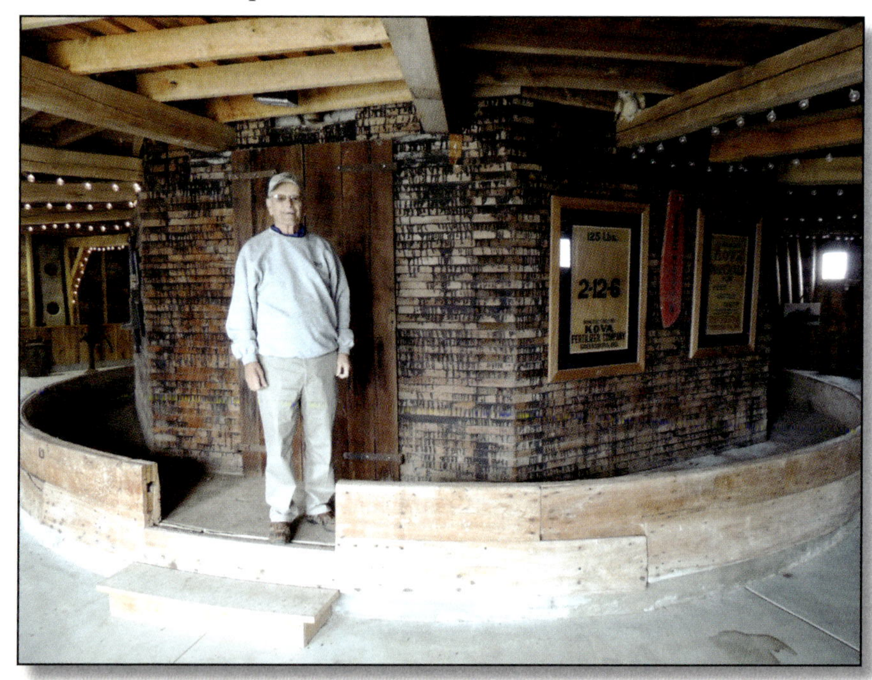

Owner Richard Reed, next to the central silo. Notice curved wooden enclosure. Decatur County, Indiana

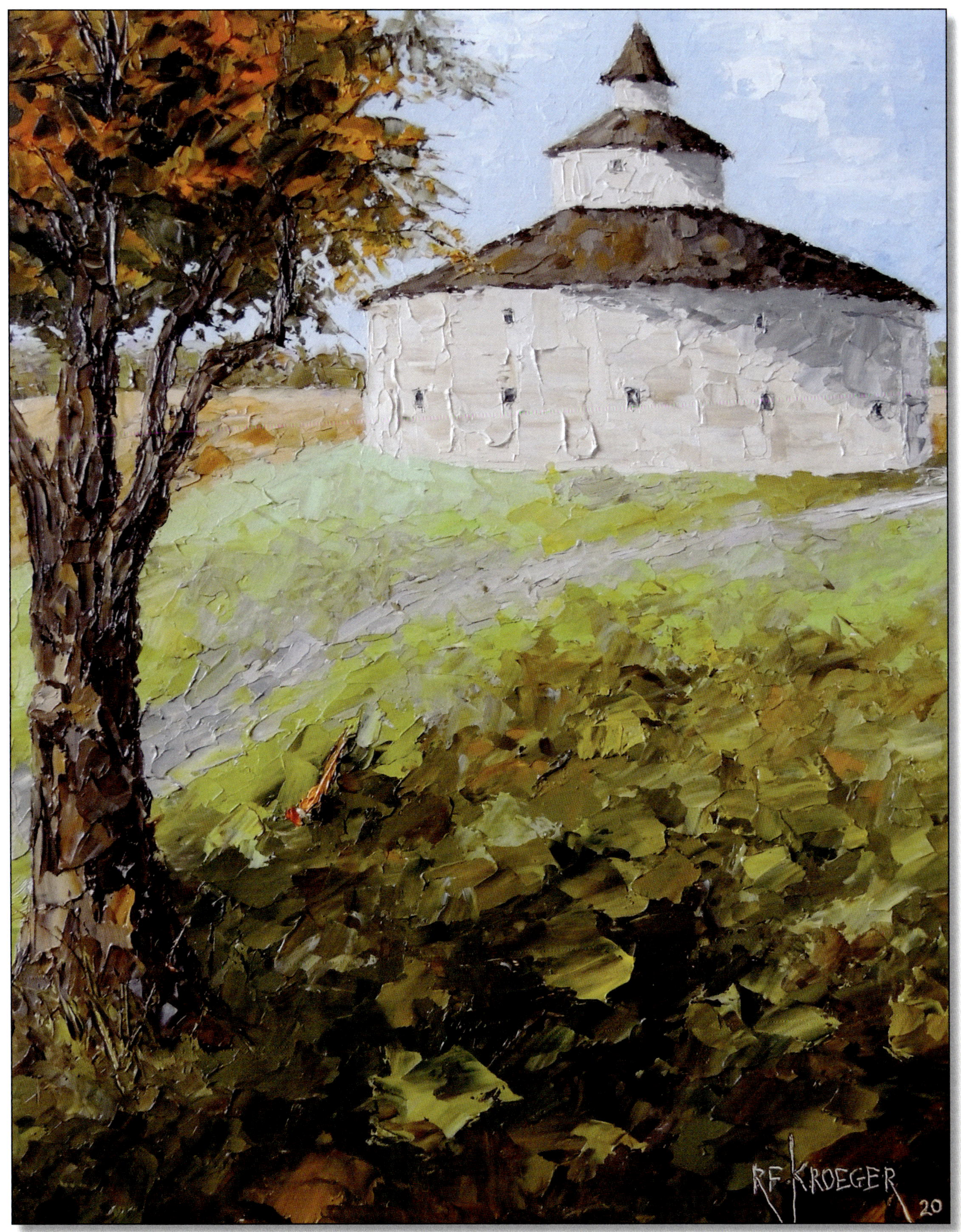

The Wedding Cake

After graduating from Purdue University, Richard returned to the family business in 1958, determined to keep it going, a task that required hard work, which did not always guarantee success. It's not uncommon to watch a patriarch build a thriving company only to see it dwindle or fail in future generations. Take Kodak for example. This iconic company was founded in 1880 by George Eastman, a poor high school dropout who supported his widowed mother and two sisters, one of whom had polio. Some will remember the Kodak brownie camera, which the company began producing in 1901 and which sold in the millions in the 1950s and 1960s, using conventional film. But when the digital filmless camera came along — ironically first invented in 1975 by a Kodak engineer — company executives dismissed it as "a cute" idea and one that should be kept hidden. But others saw the future of the digital camera, though Kodak gurus, even as late as 2007, asserted the superiority of film-laded camera. The multi-national company filed for bankruptcy protection in 2012.

On the other hand, Richard Reed grew his fertilizer business into a thriving economic engine, one which today employs not only his three sons but eight of his 11 grandchildren. His son Todd is quoted on the company website, "We are focused, we have the right people, and we challenge ourselves to do the best job possible for our customers."

Richard lives close to his stunning round barn, which he takes school children through and which he shows off to visitors from other states and other countries. The 85-year-old said he's lived in the same house for a long time, "Sixty-two years in the same house, and 62 years with the same wife." I wonder if they had a three-tiered cake at their wedding.

LAKE COUNTY

Perfection

According to Orson Squire Fowler, editor of the *American Phrenological Journal*, the circle was the most perfect form, an opinion that might go back to his days as a student at Amherst College, located less than 50 miles from the unique round barn of the Shakers in western Massachusetts. However, in his book, *The Octagon House: A Home*

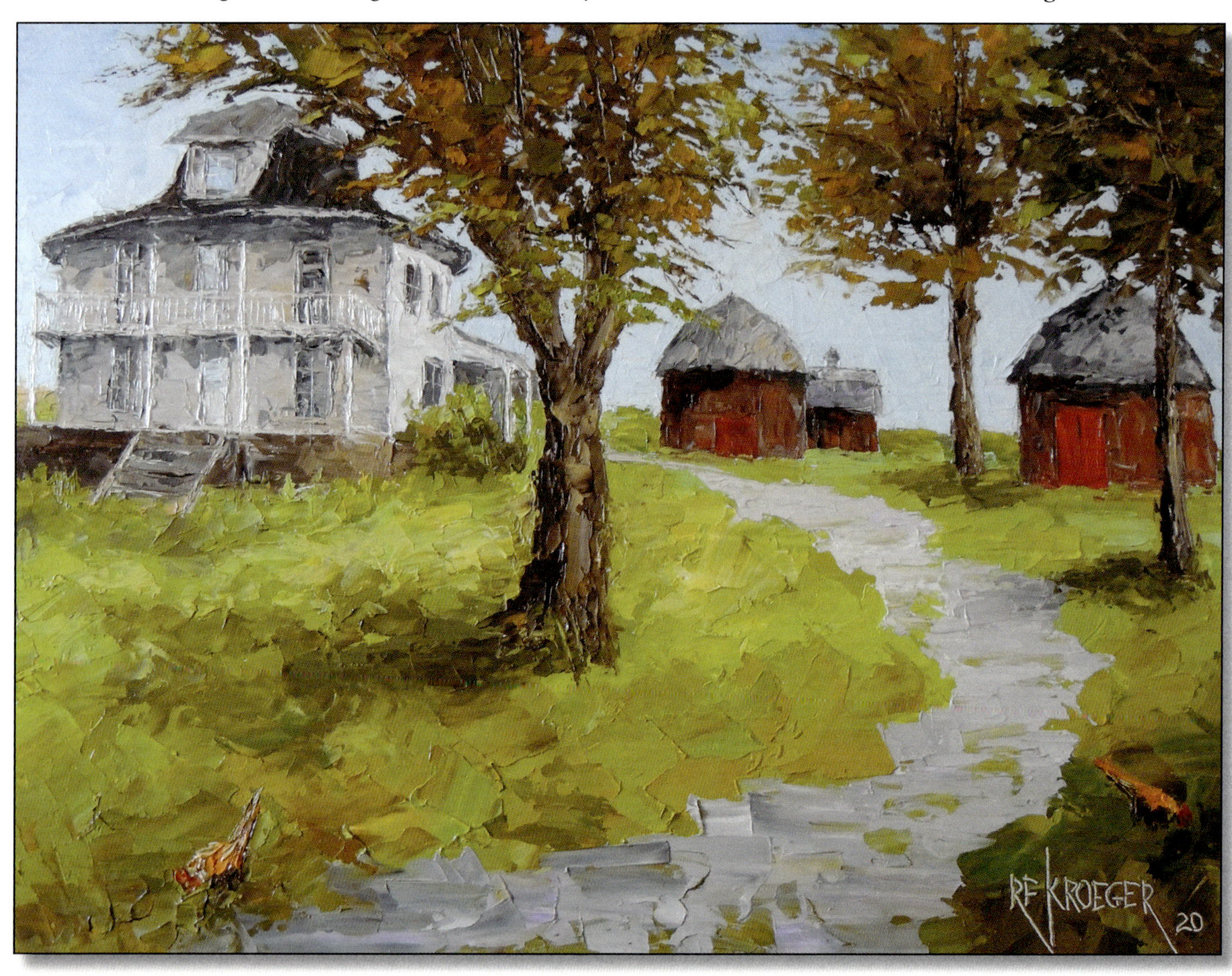

Perfection

For All, published in 1848, he emphasized the advantages of an octagonal building, not a circular one, which he felt was more difficult to construct. Perhaps the buildings of Thomas Jefferson, whose favorite design was the octagon, rubbed off on Fowler, who was well traveled in preaching his gospel of phrenology.

He continued with a third edition of his book, which he published in 1853 and which described the ideal farmstead as having both a house and barn in an octagonal shape. These books and subsequent articles prompted many throughout the east coast and the Midwest to build octagonal houses, though the barns would have to wait until Stewart's advocacy in the 1870s.

Although Indiana has many beautiful and historic barns, these two circular barns and a round farmhouse, located west of Cedar Lake in Hanover Township, may represent the only farm conforming to Fowler's concept of the ideal — a round house and round barns. Horace Duncan built them for the Echterling family around 1909, one for horses and one for dairy. The adjacent round house came after the barns.

In fact, this historic site may have been one of only a few — if any — such farmsteads remaining in America. Sadly, the barns may both be gone by the time of this book's publication and, even more sadly, the site did not make it into the National Register even though, as Fowler's ideal farmstead, it may have been one of a kind. Regardless, it merits the title of this painting, "Perfection."

KOSCIUSKO COUNTY

Dodecagon

Blame this one on the Greeks. If a hexagon is a six-sided polygon, and if a 10-sided structure is a decagon, then a 12-sided building, such as this barn, is a dodecagon. And it's a rare bird, one of the few dodecagonal barns left in America, according to its owner. It has also become a labor of love.

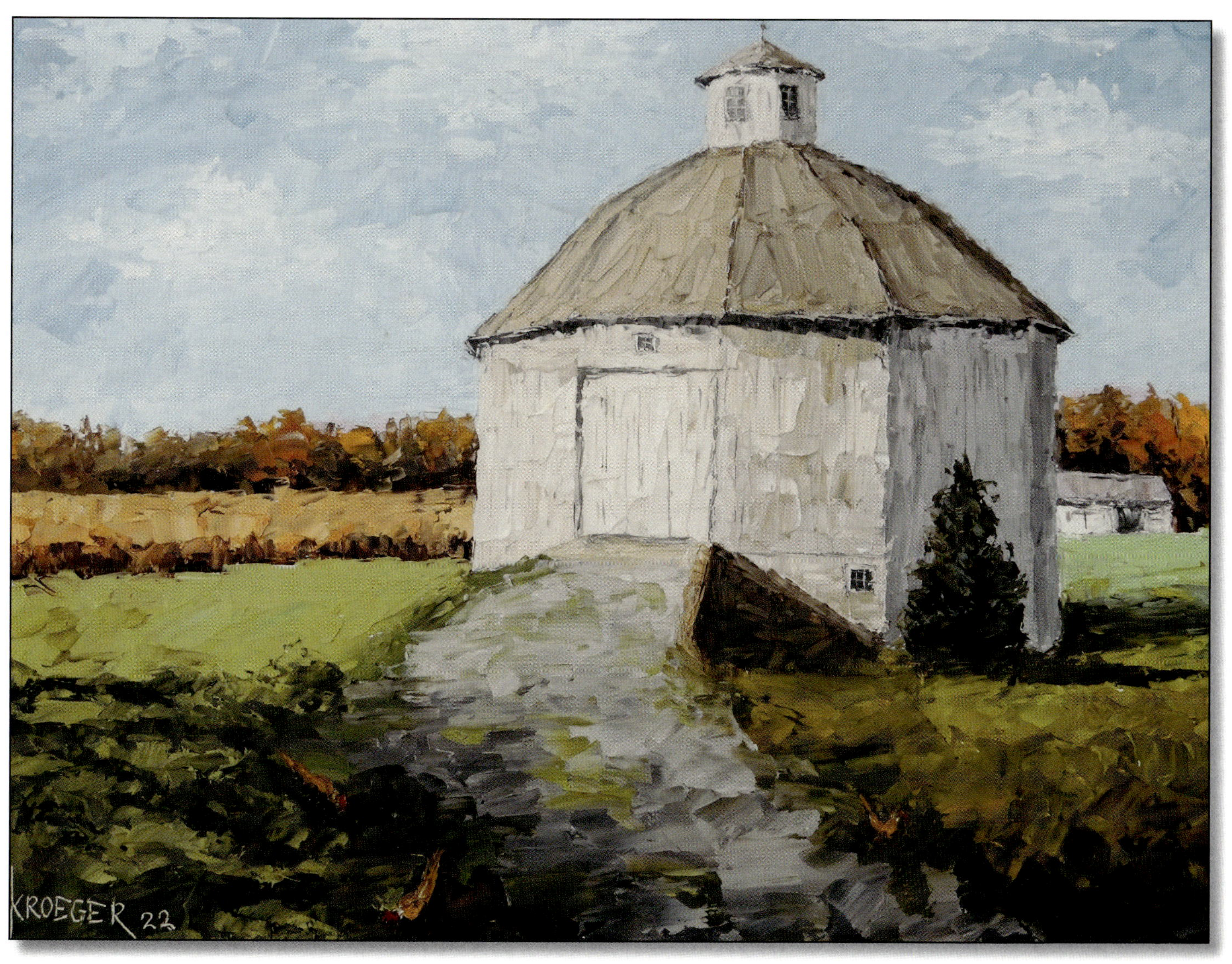

Dodecagon

Jerred and Jennifer Reiff, he a general contractor, and she the principal of Columbia City High School, bought this farm in 2002. According to Jerred, the barn was a mess. "It had deteriorated badly," Jerred explained, "but we wanted to save it." So, using his construction know-how, he poured concrete, lots of it, to stabilize the base of the barn, which was much more complicated than it sounds.

Unfortunately, they couldn't salvage the nearby old farmhouse nor the spring house, used to keep the milk "cold" after the cows produced it in the barn. Too far gone. But the barn, unique as it is, was worth keeping, one more feather in Indiana's cap — a state with many round barns still existing. In fact, nearby Fulton County is known as the round barn capital of the world. Round barn building began in Indiana in 1874 when its first octagonal barn was built.

Before round barn construction ended in the 1930s, Indiana's round barn count numbered 226, many of them in Fulton County. One of the barn builders, C.V. Kindig and Sons, though not enamored by the design, built many in northern Indiana, including 23 in Fulton County. The Reiff's barn is located in adjacent Kosciusko County, not in Whitley County, which, oddly, has none remaining. According to John Hanou, in the two editions of his book, *Round Indiana: Round Barns in the Hoosier State*, of the over 260 round barns originally in the state, 16 of them were 12-sided. In the book's first edition, published in 1993, the author found that over 100 remained, but in the second edition he cited only 71 still standing. Of course, with old barns coming down frequently, that total decreases annually.

Jerred explained that the circular design of the barn for milking cows served as the model for the modern honeycomb feeder, which can cost up to $250,000, making commercial dairy farming reserved for mega-farms. He said that this barn, begun in 1911, wasn't finished until 1913. Why did it take over two years? Regardless, the inside of this barn — and any round barn — is magnificent. Voila! — at the top of the roof, wood shoots out in all directions — without any supporting beams — and is a joy to look at, keeping in mind that this was built over a century ago.

So, what can you do with a small round barn? The Reiffs don't have a big herd of dairy cows, nor do they have a massive honeycomb feeder, but they do have a purpose for this barn. They use it for storage and allow 4-H events to be held in it, giving this old barn a reason to exist. I'm sure, if it could talk, the barn would thank Jerred and Jennifer for deciding to save it from the bonfire and for letting it earn its keep. Even barns have pride.

VERMILLION COUNTY

Unpainted

Most barns receive several, if not many, coats of paint, usually red or white, over the course of a lifetime, but this one, located in an idyllic part of Vermillion County, has never had one, a rarity in old barns. A photo, captured in an autumn setting by Marsha Williamson Mohr, was so striking that it merited two spots in her photography book, *Indiana Barns*. It also captivated me enough to use it as a photo reference for the painting.

Though there's not much history behind this circular barn, built by Purdue graduate O. Earl White in 1916, the heart of the story is its wood, cypress siding shipped from Louisiana, a state where giant water-loving cypress trees, with their sprawling trunks, dot many swamps and bayous. Current owner Roger Hazelwood reported that the railroad line was less than a mile away.

Why Mr. White chose a circular plan for his barn remains just as unknown as his decision to buy wood from such a distant location. Perhaps he knew that cypress wood can last for hundreds of years, if sealed, and still exhibit an appealingly warm, honey-brown hue. Yes, time has proven this choice to have been a good one since the barn remains unpainted now nearly 125 years later. For interior partitions, protected from the elements, White took lumber from a covered bridge near Newport, about 10 miles away, according to a 2010 article in the *Tribune-Star* newspaper, "Three round barns dot Wabash Valley landscape."

Two wooden plank ramps, both freestanding, lead into the second level, where grain was stored. The farmers kept hay and straw on the top level and housed cattle and horses on the lowest of the barn's three floors. In time, the barn got a new purpose, changing to chicken production, one with seven floors that could hold up to 84,000 chickens at a time, just like the six-story Moyer barn in Ohio's Sandusky County, another huge chicken enterprise.

The barn's gigantic size — 60 feet high and 60 feet in diameter — qualifies it as one of Indiana's largest round barns. In fact, over the years, before the age of supersonic airplanes, pilots would use the barn as a navigational landmark on flights from Terre Haute to Chicago.

But, as with all old barns, it has required maintenance. Pam Hazelwood's mother and a friend re-glazed and repaired the barn's 60 windows, a task that — I am only guessing — must have taken many weeks or months to complete. Such is a mother's love.

A few months after I had finished the painting, I stumbled upon a stunning photo by Frank Hutton, whose image shows the barn's reflection in a pond, which Frank told me was hidden in the scene that I painted. After I complimented

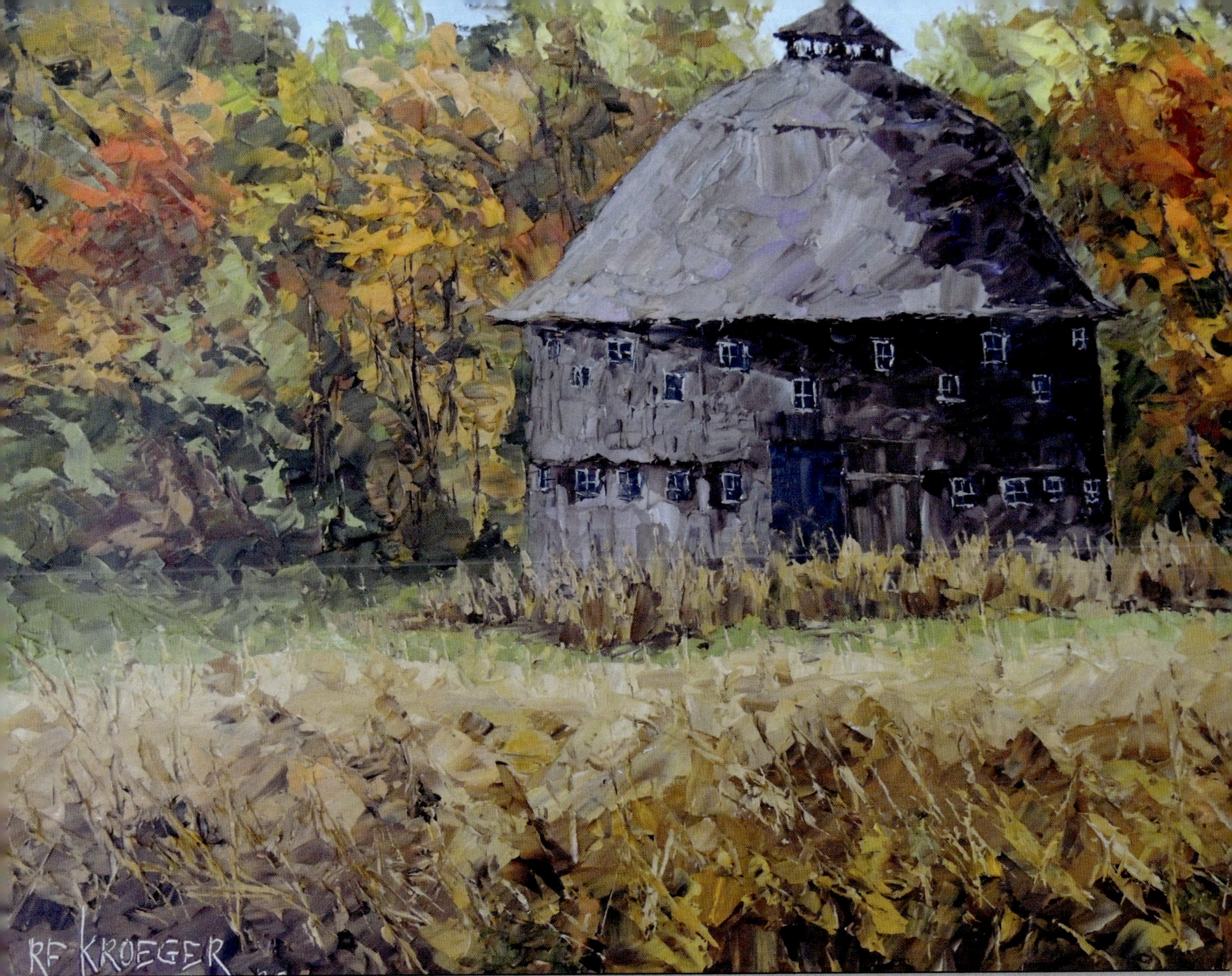

Unpainted

Frank on his work, I told him I now felt compelled to do another painting, this one showing the reflection. Today the barn still stands and inspires photographers and artists, though the Hazelwoods use it only to store equipment and firewood. Its cypress siding remains, as it was in 1916, unpainted.

SCOTT COUNTY

Heavenly Hardy

Though information on this extraordinary barn may be lost to antiquity, round barn lovers owe thanks to both the Dale Travis website with its 1972 photo of the barn, taken by Fred Yenerall, and to John Hanou's book, *A Round Indiana*. The barn was razed in 1990.

According to Hanou's research, a farmer named Oliver Hardy started the farm and the Bruce F. Hardy family built this circular barn circa 1920, an era when agricultural journals had been criticizing the round design for over a decade. Experts claimed that such barns were expensive to build, costly to maintain, and were vulnerable to collapse of the roof — when compared to the traditional rectangular barn. Still, some farmers ignored this advice and kept building the rounds.

Perhaps these farmers had seen others with a similar long extension of a central silo, such as the Thompson barn in Randolph County (built before 1910), though that barn's silo extended only ten feet above the roof line. Similar barns in Iowa with silos extending even higher may have been featured in ag journals that Oliver might have seen, triggering his interest.

The Hardy family — Bruce, Malta, and Oliver — built four round barns in Scott County within a few miles of each other — two octagonal and two circular. All four, built between 1916 and 1921, have been razed, hinting that perhaps the round barn critics had valid points, especially

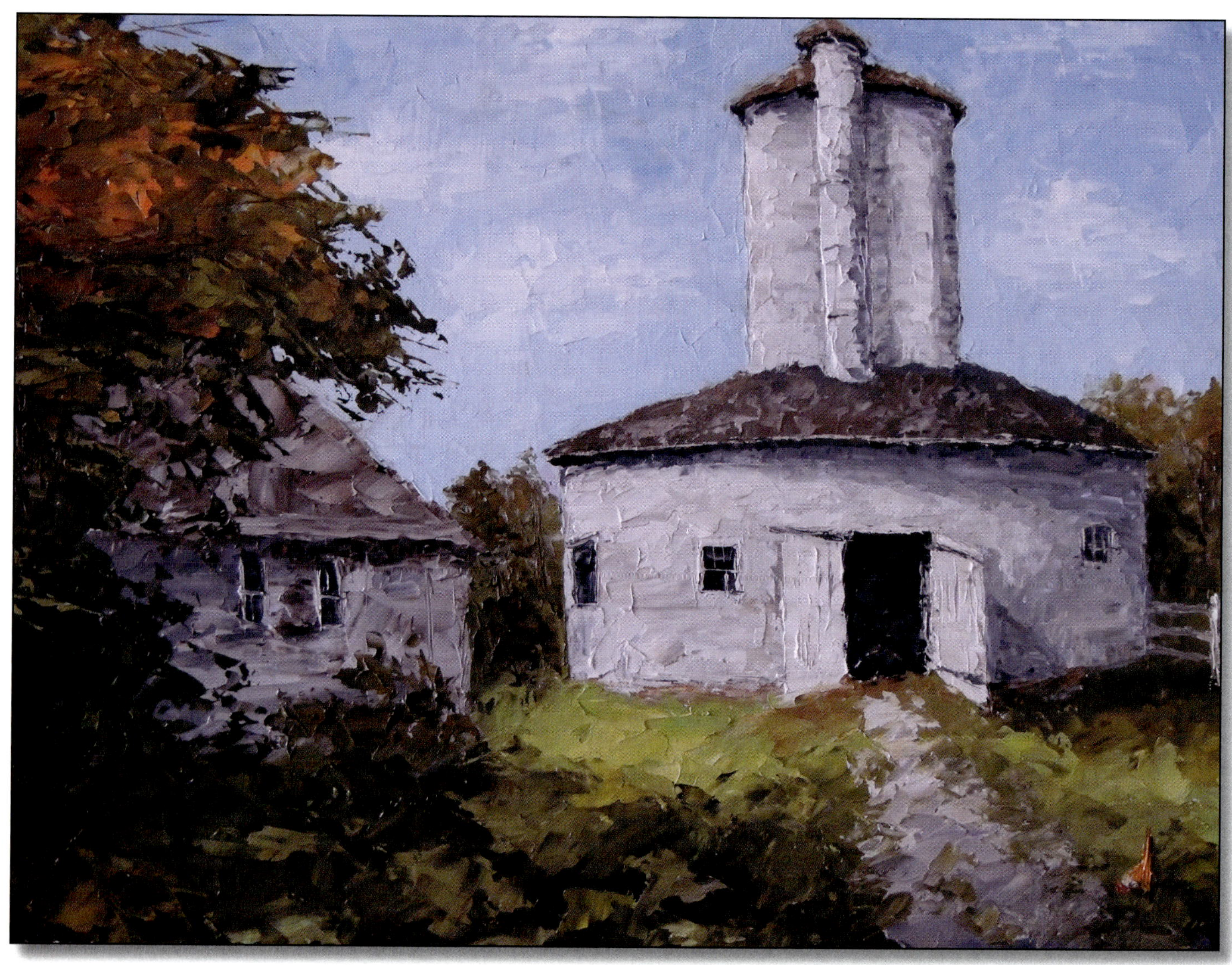

Heavenly Hardy

since many rectangular timber-framed barns from the 1800s have survived. This one, on the small size with a diameter of only 36 feet, housed dairy cattle, which were fed around the silo but later moved to a large traditional barn, according to Hanou's book.

Regardless, this tiny barn with its conical silo, rising to the sky, was one of Indiana's most unusual barns. And, although it's a shame that it's now gone, wouldn't it have been a great one to have survived? Indeed, saving it would have been heavenly.

MICHIGAN

BERRIEN COUNTY

Enter Thirsty and Leave Happy

The Round Barn Winery has been named one of *USA TODAY's* 10 best wineries and vineyards, thanks to this round barn that slipped through the grasp of its original owners in Indiana. Moral of the story: one man's discards may be another man's treasure. In 1997 the Moersch family, farmers and vinters from Michigan, discovered a round barn in Indiana's Fulton County, the county that had more round barns than any other in the state and is often referred to as "The Round Barn Capital of the World." Located near the shores of Lake Michigan and close to Benton Harbor, the Round Barn Winery and its circular barn are only 30 miles from South Bend.

The barn dates to 1912 when the Huffman family built it in Newcastle Township, Fulton County. With a diameter of 63 feet, it probably served as a barn for a modest dairy operation and likely went through several owners before the most recent ones decided that the price was right and sold it to the Moersch family. They transported it to Baroda, Michigan, to become the flagship for their Heart of the Vineyard Winery, which they renamed Round Barn Winery in 2001.

The story began when Rick and Sherrie Moersch, schoolteachers, became interested in wineries. Rick took a job in 1979 to run the wine lab of Tabor Hill, Michigan's fourth largest winery at the time. In the 1970s drinking wine was not widespread but its popularity grew each year and, after Rick was promoted to head winemaker in 1981, he and Sherrie bought a 28-acre farm. They grew grapes and sold them to their next-door neighbor, Tabor Hill. They were entrepreneurs at heart.

But the time wasn't right to strike out on their own: Rick continued to work for Tabor Hill and four years later he became the general manager — in charge of winemaking, wine sales, and restaurant operations. He learned the business well. In fact, during this time their sons, Chris and Matt, grew up learning it too, working at Tabor Hill during school years. Under Moersch's leadership, Tabor Hill Winery grew rapidly and so did Rick and Sherrie's desire to start their own wine business, which they did in 1992, choosing the name, Heart of the Vineyard Winery.

Then came the idea of finding a round barn. Why round? Matt, now co-owner in the business, said that his parents chose this unique shape so that they would produce only good spirits since, in a round barn, there wouldn't be any corners where bad spirits could hide. Ah, the advantages of a round barn. But, despite advice from architects, who told Rick and Sherrie that finding, buying, and restoring an old round barn wasn't practical, they found one and moved it to their farm in 1997. So much for the naysayers.

The rest, as the saying goes, is history. Buoyed by their entrepreneurial spirit, good management, and fortunate weather (Michigan's winters can be harsh, though the lake effect helps), they added a brewery. After all, many men prefer beer to wine. In addition to the brewery and "public house," they added a distillery for spirits and even began making red sangria, a compliment to the vineyards in Spain.

The most impressive change came in 2017 when the next Moersch generation acquired the business. Matt

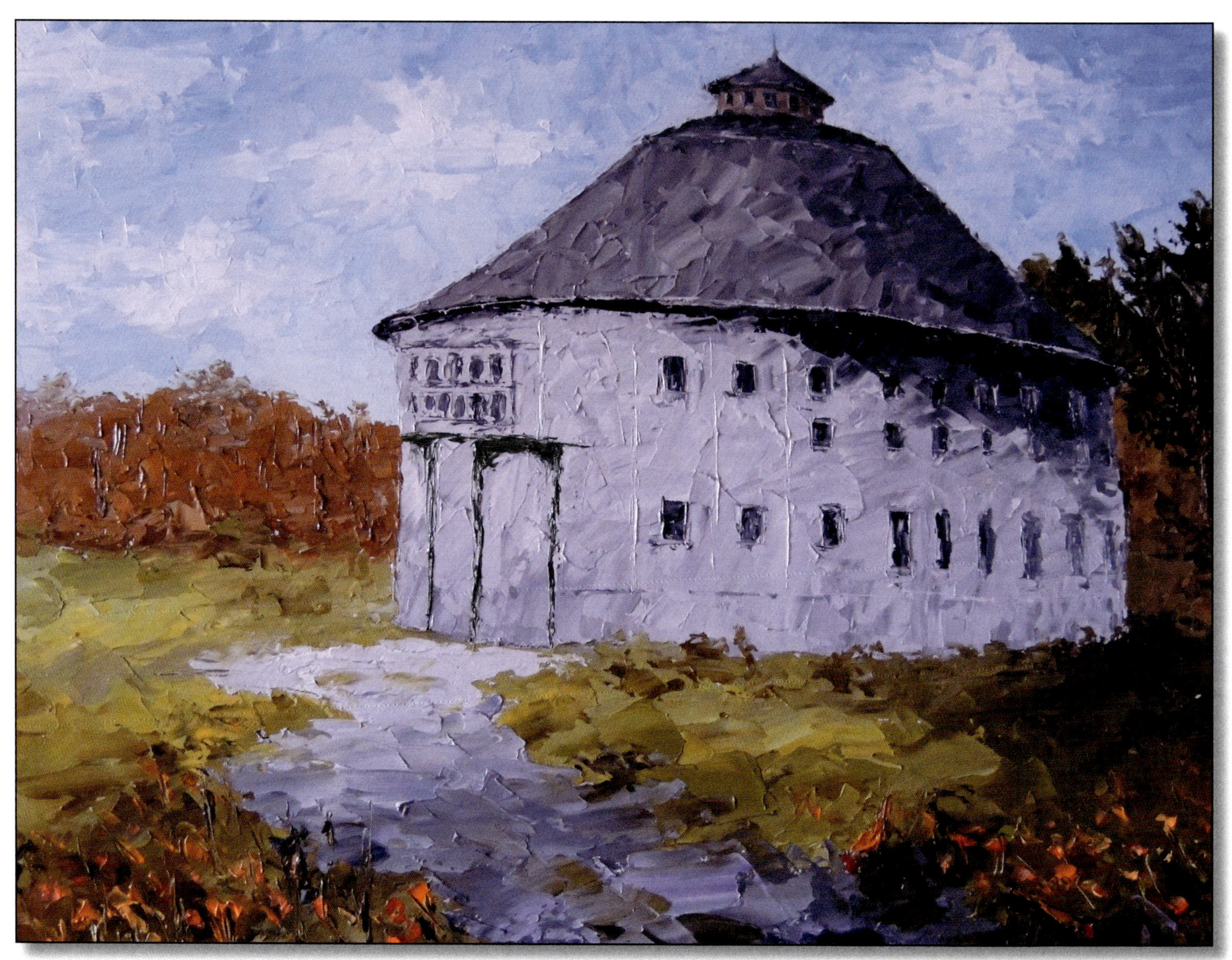

Enter Thirsty and Leave Happy

and Chris, who spent many hours in their teenaged years working at Tabor Hill Winery, purchased Tabor Hill and combined it with their Round Barn Winery, making this one of Michigan's largest wineries. Now, with cooperation from Mother Nature during Michigan's snowy winters, this venture will continue to thrive, honoring, in a sense, Indiana's Huffman family and their round dairy barn. After all, if visitors enter thirsty and leave happy, this round barn must be smiling.

TUSCOLA COUNTY

Tom's Thumb

The History of Tom Thumb, published in 1621, was the first fairy tale printed in English. In this folk story, passed down from generation to generation long before it got into print, little Tom is no bigger than his father's thumb. As the tale goes, the wife of a poor woodsman, forlorn for not having had any children, wishes she could have one even if the child were no bigger than her husband's thumb. When a good fairy, passing by the house, heard her wish, she granted it. Voila, Tom Thumb.

Though there are plenty of Toms on Michigan's Thumb, the peninsula jutting into Lake Huron (which, from an aerial perspective resembles the thumb of a hand or mitten), there's also an octagonal barn, loved enough by locals to merit preservation. It's located just east of Gagetown, a village of nearly 400, which sprang up around a mill founded by Joseph Gage in 1869. In the same year, James Luther Purdy, the one who decided to build this barn, was born.

Though originally from Pontiac, a city northwest of Detroit, he was raised in Gagetown and, at 21, he joined his father in the banking business — the Bank of P.C. Purdy and Son. Four years later, in 1894, he married and began raising two daughters.

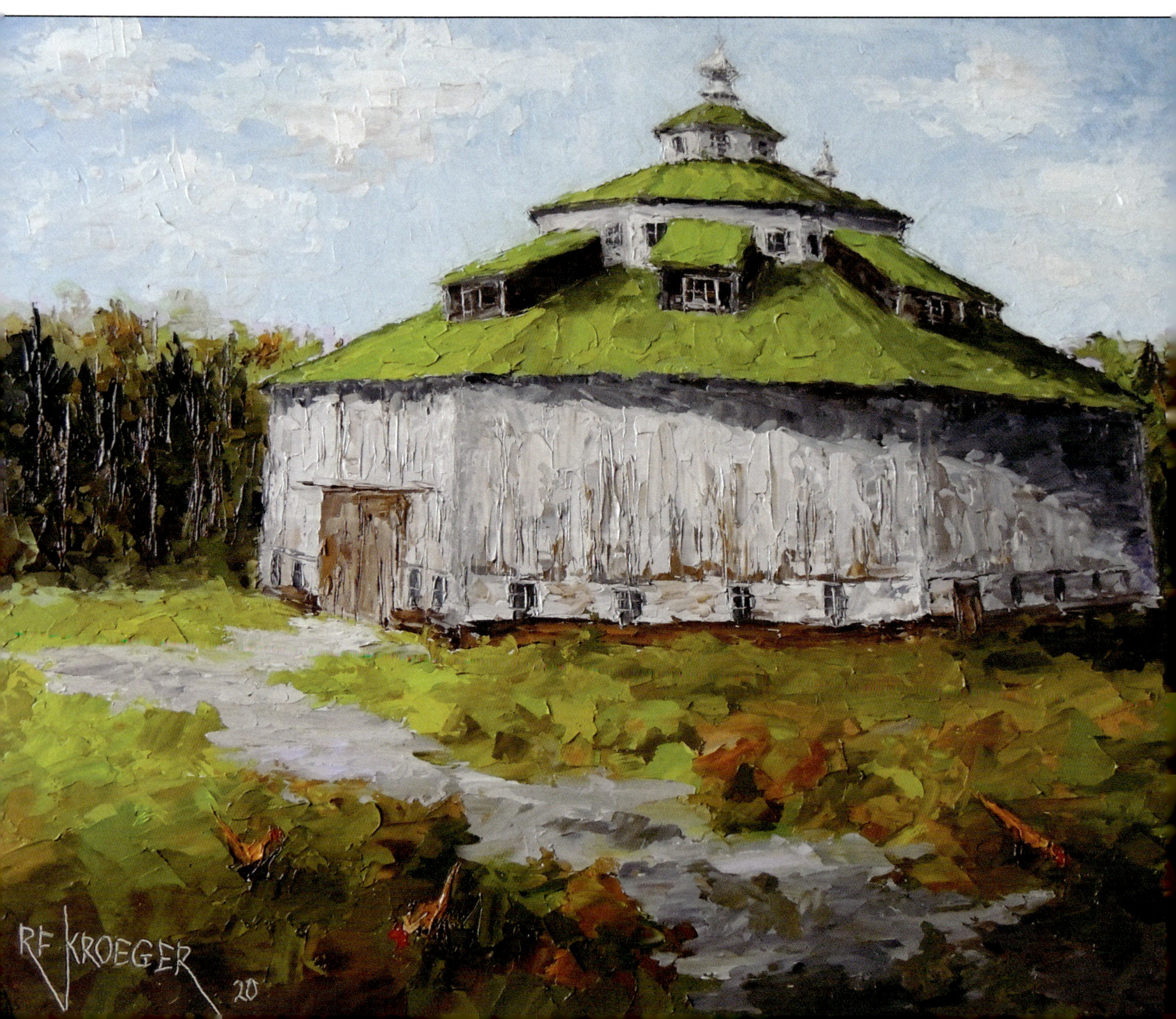

Labeled as a "natural," he became president of the bank, which flourished under his leadership and was one of only two banks in Michigan that remained solvent during the Great Depression. After having lost trust in banks, Americans were reluctant to make deposits and rightfully so — more than 9,000 American banks had failed by March, 1933. However, hoping to restore credibility in the system, James Purdy met with other bankers in Lansing, formulated a plan, and traveled to Washington to convince Michigan's Senator Arthur Vandenburg to introduce a bill to save the banking business. His trip and his idea were successful: Congress passed both the Glass-Steagall Act of 1933, which protected bank depositors, and the Banking Act of 1933, which led to the formation of the FDIC. Though originally denounced by the American Bankers Association as a questionable support of bad business as well as being too expensive, the FDIC, thanks to Purdy and his fellow Michigan bankers, proved its mettle when only nine additional banks closed in 1934.

But this Michigan banker had rural yearnings. In 1895 he bought a 50-acre parcel of farmland and, over the years, increased that homestead to 560 acres. In 1919, James and his wife Cora hired local builders George and John Munro to build a craftsman-style 15-room home on this land, which became known as "Mud Lake Estate." They moved into the home in May, 1922. Their next project was the barn.

Pleased with their work, the Purdys again hired the Munro brothers to build a barn, but not an ordinary one — instead an octagonal one, after a barn that James saw during his travels in Iowa, a state that competes with Indiana and Wisconsin as being round barn capitals of the country. The Purdys apparently gave a blank check expense account to the builders, who, to their credit, asked for help, sensing that building a round barn would require knowledge outside their expertise. They looked for advice to Russell Jaggers, the principal of Gagetown High School and a math teacher, and used his calculations, which were accurate. The result, one of Michigan's most remarkable barns, must have impressed the Purdys.

The barn stands 70 feet tall, the equivalent of four stories, has a diameter of 106 feet and eight sides, each nearly 43 feet wide. With nearly 15,000 square feet of internal space — 8,600 on the first floor and 6,200 on the second — the barn sits on a four-foot-high foundation. An octagonal cupola, harboring a large ventilator, rises over six feet and, beneath it, distinctive shed dormers project from the double cupola. The 288 individual windowpanes in 32 windows are positioned to minimize direct sunlight, reducing the risk of fire in the haymow. Originally, an internal wood stave silo, built for grain storage for feeder cattle, sat on the first floor but, after years of neglect, a later owner removed it. The Munro brothers had to be proud of their masterpiece, finished in 1924.

The Purdys stayed on their Mud Lake Estate and raised Black Angus cattle until 1942, when they returned to their Gagetown city home. They sold the farm in 1943. Seven years later James died and, in 1955, Cora passed. Unfortunately, the heirs did not take ownership and the home, farm, and barn went through four different owners, the last of whom lost it to, ironically, a bank foreclosure. In 1991 the bank sold the 80-acre estate to the Michigan Department of Natural Resources, which wanted it to link to their adjacent hunting and wildlife preserves.

With decades of little maintenance, the barn had deteriorated, forcing the new owners to consider scrapping it. When word of the barn's possible demise made news, local citizens banded together and organized the first Octagon Barn Festival in 1994 — to raise funds to repair the barn. The Friends of the Thumb Octagon Barn was formed that year and, in 1996, came to an agreement with the state that granted the group control over the eight-acre farmstead — with the stipulation that it would provide liability insurance and develop a plan for restoration.

Today, the nonprofit has not only restored the magnificent barn but has also converted the farm into an agricultural museum, which includes the barn, farmhouse, and power plant. They have also added a one-room schoolhouse, sawmill, grain elevator, cider mill, granary, and a covered bridge and they hold an annual barn festival each year and provide tours to school groups — to illustrate what farm life was like a century ago. Their motto, "Saving the Past for Tomorrow's Future," epitomizes the goal of every historical preservationist. And, thanks to these "friends" and to this painting and essay, Purdy's spectacular octagonal barn will be remembered as an important legacy in Michigan's "Thumb."

Opposite: *Tom's Thumb*

10. UPPER MIDWEST

ILLINOIS

KANE COUNTY

Teeple's Thorn

One of the selling points — circa 1890s — of round barns was their self-supporting roof, which proponents claimed was more wind resistant than that of conventional designs. This concept must have appealed to Lester Teeple, who built this 16-sided barn in 1885, about ten years after New York's Elliot Stewart wrote about his octagonal barn in widely read agricultural journals.

In fact, although Teeple wanted an octagonal shape — also Thomas Jefferson's favorite — the lumber he chose was not long enough to build this polygon, which is puzzling since he owned a lumber yard. Instead, he hired Elgin-based architect W. Wright Abell to design the barn in 16 sections, technically a hexadecagon. George Washington built one in 1794 and Ohio's only 16-sided barn still stands, "Workley's Wonder," deep in the Appalachian hills of Harrison County.

Teeple built the barn in 1885 — a large one with a diameter of 85 feet and a height of 85 feet. A dairy farmer, he intended the barn for his herd of — sorry, math lovers, not 85 — but 65 Red Poll cattle, a breed that was known for both beef and milk production. In 1952 the owners installed concrete buttresses to allow modern farm machines to be stored on the brick floor, which sat on top of a fieldstone foundation. The barn was busy in those years — housing hay, straw, grain, and a herd of dairy cows. Its hayfork system, attached to the ceiling with many pulleys, showed one more facet of this creative round barn builder.

Unfortunately, high winds often blew in that area, occasionally kicking up a tornado, one of which took off the attractive red and white cupola in 1973. Additionally, progress in the growth and development around Chicago (Elgin is only 35 miles away) meant that many old barns and farms were becoming industrial property. Randall Road, where the barn sat, became an exit off I-90, giving passing motorists a glimpse of the barn as they whizzed by it. Deservedly, it merited inclusion into the National Register in 1979 and its proximity to Chicago helped publicize its uniqueness. It had remained in the Teeple family for over a century.

However, the barn began to deteriorate during the 1980s and the family eventually sold it. Concerned preservationists formed a nonprofit group, AgTech, in 1996 and three years later they restored the striking cupola, a restoration that cost $100,000. More attention came when the National Geographic included the barn in its 2001 book, *Saving America's Treasures*, which evolved from a public-private partnership between the National Parks Service and the National Trust for Historic Preservation.

Three years later, Ag Tech, with cooperation from the Kane County Farm Bureau, started scheduling fundraisers to restore the barn, which was estimated to need $3 million for structural repairs and for a conversion into a resource center for agricultural science. By October it had raised $50,000 towards a matching grant of $149,000. With sadness, their efforts were too little and too late.

In May, 2007, strong prairie winds ripped off the roof, making the barn a total loss. The owner, a nut-processing company tried to preserve the cupola and whatever else was salvageable. This wasn't the first round barn to lose its roof to a windstorm.

But its memory lives on, not only in this painting and essay but in a scale model, built by Dick and Joann Lichthardt, who toured the barn before it collapsed. They wanted to add it to their village of miniatures, including a schoolhouse, church, buggy shed, hog barn and chicken

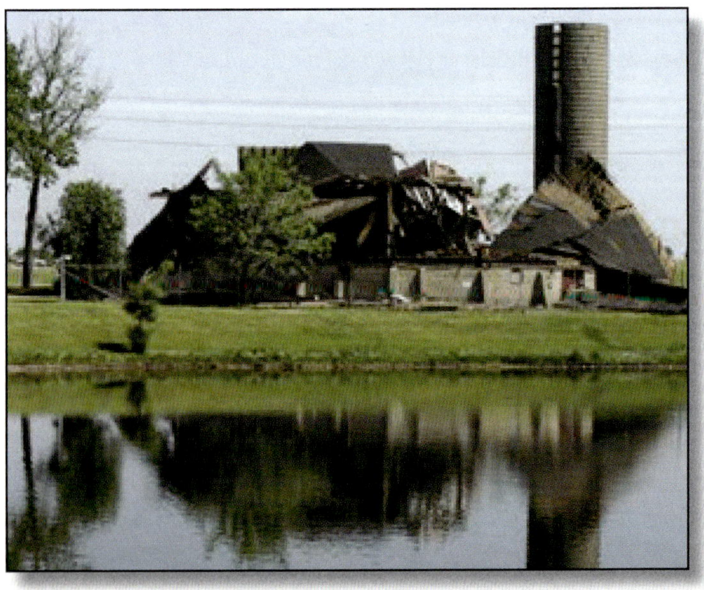

Roof collapse, Teeple Barn. Kane County, Illinois

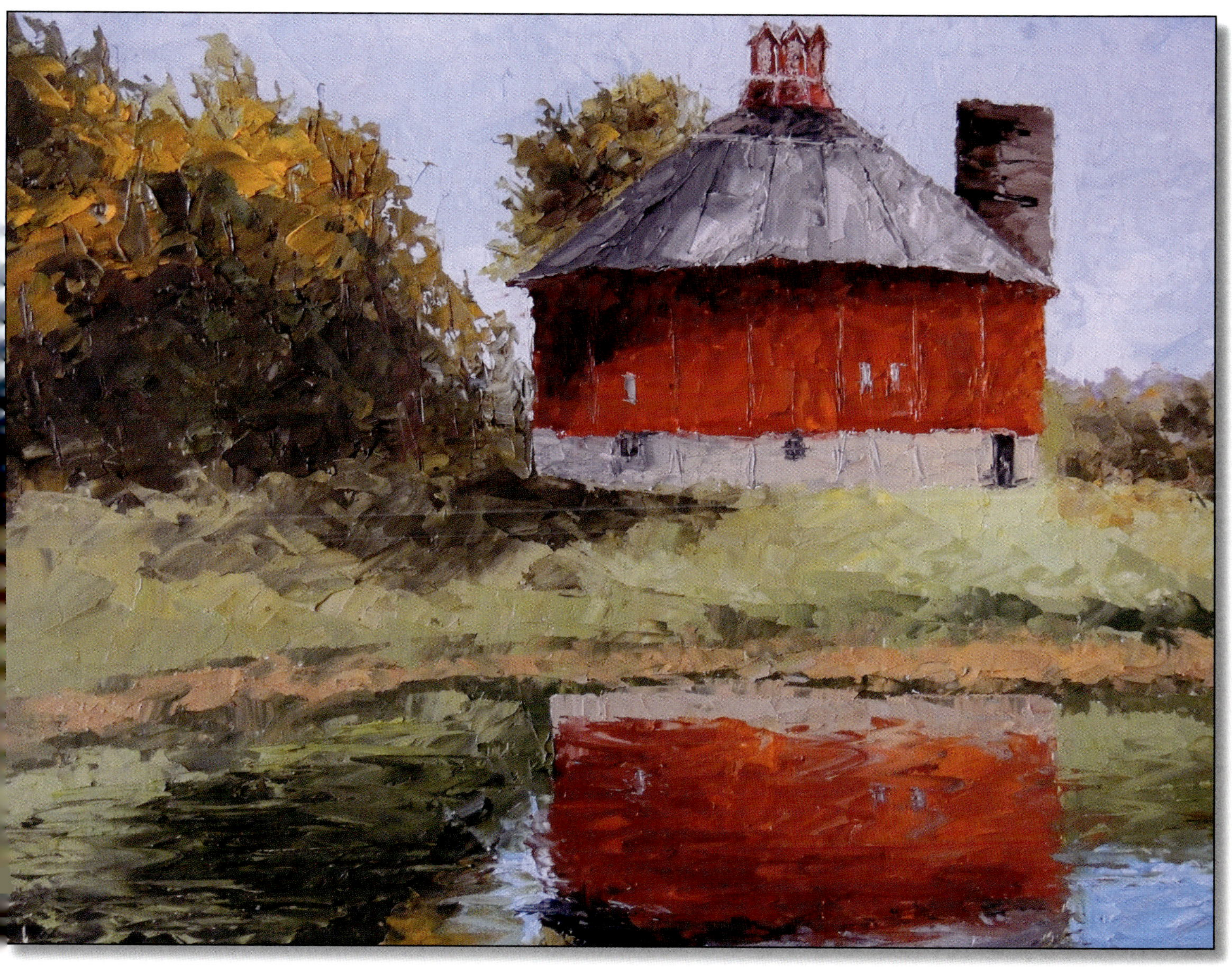

Teeple's Thorn

shed. It took these two history lovers 18 months to finish the model, which is on a scale of a half inch-per-foot and includes dairy cattle, farm workers, a dog, haystacks, and a hay fork. After the artisans completed their model, they displayed it for the first time at the Illinois Steam Power Show in 2005. Today it stands proudly in the lobby at Kane County Farm Bureau, where it will remain as a reminder of what once was before high winds became the thorn in Teeple's side.

OGLE COUNTY

The Donut

From a distance, a "donut" barn appears similar to one with an oval shape, but it differs, especially from an aerial view, because it resembles an actual donut — with a hole in the middle. Was this done to provide light into the inner parts of the barn? For time savings in feeding livestock? For exercising livestock? Or just to be different? Whatever the reason, the design didn't catch on in other counties. Outside of Ogle and adjacent Stephenson counties, there are no existing round barns of this type in Illinois. Of course, that doesn't infer that such barns weren't built elsewhere but it's unlikely that they were. Of the seven such barns in these two counties, this one was the oldest, dating to 1898, and owned by a farmer named DeVries, according to the Travis site. Interestingly, a donut barn was also built in the 1890s in Stark County, Ohio.

The findagrave.com site lists many Ogle County residents with the De Vries surname, one in particular — Arend — was born in 1868 and died in 1935. Did he build the barn in 1898, when he would have been 30 years old? Several others of the same time period are also buried in the Ebenezer Cemetery, not far from Maryland Township, where the barn was located. Presumably, the

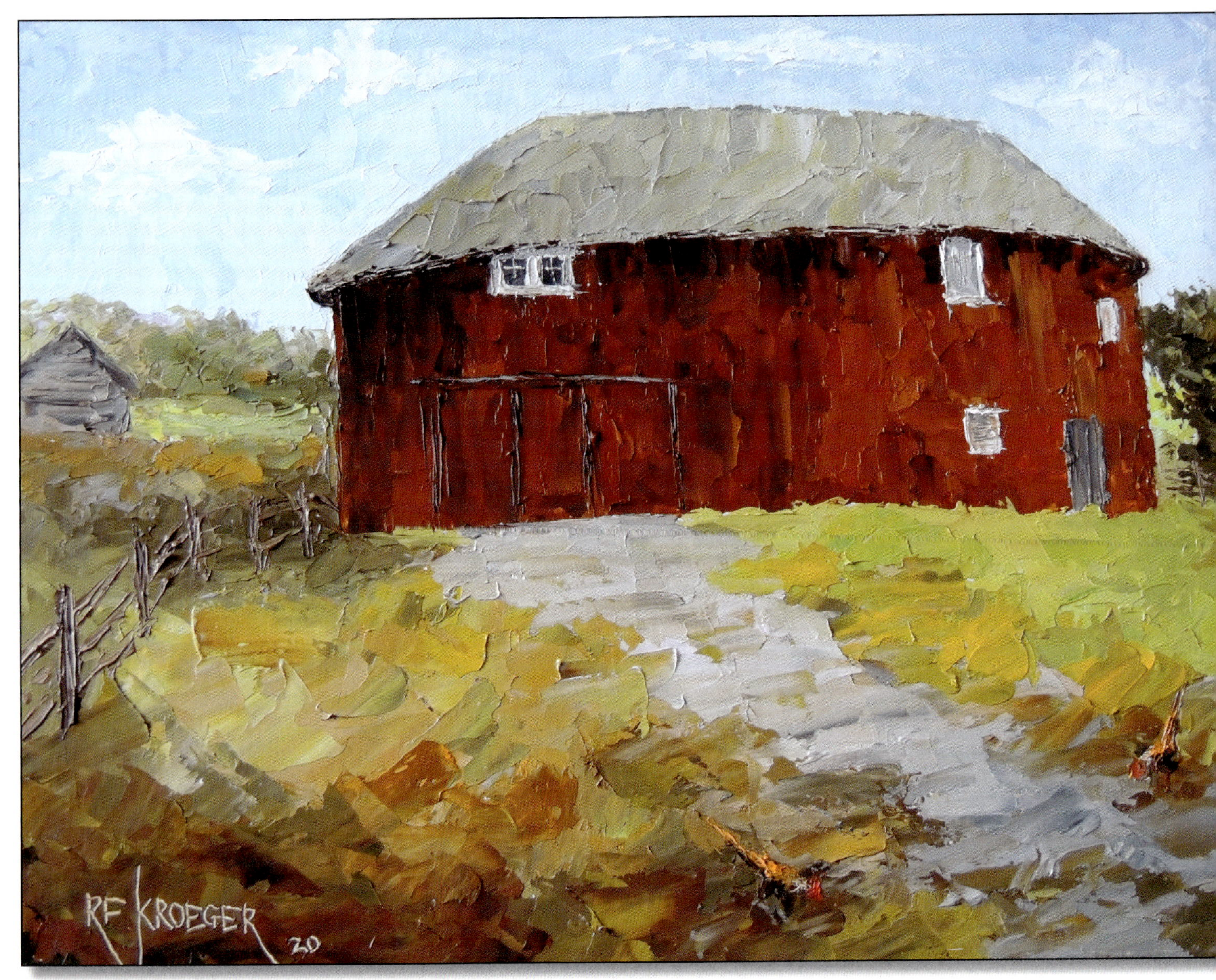

The Donut

family was prosperous as suggested by the large size of the barn — 66 feet long.

Perhaps just as interesting as this donut-shaped barn is the history of the county, named after Captain Joseph Ogle, a veteran of the Revolutionary War, who commanded a Virginia company. His heroism in defense of Fort Henry during the war is why the governor of Indiana named this county after him. After the war, his family lived in the western part of the Colony of Virginia, present-day West Virginia.

Opposed to slavery, Ogle and his family left Virginia and ventured into the Northwest Territory, which was Indian country in 1785. They settled in the southern part of present-day Illinois. Two years later Congress passed the Northwest Ordinance, opening the territory from the Ohio River to land east of the Mississippi for settlement. However, fighting with Native Americans was inevitable as the influx of farmers began to encroach on the Indians' way of life.

A frontiersman, Ogle sought land and freedom from oppression, which he found in Illinois, though the move came with danger. In 1791, Ogle was involved in a skirmish with Native Americans near what is now Waterloo, Illinois, and was chosen to lead the local militia in battles. Much later, Captain Ogle died on his farm in Ridge Prairie in 1821, at the age of eighty, a long life in frontier days. His son Joseph Ogle fought in the Black Hawk War in 1832, the last major battle in this area, effectively opening the region to settlers.

Even though little is known about this unique barn, razed prior to 2007, its memory remains in this painting and essay as a rare piece of Americana, a donut barn in Ogle County.

CHAMPAIGN COUNTY

The Experiment

The University of Illinois authorities ordered these three round barns to be constructed well after Professor King publicized his round barn concept in 1890. Two years later, Stewart, who promoted his octagonal barn design in the mid-1870s, admitted that round barns were more difficult — and therefore more expensive — to build than their rectangular counterparts. Joseph Wing, editor of *The Breeder's Gazette*, also decried the so-called advantages of round barns when he published articles in 1902 and in 1905 stating that the round barn's wedge-shaped stalls were inconvenient when compared to right-angle stalls, the barns let in too little light, and they required special lumber, especially when the boards needed to be soaked in water in order to bend. Other articles brought out more deficiencies of the round barn in early 20th century agricultural journals, including one published in *Ohio Farmer* in 1906 when a farmer, after building a small round barn, claimed that it turned out to be six times more expensive than a rectangular one. However, professors at the University of Illinois ignored these criticisms and were determined to conduct experiments to determine how to maximize milk production per acre of farmland. They thought the answer was round barns and they put their money where their mouth was in 1908.

By 1850 America was predominantly a country of small farms — 1.4 million of them — and, with expansion westwards, settlers faced challenges: tornadoes, damaging insects, droughts, blizzards, floods, and fungal diseases. Many lost their farms. In 1862 President Lincoln, despite the difficult Civil War years, not only signed the Homestead Act, which awarded 160 acres of land to a pioneer-farmer — who qualified for this land after homesteading for five years — but also created the U.S. Department of Agriculture and enacted the Morrill Land Grant College Act, which assigned 30,000 acres of land to each state to establish a college for agriculture and the mechanical arts. Lincoln was aware that such land-grant colleges could improve crop and livestock production, especially for the war effort in the north. With Lincoln's blessing, agricultural colleges sprang up: Cornell University was founded in 1865, followed by the University of Illinois (1867), Purdue University (1869) and Ohio State University (1870). Science was about to join hands with farming.

The University of Wisconsin became a land-grant institution in 1866 and about 20 years later — in 1889 — Professor Franklin King publicized his circular barn design. It became popular in the 1890s and convinced a number of carpenters to begin building and designing round barns, especially ones with a self-supporting roof. By the early 1900s they aggressively advertised and built these unusual barns, traveling to all parts of the Midwest. By 1903 C. B. Dorsey, an agricultural professor at of the University of Illinois, one of Lincoln's land-grant colleges, traveled to Indiana to view the barns built by Benton Steele, the foremost round barn builder of that time. Impressed, the professor hired Steele to construct a round barn on his farm in Gilberts.

One of his colleagues in Illinois, Wilber J. Fraser, the first head of the Department of Dairy Husbandry (1902—1913), apparently also ignored the advice against round barns in agricultural journals. After seeing Professor Dorsey's barn, he became a strong advocate of this design, claiming that round barns offered the "economy of consideration, low maintenance, and labor efficiency." He also claimed a round barn was less likely to suffer from a windstorm, compared to a conventional one. At the university's experimental farm in Urbana, Champaign County, Fraser started a dairy farm in 1908, specifically to determine how to maximize milk production per acre, and he began building round barns. The first one came in 1908.

But, rather than hiring Indiana builders — Steele, Detraz, the McNamees, or Duncan, the cream of the crop — he chose the university's own architect James M. White, as well as contractors Kell & Bernard to build the barns. Sixty feet wide, this first barn, known as the Twenty Acre Dairy Barn, was built into a hillside, had two stories and a central wooden silo, held 20 cows, and cost $3,200 to construct, almost twice as much as round barns being built in 1908 in nearby southern Wisconsin.

The second barn, the Dairy Horse Barn, though also a small one with only 60 feet in diameter, cost $2,000, a more reasonable sum when it was built in 1910. It, too, had two stories, a gambrel wood-shingled roof, a concrete foundation, and vertical wood siding. Unlike the others, it was built on flat land.

The Dairy Experiment Barn, the third one and built in 1912, was the most costly of the three — $11,000 — and the largest — with a diameter of 70 feet. A sizeable cupola provided ventilation and a rectangular wing allowed more cattle to be housed. This barn continued to spread the gospel of the experimental station throughout the country. After all, why would a university continue to build round barns if they weren't efficient? And why would it build such a large and expensive one?

In February, 1910, after a year of experimentation with the Twenty Acre Dairy Barn, the first built, Fraser published a seminal paper, *Economy of the Round Dairy Barn*, in Bulletin 143, issued by the University of Illinois Agricultural Experiment Station. Early in the bulletin, he admitted he knew about the negative viewpoints, "The objections to round barns have usually been made by those who have only a superficial knowledge of the subject ..." He went on to not only elaborate about the advantages of the round barn but he also provided complete specifications, detailed costs and construction methods of the university's first circular dairy barn. Coming from a learned and respected professor of agriculture, this bulletin spread widely throughout the Midwest, stimulating the greatest growth spurt of the round barns, from 1910 to 1920.

However, despite Fraser's continued publications and his willingness to share exact details of construction, the evidence against round barns continued to mount, instigating negative publicity during the decade. And though Fraser's experiments influenced some farmers to build round barns, they never amounted to more than one percent of all barns built. After all, farmers of the late 1800s and early 1900s had to be practical, had to support a large family, and had to watch costs. Just as Missouri is called the Show-Me State, so also the average farmer had to be shown that something worked: whether it was crop rotation, a certain pesticide, or a new hybrid of corn. It's reasonable to assume that farmers could envision the additional costs of making a curve in a building — the use of correct lumber, the soaking of the boards, and the trimming of the excess siding to fit, not to mention the difficulty in finding a carpenter to construct the barn.

Did Fraser's experiment fail? Despite Fowler's octagonal concept earning a following in the 1850s and Stewart's octagonal barn design furthering interest in the 1870s, the percentage of octagonal barns remained meager. Even after Wisconsin's Professor King publicized his circular plans in the 1890s, the numbers of round barns built were a small fraction of barns. And, yes, Fraser's bulletin in 1910 did motivate some farmers but it fizzled within a decade. Depressed agricultural prices in the 1920s, the Great Depression of the 1930s, and the understanding that a round barn was more expensive to construct ended the era of the rounds.

In 1993 the university secured a listing on the National Register for this trio of barns, which they richly deserved — acknowledging Professor Fraser's contribution to the history of the round barn phenomenon. Today these three icons of Illinois farming still stand — exactly where they were built in Urbana — and continue to be used for small dairy herd experiments and for storage. The university is wise to preserve them and to honor the legacy of Fraser's grand "experiment."

OGLE COUNTY

The Oval

Well, this type of barn is not polygonal, nor circular, nor donut-shaped, though it could be called rectangular, were it not for its rounded ends. How should this hybrid

Below: *The Experiment*

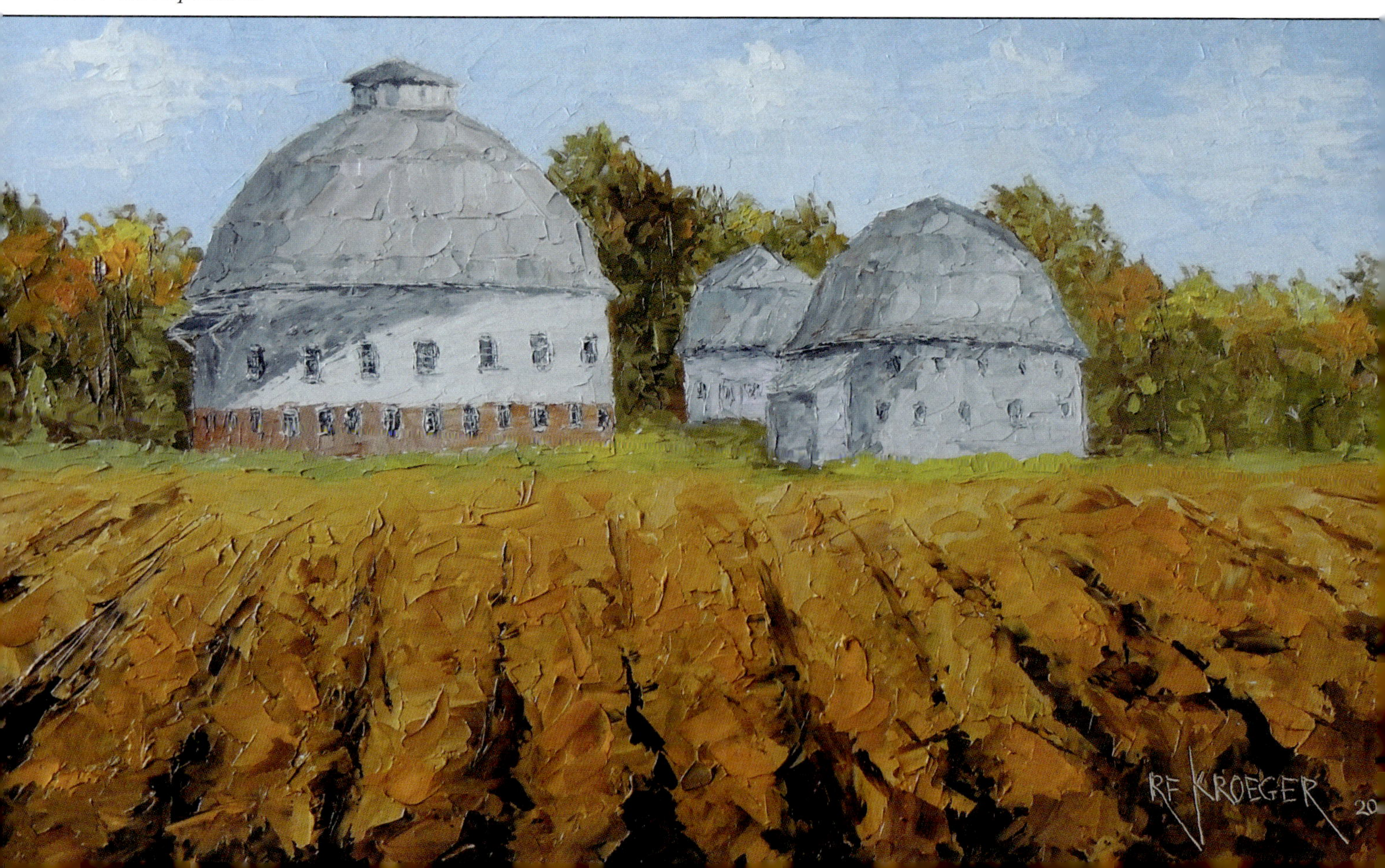

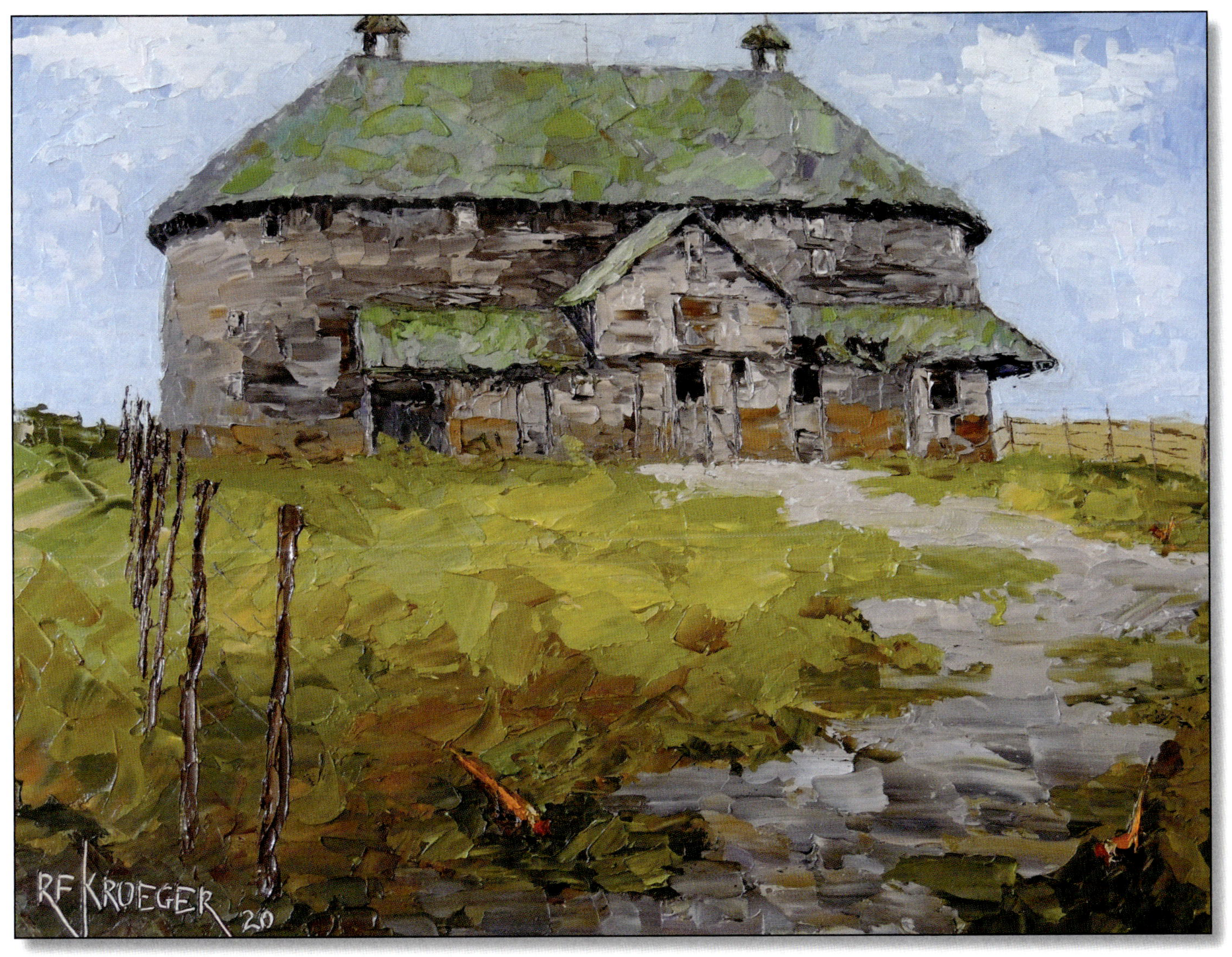

The Oval

barn be classified? When any Ohio State grad thinks of "The Oval," a large oblong green space comes to mind, located in the center of the Columbus campus and its multitude of gray stone college buildings. Dale Travis, in his website, calls this type of barn an "oval," as do the authors of *Barns of the Midwest*. The term emphasizes the esthetics of architecture — with soft, rounded corners.

In 1901, seven years before the University of Illinois began its experimental agricultural station and its three round barns, Jeremiah Shaffer and his five brothers-in-law, the Haases, began building round barns in Ogle and Stephenson counties in the northwestern corner of Illinois, bordering dairy-rich Wisconsin. Though Shaffer, born in Stephenson County, was a schoolteacher, he read voraciously, which is how he presumably acquired knowledge about round barns and Professor King's round dairy barn. In fact, Shaffer and his team built many of them in Stephenson County, which, in the 1984 group submission to the National Register, still had 21 round barns, more than any other county in America. As of 2007, five of these, on the Register, still survive, including this one, built in 1914. Most were built by Shaffer and the Haas brothers.

According to Allen Noble's *Barns of the Midwest*, Shaffer was a convincing salesman and he used a clever example to show the farmer, the prospective buyer, the advantage of a round barn. While sitting at the farmer's kitchen table and making his pitch, he would use a piece of cardboard, cut a rectangle out of it, and fill it with oats. Then, he'd shape the same cardboard into a circle, fill it with oats, proving that the circular design could hold more than its rectangular cousin. Apparently, this worked well.

What is unusual is that the design of this "oval" barn varies considerably from the squat round shape — with domed gambrel roof — of the barns built by Shaffer and company. Regardless of who built them, why did the builder opt to round off the corners as well as the roof on basically a rectangular shape? Was this a desire to be more efficient? Or just to be different? As of 2020, seven barns with this unique oblong shape — built between 1898 and

1915 — survive in these two counties of Illinois. From a pragmatic standpoint, construction of the rounded corner had to cost more than a simple rectangular end, suggesting that the owner may have wanted a bit of flair or perhaps a cross between a traditional rectangle and a circle. Few were built after the onset of World War I and none were built in the 1920s.

This barn, northwest of Adeline, is only a short distance from German Valley in Stephenson County, but, with a length of 88 feet and a width of 38 feet, it differs drastically from the smaller traditional round barns throughout the area. The most recent owner, Bernard Bagley, is listed in county records with an address in Texas. Unfortunately, a letter to him remains unanswered.

And, while a few barns built in more contemporary times feature the oval shape, most are found serving as exhibition halls in county fairgrounds, which, again, may reflect a desire for old-fashioned "curb appeal." It's just one more interesting page of Americana.

WISCONSIN

SAUK COUNTY

Honey Creek

This barn, resembling, at least in this composition, a magical scene in a fairy tale by Danish author Hans Christian Andersen, stood in Honey Creek Township, an area named for the large amount of honey found here in the 1800s. Located in Wisconsin's Sauk County, it was close to the village of Leland, which took its name from Cyrus Leland, an original settler who built a sawmill on Honey Creek in 1847. Today the village has a population of about 50.

Though there are many beautiful round barns still existing in Wisconsin, this delightful one, dismantled in 2012, deserves recognition since, if not recorded now, its memory will fade and another page of round barn history will be closed.

The story begins with Carl L. Ott, born in Prussia in 1833, who immigrated to Leland in 1867 and worked as a blacksmith in his uncle Gottlieb's farm near Cassel Prairie. His son, Carl A., was born in 1869. Together they farmed and, apparently being good carpenters, built over 50 barns in the Leland area. Constructed in 1895, this one was their flagship, even though it wasn't large — its diameter was only 48 feet. Duane Ott, one of the grandsons, remembers the hand-hewn timbers, expertly assembled to support the walls and roof. The striking cupola was icing on the cake.

Though Professor King's classic circular barn plans became available in 1890, the Otts chose an octagonal shape for their barn, possibly influenced by New Yorker Elliot Stewart and his many articles in farm journals in the 1870s. However, they did follow King's plans for a central wooden stave silo and they also erected a rail system, used for moving loose hay into the mow. This track system, made of wood instead of steel and built around the circumference of the barn, made it possible to drop hay anywhere. The Otts hitched horses to a 100-foot rope, attached to pulleys up to the roof, which allowed large amounts of hay to be lifted off the wagon at will. In later years, an elevator transported baled hay.

The steep roof, a throwback to medieval European barns, was much different than the gently sloping American gambrel roofs. In fact, Schaeffer Goerks, a local Leland lad, was the only worker who attempted to paint the cupola, which he did for three dollars in 1930. After that, Mr. Ott couldn't find anyone to risk his life to paint it.

In 1923, despite collapsing agricultural prices, these farmers were prosperous enough to add a wing to the octagon. A signature board, discovered during dismantling, showed the date, 1923, and the name of Ed Zick, probably signifying that he built the extension or at least was one of the main carpenters. The Zicks were carpenters, who built nearly all the barns and houses in Denzer, a small village close to Leland. Many of them still stand today.

The next owners — in 1946 — Harold and Esther Ott, were dairy farmers and, at one point, considered taking down the barn and building a larger one since they wanted to milk more cows. But that didn't happen and they continued using the barn until they sold it to Albert Fenske, who kept the barn and the dairy business, ending the operation in 1977. After Albert died, his wife kept the farm going, though it was seldom used. Their daughter, Palma Walker, inherited the farm when Esther passed away. Alas, its foundation began to deteriorate.

Eventually, a Texan purchased the barn, which was dismantled in 2012, with plans to reassemble it on his ranch near Fredricksburg. But, though the Wisconsin siblings lost track of this man, according to a local realtor, he suffered financial losses and wasn't able to re-build it. Now, its timbers sit somewhere in Texas, patiently waiting a re-birth and a new purpose. Nonetheless, the barn built near Honey Creek will live on in this painting and essay, preserving a little slice of early Wisconsin history.

Opposite: *Honey Creek*

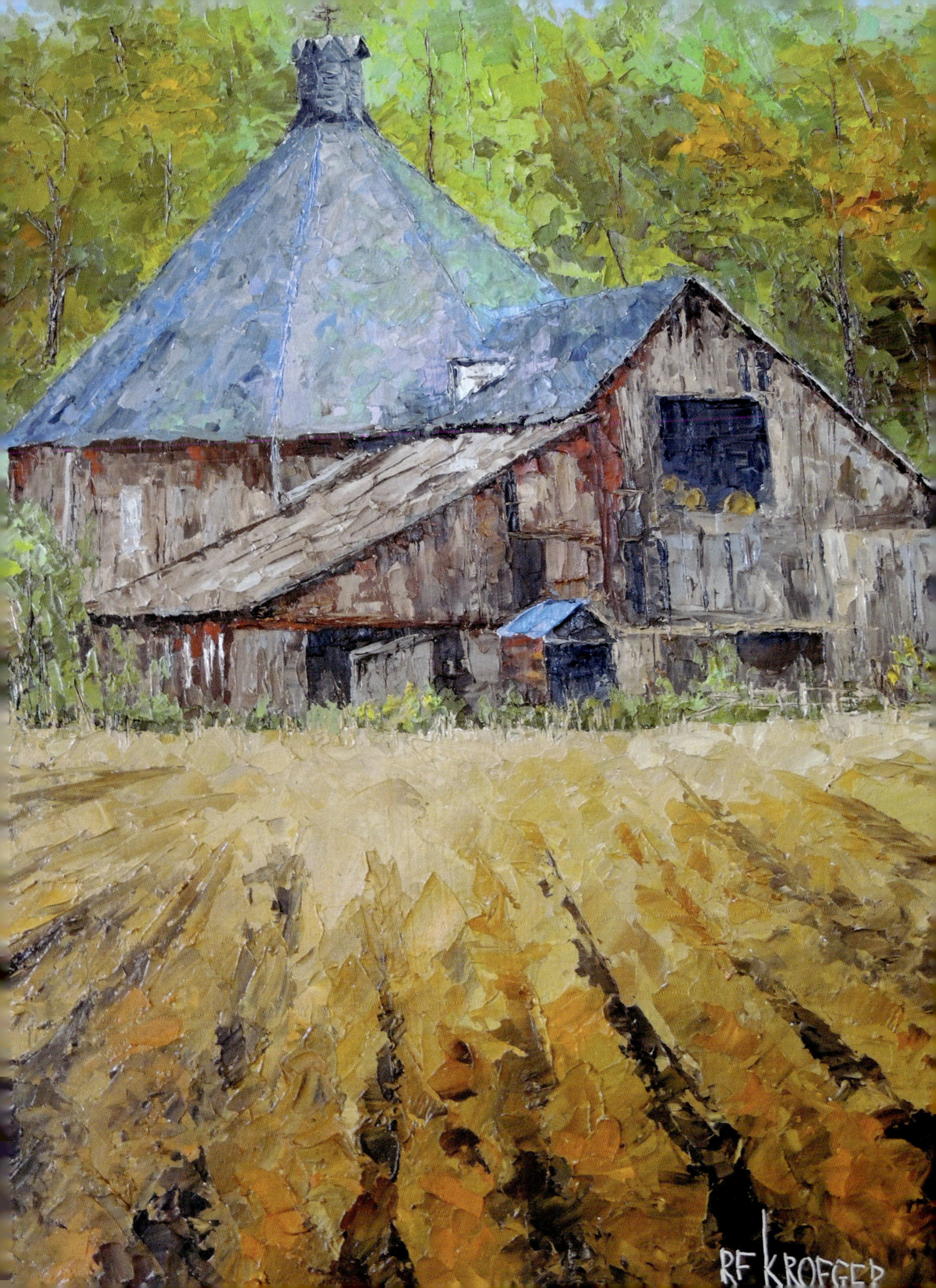
RF KROEGER

VERNON COUNTY

The Round Barns of Vernon County

Located in the southwestern corner of Wisconsin, Vernon County lies in a region referred to as the Driftless Area — a whopping 24,000 square miles that extends to southeastern Minnesota, northeastern Iowa, and the extreme northwestern corner of Illinois. Somehow, the glaciers of the last ice age, 11,700 years ago, missed this land, leaving it rugged, with deep river valleys and tall ridges — unlike flat fields, ideal for agriculture. To the east, 60 miles away, are the Wisconsin Dells, well known for 100-foot cliffs, scenic river canyons, and stunning rock formations, a photographer's dream but a farmer's nightmare.

Regardless, farmers have survived here since the mid-1800s and, during the peak years of round barns — 1900 to 1920 — somewhere between 30 and 40 were built here, giving the county legitimate claim to "Round Barn Capital of the World." However, since Fulton County, Indiana, claimed that title earlier, the Vernon County Historical Society graciously has allowed the title to remain in Indiana, especially since they had already established extensive signage to that effect.

Since 2000, the county's round barns have been disappearing — from a total of about 20 to 12 — as of 2020. Fire, natural collapse, and wind have been the culprits. By the 1930s, some have estimated that Wisconsin had up to 215 polygonal barns, most of them circular. Vernon County was, and still is, the state's leader.

Its proximity — about 90 miles — to Madison (where Professor King worked when he began to publish his round barn plans) was no doubt a factor but agricultural trends played a part as well. The first farmers to settle Wisconsin came from New England and other eastern states and they knew how to grow wheat, which quickly became the state's leading crop. By 1860 wheat — about 30 million bushels of it, at 80 cents a bushel — helped countless farmers to pay off debts, build attractive brick farmhouses, and raise large families. That was King Wheat's peak. What followed probably surprised many farmers: soil depletion, chinch bugs, smut, and rust decimated yields. By 1879 wheat growing slowed to a trickle and farmers began trying other crops; among them were tobacco, sorghum, hops. By 1900 although potato growing had become popular, storage was a problem in Wisconsin's frigid winters. Corn crops and hog raising helped but it was the dairy business that took over the state and spurred the growth of the round barn with a central silo, a plan that university experts promoted extensively. Dairy farming, though labor intensive — milking cows twice daily, feeding them, and removing manure — became the state's agricultural leader, leading to its title of "America's Dairyland." In 2019 Wisconsin led the country with 3.36 billion pounds of cheese produced. And, though round barns comprised only a small percentage of barns, they were built primarily for milking cows.

Wisconsin's round barn builders ranged from Germans, Swiss, and Scandinavians to other nationalities. In Vernon County, as related by a descendant, Ernest DeWitt built the family round barn as well as others in the Cheyenne Valley and Frank Lisker and his sons built their own round barn. But one of the most intriguing round barn builders was Alga Shivers, son of an emancipated slave.

In decades before the Civil War, Wisconsin was Indian territory. In April of 1832 Chief Black Hawk, a 65-year-old Sauk warrior, led some 1,000 Sauk, Fox, and Kickapoo men, women, and children, including about 500 warriors, across the Mississippi to reclaim territory in Illinois that other leaders had surrendered in the treaty of 1804. After initial victories, the Indians were defeated by the end of the summer and, by 1837, most had migrated westwards, leaving Wisconsin open for settlers and farming.

In 1855 six black families, freed slaves, settled in Vernon County's Cheyenne Valley, intermixing with Native Americans and white New Englanders. Word spread, as it did, albeit slowly in those days, and, thanks to Wisconsin's defiance of the Fugitive Slave Act of 1850, more enslaved blacks migrated here via the Underground Railroad.

One of them, Thomas Shivers, was born into slavery in 1857 on a Tennessee plantation, which almost always meant a life of hard labor. However, his owner, noticing intelligence in the child, allowed Thomas to attend elementary school (Tennessee was one of the few southern states that allowed slaves to be educated). At age five — in 1862 and during the Civil War — he walked five miles each way to the schoolhouse. Two years later he was orphaned and was then raised by an enslaved woman named Charlotte. After the war she married a black Union soldier and they adopted Thomas and his brother Ashley but gave up trying to live in the Jim Crow South and headed north. Ashley, Thomas, and Mr. and Mrs. Harris arrived in the Cheyenne Valley in 1879 — after walking here on foot, a journey that lasted two years. Ashley and Thomas were given the last name of their slave owner.

Thomas married and became a successful farmer; by the end of the century he owned 260 acres of land and had the largest black-owned farm in the state at that time. In fact, this region probably had the largest population of African Americans in farm country in the Midwest. Thanks to his owner in Tennessee, Thomas had been one of the few slaves permitted to attended school and was considered to be a man of ideas and innovations among his fellow farmers in this unique valley where marriage between blacks, Native Americans, and whites erased racial barriers.

Shivers was the first in the area to install electricity, he bought the first tractor in the county, and, by 1920, he was the first farmer install a hot and cold-water system in his home. There's no doubt that his ingenuity and solid work ethic rubbed off on his son, Alga, who was born in 1889. As other farm children did, he learned farming from his parents and, in 1906, at 17, he helped build a round barn for George Harris, a dairy farmer who moved here from Virginia after the Civil War. The George Harris and Burl Harris families used the barn to house their herd of Jerseys. Before that, Alga helped build a round barn on his father's farm. The Harris barn still stands.

Alga, known by many as Algie, attended the George R. Smith College in Missouri, a historically black institution that operated from 1894 until it burned down in 1925. After studying carpentry and engineering, he served in France in WWI and, surviving the war, he returned to his family farm. After marrying Flora, he continued farming and building round barns. Though they never had any of their own, they raised many foster children on their farm. Fifteen round barns in Vernon and Monroe counties are attributed to him.

His building style followed Professor King's plans, though he adapted each barn to suit the farmer's needs. Typically, Shivers would minimize costs by cutting logs from the farm property and let them cure for a year or two. He'd also use stones from the farm for the foundation and sometimes for fieldstone walls. Besides a gambrel roof and a substantial cupola over the central silo, his barns usually had vertical siding, which was easier to install, compared to a horizontal application. After the logs had cured, Algie and his crew would return and could build the barn in two or three months.

Besides round barns, they also built conventional barns and outbuildings, even into the late 1920s after the round barn design had become outdated. Though Alga had plenty of work in Vernon County, he preferred not to venture out of that well integrated community for fear of encountering racism. Throughout the 20th century he continued farming, milking cows through the 1960s. He passed in 1978, nearly reaching 90. His round barn burned down two years later.

Though this county does not claim the title of the round barn capital of America, its history shows that men and women of all races can coexist comfortably, which might be easier in farm country than in an overpopulated city. Today its round barns, 11 still standing, no longer house dairy cows, except for one purchased by an Amish family, who still use the barn for milking.

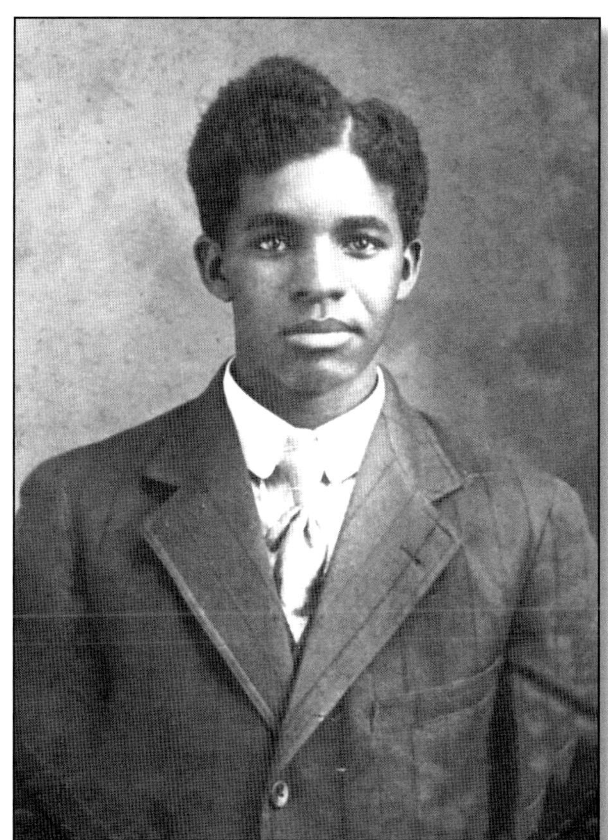

Alga "Algie" Shivers, round barn builder, Vernon County, Wisconsin. Courtesy of the town of Forest

Honorable

In 1906 Alga Shivers was 17, an age when much was expected of young men in rural communities — milking cows, harvesting crops, repairing barns. But building them? Local legend attributes this barn to Alga Shivers, though it's more likely that he assisted experienced builders. After all, farmers were pragmatic, even those progressive types who chose to build a round barn over a rectangular one, and they'd be more likely to entrust their hard-earned dollars to a builder with experience rather than to a 17-year-old.

George Harris, a dairy farmer from Virginia, moved to Wisconsin after the Civil War. Perhaps unhappy with the history of slavery in the South, he apparently did not object to having an African American, son of slaves, work on his barn at the turn of the century. Maple wood was used for barn construction and was cut from trees on the farm, air dried, and then steamed on a mold, though the planks were placed vertically, not horizontally. Fieldstones used in the foundation were also harvested on the property.

George and Mable Harris and the Burl Harris family raised Jersey cows, operating a modest dairy business in this medium sized barn (60 feet in diameter). The central

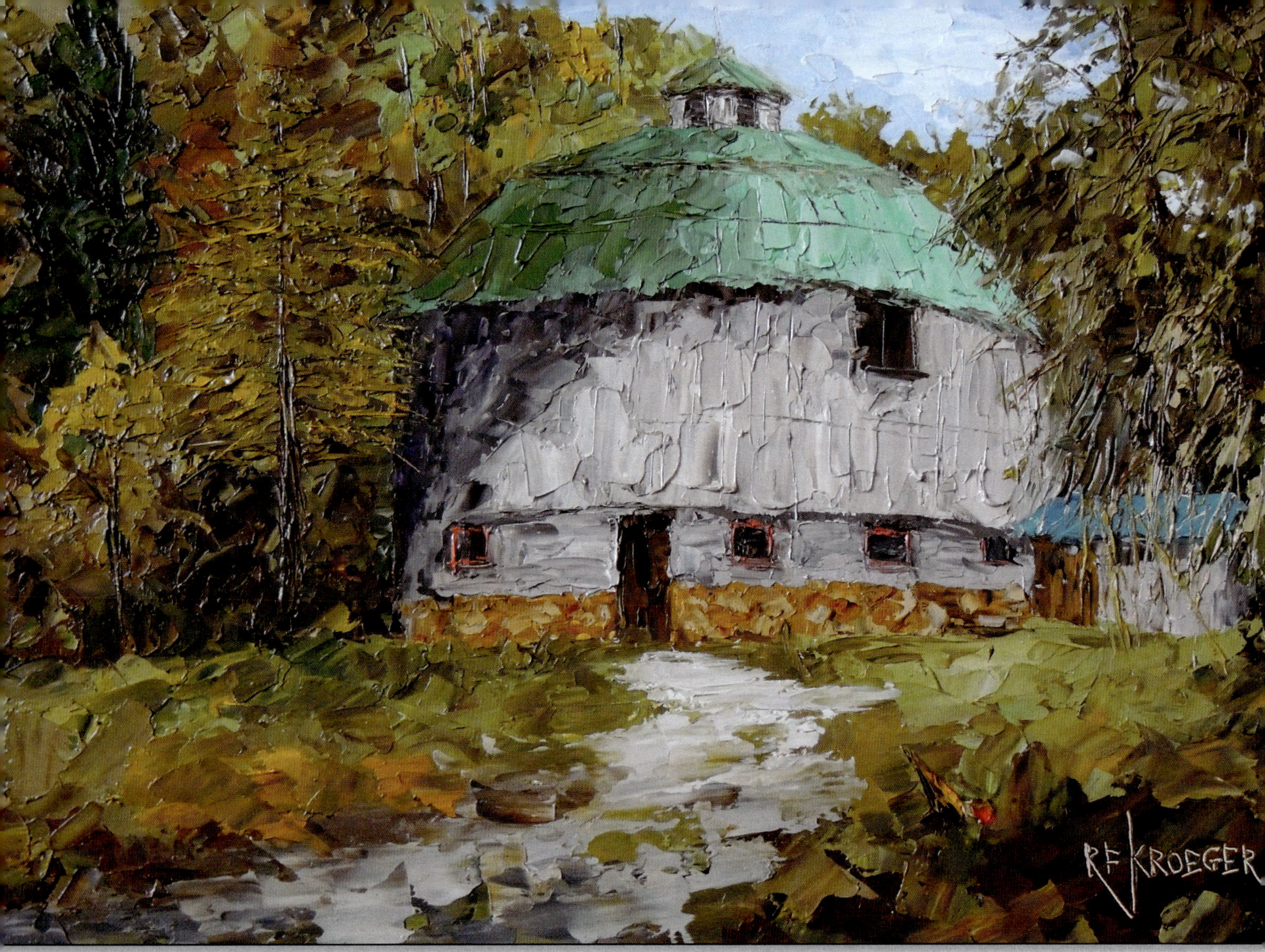

Honorable

silo appears to have been made from a mix of concrete and fieldstones, a unique form of silo construction, and, after a century of use, it has proved to be durable.

In 1980 the family sold the farm to Marcus Kaplan, who has maintained the barn and has repaired the roof, always the Achilles heel of an old barn. Though more expenses loom in the future, the barn will be preserved in this painting and essay, a tribute to both Vernon County and the former Virginia farmer, who ignored racial bias and will always be remembered as honorable.

The Individual

Frank Lisker and his sons, Joseph and Adolph, built this barn in 1910 — at the peak of round barn construction in Wisconsin. Their neighbors, Frank Jeffek, Frank Sladek, and George Abbot pitched in and Albert Sterba laid the colorful stone foundation. Lisker harvested trees on his farm for the lumber and used a specially made handsaw to cut the boards. They used large boulders of sandstone, hauled via a steel-wheeled wagon from a nearby farm, for the lower level's foundation. Besides following Professor King's circular plan, the Liskers borrowed ideas from a neighbor, George Pepper, whose round barn, according to descendants, may have been built by Alga Shivers.

With remarkable foresight, Mr. Lisker covered his barn with stamped zinc, a metal, not only inexpensive and durable, but one that eliminated the need for constant repainting. Its uniqueness has stood the test of time. The round ventilator in the cupola is still intact.

Lisker paid his workers $2.50 a day, a fair wage in 1910, and estimated that his total cost was $1,800, a reasonable amount for a barn with a diameter of 60 feet. The current owner, Edward Lisker, reasoned that his grandfather chose the circular design to make milking and feeding cows more efficient.

He said that the family made changes over the course of the 20th century, including adding electricity and a barn cleaner. When he took over the farm in 1947,

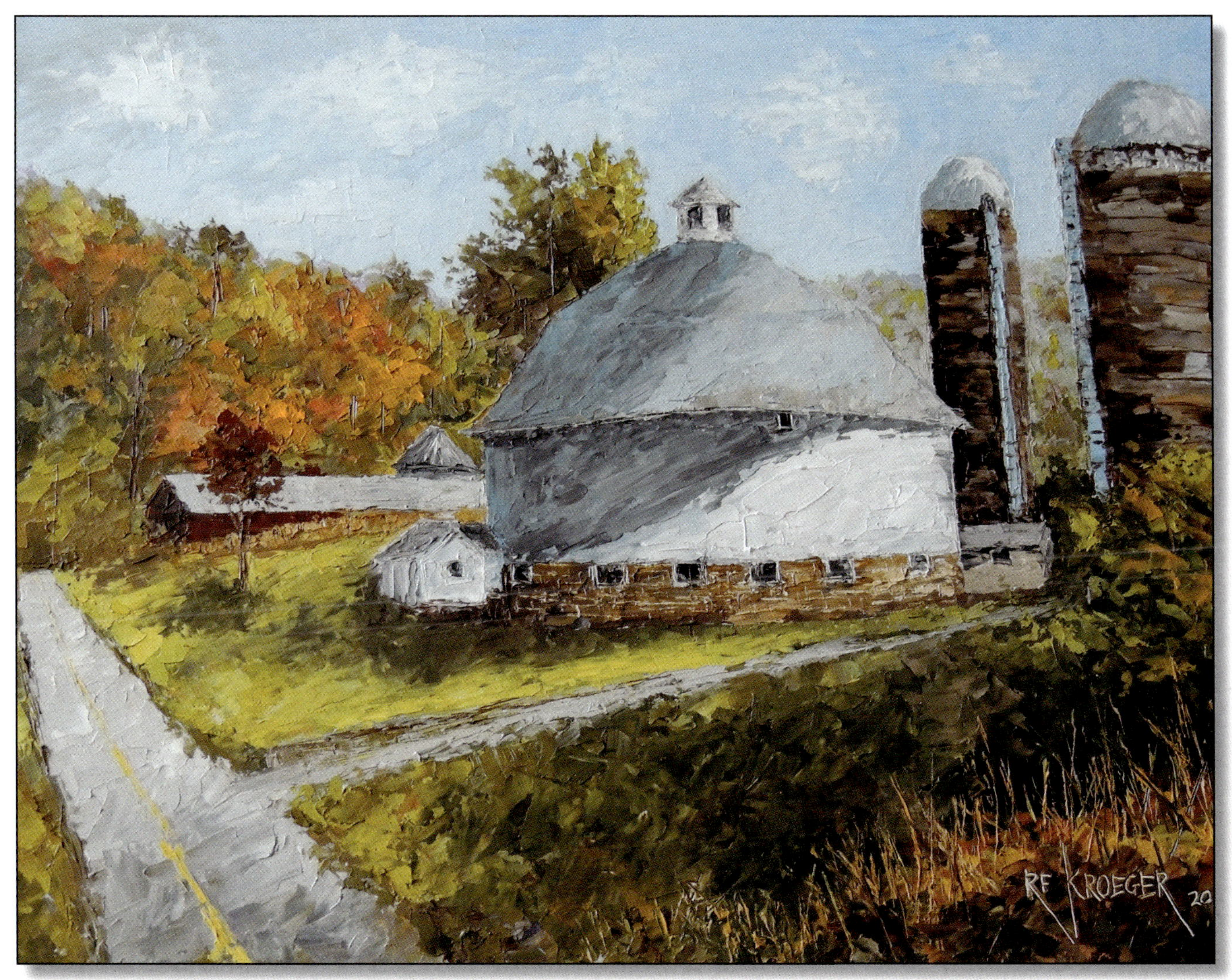

The Individual

he continued upgrading, eventually removing stalls for calving and adding more stanchions so that they could milk 40 cows instead of 30. By the 1960s they had stopped using the central silo and instead built three new silos. The dairy business was good. However, Edward Lisker, who bought the farm from his father in 1951, no longer milks cows and uses the barn today only for storage.

The scene from on top of a hill, looking down on the barn beside a road, shadows falling and autumn colors in the distant hills, was hard to pass up. And I'm sure the family enjoys this sight this every day, although they honestly admit that maintaining a circular barn costs money. The barn cleaner and the milk pipeline would have been much less costly than if fitted for a rectangular structure. Of course, conventional barns are a dime a dozen in some respects. This one, besides being a rare round barn, stands out with its unique metal siding. A rare gem, indeed — a real individual.

The Reflection

Ernest DeWitt, according to his grandson Melvin DeWitt, built this round barn in 1912, along with several others in the Cholvin Valley, a picturesque region located near Wildcat Mountain State Park. However, despite the claims of durability of round barns, this is the only one that DeWitt built that's still standing. A bit smaller than most round barns in Vernon County — only 54 feet in diameter — this barn is unique in that its interior has lathe and plaster construction. The 10-foot-wide central silo follows Professor King's plan of the ideal dairy barn.

The DeWitts sold the farm to Elzie and Dorothy Parish, who used it for 11 years before selling to the McClure family in the early 1980s. In 2005 Kristi and Craig King took the reins and, historically inclined, began restoring the barn. From a photo, taken prior to restoration, many of the horizontally placed side boards had warped, ends springing out, testifying to the inherent problems of soaking

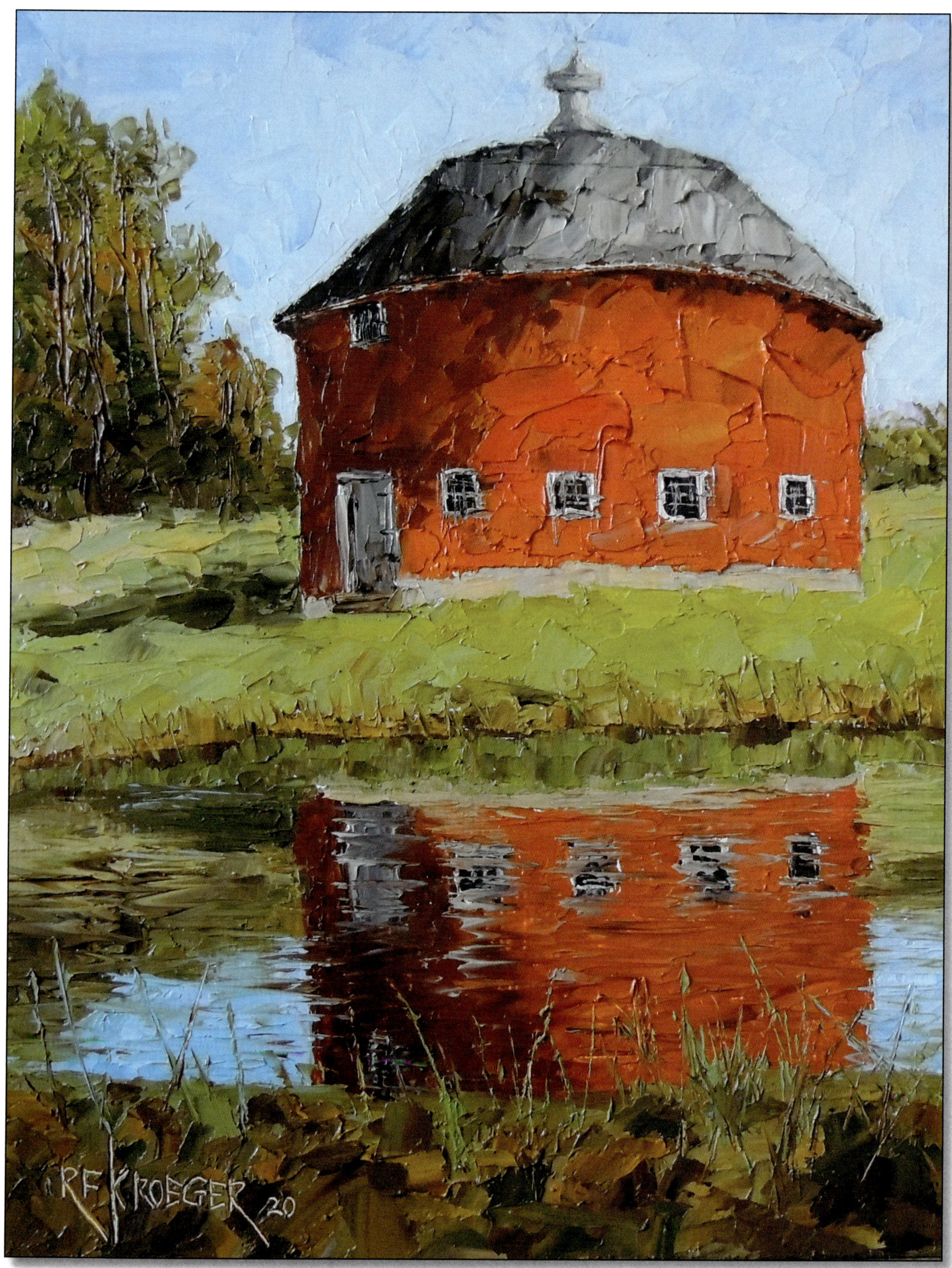

The Reflection

boards, done prior to construction in hopes that the boards wouldn't return to straight.

However, the Kings remedied the issue with sprung boards, re-sided the barn and added a fresh coat of red paint, adding a striking complementary color contrast with adjacent green foilage. According to Kevin and Patsy Alderson, authors of *Barns Without Corners*, they also excavated the original bank entrance and built a retaining wall as well as a new bridge entrance to lessen pressure on the foundation. The owners hope to continue maintaining this Wisconsin icon, one that sits above a pond, which, on a clear day would inspire any photographer or artist to capture its priceless reflection.

The Twister

Though old barns can suffer from shifting earth, which weakens foundations, and their paint can peel and their roofs can leak, most of the times these problems can be fixed. But old barns can't survive lightning strikes or tornadoes, which often put the final nail in a round barn's coffin — as happened to this round barn.

Its demise was tragic since it was one of the first that Algie Shivers built after he served in World War I. Before he enlisted — hoping to gain respect, which many African Americans sought in that era of blatant racism — he had studied carpentry and engineering in a college in Missouri, giving him a solid foundation for his passion — building round barns and other buildings. Returning as a war hero — he served in France, where the French gave black soldiers respect — was no bonus for an African American in the early 1920s. But coming home in 1919 to racism-free Vernon County, living and working on his farm, was all that Shivers wanted. He did not like to travel outside the county. No wonder.

In 1921 dairy farmer Joe Dank, a Bohemian immigrant, hired Algie, who by now held an impressive résumé as a round barn builder. With a crew of neighbors and carpenters,

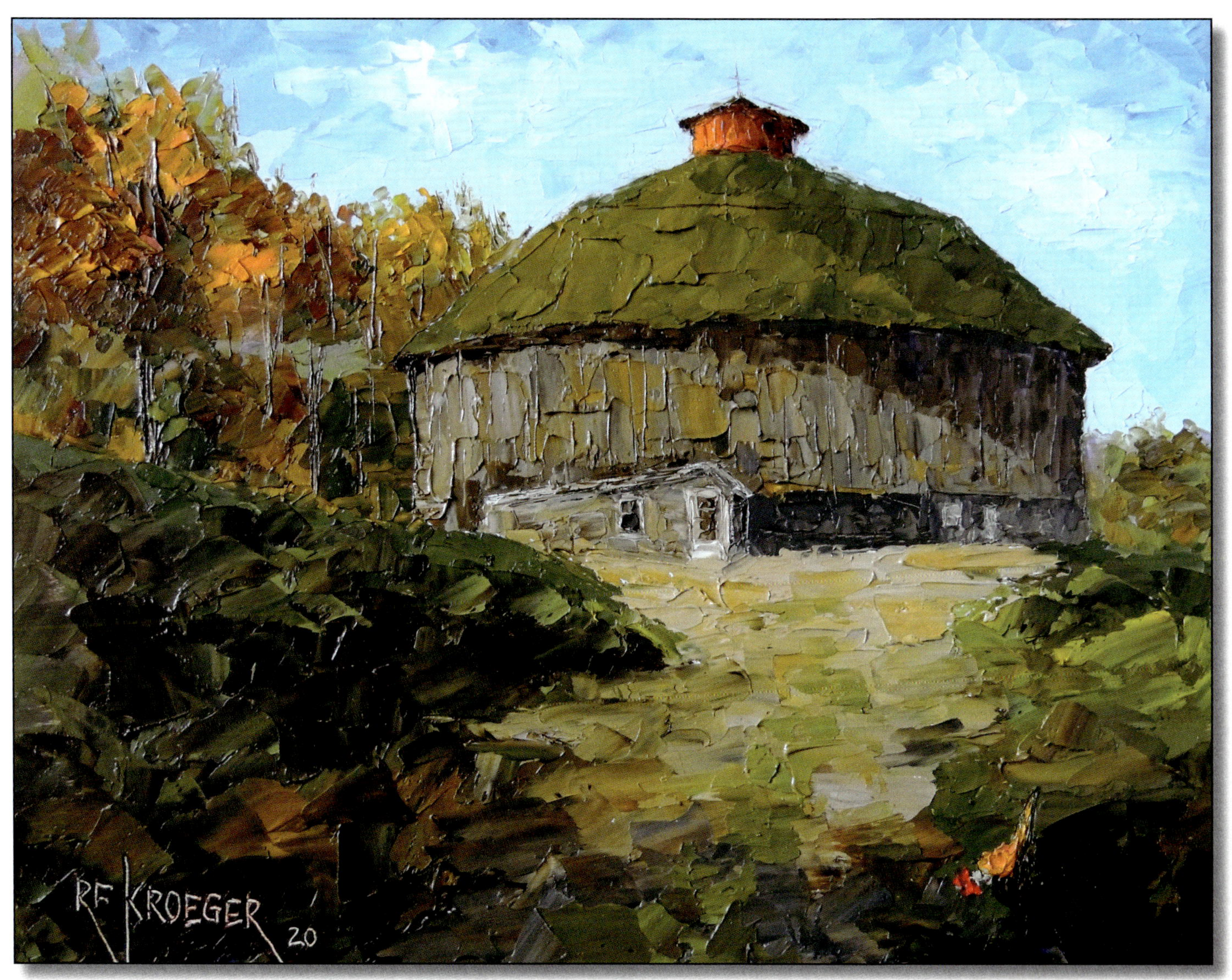

The Twister

he designed and built this medium-sized barn. Its 60-foot diameter and 12x48-foot central silo meant that it could service a small dairy herd. Algie probably cut trees on the farm for the barn's lumber and, as he typically did, cured the logs for one or two years before sawing them. Eight-on-eight windows, only a few feet from one another, rimmed the lower level, providing needed light along with ventilation, and a ramp allowed wagons access to the second floor. A two-pitched gambrel roof and small cupola, two trademarks of a Shivers barn, added a bit of flair.

Joe passed the farm to his son Frank, who, in turn, kept it in the family — with his son Laramie taking over. He made improvements: a milk house in the 1950s, a bulk tank in 1976, a barn cleaner in 1979, and a pipeline milker in 1981. Then disaster struck.

A vicious tornado (Is there any other kind?) hit the barn in 1983 and twisted the barn and silo, damage that couldn't adequately be repaired even though a construction firm tried. After that, according to the Aldersons in *Barns Without Corners*, "It was never quite the same."

The next owner was the James Noecker, Jr., family. After restoring the milk house — to meet regulations to ship Grade A milk — they continued dairy farming, a business that kept going until 2010, nearly 90 years after the barn's construction. Unfortunately, a strong storm in 2019 caused its collapse, due in part to the tornado's damage. And, although it's now only history, it will always be alive in this painting and essay, a tribute to its builder, a veteran of World War I, as well as a statement about the enemy of all old barns, the deadly twister.

IRON COUNTY

Little Finland

Like Finland, northern Wisconsin and Michigan's nearby Upper Peninsula have cold weather and lots of snow. In fact, this area, known as Copper Country, gets more snow than anywhere else east of the Mississippi in the U.S. — not ideal for farming crops. The region was, however, full of iron and copper deposits; this county was named Iron for good reason. After more than a century of mining iron ore in this region, ending in the 1960s, the famous 2,000-foot ore dock in Ashland, Michigan, was dismantled in 2012.

Copper mining, dating to 3,000 B.C., when Native Americans dug it out of small pits, also flourished from 1845 to the 1960s, and drew European immigrants. Along with the Irish, fleeing from the potato famine, Cornish, Germans, and Scandinavians began to colonize this area. Immigration of the Finns peaked from 1890 to 1920. One of them built this barn.

In 1902 the Annalas were among the first five families to settle the rural countryside near Hurley, land that had been cleared by logging, leaving tree stumps behind as well as boulders, remnants of the glaciers. Besides long winters and a short growing season, the soil was clay-based, not conducive to crop raising. That left dairy farming.

Matthew Annala, a Finnish carpenter and stone mason, quickly decided on that option, in hopes of supporting his wife and 12 children. By 1917 — when he began working on the barn — he had built several buildings, including the Oma (a Finnish word for "our home") School, which has since become the town hall. According to his daughter Mildred, he chose a circular design after visiting round barns in east central Wisconsin, a state that exploded with the circular design and central silo, thanks to Professor King's publications. Also, concerned about the destruction caused by tornadoes, Annala decided to make his barn tornado-proof and, with a never-ending supply of rocks, he built his barn with fieldstones. Though many of Wisconsin's barns have fieldstone foundations, this is the only one with complete walls of stone.

One of his daughters explained his method: heating the boulders in a fire and then dropping them in cold water — to make them crack. Matthew then used his stonemasonry skills to fit the pieces tightly next to one another, creating a two-foot-thick wall of stone, requiring little mortar. She explained that engineering professors would bring their students to view the free-standing roof, converging on the central silo (also fieldstone), with only a drum and hoop support of hemlock rafters. Annala and his sons worked on the barn during five short summer seasons from 1917 to 1921, when they finished. Oddly, though his barn was an esthetic masterpiece, other farmers didn't follow his lead, choosing instead a conventional barn design. And, by this time, farm journals had published many articles, criticizing the round barn design as being more costly and perhaps less efficient.

The barn's size, 60 feet wide and 60 feet high, was large enough for a small dairy herd; its 24 metal cow stalls circle around the white-painted fieldstone silo. After years of success in the dairy business, Annala built a 15-foot-high circular milkhouse in 1928 — out of fieldstone that matched the barn — so that fresh milk could be piped from the barn directly for bottling and shipping. His plan was to fashion the fieldstone chimney into a milk bottle but that was never finished, possibly due to the emergence of the Great Depression.

Still, during these hard times, Mr. Annala continued to improve his barn, adding the adjacent clay tile silo around

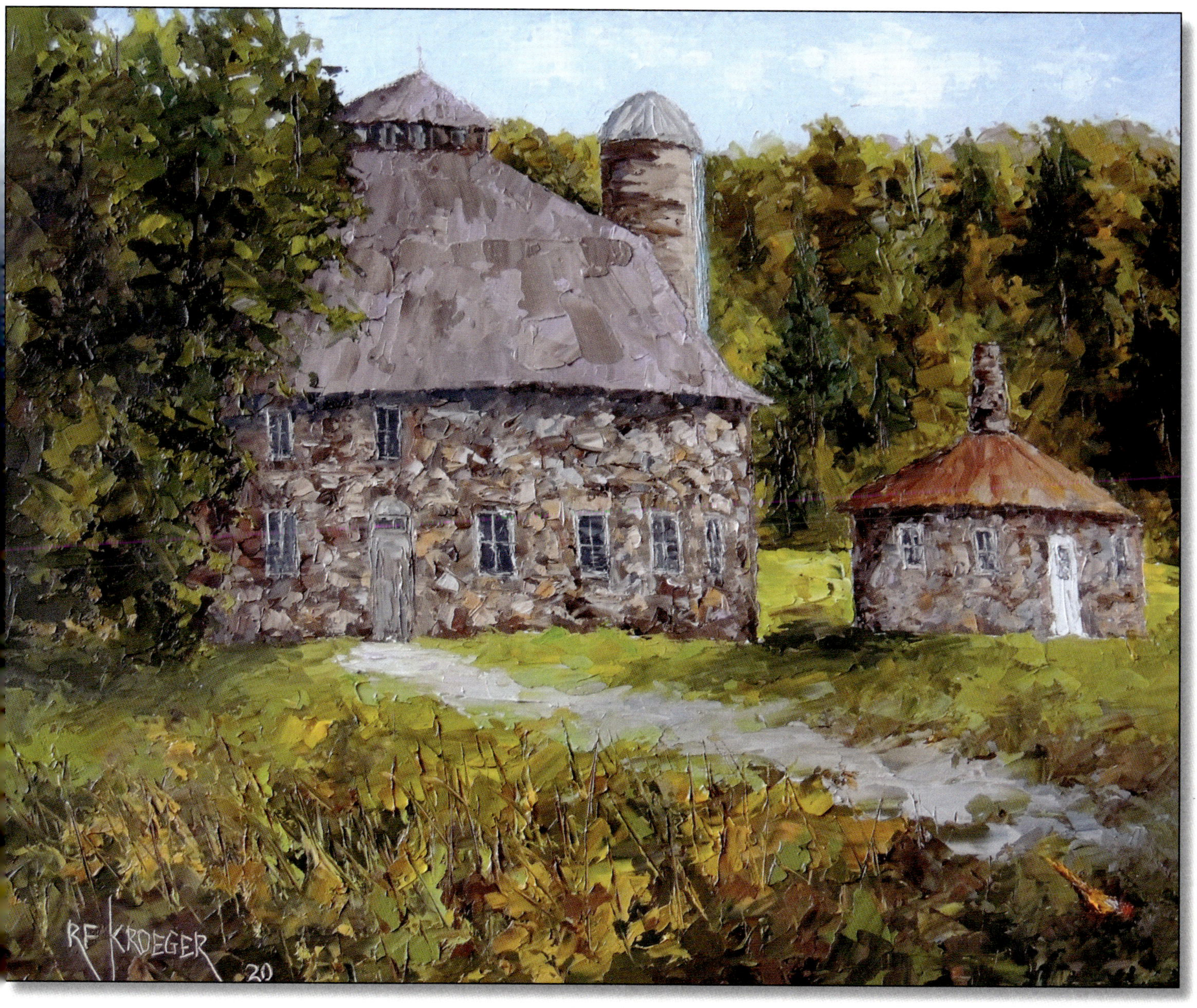

Little Finland

1938 and in 1943 a 40-foot long ramp of fieldstone that led to the double-door entrance of the second level. The haymow could hold 100 tons of hay. Stalls for the bull and calves were located beneath this ramp.

During WWII the family delivered their own milk but stopped the bottling process in the mid-1940s. In Wisconsin, farmers would add extensions to their barns for increased production as their dairy herds increased in size, but stone walls in this barn prohibited that. Unfortunately, its dimensions limited the number of cows it could hold, eventually leading to the family's exiting the business and selling the farm in 1973.

The next owner, Paul Janoska, must have felt a sense of history when he secured a listing for the barn and milkhouse on the National Register in 1979, though the nomination form noted that the gambrel roof was in poor condition. In fact, when photographer Frank Hutton visited the barn in the 1980s, he began to observe a gradual deterioration and, worried about vandalism and fire, he placed the barn high on his bucket list. In 2011 he visited again and was lucky to find the owner, Paul Bauschke, not only at home but gracious enough to permit him to take photos in various seasons.

The Bauschkes purchased the farm in 2003 and have taken good care of it, using it mostly for storage. They hired professional restoration workers to bring it back to life, which incurred a great amount of money, though Paul refitted the windows by himself. Its walls, bursting with color from fieldstones fitting together like clockwork, revive the memory not only of this master stonemason and his sons but also of the early Finnish immigrants who settled here, in "little Finland."

GOODHUE COUNTY

The Good Humor Barn

Sorry, but the county's name, Goodhue, conjures up pleasant childhood memories. In 1950 a movie was made, *The Good Humor Man*, and in 2005 a Showtime channel movie of the same name was released. Both refer to white-clad salesmen, who drove through neighborhoods in trucks, blaring their jingles — much like the Pied Piper playing his flute — to attract children to buy ice cream. In the early 1920s this iconic ice cream, the Good Humor-Breyers brand, began in my hometown of Youngstown, Ohio. When we kids heard the music, we'd ask mom for permission and then run like crazy — with a dime or a quarter — to buy the delicious chocolate-coated ice cream bar on a stick. In the 1950s the company had nearly 2,000 Good Humor trucks around the country. Who doesn't like ice cream?

But this is Goodhue County, not the land of ice cream trucks and their frozen treats. Created in 1853 and located about 50 miles southeast of Minneapolis, the county took its name from James Madison Goodhue, who published the first newspaper in the territory. The county seat of Red Wing was named after an early 19th-century Dakota Sioux chief, Red Wing (Shakea). It translates to "Wing of the Wild Swan Dyed Red."

Initially, New Englanders colonized the region and laid out farms. Germans and Scandinavians followed in the late 1800s. Today, a reservation, Prairie Island Indian Community, comprises most of Red Wing, a charming village alongside the Mississippi River, which the National Trust for Historic Preservation placed on its 2008 distinctive destinations list. And, yes, both Red Wing Shoes, founded here in 1905, as well as the city, feature the familiar red swan wing logo.

This round barn, built around 1914 by local carpenter Oliver Landick for the Dammons, signified a farming transition in the state. Wheat, the principal crop grown here throughout the 19th century and the first crop grown commercially, helped Minnesota to be the country's leader in wheat production by 1890. But, as it did in neighboring Wisconsin, the well ran dry; wheat had depleted the soil, a fungal disease called "rust" occurred repeatedly, and invasive reeds hurt crop yields. By the late 1890s agricultural experts warned farmers to diversify and, with farm incomes plummeting, such a decision came easily. The answer was dairy farming.

However, when farmers tried to convert their threshing barns into ones suited for dairy cows, they struggled at first but eventually succeeded, sometimes building rectangular additions for housing the animals. Others chose to build round barns, most of which are now gone, though, according to John Roscoe in his book, *Minnesota's Round Barns*, there were 72 still existing when he began searching in 2007. Even though Wisconsin's professor King published his findings that advocated the circular barn design with a central silo in the early 1890s, Minnesota farmers weren't convinced. Most round barns in Minnesota came later — after 1910.

Henry and Mary Dammon must have been proud of their unusual barn, with horizontal siding and an impressive fieldstone foundation, thanks to a plentiful supply of boulders in Minnesota glaciated fields.

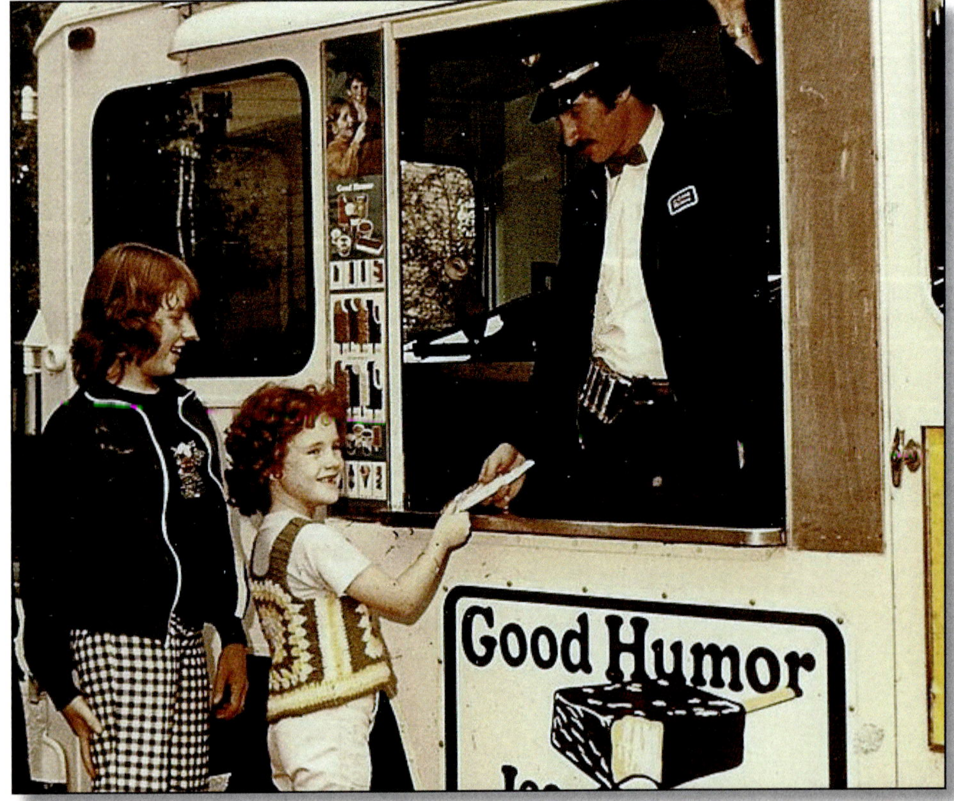

Left: *The Good Humor man, circa 1975. Wikimedia, Grubbgxdn*

Below: *Red Wing logo. Courtesy, city of Red Wing, Minnesota*

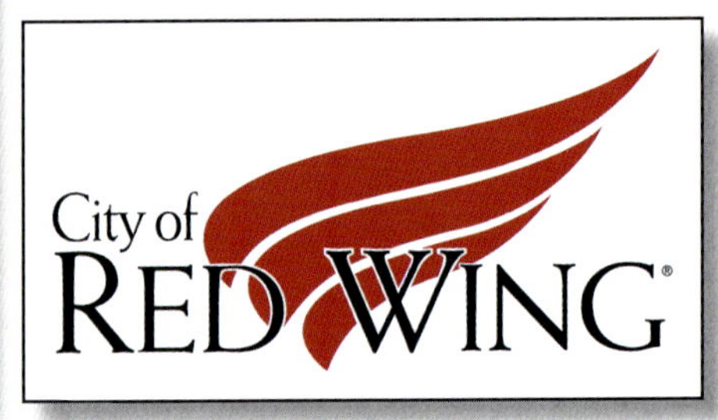

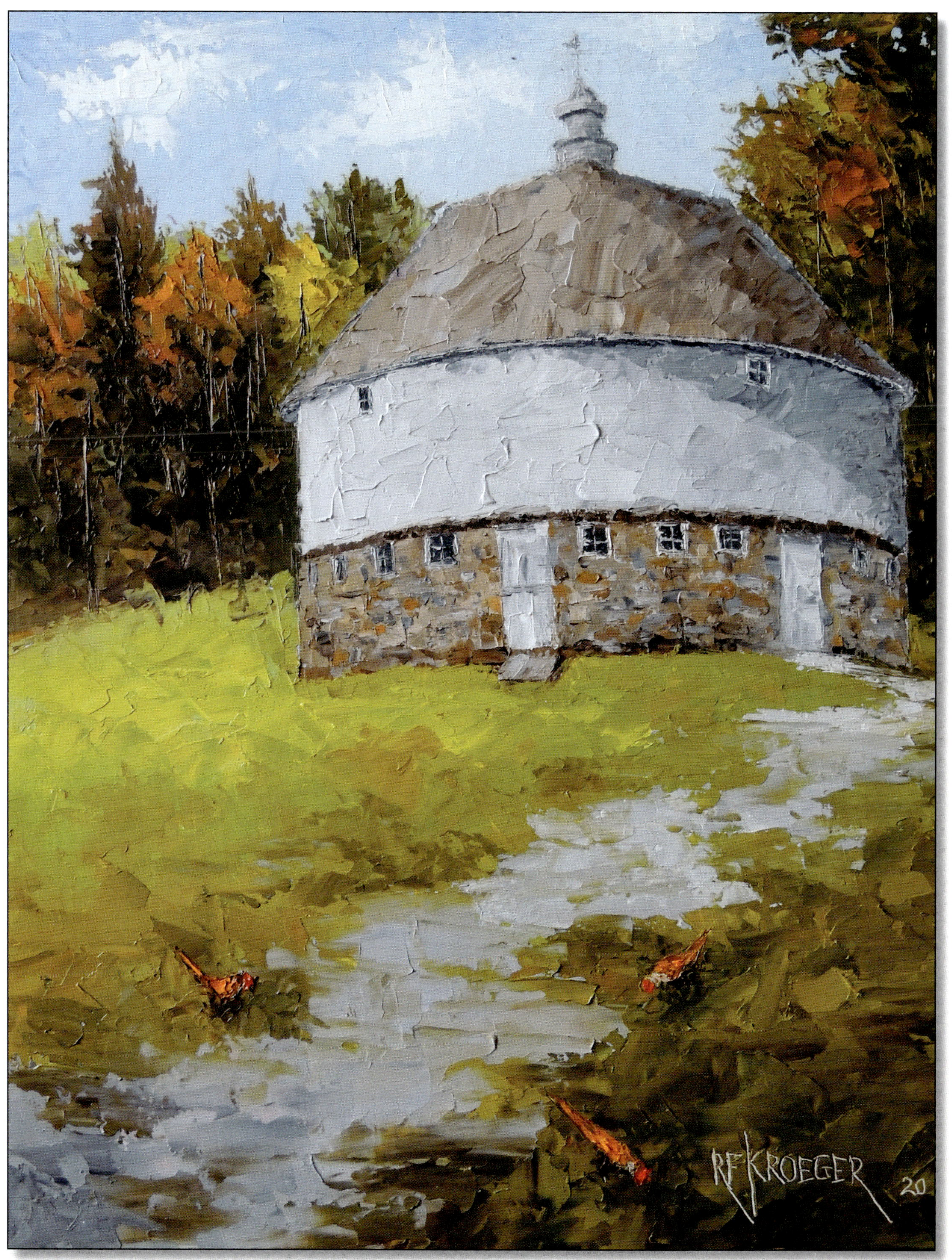

The Good Humor Barn

The barn size, 60 feet wide by 60 feet high, housed more than 20 cows and provided space for horse stalls and a calving pen. Cows, huddled around the central silo, created enough heat to keep the silage from freezing in sub-zero Minnesota winters and, thanks to an overhead circular track, they could be fed with minimal labor. Lighting was considered, too — Henry Dammon had plenty of it while he milked his cows, thanks to 22 windows. Built into a hillside, the rear doors opened wide enough for a wagon full of hay and, on the ground level, a person could enter the barn from either side. It was an efficient barn for dairying.

Eventually the farm passed on to Earl and Retha Griffith, who used the barn for a honey-processing plant from the 1950s through the 1980s. Their son Ronald, showing his love for this rare barn, built a one-twenty-seventh scale model of it, complete with barrels of honey, which the eventual owners, the Kleffmans, kept in their farmhouse. Michael Zuckerman prepared an application for the National Register in 1978, which listed the owners as Leroy and Joann Wehrle of Springfield, Illinois. Oddly, the listing was not approved until 11 years later in 1989. Then the farm changed hands and once again brought the old barn to life.

In 1998, to fulfill a lifelong dream to own a bed and breakfast, Robin and Elaine Kleffman bought the farm. They spent a summer cleaning the barn, which hadn't been used in 10 years and then, after tearing down the old farmhouse and being historically minded, they built a new one, based on an 1861 design by architect Samuel Sloan, an influential Philadelphia-based architect, who worked in the mid-19th century. Not only was he one of the most prolific architects of his generation, one of the few nationally known to work in the antebellum South, but he published *The Architectural Review and American Builder's Journal* (1868-1870), referred to as the first American periodical devoted exclusively to architecture.

After the Kleffmans entertained their first guests in their new B&B, income began to flow, enough to justify restoring the old barn. They straightened walls, replaced original pillars for support, and leveled the ground floor. Sensing history, they also preserved the pre-Civil War smokehouse. And, to add the final touch to the property, they improved the landscaping so much that it garnered the 2005 Minnesota Nursery Landscape Design Award.

Another couple, also holding the dream of owning a B&B, stayed here as guests one year when they learned that the business was for sale. Wendy and Kirk Stensrud didn't hesitate, buying the property in 2017. Entrepreneurs, they continued to expand services by adding a large pavilion next to the barn where they could stage weddings and other events. These days the roundbarnfarm.com advertises both B&B accommodations and weddings and proudly lists its awards, one of which, according to Buzzfeed, ranks this event center as number 13 on the list of coolest places to get married in America. There's no doubt that the Good Humor Barn plays a key role in this enterprise.

ISANTI COUNTY

Springtime in Minnesota

I took this composition from a photo by Henry Hintermeister, a Minnesota photographer, who posted it on Facebook in March, 2021. The warm beige colors of the concrete stone walls contrasted nicely with the black windows outlined in red. I thought the painting, even though not of an Ohio barn, would help the fundraiser in the historic Pump House Art Center's event in August in Chillicothe, Ohio's first capital.

The barn landed a spot in the National Register in 1980, when it was listed as in "good" condition. However, Henry's photo shows the cupola ready to fall off and the cap of the silo gone. A photo taken in 2002 showed an intact cupola as well as a distinctive and elaborate cap on the silo. While the concrete walls will stand the test of time, water penetrating from the broken cupola may eventually lead to collapse of the roof. The wood stave silo, missing its top, may also succumb someday, too.

At the time of the National Register listing, the barn owners were Allen and Edward Linden, descendants of Olof Linden, who left Sweden, came to America's northern region, and began farming here in 1874, a time when there were still conflicts with Native American tribes. By the turn of the century, the Linden family had prospered enough to warrant this new barn, which was built by local carpenters John, Victor, and Alec Wicklund in 1914. Linden had probably seen round barn plans not only in agricultural journals but also already existing in nearby counties. It must have seemed to be the ideal solution to expanding his dairy herd.

And, rather than wood siding, he used 10-inch concrete blocks for the walls, 18 feet high, with visions of future generations of Lindens continuing the family farm. Inside, he covered the walls with clay tile, a popular choice of Iowa's round barn builders — one which improved sanitation, and which would last longer than wooden siding. Dozens of square windows, now framed smartly in bright red, provided light on both the first and second floors, so necessary for housing livestock during long northern winters.

On the ground level there were six horse stalls and a harness room next to the large cattle area of 20 stanchions, a calf pen with six stanchions, and a cream separator. A stairway led to a huge hay storage area, from which hay

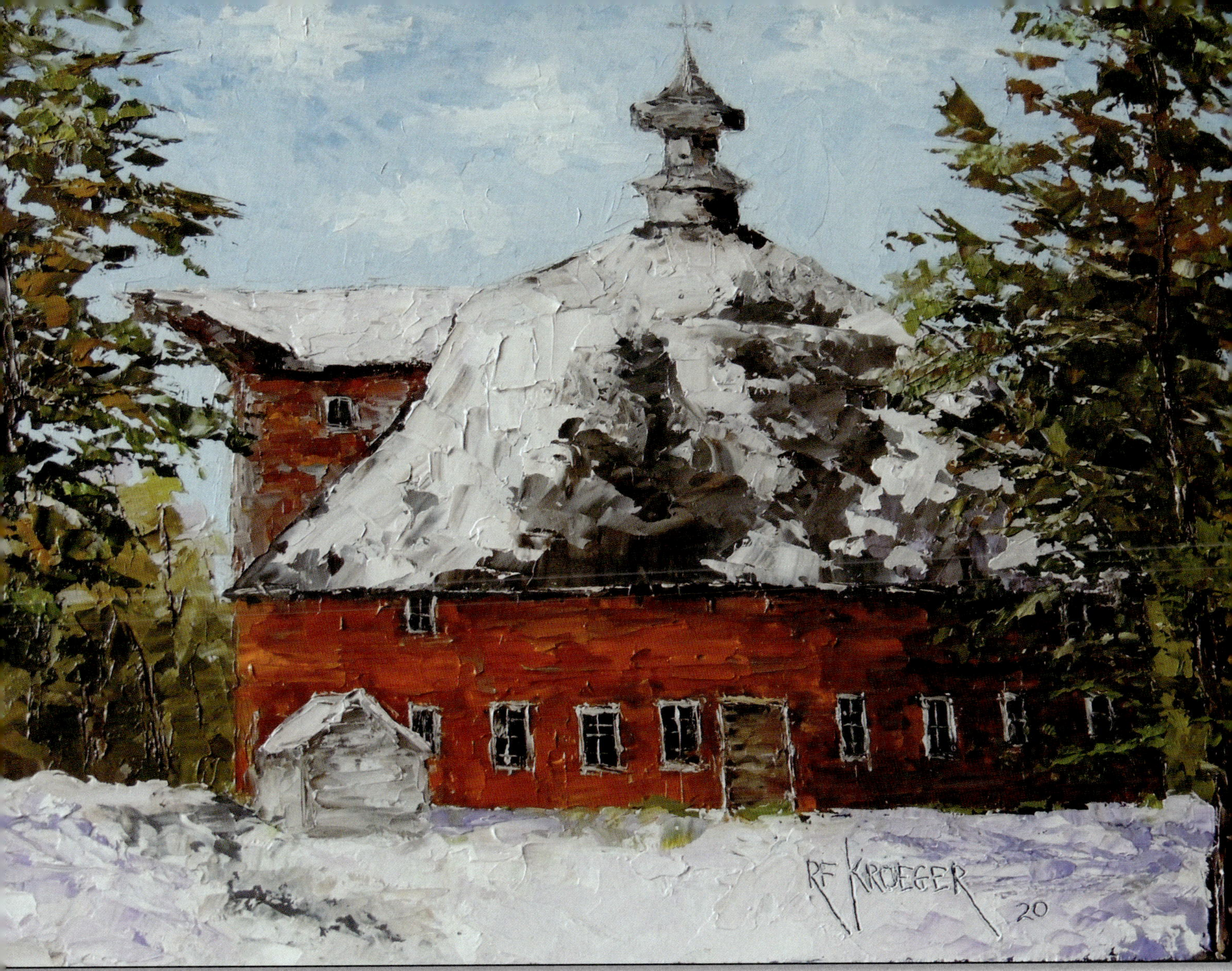

Springtime in Minnesota

could be tossed down to the ground floor. However, the Lindens chose not to follow Professor King's design of a central silo, instead building an outside silo of redwood, topping it with an attractive gambrel hexagonal cap, matching the conical gambrel roof of the barn. It was a large, stylish barn, a popular landmark in the area in 1914.

However, at the time of the National Register application in 1979, the barn was not being used for dairy farming — no cows — though a neighboring farmer stored hay in it. John Roscoe, in his book, *Minnesota's Round Barns*, reported that, during his visit, Jerome Jirovec, the current owner, said that, after the seamed metal sheets covering the roof had come loose, allowing water to penetrate, he removed every nail over a period of two years — probably thousands — and replaced them with longer lasting screws. He wanted the rafters, made of durable Washington State fir, to continue their job of supporting the roof. Talk about a labor of love.

And, with good fortune, the Linden barn will continue to survive, a tribute to a forward-thinking Swedish immigrant, one who spared no expense in constructing this round barn and its wooden silo, wonderful remnants of the past, as seen in this snowy Minnesota springtime.

BECKER COUNTY

Cuba of the North

Located in Cuba Township, population 208 in a recent census, this round barn symbolized the hardy farmers in this snowbound state. Founded in 1872, the township took its name — not from the island south of Cuba, famous for President Kennedy's famous missile crisis of 1962 — but rather from Cuba, New York, the former hometown of the township's first settler Charles W. Smith. Temperatures in Havana are much different from those in Becker County.

Surrounded by lakes (Minnesota isn't called the Land of 10,000 Lakes for nothing), the township's 35 square miles is almost four percent water: Cuba Lake, Duck Lake, La Belle Lake, Lime Lake, and Stinking Lake. Though the last one doesn't sound inviting, the others have strong appeal. The closest city is Lake Park, whose motto is "Gateway to the Lakes," a phrase that is more than appropriate.

Fur traders settled the area in 1841 at the same time that a band of Dakota Indians lived in a camp near Lake Flora, which the current city park now borders. These were known as the Eastern Dakota, the original Santee, a tribe that migrated in the 17th century from the colony of South Carolina — where the Santee River still bears their name — through the Ohio Country, and finally further north. In the 19th century they lived in the Dakota Territory — also named after them. The tribe was a Woodland people, exceptionally hardy to transition from the heat of the south to the cold of the north. They hunted, fished, and farmed but, as settlers moved in, their way of life began to change.

By the late 1850s, treaty violations by the United States and late annuity payments, a form of welfare given to the tribes in exchange for their land, created much hardship for the Santee, whose traditional way of life was quickly ebbing away. For some reason, the government began giving the payments directly to the Indian agents, who probably manipulated them, fueling frustration and eventual conflict.

On August 17, 1862, a small hunting party of young braves killed five settlers and that night a tribal council decided to begin attacking settlements in an effort to drive whites out of this region. In President Lincoln's second annual address, he estimated that about 800 white settlers had been killed in these attacks. Of course, at that time he had other, more pressing concerns, such as the Civil War.

Over the next few months, war raged between the army and the tribe, ending with the surrender of most of

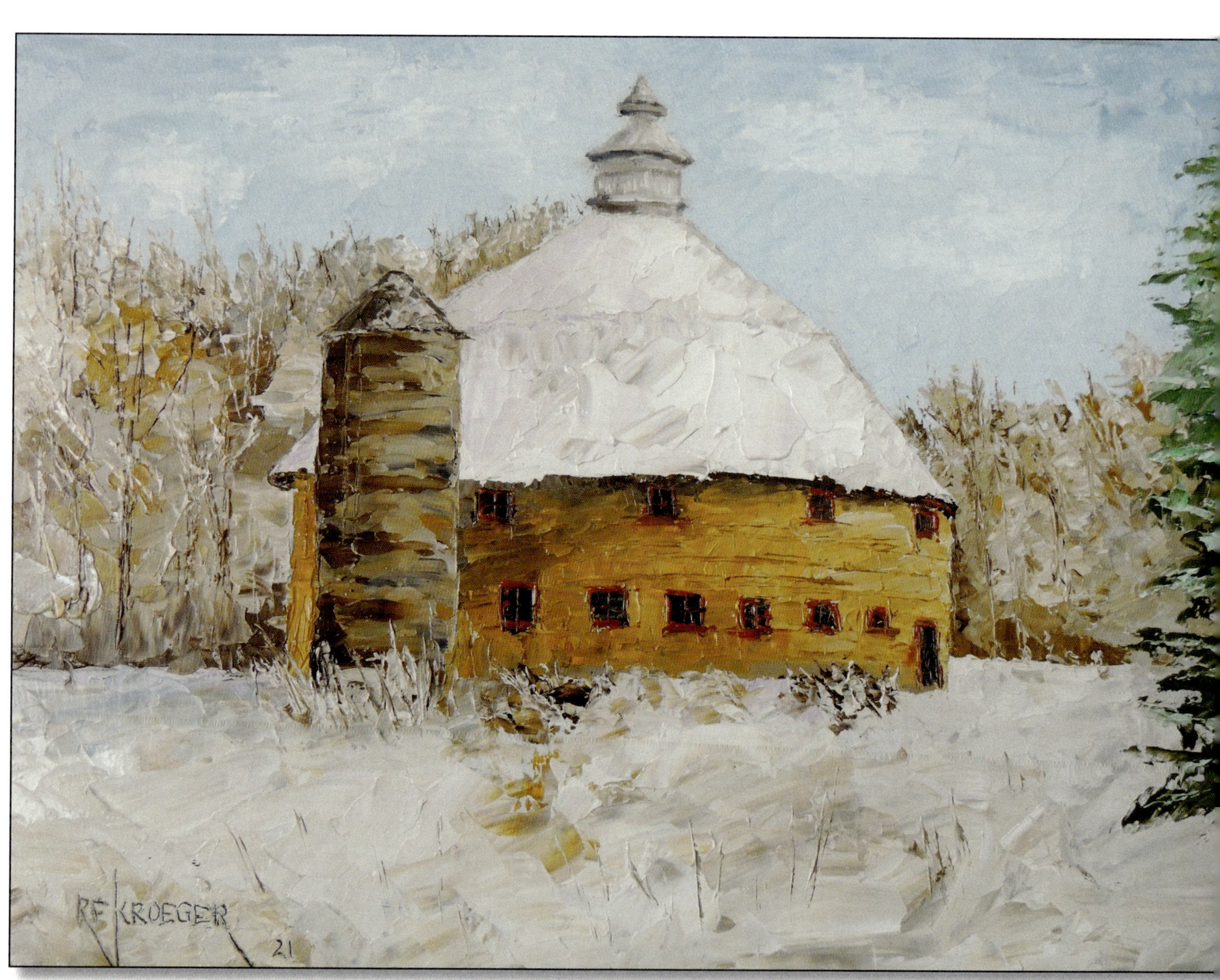

Cuba of the North

the Dakota bands. By late December the US Army had captured more than 1,000 Indians, who were kept in jails. After trials — and thanks to some clemency granted by President Lincoln — "only" 38 Dakota men were hanged, the largest one-day mass execution in America. By April of the next year, the government expelled the rest of the tribe from Minnesota to Nebraska and South Dakota.

Today the majority of the Santee live on reservations in Minnesota, Nebraska, South Dakota, North Dakota, and Canada. However, their legacy remains in this area: the name, Lake Park, comes from a Dakota phrase that means "where the prairies meet the waters."

Slowly, settlers moved in, bought land, built houses and barns, and began farming. In the late 1800s, Lake Park's founder, James Canfield, helped the town by securing a station on the Great Northern Railway, a line that stretched from St. Paul to Seattle, forming the northernmost section of the transcontinental railway. This provided jobs and stimulated growth, including lefse factories, which led to the area being known as the "Lefse Capital of the World." The factories continued their high production through the mid-1980s when a recession and the end of regular rail freight caused their demise.

Lefse, a traditional soft Norwegian flatbread, is usually made with potatoes and rolled on a large, flat griddle. At holidays Norwegian grandmothers would get out their rolling pins and make these treats for the family. When Norwegian immigrants left their country, they brought folded lefse to eat during the early part of their journey across the oceans. And when they began to populate the northern states of the Midwest, they introduced this tradition.

During World War I, the government encouraged Americans to grow and eat potatoes — since wheat was used to feed troops overseas. This patriotic duty made it even easier for Norwegians to consume one of their favorite dishes. Today, a factory in Rushford, Minnesota, Norsland Lefse, produces about a half million rounds of lefse each year and other smaller lefse factories dot the landscape throughout these northern states.

Whether this barn, which was built in 1916 and razed exactly a century later, ever stored potatoes may remain a mystery. From its appearance, thanks to a fine photo on the Dale Travis site, posted by John Roscoe, author of Minnesota's *Round Barns*, it may have been a dairy barn. Was it owned by Norwegians? Did they celebrate holidays with their traditional lefse? These questions may go unanswered but the beautiful snowcapped barn will be remembered in this painting and essay, a memorial to little Cuba of the North.

BENTON COUNTY

The Veterinarian

Before the first European settlers came, the land of present-day Benton County was home to the Sioux and Chippewa. Wild game and buffaloes were plentiful. Though skirmishes made pioneering risky, David Gilman established a trading post on land along the Mississippi River in 1848. Immigrants from Scandinavian countries, Germany, and Poland began arriving and by 1880 much of the land had been claimed by farmers. By the turn of the century, there were enough farmers to warrant a veterinarian.

One such animal doctor was Alphonse Cota, who also farmed. However, Al had a flair for being innovative and gave up his veterinarian practice in 1913 to pursue his real passion — construction. His theory was that a building made of concrete, though initially more expensive than wood, would pay dividends in the long run. He became a concrete contractor.

As his reputation spread among local farmers, he built foundations for barns and homes and eventually poured concrete silos, which were becoming popular in the early 20th century. As his business grew, he expanded into barns, beginning with these two circular ones on his own farm, which, he hoped, would advertise his services. Both have walls of reinforced concrete, highly unusual in circular barns.

He built the first barn on the westernmost section of his farm (on the right side of the painting) in 1921, at a time when round barn designs were falling out of favor throughout the Midwest. Measuring 60 feet in diameter, the barn's gambrel roof, originally covered with cedar shingles, surrounded a 35-foot concrete silo, which rose slightly above the roof line. Three doors and 18 evenly spaced windows provided some light, although the barn's interior had to be fairly dark. Hay was stored on the second level.

The barn on the left side of the painting — easternmost on the farm — was built in 1923, after his concrete business had become successful. This barn, a bank variety, though slightly smaller than its sister barn, had a 44-foot central silo.

Though only one other concrete round barn, attributed to Cota, still survives, in the 1920s Al Cota's concrete business must have been doing well — since he was able to hire and train several crews. Apparently a good businessman, he expanded his company through the Great Depression until his health deteriorated in the mid-1930s, forcing retirement. However, Al's crews continued erecting silos through the 1940s.

In 1982 the owners, Willard Lorette and Dennis and Mari Neis, listed the barns on the National Register, a recognition these unusual round barns deserved. The farm

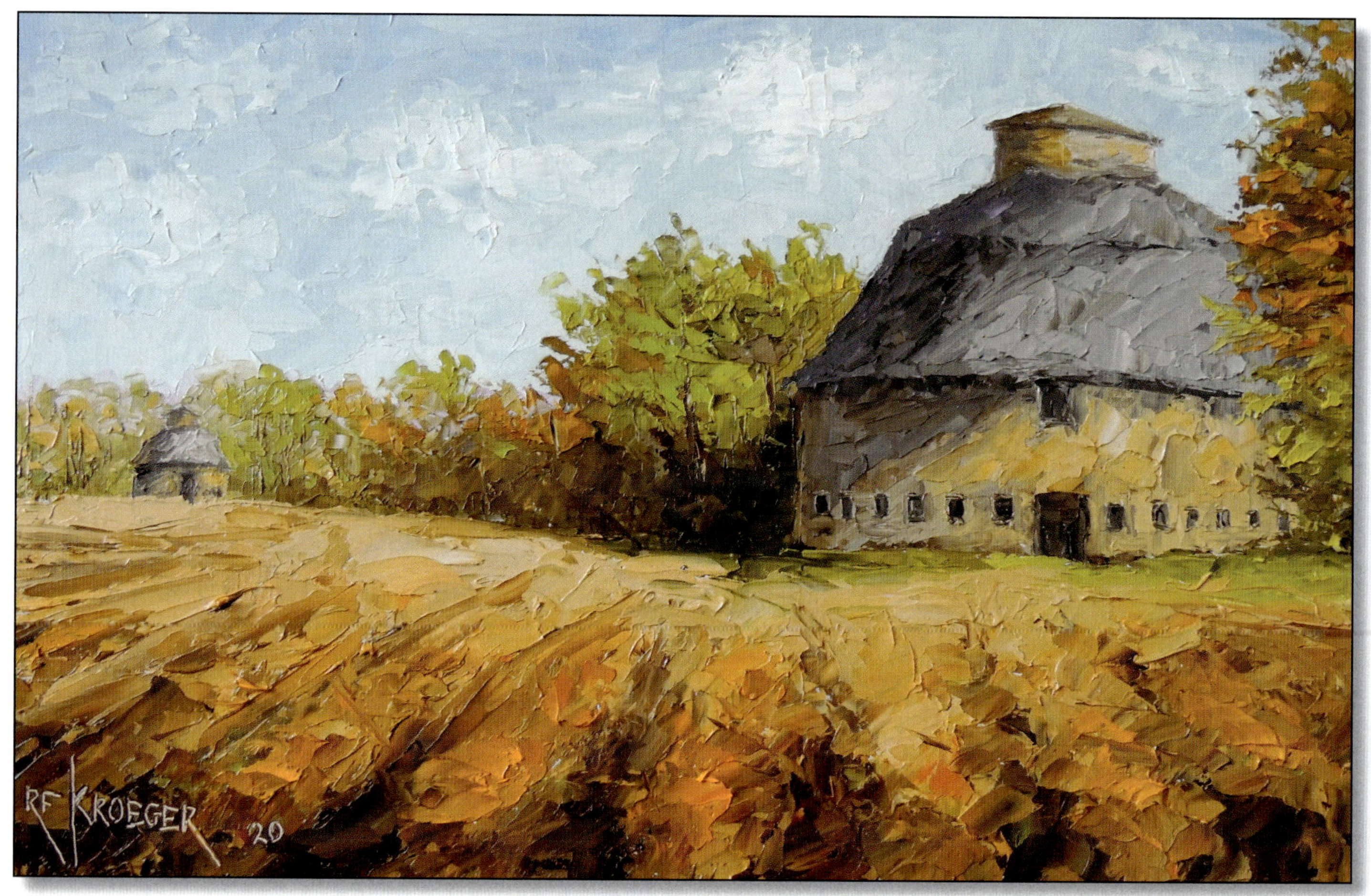

The Veterinarian

eventually split into two, with each owner keeping one of the Cota round barns.

One of them, Rising Moon Farm, owned the smaller barn, the one built in 1923. Catherine Friend, the owner, raised lambs, sheep, llamas, goats, steers, peacocks, ducks, and chickens — without the use of antibiotics or growth hormones. But after 24 years of farming, she decided to switch to writing and fiber art.

As long as the roofs get maintenance, these two concrete round barns should last many more years, a tribute to their builder, Dr. Al Cota, concrete contractor supreme, though he probably would want to also be remembered for his first occupation — a veterinarian.

STEARNS COUNTY

The Beginning

Just as "Granville Gray," an old deteriorating barn in Licking County, stimulated my Ohio Barn Project when I first laid eyes on it in 2012, likewise this barn inspired John Roscoe to research and write about round barns in his state, now recorded in *Minnesota's Round Barns*. The barn is located in central Minnesota in Sartell, a city unusual in that it straddles both sides of the Mississippi River.

The barn's story began when Peter Fasen built it in 1928, a feat recorded in a granite plaque embedded in the barn's cement wall. Peter apparently was a farmer of vision and wanted a barn that would endure the rigors of northern winters and the heat of summers, weather factors that take their toll on wood, especially barn siding placed horizontally on a round barn. So Peter chose cement. And he must have been an affluent farmer since depressed agricultural prices wreaked havoc on farming during the 1920s.

Though the barn has been abandoned, its cement walls have endured Minnesota's weather for nearly a century — as have the two Cota concrete round barns in nearby Benton County. In fact, these two barns might have been the motivation for Peter's choice of a round cement barn. All three have gambrel roofs and interior cement silos. At one time, stalls for dairy cows encircled the silo. Dairy farming played a major role in agriculture in Wisconsin and Minnesota, though the Great Depression created hardships for many farmers, beginning only a year after Peter built this barn.

Fifty years later — in 1978 — brothers Michael and Wilfred Weyer purchased the farm and continued raising beef cattle, keeping hay in the loft and silage in the silo. However, they gave up farming in 1993 and stopped using

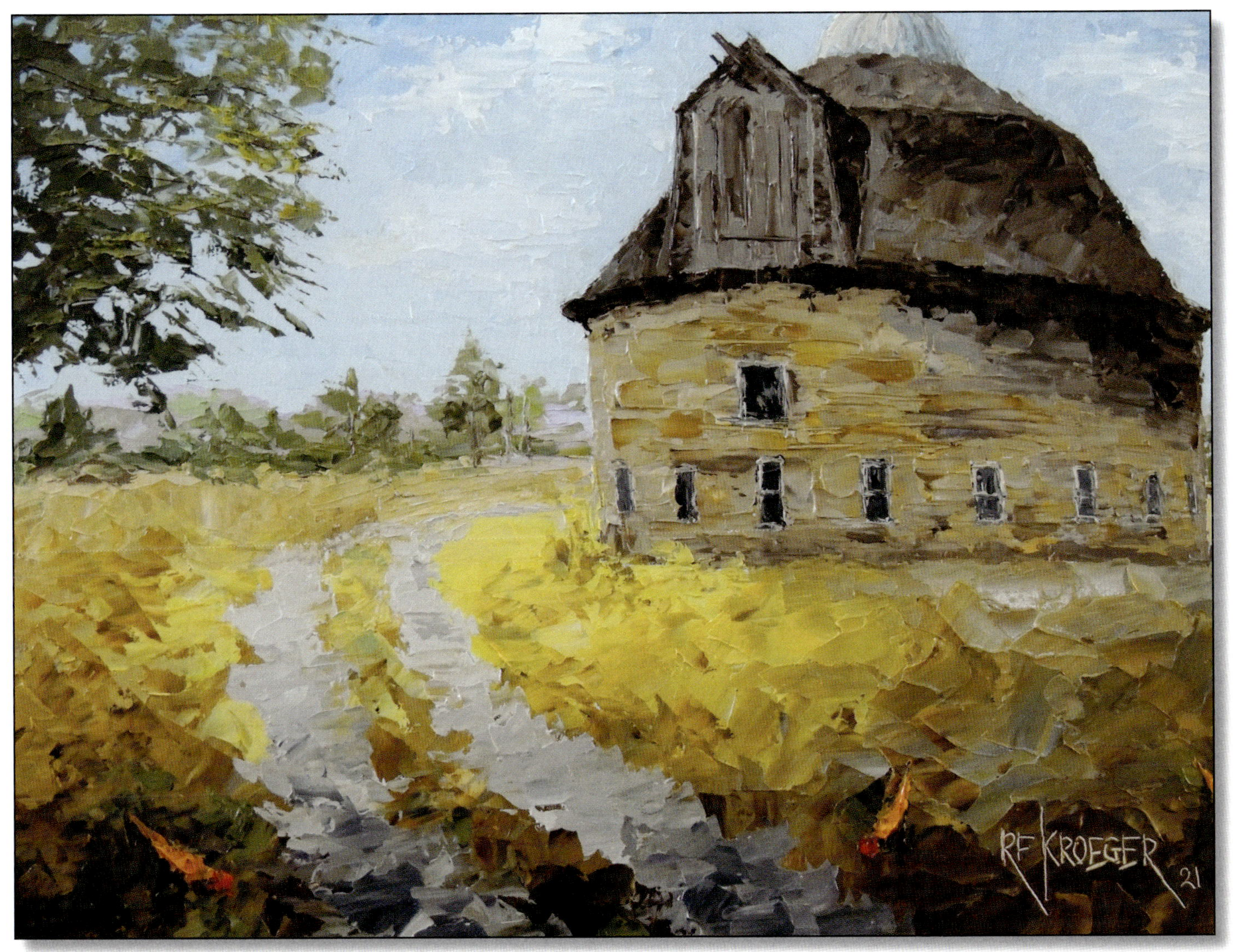

The Beginning

the barn. At one time, farm fields surrounded the barn, but now suburban sprawl is slowly creeping in.

The Minnesota Preservation Alliance placed the barn on its 2006 "Ten Most Endangered Sites List" and around 2009, when Mr. Roscoe saw this barn, local citizens made plans to save it and repurpose it into a historical center. However, publicity about this effort failed to attract attention and no one offered to buy the barn from the Weyers. These days, homes and businesses continue to encroach on the barn and, even though it may eventually be demolished, it served a purpose in giving birth to a book on historic barns. For John Roscoe, it was the beginning.

IOWA

Like Indiana, Illinois, and Wisconsin, Iowa is a state where round barn building took off. In his book, *Without Right Angles — The Round Barns of Iowa*, author Lowell J. Soike, found 160 round barns in his 1978 survey — with 127 still existing then. In the ensuing 50 years, many have collapsed, burned, or been dismantled, the fate of many old barns. What's interesting is that Iowa, unlike Wisconsin (the leader in still existing round barns with 180) was predominantly a corn state, not dairy, which the round barns were designed for.

Regardless, Iowa has many unique round barns and its Iowa Barn Foundation, established in 1997, is dedicated to preserving these American treasures.

FAYETTE COUNTY

Arlington's Aristocrat

If the definition of aristocracy — including such words as rank, elite, superior, nobility — would apply to barns, then this one would qualify, hands down. Its striking tiled central silo extends well above its low-pitched roof, which gives it a spectacular appearance, especially when silhouetted

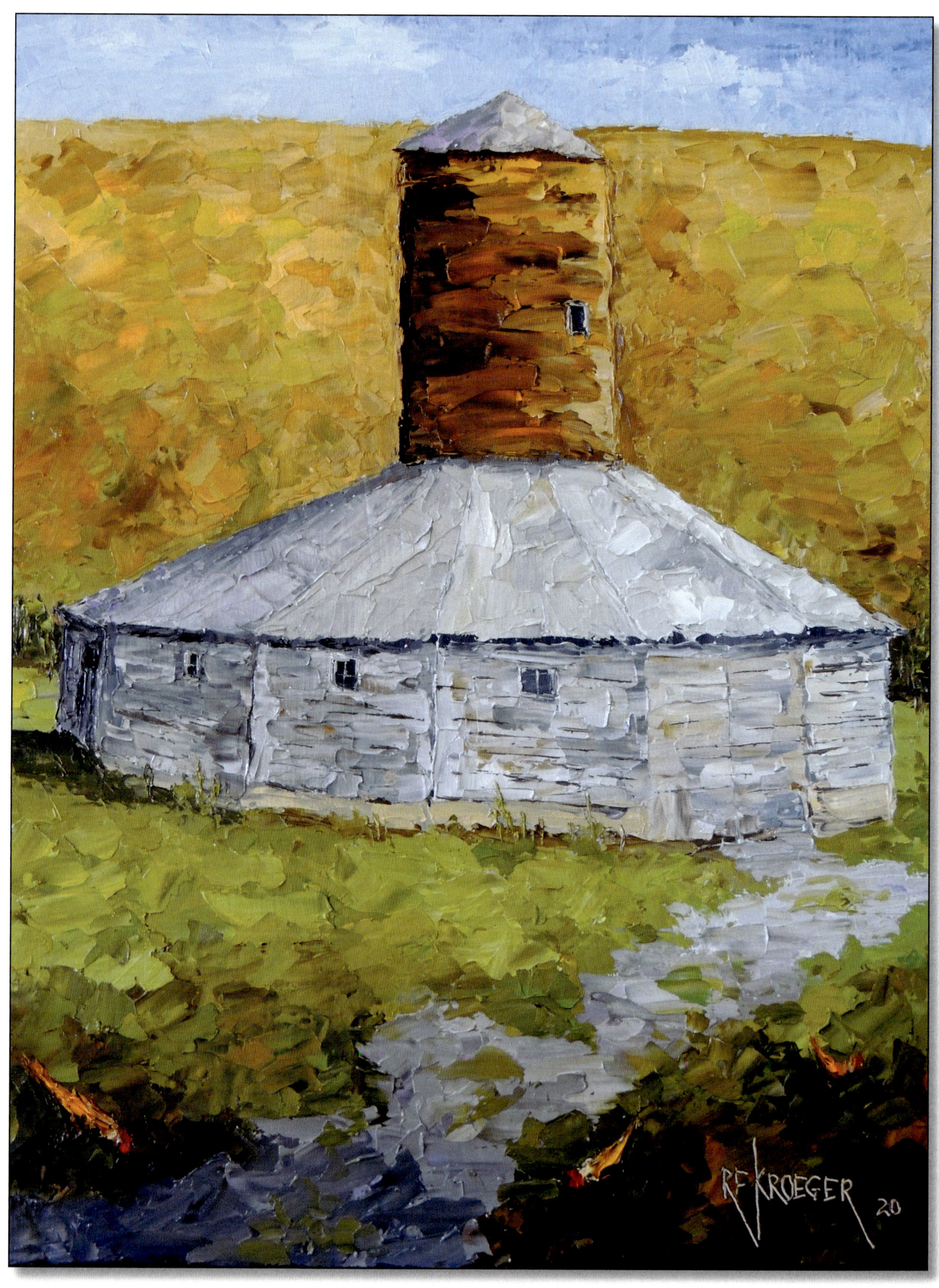

Arlington's Aristocrat

against a wide field of golden corn. Built in 1906 by owner August Nus near the little village of Arlington, Fayette County, the 12-sided barn may have influenced other Iowa farmers to build similar prairie styled barns since it was the first of this type in Iowa.

The county, one of Iowa's 99, takes its name from the Marquis de Lafayette, a French aristocrat, aptly enough, whose actual name was La Fayette. Commissioned as an officer at 13, not unusual in wealthy families, he felt that the American cause was heroic and in 1777, seeking fame and action, he decided to fight for the colonies. Promoted to a major general at 19 by the young congress — which had scant funds — Lafayette used family money to buy a ship to transport himself and other volunteers across the ocean. After three years of fighting, he returned to France to beg the king for more troops, which he granted. The 4,000 additional French soldiers turned the tide of the war and in 1781 Washington put Lafayette in charge of the American army that cornered Cornwallis at Yorktown, culminating in an American victory.

But why did August Nus decide on this design? Did he want others to take notice of his imagination? Or did his dairy herd require a large silo (14-foot diameter) for its feed? The size of the barn — only 60 feet — suggests a modest dairy operation, which lends credence to the first assumption: Mr. Nus was affluent enough to build this eye-catcher and wanted to leave his mark. In retrospect, he was successful when the barn became listed on the National Register in 1986. In choosing a composition, I decided to omit the other farm buildings and the windmill, instead leaving the barn to speak for itself — in front of an endless field of corn.

Although the barn will never garner attention from the Queen of England and although it will never be given the title of knight, duke, earl, or lord, it's just as much an aristocrat as was the young French general who helped the colonies gain their independence and whose name is remembered in this county.

VAN BUREN COUNTY

Hog Heaven

Long after Brigham Young and his wagon trains crossed through Van Buren County in 1846, a farmer in Cantril started raising hogs. And he was good at it — so good that his reputation as a breeder and salesman had spread far and wide, convincing him to build a barn to conduct his auctions, which he did in 1918.

Frank Silver hired Alva Hunt of nearby Pulaski to design and build a circular barn. Hunt, who was a farmer in 1900 — according to census documents — a carpenter in 1910, a house carpenter in 1920, and a building contractor in 1930, clearly had a flair for construction, evident in this impressive barn with its 12 dormers jutting out of two floors, its attractive tile siding, and a large metal ventilator capping the roof. Though it had a diameter of only 50 feet, the barn's first floor was large enough to hold Frank's office, an 8x8-foot show ring, and bleachers to seat over 700, many of whom traveled considerable distances. And, since the twice-a-year hog auctions would last several days (one lasted three months), Frank added eight guest rooms on the second floor. The top floor was reserved for playing cards, drinking, and socializing. In the basement, Alva included an electrical plant, a rarity since many farmhouses, let alone barns, did not have electricity in 1918. He also included a kitchen, dining room, pantry, and fruit cellar. The result, a barn as stylish as it was functional, was reflected in its cost of $20,000, a huge amount in 1918.

It did not, however, hold the hogs, who were kept outside, where they were housed and fed. Frank apparently knew his business, operating the largest Hampshire hog farm in America, in one year raising 1,500 animals and auctioning them twice a year.

Try to imagine the scene. The bleachers were filled with hundreds of buyers, all trying to impress the other with their bids as they examined one hog after another, which were brought in through the wide double doors. Were drinks provided or was it a bring-your-own party? Did the prices escalate in proportion to the amount of alcohol consumed? Perhaps this happened when one prize hog sold for $5,000, another giant sum in the early 1920s. Now, that's a lot of bacon!

In 1923 the sales included six grand champions, 12 champions, and 59 firsts. Some of the famous hogs merited names, such as Lookout Lad and Lieutenant Wickware, honors similar to what another round barn owner bestowed on her "tuxedo pigs." Edith Kuykendall of Hampshire County, West Virginia, imagined that her hogs, dressed smartly in black and white, to be of noble English descent and gave them names such as Sir Walter Raleigh, Jane Eyre, David Copperfield, Winston Churchill, and Lord Byron. After all, the Hampshires aren't just any breed of hogs.

However, the economic downturn of lowered farm prices and a cholera outbreak hit hard, forcing Silver to end the business, sell the farm, and leave town in 1926. Rumor has it that the new owners turned the barn into a private club, which operated as a "speakeasy" during the era of prohibition. However, the hogs couldn't frolic with the party goers; they were long gone.

In 1986 the barn, named the Wickfield Sales Pavilion, was added, with several other round barns in Iowa, to the National Register, recognizing its unique design and historical

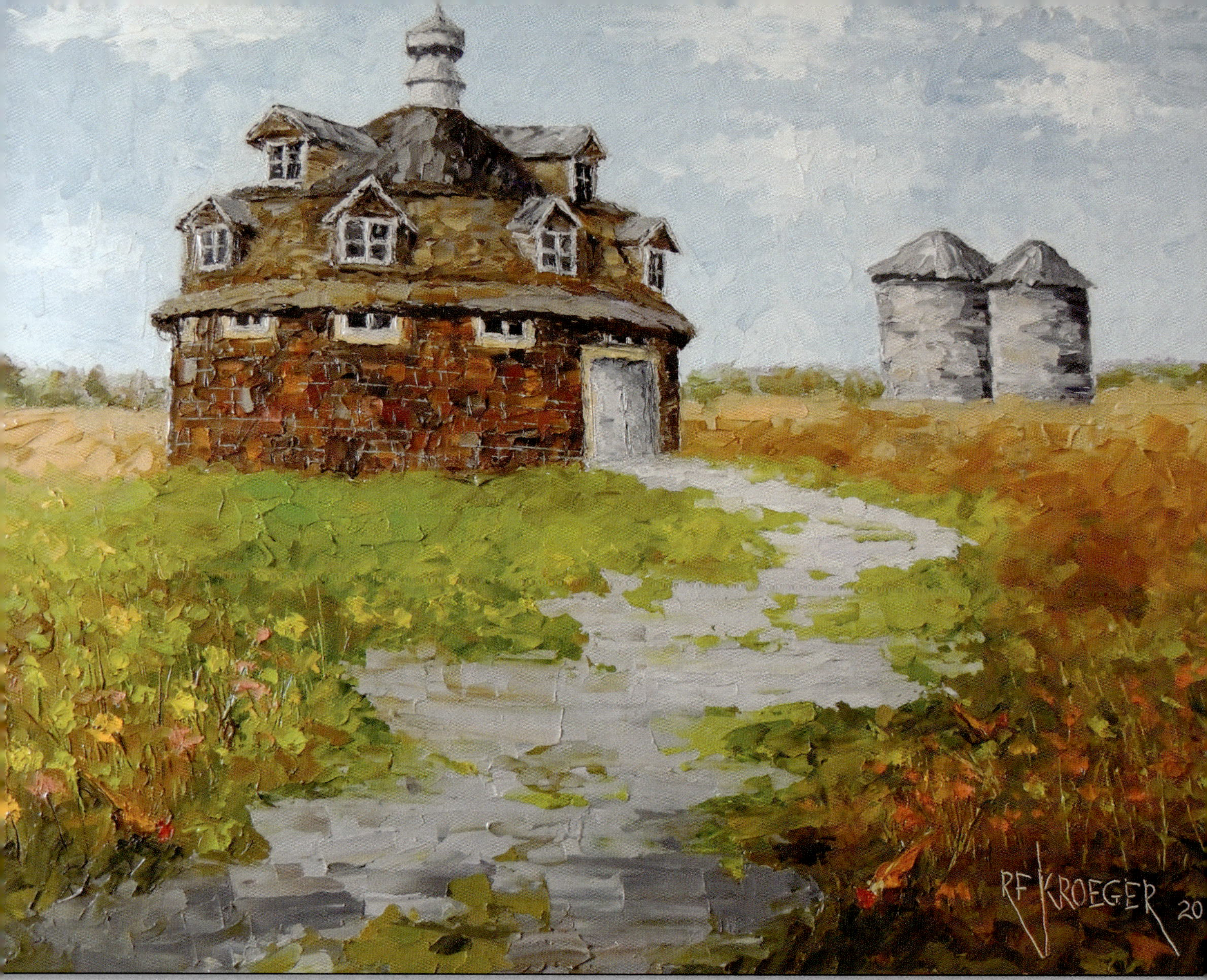

Hog Heaven

importance. In a conversation with 82-year-old Max Wellborn, former president of the local historical society, he explained that his dad worked as a driver to transport the hogs to shipping companies and that his uncle and aunt took care of the cooking in the barn's kitchen. When the barn began to deteriorate, Max and his group successfully applied for grants and raised over $130,000 to restore the barn.

Current owners Jack and Linda Sharp put the barn up for sale in 2021. Its multi-colored terra cotta hollow tile still glistens in sunshine, its distinctive dormers dramatically stand out, and the giant metal aerator sits safely on top, all waiting for a buyer, hoping that the new owner will decide to preserve it and turn it into a museum, something it richly deserves — a page in agricultural history. In fact, according to locals, one hog, an illustrious champion, must have impressed Frank so much that each day he made sure that the hog was taken to the basement for a shower. Truly, for this champion at least, this barn was indeed "hog heaven."

JACKSON COUNTY

A Beautiful View

Octagonal barns built in 1921 weren't plentiful, especially in Iowa, a state where the circular shape became the most popular round barn type after the turn of the century. One of only four such barns with a flattish roof and central projecting silo in the state, this is the last round barn that remains in Jackson County. The county took its name from President Andrew Jackson in 1837, his final year of the presidency. Nine years later Iowa gained statehood.

The county is small, with a population of 20,000, and mostly rural. Its second largest city, Bellevue, where the barn sits, was named by French trappers — travelling up and down the adjacent Mississippi River — by combining two words, belle (beautiful) and vue (sight). Their assessment was correct since the city lies in between two tall bluffs, affording scenic views, thanks to this land being the southernmost part of the Driftless Region, an area that the last ice age missed, explaining the many tall ridges and deep canyons.

With a population of 2,000, Bellevue is tiny, just like its county, and, as so many small rural villages, it has tried to reinvent itself to stimulate its economy. In a brainstorming session years ago, a few dozen residents gathered to figure out what would attract visitors. They came from diverse ways of life: farmers, business owners, and 4-H and FFA high school students. Some came from a U-pick apple orchard, one from a winery, one raised organic beef, another farmed strawberries, and yet another kept bees, selling honey and beeswax.

An expert, affiliated with Iowa State University Extension, hosted the day-long event by telling her story. In the early 1980s she and her husband farmed, raising hogs and growing corn, and were doing well until the farm crisis hit. They lost everything. Switching to a job in her town, she eventually became interested in helping others combine farm life with economic success. She commented that, even though Bellevue sits on the mighty Mississippi and still has one of its historic locks, which attracts visitors in the summer, and even though bald eagles fish in the wintry river, the economy sputters from October through May. The expert's answer was agritourism.

As she explained, it's a rising trend and one that has grown from $3,000 per farm in 2007 to $950 million nationwide in 2017. Besides setting up petting "zoos" and corn mazes, farmers with old barns, especially unique round ones, can invite visitors for a tour back into history. This

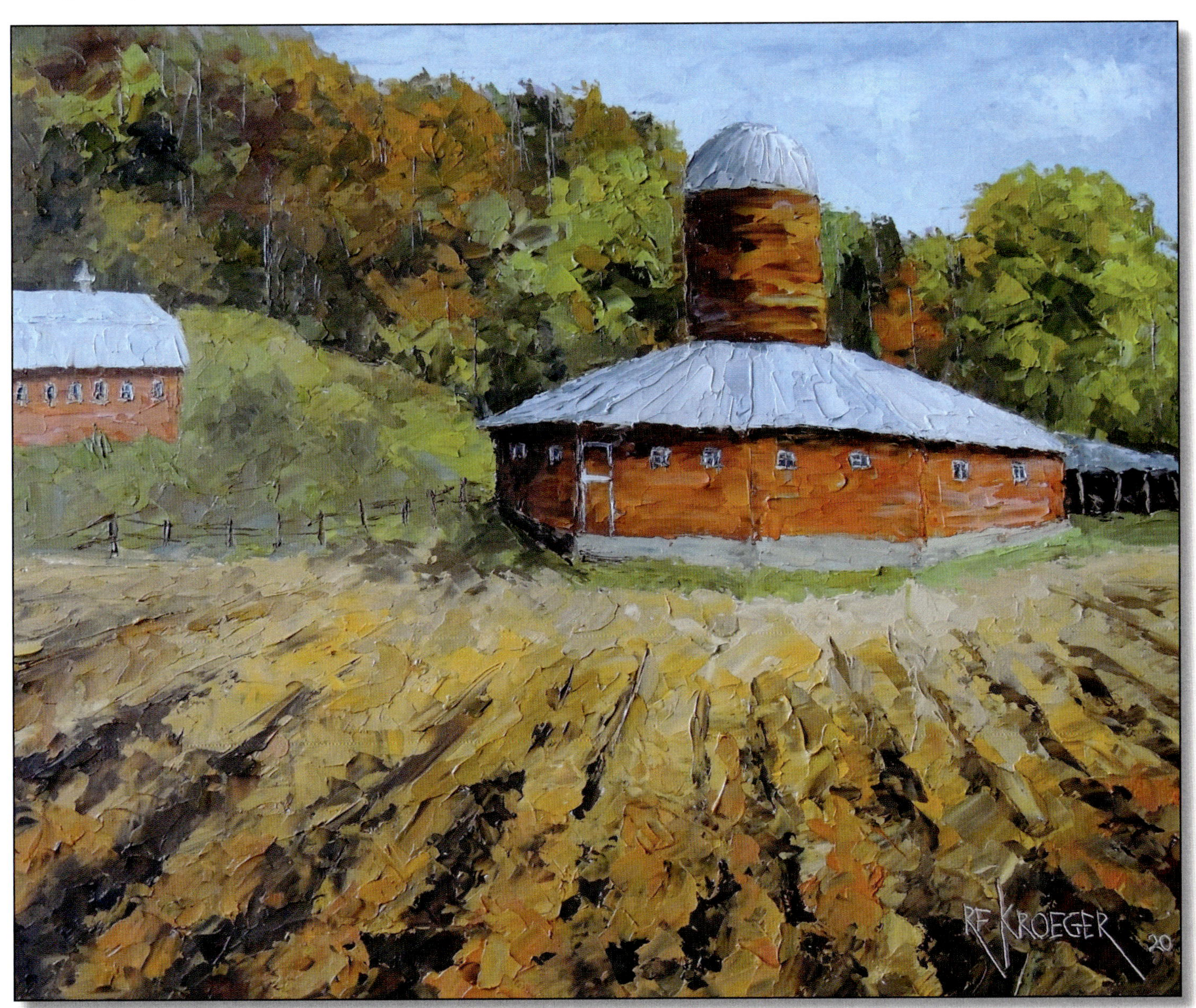

A Beautiful View

barn is no exception. And, while stepping inside an old timber-framed conventional barn — one with mortise and tenon joints secured with wooden pegs — never fails to inspire, setting foot inside a round barn and looking up into the magical roof and central silo is a wonder that few ever get to experience.

Entered into the National Register in 1986, this barn celebrated its centenary in 2021, which brings up another piece of history. By 1921 — when the barn was built — many articles had been published that discredited the so-called advantages of round barns. Regardless, it was built for a farmer named Dyas by a carpenter named Stuart and survived both the farm crisis of the 1920s and the Great Depression of the 1930s. A metal roof has protected its central wood stave silo, around which are arranged pie-shaped animal stalls. The sides have also been covered with metal, thanks to preservation-minded owners. Strangely, even though the barn has eight sides, it's known by two names: the Dyas Hexagonal Barn and the Dyas Octagonal Barn. Go figure. Also, three other round barns were also built on this farm, which is just waiting to be discovered by city-dwellers. Such a beautiful sight!

MISSOURI

GREENE COUNTY

Gilmore's Gem

Stone barns are rare and stone circular barns such as the Shaker barn in Massachusetts are even more unique. But, just as remarkable are the octagonal stone barns, such as this one, another in Clark County, Ohio, and a third in Sheridan County, Wyoming. Unlike their wooden compatriots, stone barns, if maintained, can resist natural disasters such as wind, snow, and fire (excluding the roof). They're the rocks of Gibraltar.

Located in the quiet city of Ash Grove — named for local ash trees — this round barn was built around 1899, a time when one of its 26-year-old residents, the infamous Ma Barker, born here as Arizona Barker in 1873, was raising a family of notorious criminals. She and her husband George had four sons — Herman, Lloyd, Arthur, and Fred, all of whom waffled between time in penitentiaries, robbing banks, kidnapping the wealthy for ransom, and killing police officers. While father George didn't condone their wicked ways and eventually left his family, Ma Barker always looked the other way as her sons moved throughout the Midwest, leaving a trail of crimes and blood.

She earned such a reputation as a crime boss that J. Edgar Hoover described her as "the most vicious, dangerous, and resourceful criminal brain of the last decade," quite a comment from the director of the FBI, who led the bureau from 1924 to 1972.

Finally, the end came in 1935 when the FBI tracked down Ma and her son Fred, together with the Karpis gang, in a house in rural Florida. When the agents ordered them to surrender, Fred opened fire. Then, after an intense shootout lasting hours — one that attracted locals, who watched and even held picnics during the fire fight — the gunfire from the house finally stopped and, upon inspection, both Fred and Ma Barker were dead (other members of the gang had fled). Though Fred's body was riddled with bullets, Ma died from a single bullet wound — with a Tommy gun lying in her hands. At 61, her days had ended, earning her a place in history — a rare female crime matriarch in an era when male figures dominated the underworld, such as Al Capone, Bugs Moran, John Dillinger, Baby Face Nelson, Pretty Boy Floyd, and Machine Gun Kelly. All this happened during the Great Depression while the Gilmores were scratching out a living on their Missouri farm.

Their story, a bit less sensational than that of Ma Barker and sons, began when James A. Gilmore and his wife moved here — like many other families did from Tennessee — and bought a tract of land in 1835, only five years after the Delaware, Kickapoo, and Osage Indians had been removed to reservations further westwards. Greene County and the Ozarks were now open for settlement.

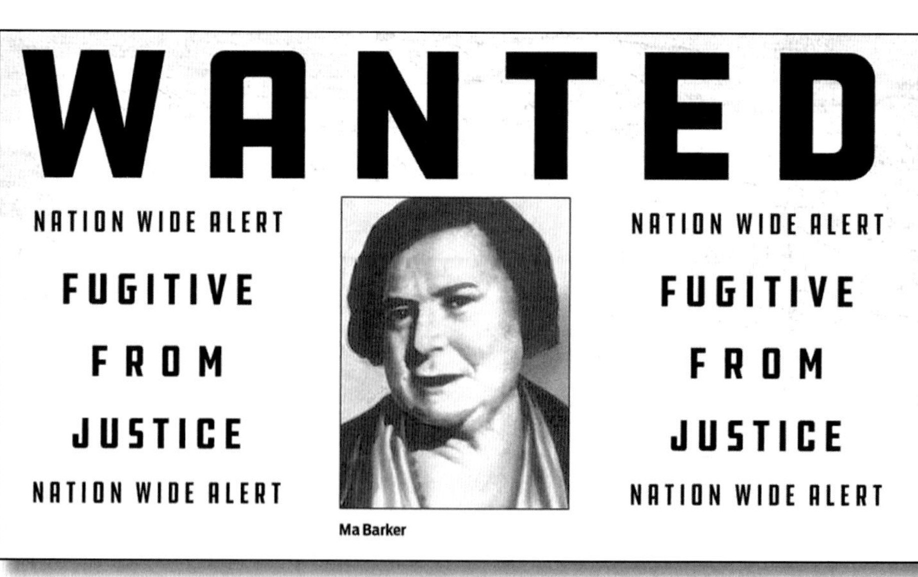

Ma Barker wanted poster. Courtesy, White Bear Lake Historical Society, Minnesota

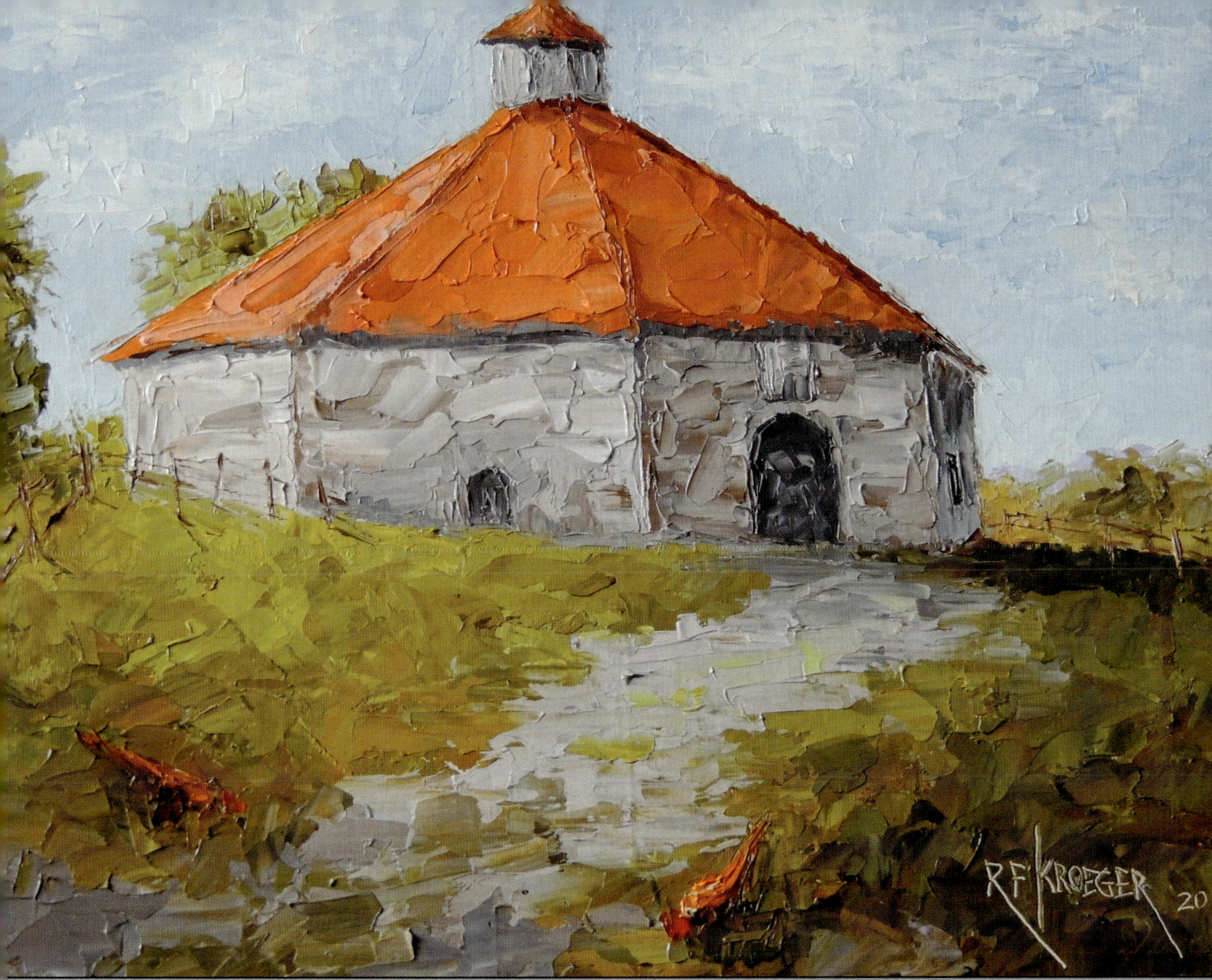

Gilmore's Gem

James bought 40 acres, paying $1.25 an acre to the government, now determined to speed development of these new lands. One of their sons, James Kannon, bought land from his parents in 1849, paying $10 per acre, and began farming, which proved successful enough for him to pay $720 in 1871 to buy more acreage from the Atlantic and Pacific Railroad, which included the land where this barn would be built. James and his wife raised 10 children and in 1896 he sold 490 acres to one of them, Francis, whose purchase included the barn site.

According to a history of Greene County in 1883, James Kannon Gilmore "owned 700 acres and was one of the most substantial citizens of Greene county." However, his son Francis was different and was described as "a dreamer," according to his family, and restless, wanting to try new things. Perhaps his boredom with the mundane routines of farming prompted him to experiment with the octagonal barn.

Francis may have heard about — or even seen — another large stone octagonal barn, one with a formed concrete foundation and a rubblestone first story. This one, built around the same time, was located near Bois d'Arc, about five miles south of the Gilmores. It burned in 1988 and was not restored.

In 1899, about when they built the barn, James, aged 72, and 32-year-old Francis farmed together in a de facto partnership, as a 1904 plat map shows. They raised cattle and stored corn, hay, a perhaps other crops in the barn. The Gilmores continued to use the barn and farm the land through the Great Depression until new owners took over. James and Ida Gold sold it in 1993 to the McGilvrey family, who continued farming. They also secured a listing on the National Register in 1994. Photos taken in 2002 by Jerry Freeze showed the roof and cupola intact, though the barn appeared unoccupied.

Although Francis, who presumably convinced his father to consent to a round barn, was considered a dreamer, he was intelligent enough to build this barn into a bank of solid limestone, which acted as a perfect foundation and was perhaps where the stone was quarried for the barn's walls. With a diameter of 70 feet, it was — and still is — the largest polygonal barn in the state and its two-foot-thick limestone walls continue to defy the ravages of Mother Nature.

The second floor opened to the ground level on the upper side of the bank and the first floor opened to the lower side, both doors having a stone arch form, which displayed skills of the stonemason. Though the beams were sawmill-cut, they were connected by mortise and tenon joints and wooden pegs, a transition from hand-hewn timber framing to dimensional lumber construction. Instead of a silo (which had yet to become popular), a central 12-foot-wide octagonal corn crib stored ear corn and rose from the ground floor to the third level. Also on the ground floor were eight livestock bays, five of which were enclosed.

Wagons, full of hay or corn, could enter through the second story doorway, its floor built with two-inch thick oak planks. Here the crops were unloaded, where they could be stored or moved to the third-floor hay mow. Dr. Robert Gilmore, grandson of Francis, reported that the mow held as many as 6,000 bales of alfalfa. On this top floor, the octagonal cupola provided both ventilation and light.

An octagonal trough, 30 inches high and four feet wide, sat just outside the central corn crib, which, with approximately 8,000 square feet of storage space, could hold over 3,000 bushels of corn, more than enough for winter feeding, though winters were usually mild in the Ozarks. All in all, the dream of Francis culminated with a barn for the ages, one that now has passed the century mark and may pass many more.

Farming had stopped by 2002 and the barn received little attention. However, thanks to some enterprising and historically minded entrepreneurs, the Dean family, the barn was repurposed, serving as an event center and known on Facebook as The Round Barn on Clear Creek, which has resumed pricing in 2022, after recovering from the COVID pandemic.

New wooden doors now grace both entrances and the upper level has a wooden façade over the limestone walls. Inside, a sparkling wood floor reflects shimmering lighting throughout, highlighting the magnificent struts that support the roof. Wedding and reunions have been held here, proving that old barns, like old dogs, can learn new tricks, even though they don't include housing livestock and crops. Gilmore's gem continues to sparkle in Greene County.

11. WEST

NORTH DAKOTA

EDDY COUNTY

The Marriage Barn

Denise Reis, who purchased the farm and this octagonal barn in 1981 with her husband Ken, related a story that years ago a physician, dressed in her wedding dress, visited the barn with a photographer. Under the impression that this was a "marriage" barn, she wanted her wedding photos taken here. Not quite right. Yes, the marriage part is correct but it refers to Sylvanus Marriage, the farmer who had it built in 1901. Hopefully, doc wasn't too disappointed.

It's unknown if this octagon replaced earlier barns, as happened in the case of New York's Elliot Stewart, who started this trend in the 1870s, erecting an octagonal barn, after not one, but four, of his conventional barns burned. Whether Mr. Marriage built the barn himself or hired a carpenter also remains a mystery, though, since he was a stonemason, he probably laid the original cut stone foundation. Not much is known about the original construction.

Most round barns were built for dairy cows and this one, with a diameter of 64 feet and with eight sides of 29 feet each, was large enough to service a small herd, house the hay, and provide enough milk and dairy for sales. However,

Below: *The Marriage Barn*

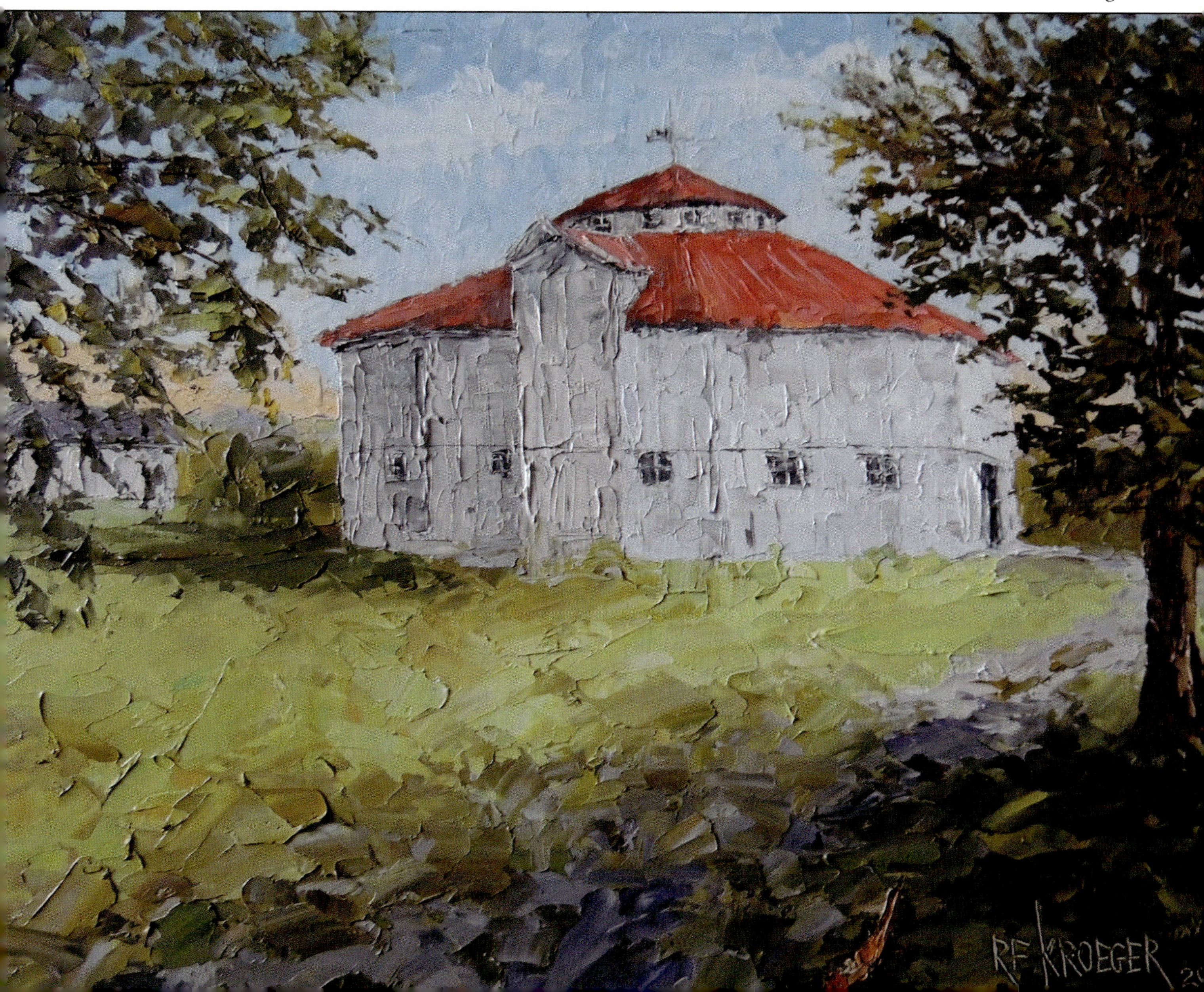

according to elderly locals, there were no stanchions for cows, suggesting that Sylvanus used the barn for raising horses. A sliding carrier was suspended from a track above the feed trough, allowing all the animals to be fed with minimal effort. The distinctive gable-roofed haymow and the octagonal cupola, containing three-over-three fixed pane windows, set this barn apart from others nearby. In fact, the 1919 Jens Myhre barn, another round barn built in Eddy County, was a plain Jane, when compared to this one, even though it was probably more expensive to build, due to its domed gambrel roof and circular wood design.

The barn's unique look might have been the main reason why Albert Haas bought the Marriage farm in 1946 since being here might have worked as therapy for him — a retreat away from a busy dealership in New Rockford. But the barn needed help. By 1952 the stone foundation had shifted and, badly deteriorated, needed replacement. Even though Mr. Haas didn't farm and didn't house livestock or crops in the barn, he must have been attached to it, as shown by his efforts — pouring a new concrete foundation and adding wooden boards over it. In the early 1970s, he covered a major part of the barn with metal siding to protect the wood underneath, which, after 70 years, had begun warping. Winters in North Dakota are not kind to wooden barns.

Ken Reis grew up one mile north of this barn and, in 1981, he and Denise became its new owners, returning the 230 acres to farmland. They raised cattle, corn, soybeans, wheat, and oats, and brought the barn back to life. In 1986 the state historical society secured a listing for it on the National Register, elevating its prestige and attracting visitors.

Denise and Ken must have also had a sense of historic preservation, as they replaced the shingled roof with a bright red one, further ensuring a long life for the barn, while keeping its original configuration. The cupola, topped with a Black Angus standing on a weathervane, looks brand new. Thanks to a photo reference from Denise, the painting has two tall trees to frame the barn, now in the hands of their daughter Jenna Helseth and her husband Brent, who purchased the farm in 2020. With good fortune and responsible maintenance, the "Marriage barn" will continue to serve for many years to come.

DICKEY COUNTY

Patterson Land

This barn collapsed between 2006 and 2009, as reported by the state historical society from their observations of aerial views. It was located near Oakes, a "town on the move," according to the city's website. Founded in 1886, it now numbers roughly 1,800 residents and it's still primarily agricultural, producing corn and soybeans. Its website continues, "Oakes is proud to have not one but two 110-car elevator facilities." And it also mentions several dining options: American Legion (evening meals and pub grub), Tornado Stop, The Last Shot Bar & Grill, Angry Beaver Lodge, B&B Gardens and its expresso coffee bar, Circle R and its pizza, Donna's Diner, Casey's General Store with "easy access for trucks and semis," Northside Treats & Eats, Sweets 'N Stories, and a bit further away — The Ranch House and Ludden Tavern. For a population of under 2,000 that's a lot of dining choices and it's truly Americana at its best. Also, it was once the location of one of North Dakota's most interesting octagonal barns ... with an equally compelling story, which began with the formation of the Patterson Land Company on November 14, 1905.

Four Patterson brothers, traveling westwards towards Bismarck, North Dakota, stopped at a country store in Mankato, Minnesota. The brothers, telling stories that evening around a potbelly stove, met two sons of the store's owner, Earnest Duemeland. George and Henry, recent graduates of Mankato Business College, were looking for jobs and the Pattersons asked them if they'd like to sell land in Bismarck.

Indeed, they were interested in going to Bismarck, but for different reasons. Henry, like his father, wanted to run a general store and so he started one on Sixth and Main Streets, selling supplies to settlers. George, on the other hand, saw opportunity in real estate but demanded a percentage of the Patterson Land Company. He received 20 out of 1,820 shares and was put in charge of land sales when the Pattersons traveled eastwards, presumably to advertise their company. Many German and Scandinavian immigrants moved here, enticed by cheap land, thanks to the Homestead Act of 1862, but wanted more than the 160-acre allotment. The Patterson Land Company had a lot of land to offer and the price was right. And these northern Europeans could handle the cold winters of North Dakota.

The third generation to own the company, 79-year-old Skip Duemeland, reported in an email in 2021 that his ancestors had acquired 1.6 million acres between Bismark and Jamestown, north and south of the Northern Pacific railroad line in the early 20th century. For ten cents down and a dollar per acre, they bought this gigantic plot of land, buying it in squares in a checkerboard pattern. Although his family did not build this barn, Skip suggested that one of their farm buyers did.

However, the Great Depression took its toll and the land company lost much of its acreage to banks. Eventually it

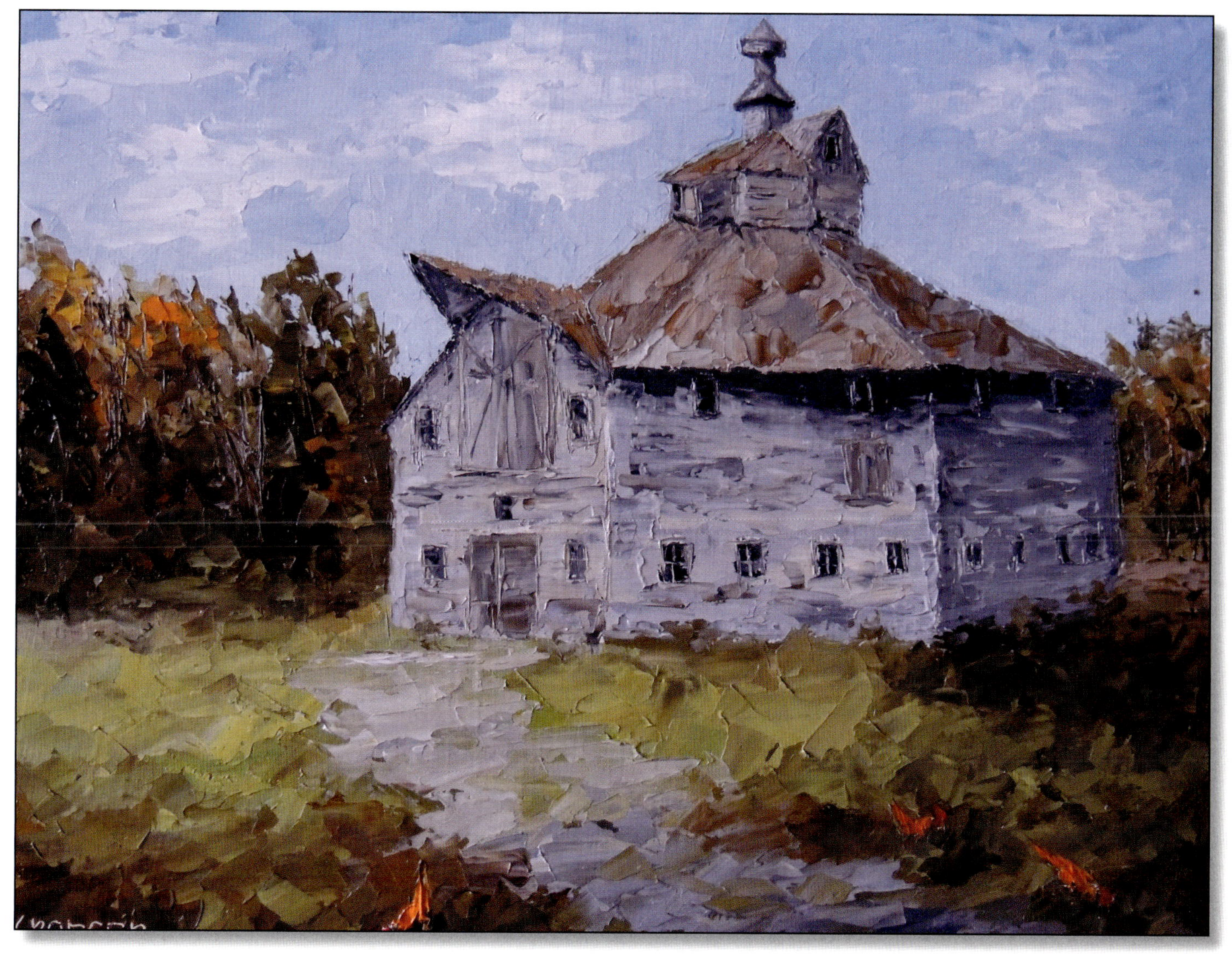

Patterson Land

recovered, bought back its land for four dollars an acre, and resumed sales. Then World War II intervened, and sales plummeted again as many young men left the state to serve their country. During these years the company accepted barter payments: chickens, cows, or hogs. Times were so hard that the Pattersons wanted out of the land business and offered to sell all their shares. George Duemeland and his son Lorin scraped together all the cash they could and bought the company, paying about $20 a share. By 1987 nearly 70 percent of the ranch lands had been sold.

Today, the fourth generation of Duemelands is part of the company. Lorin's son Skip, who can recall making many trips selling land with his grandfather, serves as CEO and his daughter Jill and her husband Aron Stenberg have become senior associates of Deumelands Commercial, a realty and investment firm that evolved from the Patterson Land Company.

The barn, built in 1905, was magnificent, although why the farmer chose an octagonal shape may remain a mystery. Could he have been aware of the F. William Boettcher round barn, designed with a three-pitch gambrel roof by Indiana's Benton Steele and built by his carpenter Horace Duncan in 1902? This was Duncan's first solo job, and was located in Emmons County, only a short distance from the Oakes area. There may have been others nearby, as well, which are now lost to antiquity. Why octagonal instead of circular? Perhaps the builder realized that the former design would be easier less and expensive to construct.

A hayhood, common in barns of the West but rare in Ohio barns, protruded from large doors to the haymow. A central wooden silo supported the roof and ascended into a classic octagonal cupola, pointing south. Numerous windows allowed light to enter and a metal ventilator provided needed air circulation, which was adequate since the barn had only a 58-foot diameter.

Thanks to a photo, taken in the 1980s and provided by the State Historical Society of North Dakota, I was able to preserve the memory of this barn in a painting.

The crowning glory was that the barn was included in the National Register in 1986. Sadly, only 20 years later, it had collapsed, ending another page in the history of round barns, though it provided a glimpse into an early land baron, the Patterson Land Company, and the many European immigrants who settled here.

SOUTH DAKOTA

DEUEL COUNTY

All the Way from Norway

Scandinavian immigrants preferred land with a climate like that of their homeland — with cold winters and lots of snow. Many chose the upper Midwest, stretching from Wisconsin to North Dakota. Norwegians, in particular, settled in the Dakota Territory, especially after the treaty with the Yankton Sioux, signed in July, 1859. More from Norway followed 10 years later, once their relatives told them the land was safe and that such a move would lead to a better life. One immigrant, Jacob S. Deuel, settled here and had the distinction of having the county named after him.

In 1862 it was land of the buffalo and the Indian. And these Norwegians were a hardy lot, just like the pioneers in the plains of Nebraska and Kansas, often living in sod houses or small 10x10-foot dug outs, which were cut into a hillside. On the Gary Historical Association's site, Marietta Thomas wrote, "My father came in the spring of 1879 to take up his claim where my brother and sister still live. He built a little claim shanty, 16x24 feet sitting on large rocks for a foundation, put up a sod barn, dug a well by hand, broke up some land and went back to Minnesota for the winter. The next spring he brought his wife and two small daughters back to the wilderness ... This claim shanty with two small additions added later, was our home until 1908 when we built the new house. ... At the time my father came there were still a few buffalo and antelope and Indians. The Sioux Indians were at peace then but still use their trails across the prairie, and the rings of stone still lay where they had weighted down the flaps of their teepees. The buffalo rings still plainly showed where the bulls had stood stomping flies, with their heads to the outside, to protect the cows and calves, which were in the inside of the ring, from the wolves and coyotes, which were many in those days. I still can remember the chilling howl of them in the dusk of the evening." The Dakota territory was one of the last regions of America to be settled and was finally split into two in 1889, resulting in statehood for North Dakota and South Dakota.

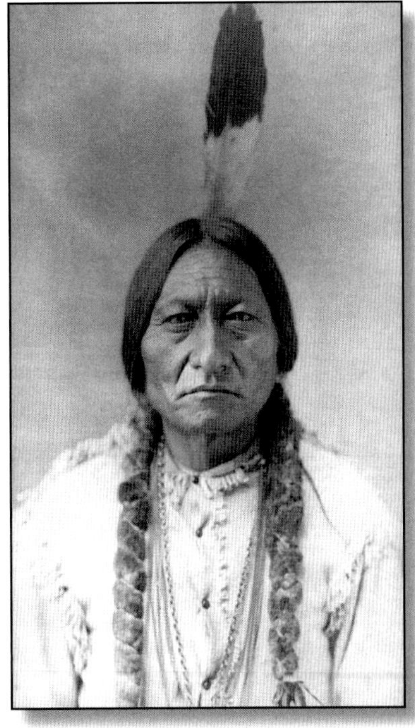

Sitting Bull, 1885. Wikimedia. David Francis Barry

Anton Brevik, the builder of this round barn, emigrated from Romsdalen, Norway, about 1892 and married Cloie Herrick, a native of the area, in 1898. A year later they established a homestead near Lake Cochrane, close to the Minnesota border, where they raised seven children, all born in the farmhouse. In 1901 he began planting evergreens around the house, trying to re-create his homeland of Norway.

Soon Anton began hog farming, specializing in purebred Poland China hogs. He'd travel far and wide to find a quality hog to strengthen his stock. In 1909 the *Canby News* reported that Brevik's Poland China hogs had a successful exhibit at the Yellow Medicine County Fair. "Mr. Brevik believes that a purebred hog ought to have as much care and attention as a good horse ... he may often be seen out in his yard on a sultry day fanning his hogs with his straw hat and feeding them chocolate creams." Anton also liked to name each one and he included all vital statistics in sales brochures.

In 1910 he built an octagonal hog barn, one with a sectional conical roof, a central roof ventilator on the cupola, and plenty of windows. He arranged pens along the outer walls. A stove, piped through a central chimney, and the barn's concentric form afforded warmth, especially important for piglets.

His hog business thrived in the early 1900s — so much so that he could afford to build a large sale barn in 1923, taking his enterprise to a higher level. The 12-sided barn (featured in this painting), with an attached rectangular hog house, was distinctive: an octagonal cupola with 16 windows, a central sales area and seating, and a matching dormer, all tinted a regal burgundy. In sale events twice a year, the entire family pitched in, preparing sales literature, detailing the name, age, and weight of each hog. Newspaper advertising showed photos and stats of the animals, enticing buyers from as far away as Minneapolis. Additionally, the family arranged for free transportation to the farm from the local train depot and provided shipping crates for the winning bidders. For

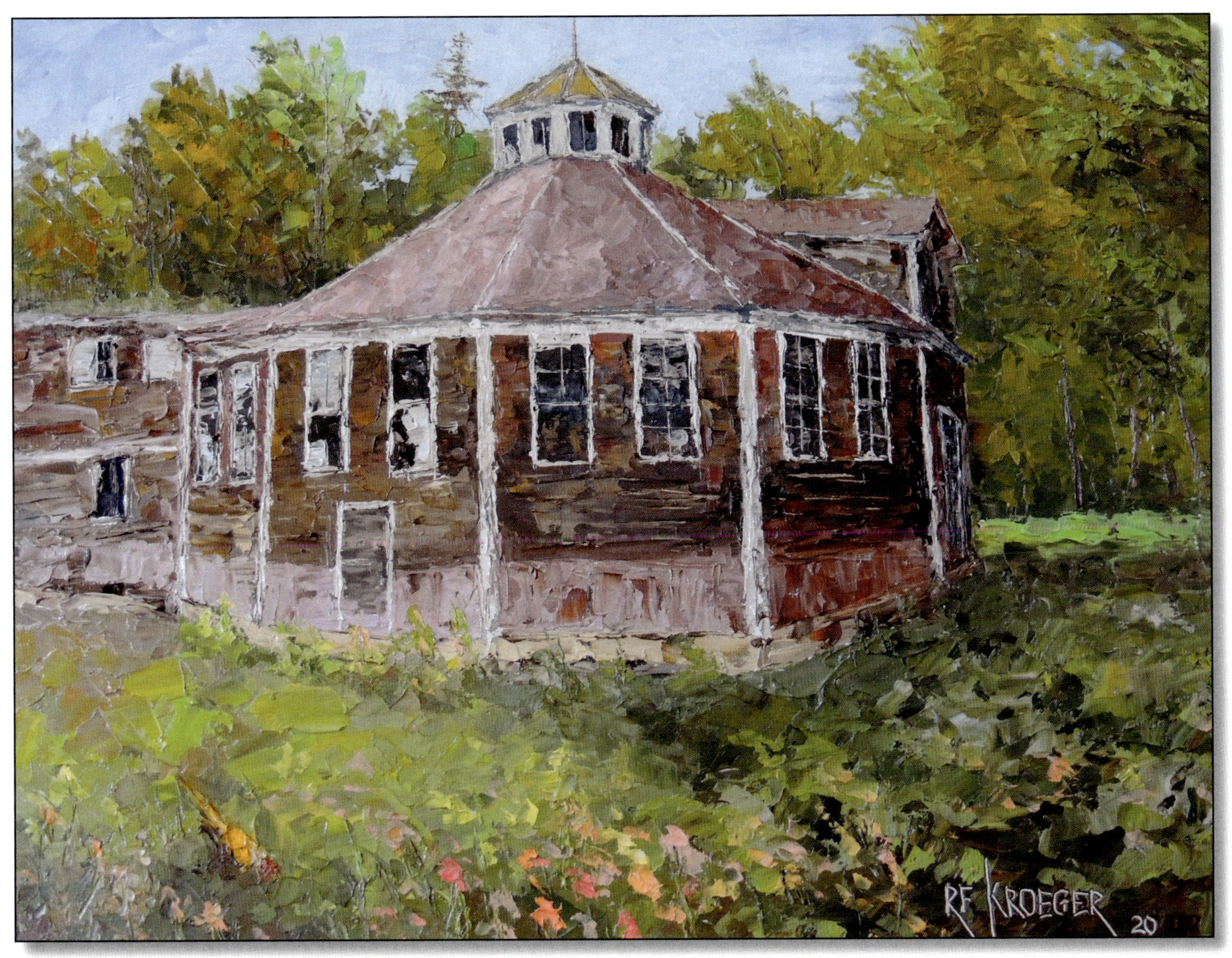

All the Way from Norway

months ahead of the auction, Cloie canned mincemeat for the 40-plus pies she'd make, fresh for the day of the sale. Lunch, including ham sandwiches, pies, and coffee, was served without charge. All seven children helped. By this time the farm had been named, Plain View Farm. In the first sale in the new barn in 1923, 250 attended and paid good prices for the stock.

However, as the 1920s progressed, bad crops and weak prices made farming difficult, forcing Anton to sell to a Mr. Gottsch in 1927. During the Great Depression, in years 1936-1937, the Breviks traveled west to Oregon, hoping for a rebound, picking berries, doing road repair work, and various farm labor jobs but, after six months they returned home. Even though Anton lost his farm, he continued raising his prize Poland China hogs until he died in 1941.

Sadly, in an article written by Anton's grandchildren, the farmhouse had deteriorated badly by 2003 but family descendants were reminded of how it looked in its heyday by a painting by Jerry Barlow, the wife of Anton's oldest grandson. Likewise, even though the barns are now gone, thanks to a reference photo from the Dale Travis site, at least the sale barn will live on in this painting and essay, a reminder of a hardworking South Dakota family and their patriarch, who took a chance in coming here, all the way from Norway.

NEBRASKA

NUCKOLLS COUNTY

A Mail Order Bride

As the United States became more populated in the late 19th century, demand for housing increased and entrepreneurs began to advertise mail order kits for homes … and barns. In the early 1900s there were several companies that sold plans, lumber, and all the needed materials in a single mail order kit. Among them were Sears, Roebuck and Company of Chicago, and the Louden Machinery and the Gordon-Van Tine companies of Iowa. Another Iowa company, Permanent Buildings Society of Des Moines, designed round barns but sold the plans only. However, the most interesting of these companies was The Chicago House Wrecking Company, which furnished Barn Design No. 206A, which, for $898, included the kit, lumber and plans, which were used to build this 14-sided barn in Nebraska in 1914. Other companies with house and barn plans soon emerged.

The first of these mail order companies started in 1906, when William Sovereign, an advertising expert in Bay City, Michigan, noticed plans for a pre-cut boat. He figured that such a system would also work for a house, and accordingly he asked for a pre-cut boathouse kit to be designed. Since this became popular, William joined forces with his brother Otto, a lawyer from Ohio. Together they started the Aladdin Company, named for the mythical genie who built a castle overnight for his master. Aladdin initially sold kits for cottages but quickly expanded to small houses. Thus began the wave of pre-cut homes and barns.

At first, Iowa's Louden company shrewdly sold only barn blueprints and would offer a customized drawing — without charge — which the company hoped would allow them to sell their labor-saving barn equipment. On the other hand, Sears, Montgomery Ward, and the Gordon-Van Tine companies included pre-cut lumber so that the farmer and his carpenters could quickly assemble the barn. This appealed to the farm wife since she wouldn't have to house and feed the carpenters for weeks.

The Chicago House Wrecking Company, founded by four Harris brothers, began as an architectural salvage business in the late 1800s, selling used materials for home building. Incorporated in

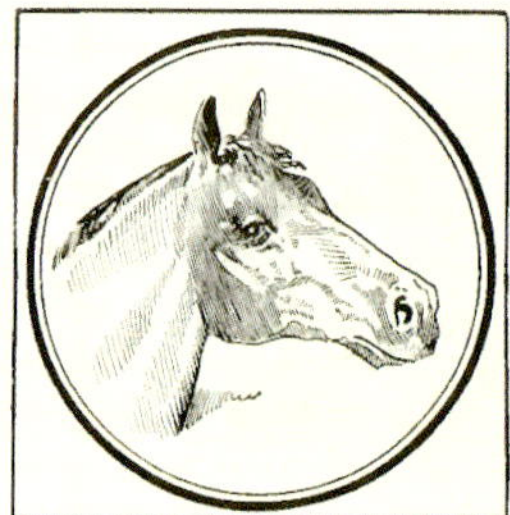

BARNS

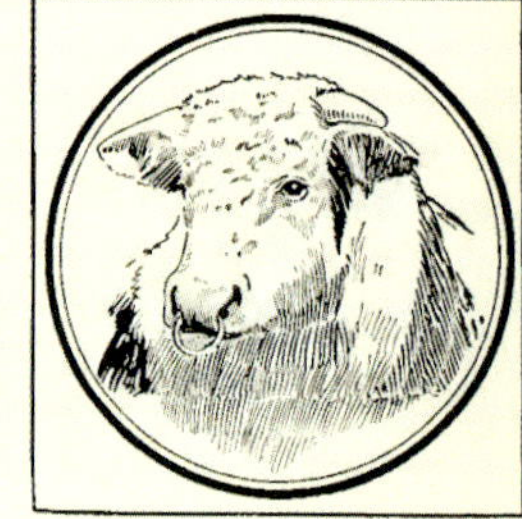

The barn is the Farmers workshop. It is as needful to his success as the store is to the merchant. The farm animals are his helpers. Proper housing and adequate provision for their health and comfort, with a minimum outlay for feed and labor, will return as big a dividend as a well-built, well equipped factory does to the manufacturer. A modern barn lends cast to the whole surroundings and enhances the beauty and value of the farm many times its cost. Do not be without one. Read what follows, then write us. We are at your service and can save you money.

OUR BARN PLANS

In the following pages we illustrate a number of barn designs to meet the various demands of the American farmer and stock raiser. In developing these designs, our aim has been to reduce waste to a minimum and select only such materials that will not only serve the purpose for which they are intended to the best advantage, but may be placed in position at the smallest possible cost. The old method of heavy timber construction is no longer followed by experienced builders and architects, because of excessive and entirely useless expense. For this reason we have adopted the built-up, or joist frame, design wherever possible.

FREE PLAN PROPOSITION

The cost of preparing reliable plans, specifications and material by competent architects is a considerable item of building expense, We furnish our customers with complete sets of drawings fully explaining the construction of every part of the building absolutely free. All that we require is a deposit of $2.00 to protect ourselves from the merely curious, and when material is purchased from us we credit you with the $2.00 paid for the plans. We furnish a complete set of specifications and a material list describing material and location, so that anyone reasonably familiar with building construction will have no difficulty in erecting any one of these designs. Our plans are made by experienced and practical men who have been in touch with building operations of all kinds for many years, and are familiar with conditions in different parts of the country, so that the plans are entirely practical.

CONSTRUCTION

So simple is joist frame or built-up barn construction, that the farmer with a little above average intelligence can, by studying the Blue prints, Material List and Specifications during spare time, easily superintend the building of his own barn. In fact, he can build it with the help around the place, during the months when work is not pressing. The advantages of this style of construction are too numerous to mention. Principal among them is economy in the cost of material and labor, and any time when enlargement or repair work is necessary, it can be accomplished a great deal more readily than with the old timber construction style of barn frame. Anyone who has studied the Department of Agriculture Bulletins on Farm Buildings, can get sufficient information and proofs from same that will convince the most skeptical in short order, and the fact that a large number of State Agricultural Departments are building barns constructed in this manner, in itself should be evidence enough that this method is a superior method in every way.

$3.00 SPECIAL MADE TO ORDER BARN PLAN OFFER $3.00

On page five we describe the most extraordinary Architectural Offer ever published and feel that our barn customers are entitled to the same consideration. We are making a similar offer, for considerably less money, and following is our offer:

In the event you do not find a barn in this Book that meets with your approval, or cannot be made so by making slight alterations, send us a rough sketch and description of what you have in mind, stating the width, length, height and whatever other information you have handy, accompanied by remittance for $3.00, and we will send you a pencil Plan architecturally drawn to the scale of ¼ of an inch to 1 foot, showing Floor Plan, one Side Elevation, one End Elevation and details, accompanied by our GUARANTEED Material Specification—describing the quality, kind and size of the material to be furnished for the entire barn, and naming you a GUARANTEED DELIVERED price, free of all freight charges, F.O.B. cars your station. SAFE DELIVERY GUARANTEED.

This valuable architectural information will be the means of saving you a great deal of money, waste of time and trouble later on, and enables you to tell at a glance how your ideas will work out in the actual building, how the barn will look, and above all, how much it is going to cost you. If our proposition meets with your approval and you decide to favor us with your order for the material, we will furnish you FREE OF CHARGE complete Blue Prints with all details, our Standard Specifications and detailed Material Bill, giving full instructions as to how and where to use the material, giving the size, style and catalog numbers, the $3.00 you have advanced will be deducted from the total amount of your bill, so that in the long run all this Architectural service comes to you FREE OF CHARGE.

Either by mail or if you are close enough to visit us in person, you may rest assured that our Architects will join you in carrying out your ideas in every detail, and give you full information and advice absolutely FREE; also demonstrate to you how you can get the best possible building for the least amount of money. **In writing, be sure and mention SKETCH PLAN OFFER 23-633.**

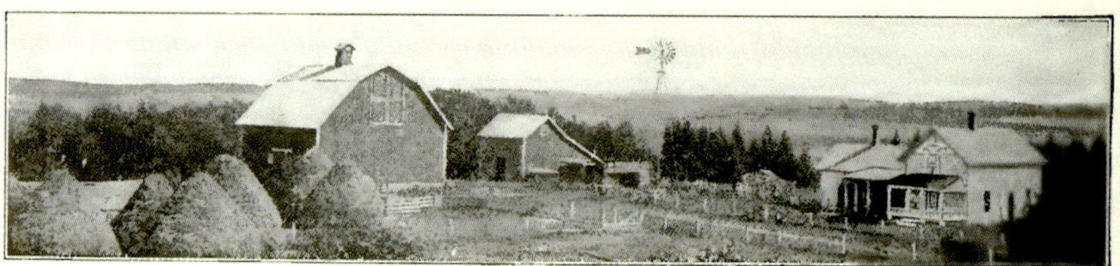

CHICAGO HOUSE WRECKING CO., 35th & IRON STREETS, CHICAGO.

80

Chicago Wrecking Company, barn plans. Courtesy of Digital Research Library of Illinois History Journal. Dr. Neil Gale

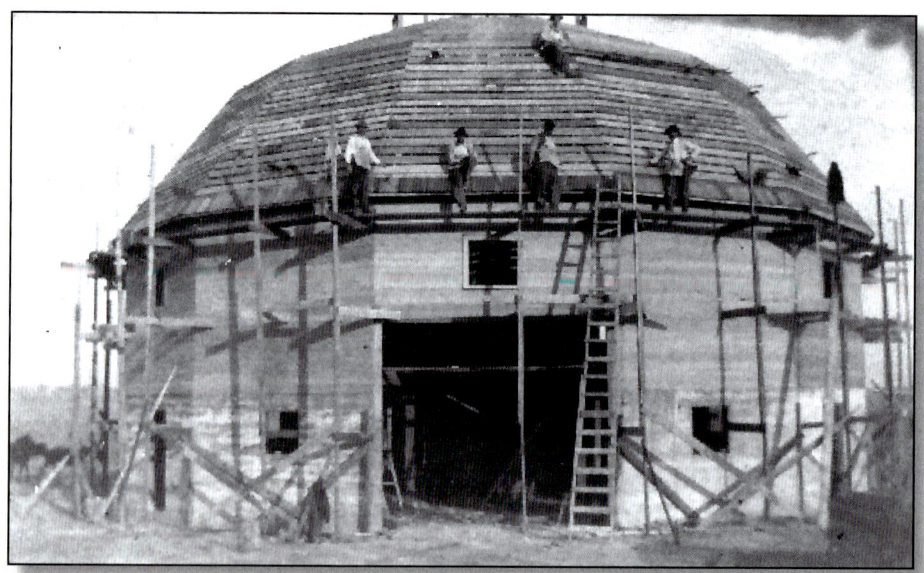

Malsbury barn construction. Dale Travis site, courtesy of Claire May

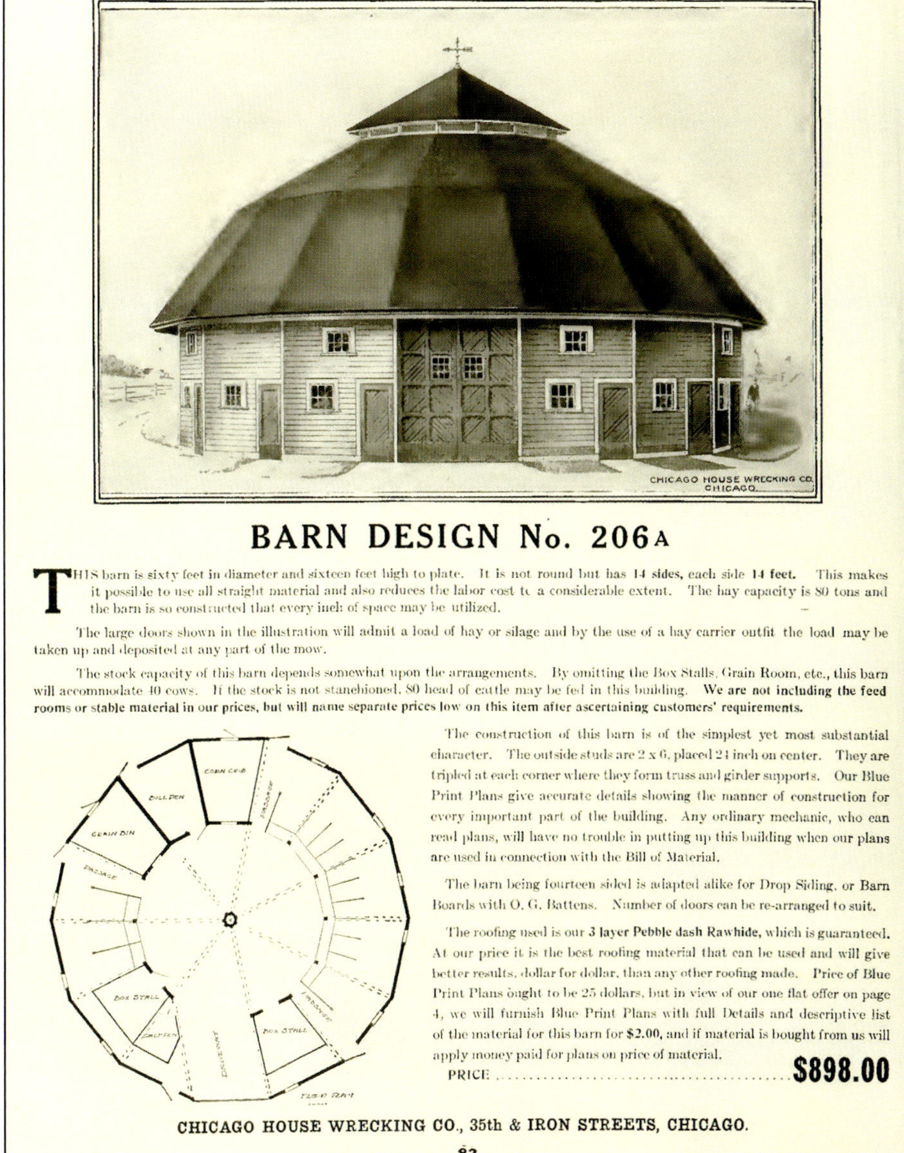

BARN DESIGN No. 206A

THIS barn is sixty feet in diameter and sixteen feet high to plate. It is not round but has **14 sides, each side 14 feet.** This makes it possible to use all straight material and also reduces the labor cost to a considerable extent. The hay capacity is 80 tons and the barn is so constructed that every inch of space may be utilized.

The large doors shown in the illustration will admit a load of hay or silage and by the use of a hay carrier outfit the load may be taken up and deposited at any part of the mow.

The stock capacity of this barn depends somewhat upon the arrangements. By omitting the Box Stalls, Grain Room, etc., this barn will accommodate 40 cows. If the stock is not stanchioned, 80 head of cattle may be fed in this building. **We are not including the feed rooms or stable material in our prices, but will name separate prices low on this item after ascertaining customers' requirements.**

The construction of this barn is of the simplest yet most substantial character. The outside studs are 2 x 6, placed 24 inch on center. They are tripled at each corner where they form truss and girder supports. Our Blue Print Plans give accurate details showing the manner of construction for every important part of the building. Any ordinary mechanic, who can read plans, will have no trouble in putting up this building when our plans are used in connection with the Bill of Material.

The barn being fourteen sided is adapted alike for Drop Siding, or Barn Boards with O. G. Battens. Number of doors can be re-arranged to suit.

The roofing used is our **3 layer Pebble dash Rawhide,** which is guaranteed. At our price it is the best roofing material that can be used and will give better results, dollar for dollar, than any other roofing made. Price of Blue Print Plans ought to be 25 dollars, but in view of our one flat offer on page 4, we will furnish Blue Print Plans with full Details and descriptive list of the material for this barn for **$2.00,** and if material is bought from us will apply money paid for plans on price of material.

PRICE **$898.00**

CHICAGO HOUSE WRECKING CO., 35th & IRON STREETS, CHICAGO.

82

Chicago Wrecking Company, round barn plan. Courtesy of Digital Research Library of Illinois History Journal. Dr. Neil Gale

1893, they successfully bid to dismantle Chicago's World Fair in 1893 and the St. Louis World Fair in 1904, giving them ample supplies to sell to homebuilders. By 1908 the company offered its first set of plans for homes and barns; other companies followed and some began to include all building materials needed to complete the project.

The Chicago company offered bolted-together "Pres-to-Up" buildings as early as 1912, which meant that houses, garages, and barns could be quickly and less expensively assembled, compared to hiring a contractor. Soon, other companies followed their lead and competition became intense. So, in 1913, realizing that their name, essentially a demolition company — not a building company — might be giving an edge to their competitors, the Harris brothers decided it was time for a new name. The Harris Brothers 1920 catalog explained: "In our earlier career we were incorporated under the name of the Chicago House Wrecking Company. For years we were known to the public, under this name, as the Bargain Mart of the world, but as time passed we were, by reason of the great savings made on new lumber and mill-work materials purchased for customers, forced into the new material business and we realized that the old name gave the wrong impression." The Harris Brothers sounded much more constructive than the former title and the company continued to sell home and barn building kits until the Great Depression hit. The company stopped selling homes around 1932 and filed for bankruptcy a year later.

In 1914 William Malsbury of Nuckolls County, Nebraska, bought their round barn kit and erected this barn, which included a concrete lower level, which he made from sand and gravel, hauled by wagon from the Republican River, eight miles away. A photo, courtesy of the Travis site, shows four carpenters installing the roof — with scaffolding in place surrounding the 14-sided barn.

The barn plan's advertisement claimed that using horizontal straight siding would "reduce labor cost to a considerable extent." This was correct: having to soak lumber for days to make it flex around a curve costs time and labor. Placing horizontal siding on 14 sides meant that the builder could avoid the circular curve. In fact, Malsbury could have saved more money by buying the blueprints only — for two dollars. And, as the advertisement offered, this payment could be applied to the cost of $898 "if the material is bought from us," which is what he probably did.

However, Malsbury deviated from the plan by pouring a concrete lower level, which reaches into the hayloft, and he installed a central silo, also not in the building plan, which was made from Oregon cypress wood. Oak beams, 8x10 inches, support the roof. With concrete reinforced with steel rods placed three feet apart, this unusual tetradecagon was built to last.

Vincent Loveall, in his Facebook site, *Round Barns of America*, reported his opportunity to interview David

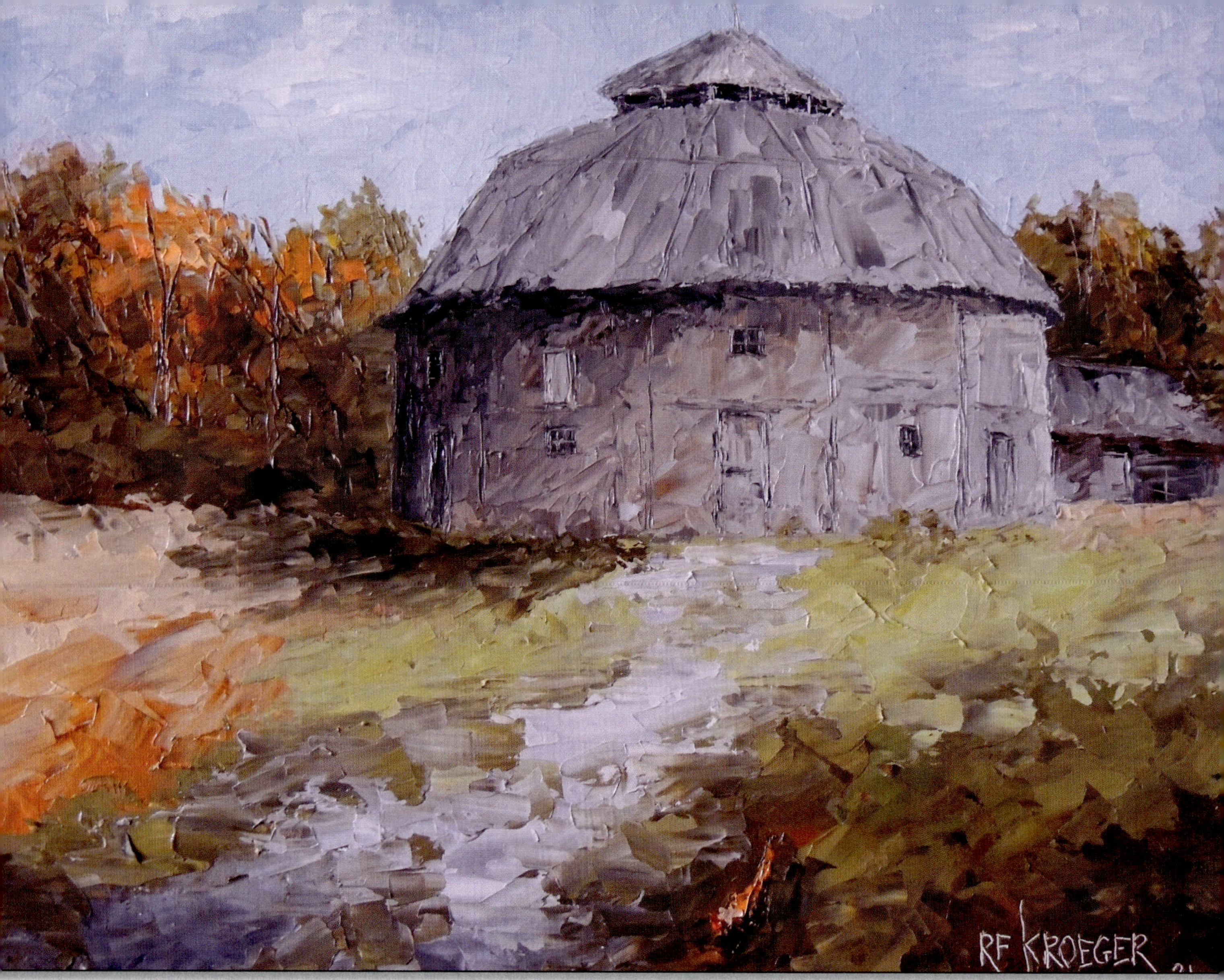

A Mail Order Bride

Barnhart, whose grandfather built the barn. He explained that William devoured agricultural journals and had a stack of them, hundreds on top of one another, which probably influenced him towards the polygonal design, even though journals had become critical of the round designs by this time.

Originally, Malsbury settled the farm in the late 1880s on the Homestead Act's 160-acre grant. A hard worker, he expanded the farm to 2,600 acres by the 1920s, which suggested much prosperity. But, alas, he must have overextended, relying on mortgages and notes from banks, which was all too common in the early 20th-century, and during the Great Depression years, like many farmers, he lost his farm and had to move.

According to Loveall's posting, current owners Jerry and Kirk Grove said that their grandfather Elza Grove bought the farm in 1940. It might have been in a sheriff's sale, common in those dark days — as America slowly emerged from the depression and was about to enter World War II. Though initially the barn remained unpainted and still had the original wood-shingled roof, the Groves painted it white and installed a new roof of interlocking tin shingles, which should protect the barn for decades to come. After all, no one would want to subject this round gem to a wrecking company. Would they?

KEARNEY COUNTY

The Sodbusters

This rare set of two round barns, now gone, was located within a few miles of Ft. Kearney, the first fort built — in 1848 — to protect travelers on the Oregon-California Trail. Wagon trains, full of immigrants seeking a new start, drove their mules and oxen along this trail as did opportunistic prospectors, bound for California's gold fields. And this was Indian territory, home to the nomadic tribes of the Pawnee, Omaha, Lakota, Sioux, and Cheyenne, who migrated with the herds of buffalo. Their grip on the Great Plains was slipping away as settlers arrived, hardy enough to survive winters on these vast treeless expanses of prairie. These pioneers laid down roots, often building sod houses if timber wasn't available. They were the sodbusters.

Photographer Solomon Butcher recorded these pioneers and their mud homes, which often leaked or collapsed, throwing havoc into lives that were already challenged by hot, dry summers and frigid winters. Roger Welsch, a Nebraska historian, in his book, *Sod Walls*, shares many of Butcher's photos and explains how these brave folks built their sod homes and eked out a living. Some of the barns had thatched roofs, reminiscent of 17th-century Europe.

It was a far cry from Somersetshire, England, where William Radford was born in 1852. Two years later his family immigrated to Canada, then into New York State, and finally to Illinois, where William was raised. In 1876 he moved with his family to Nebraska, at that point, still full of sod homes, which Butcher began documenting a decade later. William began farming with his family but it's unknown if they lived in a sod home at the beginning — probably unlikely since they chose a site near the famous Platte River, where trees were abundant.

In 1883, now 33, William married an Ohio woman, Lizzie Shaad, and paid $1,000 for a 160-acre farm owned by the Prescotts. He began farming and gradually added acreage, expanding his business to include horses, cattle, and hogs, along with crops such as corn, wheat, oats, and hay. By 1910 the Radfords were doing well, plowing their fields with a steam-driven tractor, as displayed in a Solomon Butcher photograph.

His two sons, both in their 20s, had become equal partners

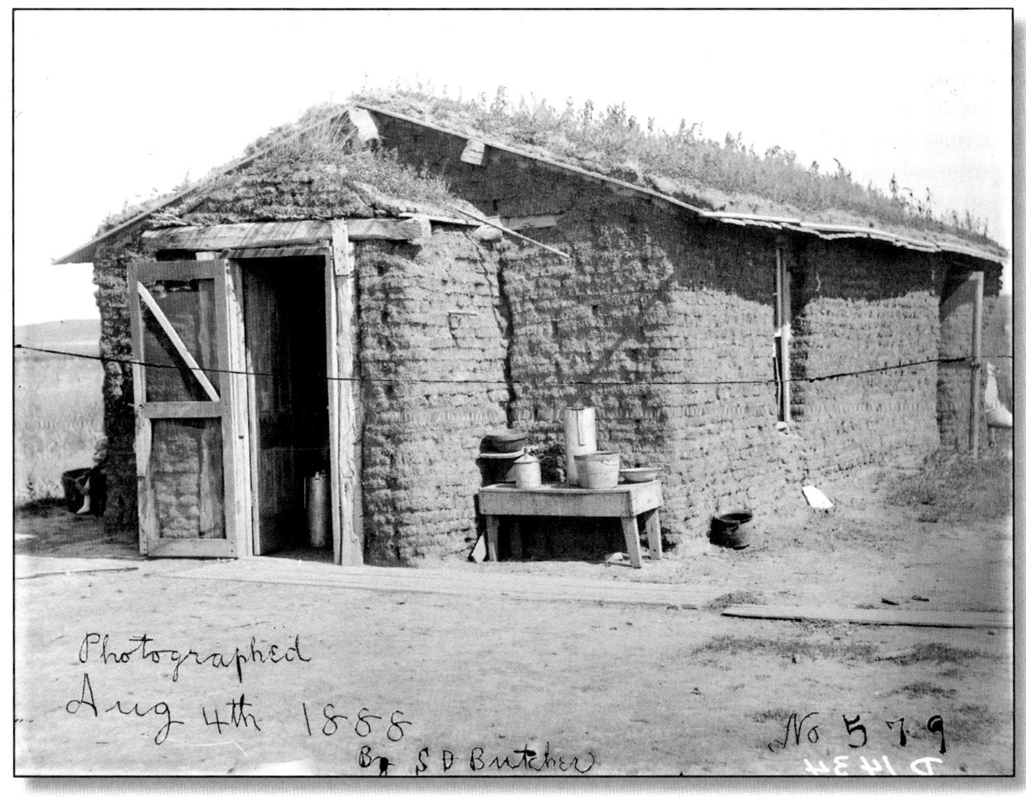

Sod wall house, Nebraska, 1888. Courtesy of the Nebraska Historical Society, Solomon Butcher

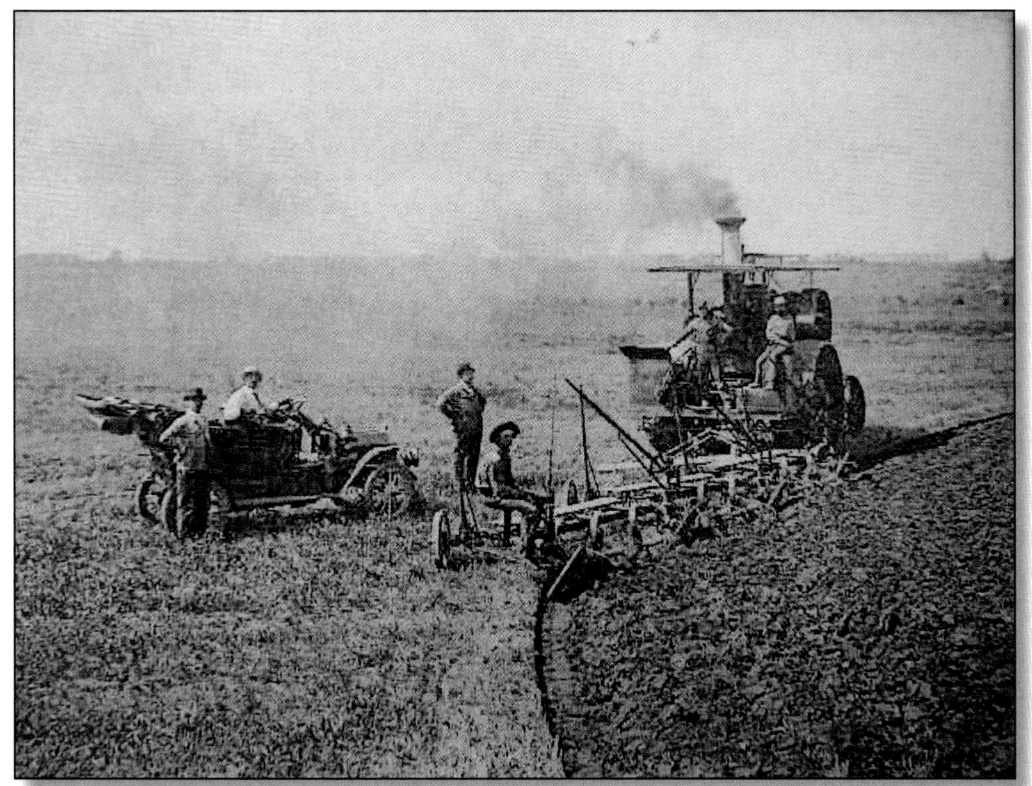
Radfords plowing field, Nebraska, 1910. Courtesy of the Nebraska Historical Society, Solomon Butcher

with their dad in the ranch-farm, a strategy that some farmers used in an effort to keep their sons on the farm and continue family ownership. It worked: by 1910 the ranch had spread to over 1,300 acres, making the Radford farm one of the most esteemed in the region. And, with about 300 head of cattle, hundreds of hogs, and plenty of horses, they needed more storage.

So, in 1917, William, now 65, and his son Boyd, decided to build not one barn, but two, connecting them (which was often done in northeastern states) with a covered runway. And these were not traditionally shaped barns, but round ones, which weren't small. Boyd wrote "Double Round Barns Save Time and Cost," an article in *System on the Farm*, published in 1920, in which he claimed that the advantages of a round barn were limited to one with no more than a 60-foot diameter.

Accordingly, he joined two barns, attaching them with a covered connector. With a diameter of 60 feet and a height of 58 feet, they could service a large farm. One housed cattle, purebred Hereford stock, and the other sheltered horses. Corn, wheat, and oats were stored along with an annual crop of 500 tons of hay. Hogs were kept in a smaller building.

Building the barns took three carpenters and three masons a year to complete. Large distinctive ventilators capped each roof, which required a train car full of wood shingles. Brown ceramic tile blocks, lining the walls, came from Seward and were laid for three cents each. The lumber, though rare in the plains of Nebraska, came from cottonwood trees, cut a few miles away. Flooring was made from creosote-soaked wooden bricks. A stairway led to the haylofts, 18 feet above the floor, and a track around the inside helped in transporting the bales. When full, each loft would hold 96 tons of hay. Two clay-tiled silos towered behind the barns. Only an affluent farmer could afford such a project.

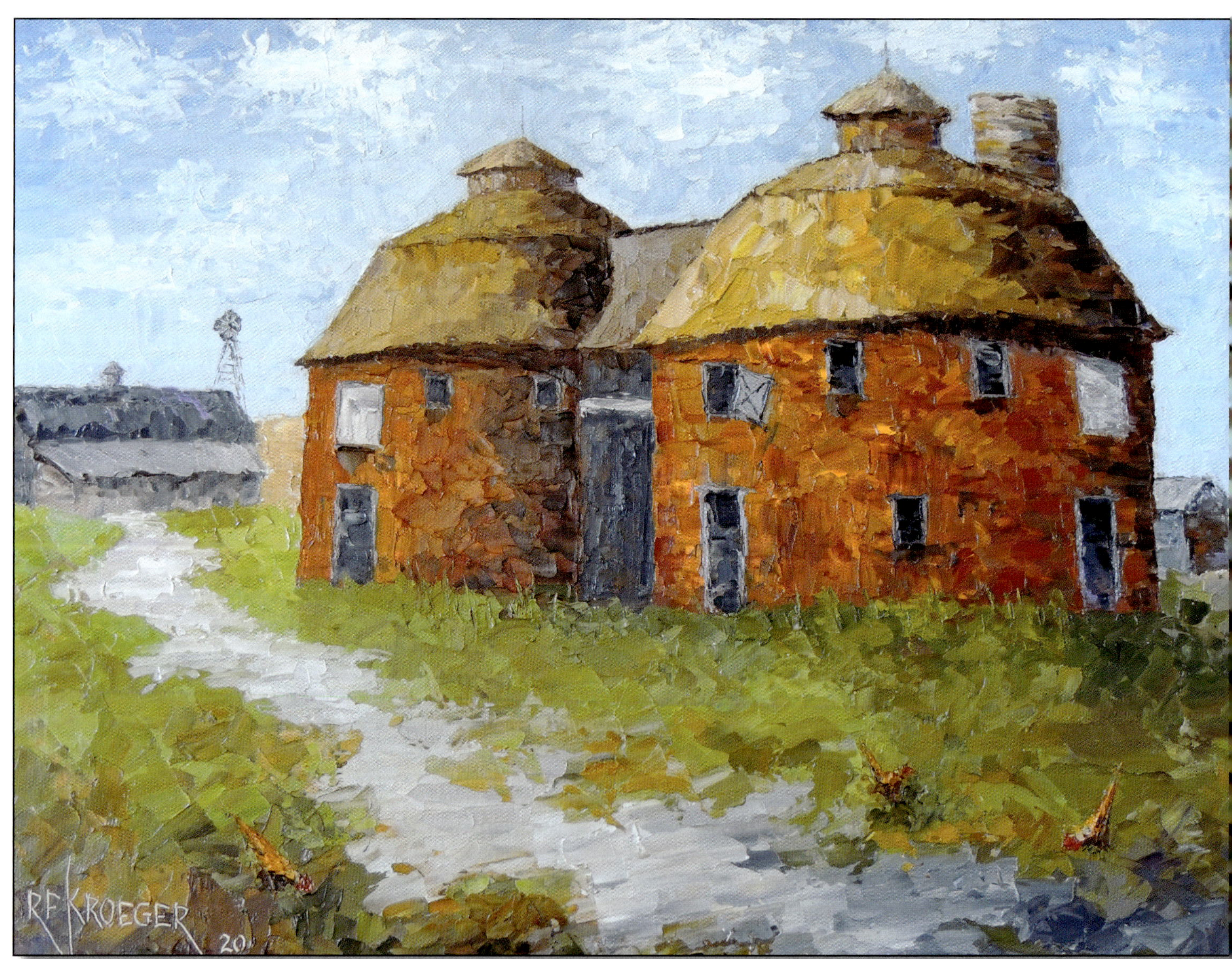

The Sodbusters

Being patriotic, the Radfords hosted Red Cross fundraisers in the barns during the remainder of World War I. One barn dance, on July 4, 1918, attracted over 1,500 townspeople and lasted until the wee hours the next morning. Two years later, in 1920, wanting to promote the concept of double round barns, Boyd Radford published an article, "Double round barns save time and cost," in a book, *System on the Farm*. Did the Radfords of Chicago, who published many books and building plans, help him get it published? Although it never caught on, its lack of acceptance — in part due to the farm depression of the 1920s — made this double round set all the more unique.

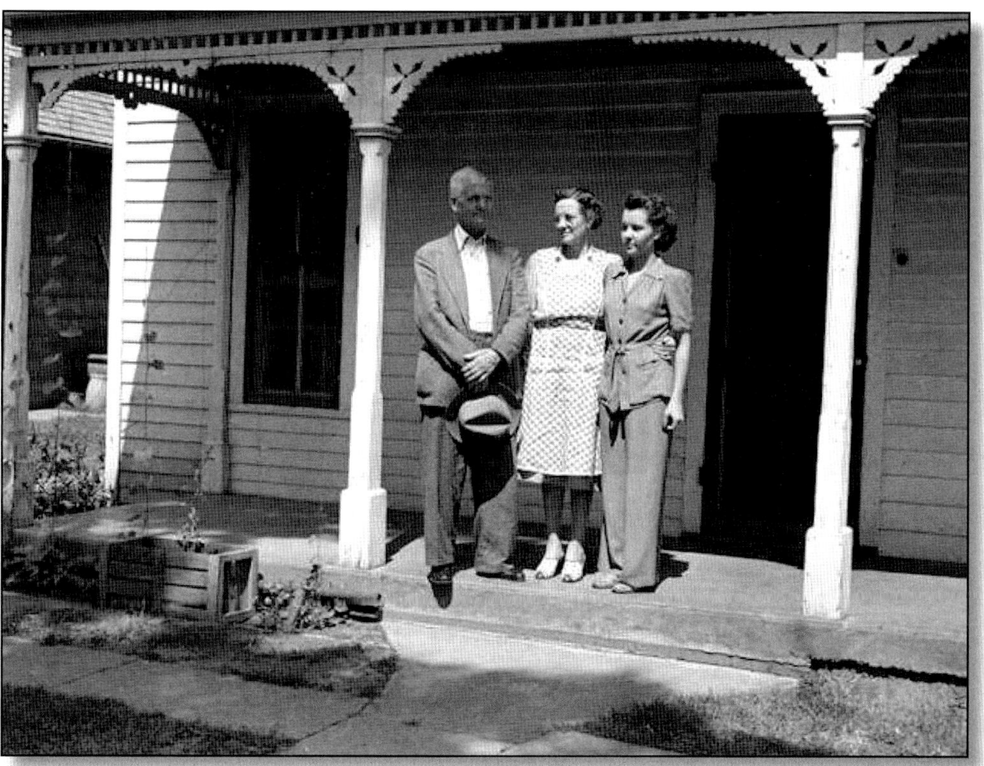

Thompson family, circa 1920s. Dale Travis site, courtesy of Marsha Mathes

However, despite their charitable giving and their expertise in farming, the farm slipped out of family hands. Was it the Great Depression? An expensive loan to build the barns? Did the bank foreclose? How about the punishing Dust Bowl of the 1930s?

The Younkin family eventually became owners and, after a tornado in 1950 dislodged one of the silos, possibly weakened by hogs digging around the foundation, they were forced to dismantle one of the barns. And then, sometime later, the other barn was taken down, ending another chapter in Nebraska history. Unfortunately, this rare architectural marvel never made the National Register, though its uniqueness and construction were enough to merit a listing. Despite its exclusion, it will be remembered in this painting and essay as a tribute to the sodbusters of the Great Plains.

KANSAS

HARPER COUNTY

A Cornfield Castle

It's fortunate that this monumental round barn became listed on the National Register in 1985, thanks to a nomination by then-current owner Dale Wohlschlegel, because, by the time of this writing, it may no longer be standing. Architecturally, it ranks as one of the most elaborate round barns in America.

The family patriarch, Zachariah Caleb Thompson, born in Iowa in 1860, and his son C.R. Thompson drew up plans for this barn, after probably reading about round barns in agricultural journals. In 1910 they poured concrete on site — forming the concrete block walls and foundation — but they ignored Professor King's concept of a central silo, instead placing two towering silos on the outside, flanking the entrance and, with pointed conical turrets, made the structure seem more like a European medieval castle than a Kansas barn. In 1912 a team of 15 carpenters — using cottonwood from the area for the joists and walls — began building it, under direction of the contractor, Bill Russell of nearby Anthony. The year-long project ended in 1913, costing $16,000, a huge sum in those days. These affluent farmers wanted to build a masterpiece and they succeeded. They used the barn for dairy, hay storage, and possibly other crops.

A large barn, with a diameter of 80 feet, silos 70 feet high, and a three-tiered domed roof rising to 75 feet, it had to be the talk of the county, if not the state. A similar castle-like barn in Allen County, Ohio, though built earlier, also reflected the affluence of its owner. And, despite hard times for farmers in the 1920s and the Depression years of the 1930s, the farm and barn remained in the Thompson family.

A year before Zachariah died in 1943, the farm was sold, eventually passing to Dale Wohlschlegel in 1981, who thought enough of it to list it in the National Register four

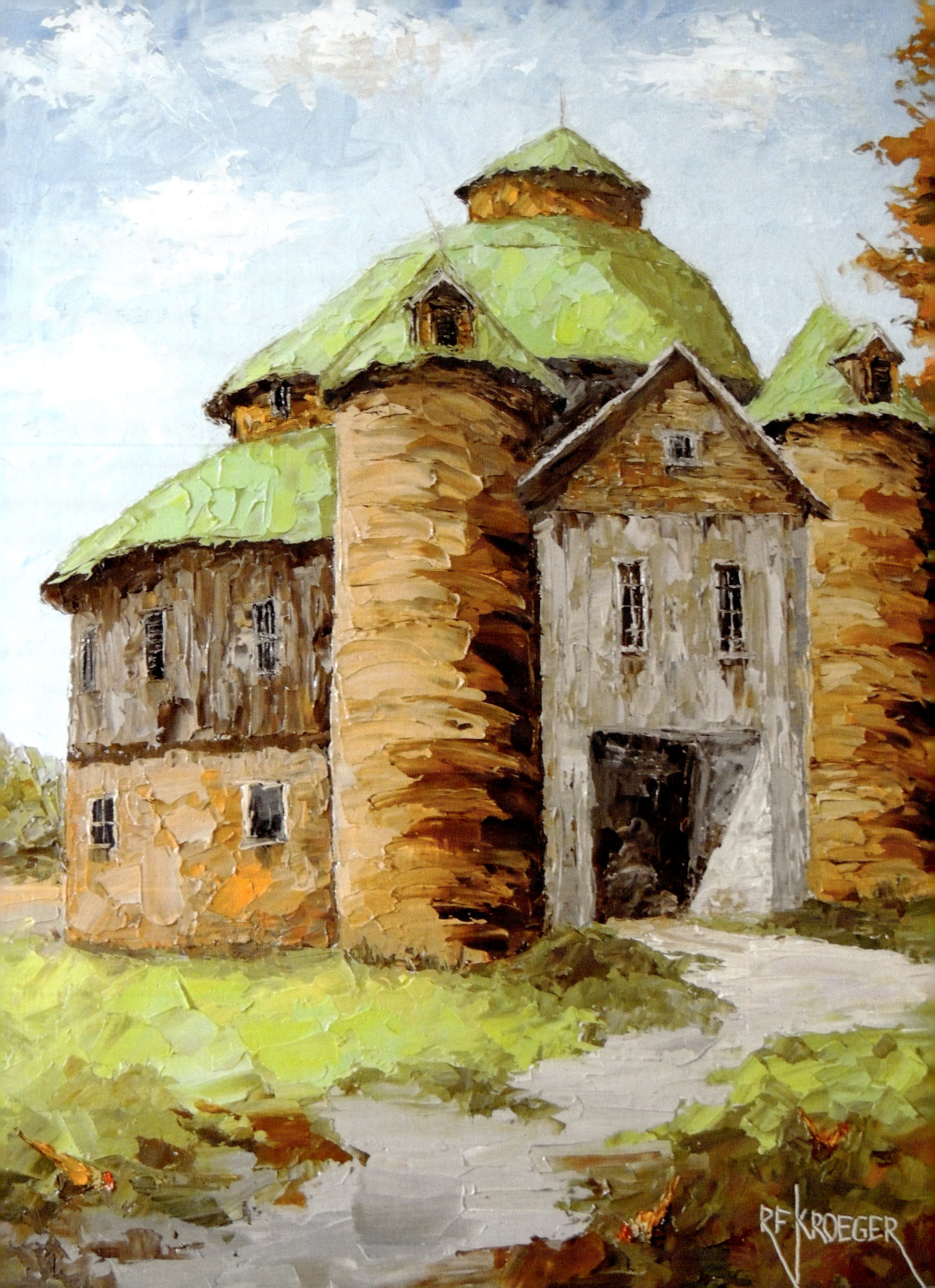
RF KROEGER

years later. However, without much maintenance, it slowly began to deteriorate, ending another episode of round barn history … a pretty good page, at that. Regardless, the barn's magnificence will endure, at least in this painting and essay, and in its title, "A Cornfield Castle."

OKLAHOMA

OKLAHOMA COUNTY

Route 66

Although it may seem strange for a barn painting to be titled "Route 66," such an appellation is well deserved since this true round barn has stood for nearly a century within yards of this iconic highway. Initially it was a dirt trail, later State Highway 7, and finally, coated with asphalt, it became classic Americana. It's nostalgia at its best.

Long ago, Indians and mountain men used trails through this region — in their search for game and, eventually, for any animal whose fur was valued for hats and coats. As wagon trains brought settlers westwards and as the 1850 Gold Rush of California lured prospectors, trails became more defined. Railroads came next. One, the Missouri-Kansas-Texas line, passed by this farm, owned by William Odor, prompting him and a few others to develop the town of Arcadia, naming it after a region in ancient Greece, known for its bucolic harmony.

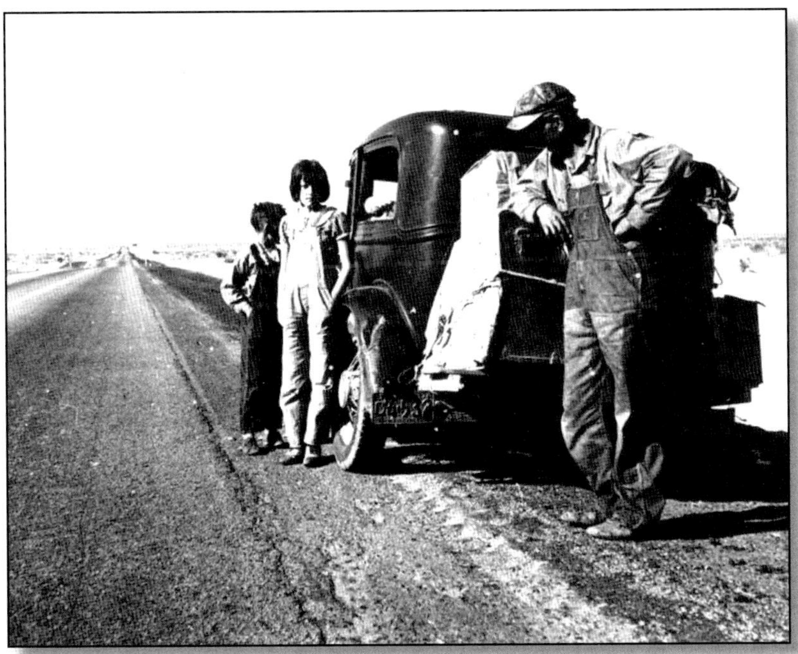

Dust Bowl migrants, circa 1930s. Courtesy of the Oklahoma Historical Society Research Center

Then came Henry Ford and his Model-T, which revolutionized travel. The dirt road passing in front of the barn became numbered — as did many others during the government's development of a national highway system. It became State Highway 7, but it was still dirt and gravel, not particularly kind to rubber car tires.

Cyrus Avery, a prosperous Oklahoma businessman, lobbied in Washington to establish a route through the West and battled a group that wanted to use the Old Santa Fe Trail, which would have bypassed Oklahoma. Avery, realizing the economic impact such a highway would have, won the bid and, in 1926, Congress decided that Route 66 would follow an old California Gold Rush Trail through Oklahoma. The 2,400-mile road connected downtown Chicago with Los Angeles, becoming a major part of the new American Highway System, although it was not fully paved until 1938. It became the "Main Street of America" and represented the transition from named roads such as the National Road and the Lincoln Highway. It brought prosperity to the many little towns it passed, such as Arcadia, which, only about a mile and a half square miles, had a population of 800 in 1904. Life was fine there until the Great Depression hit.

Many sharecroppers, trying to scrape a living out of hard ground, lost everything and had to move west. They packaged their meager belongings into a few suitcases, filled the car with family members sitting on top of each other, and headed down the highway.

Unforgiving droughts hit and dried up the land, and "black blizzards," dust storms that often reduced visibility to three feet, blew through Oklahoma and the panhandle of Texas throughout the 1930s, earning the title, "The Dust Bowl." Poor families moved west, hoping for a better life, and traveled along Route 66, which Nobel Prize author John Steinbeck called "The Mother Road," in his Pulitzer-winning novel, *The Grapes of Wrath*. He wrote, "Highway 66 is the main migrant road. … the mother road, the road of flight" as he compared the mass migration of farmers to the exodus of the Israelites out of Egypt, led away by Moses to escape the army of the pharaohs.

However, when William Harrison Odor, also known as "Big Bill", born in 1871 in Illinois, came with his new wife Myra to Deep Fork Township in 1892, Oklahoma was good farming land, at least in this fertile valley. Married only a year, they left Kansas, where they rented a farm, and sharecropped another when they arrived. After a few years of successful farming, Big Bill purchased 320 acres along the Deep Fork River in 1896 and continued to prosper, enough to advertise his newly found wealth. How? By building a round barn in 1898. Surely this would attract attention, especially if built close to the main trail through the new town of Arcadia.

Since Wisconsin's Professor King's plans for a round barn, first described in 1890, had been publicized in many farm journals throughout the 1890s, it's possible that Odor had read about them, and, captivated by the unique shape and the superiority of the round barn — as touted by many articles — he decided to build one himself. The task wasn't easy and it took six months to complete.

Although he worked as a schoolteacher in Kansas, he must have had some construction experience since he had enough sense to soak the native burr oak 2x4s in the river, making them pliable, and then dry them over a curved form. But, when the other farm hands and his brother-in-law who helped him refused to climb to the top of the 43-foot ladder to install the top two rafters, the task defaulted to Big Bill. Then, as they were about to lay the top floor, the workers, thinking that this large round floor — without center posts for support — would be ideal for community dances, they offered to pay the difference in flooring — rough plank versus smooth hardwood — if Odor would allow it, which he did on the condition that only "good music" be played. The large floor, 60 feet in diameter, served as a neighborhood dance hall for decades.

Initially Odor used the barn for hay, grain, and livestock but later he turned it into a livery and harness business. He also organized the first bank in Arcadia in 1905, started a hardware store, and had the first phone in town, which led to the Arcadia Telephone System. By 1920, the town had telephone service, two cotton gins, two banks, seven general stores, and, of course, the striking round barn. Though Route 66 helped the town's economy, a 1924 fire destroyed almost all of the business district, except for one building that survived, Tuton's Drugstore, now listed in the National Register, along with the round barn, a block away.

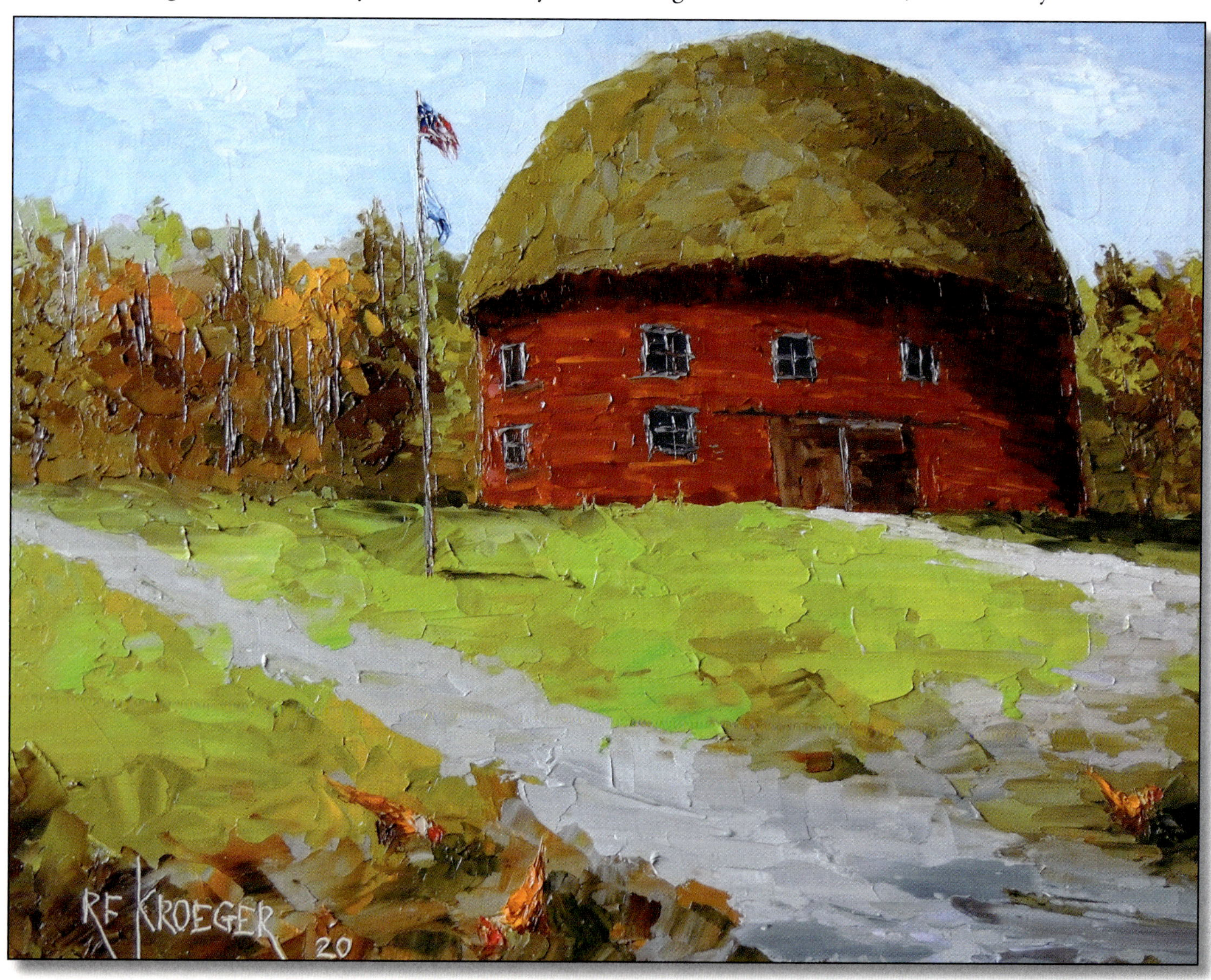

Route 66

Big Bill continued ownership through the Great Depression and World War II, eventually selling the farm to Frank and Katie Vrana. They continued to use the barn — but only for hay storage. To make room for larger equipment, they cut a large door in one of the barn's sides, weakening it and eventually causing it to tilt, signaling the end.

The next blow came in the form of America's interstates. A new "America's Road," I-75, connecting Michigan with Florida, was completed in 1957 and I-44 followed in 1964, bypassing Arcadia and its famous highway. Over the years the barn suffered from neglect, though Mrs. Frank Vrana successfully submitted it in 1977 to the National Register, though there were questions by the official reviewing it, "Will this barn be restored?" That was a good question.

Apparently, the townspeople asked the same question and eventually formed a foundation, The Arcadia Historical and Preservation Society, spearheaded by a retired builder and carpenter, Luke Robison, who decided that the barn needed to be saved. In May, 1988, the Vrana family donated the barn to the society. A month later the roof collapsed. Talk about timing.

But Luke, a soldier at heart, assembled a team of workers, a group he described as "the over the hill gang" since most of them were over 65, and continued restoring the barn. Starting with the roof, Luke inherited the job, as did Big Bill a century earlier, of being the one to connect the top two rafters, by climbing 43 feet up a ladder. After cleaning up the inside, adding new brown shingles to replace the weathered green ones, and giving the barn a coat of red paint, the geriatric carpenters had succeeded in preserving one of America's treasures. The dedication ceremony in 1992, was followed by a National Honor Award a year later, given to the society by the National Trust for Historic Preservation. Luke died shortly after this.

Today, even though Arcadia has served as a site for three Hollywood movies — the most recent, Matt Damon's *Stillwater*, shot in 2019 — its cotton gins and banks are gone and its population has dropped to under 300. But the old drugstore remains and Big Bill's round barn, now a tourist attraction, still sits proudly next to Route 66, a pleasant reminder of an America when the pace moved a bit slower on this, "The Mother Road."

MONTANA

CHOUTEAU COUNTY

Bootlegger Trail

In 1993 a destructive hailstorm ravaged the roof of this circular barn, spelling the end and, with its passing, a bit of the Wild West disappeared, too. A large barn, with an imposing arched false-front wall over the entrance, it conjured up images of storefronts in frontier towns, gunslingers, sheriffs, and weary cowboys in town for a cold beer after a long day's work on the range. Fittingly, it was located on state route 225, appropriately called Bootlegger Trail, which stretches from Great Falls and through Chouteau County, ending in Canada.

Montana — and this county in particular — in the 18th and 19th centuries, was Indian territory, full of beaver and other fur-bearing animals, whose pelts were in demand in the East. The county's namesake, Jean-Pierre Chouteau and his son, Pierre Chouteau, Jr., established fur trading companies, including Fort Benton, the last fur trading post on the Upper Missouri River.

Around 1800, Montana became prime real estate for harvesting the beaver and its pelts. Mountain men and fur trappers made their living in this way but, as fur trading escalated in the 1820s, so did conflicts with local Indian tribes, who, legally, were the only ones who could take game on these federal lands. By the 1840s, European fashion trends changed and, due to the decline of the beaver population, hunters shifted to the buffalo. Once estimated at 30 to 60 million in the 1500s, less than 400 buffalo were alive in 1884. Gradually, thanks to conservation efforts, over 500,000 exist today and, in 2016, the buffalo was declared the official national mammal, joining the bald eagle as symbols of America.

Less than 200 years ago, this area of Montana flourished with wild animals, Indian tribes, and the fiercely independent mountain man, a rare breed that could — but sometimes didn't — survive a solitary existence through snowstorms, bitter cold, and grizzly bears. With buffalo herds nearly extinct, ranching took over, which attracted cattle rustlers. Outlaws of the Wild West replaced the rugged mountain men, among them Butch Cassidy, the Sundance Kid, and Montana's own Kid Curry. And when the railroads arrived, the bandits flourished in robbing trains. But peace finally arrived in Montana.

After the turn of the century, the ladies of the temperance movement fought for prohibition, which gave rise to moonshine liquor and prompted the historic naming of this trail from Great Falls to Coutts, Canada. In 1916, Montana voters passed a state law banning the sale of alcohol, which went into effect in 1918, even though the national ban didn't become law until 1920. And so, creative entrepreneurs began making moonshine — for either personal consumption or sales. Bootlegging became a big business in the state, second only to farming. But the whiskey wasn't entirely safe.

According to George D. Mueller, in his 1920 publication, "Bootleggers and Crooked Cops," written about

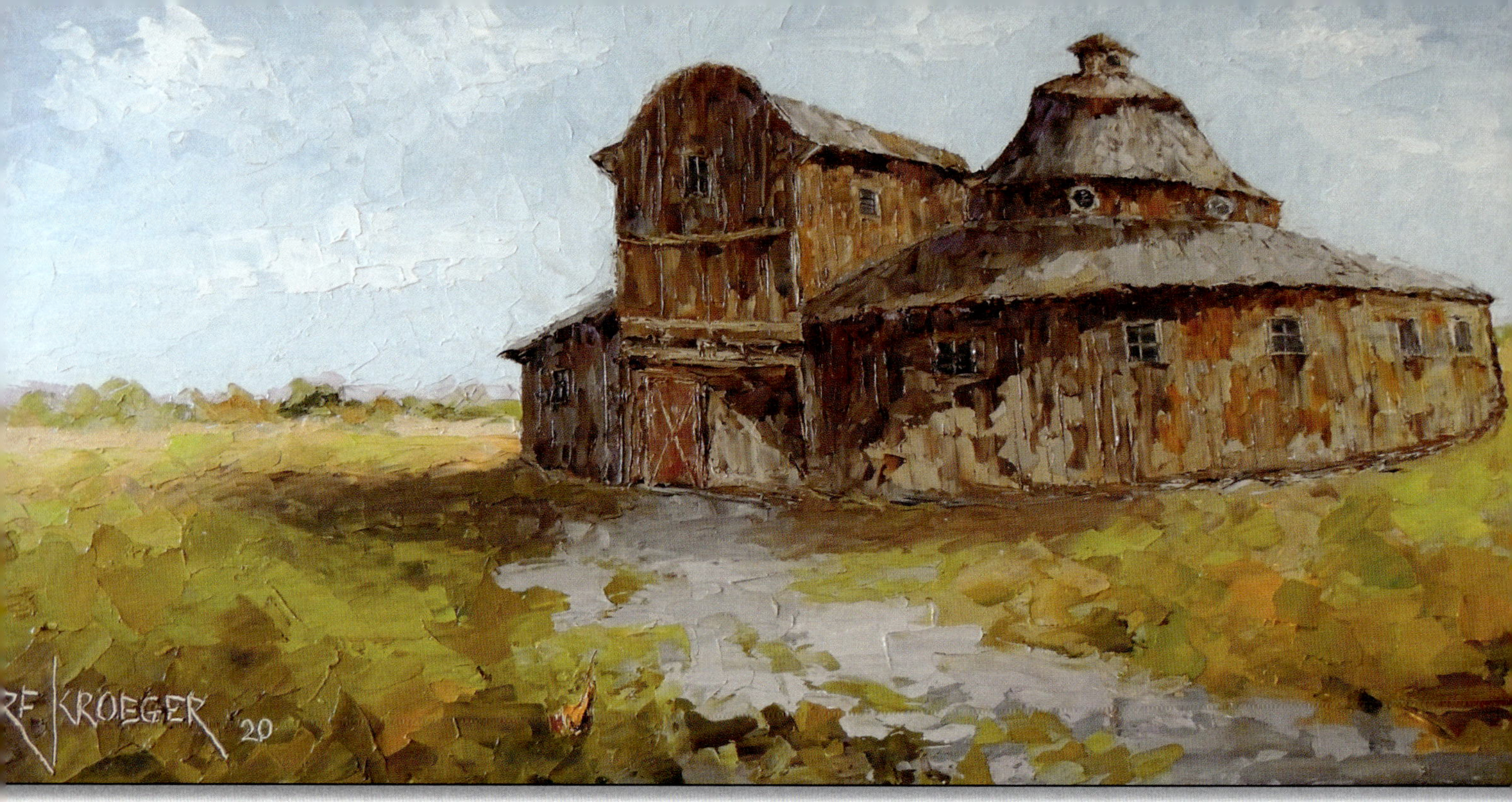

Bootlegger Trail

prohibition days in Lewistown, Montana, there were tests to do before drinking. "One was to put a finger in the bottle or jug for three minutes. When pulled out, if the fingernail was missing, it wasn't a good buy. The other test was to pour some on the fender of a car. If the paint started to peel in three minutes, it also wasn't a good buy." But it was probably less expensive than the Canadian beer and whiskey, smuggled in via this trail.

For fifteen years, whiskey runners outsped the Model Ts of policemen along this trail, and, thanks to some colorful politicians, the name stuck. Even today, news reports of accidents refer to the road as "Bootlegger Trail" and not State Route 225, which is a bit too tame for westerners. There's even another road, Bootlegger Lateral, an offshoot of the main road.

And, yes, even though this barn, located on Bootlegger Trail, wasn't around to see any mountain men, fur trappers, herds of buffalo, nomadic Indian tribes, or outlaws, it may have witnessed gangsters speeding by on their way to or from Canada.

M.J. MacDonald founded this farm in 1910 and, after several years of prosperity, hired a Mr. McManus of Washington to build this circular barn in 1917. His son Ross, about 18 in 1917, remembered that it took two railcar loads of lumber, shipped from Eureka to Brady. From there, wagons pulled by horses hauled the wood to the farm.

MacDonald could have built a conventional barn but, thanks to either the 16-sided Doncaster round barn, built in 1884 in Twin Bridges, or the many articles and round barn plans in agriculture journals, he opted for a circular design and added the striking false-front entry wall for the look of the Wild West. The builder, McManus, was probably familiar with circular and polygonal barns built earlier in his home state.

With a diameter of 83 feet and a circumference of 262 feet, the barn had plenty of room for 20 horse stalls in the center and stanchions for cows on the perimeter. They stored hay on the second level. The most recent family owner, Ross MacDonald, said that the barn was built to resist harsh prairie winds but acknowledged that the barn had less room for hay in the mow, compared to a rectangular barn.

In 1944, the MacDonalds sold the farm to the Elmer Rossmiller family, who were the last to own it. Today's Rolling Acres Farm, still located on Bootlegger Trail in Chouteau County, primarily produces wheat and, even though its iconic western barn is gone, its memory lives on in this painting and essay.

CARBON COUNTY

Versatile

The history of this barn interweaves western lore of Zane Grey, the Crow Indians, and, believe it or not, a round barn builder, who traveled here from Indiana long after the round barn craze had ended. Carbon County, located southwest of Billings, was created in 1895 from portions of Park and Yellowstone counties and, nestled among the Beartooth and Pryor Mountains and the Big Horn River to the east, it was named after abundant amounts of coal. Ironically, the county was home to the state's first oil well, too.

Author Zane Grey was the first to establish the unwritten code of western living, when he published his book, *Code of the West*, in 1934. According to Grey, the men and women who came to this part of the country during the westward expansion of the United States were bound by certain rules and values like integrity, self-reliance, and accountability. Carbon County's website has adapted Grey's ideas for those considering moving into the area, "Rural counties survive on volunteerism. Costs are kept down by the willingness of the populace to go without many things suburban and urban people regard as necessities." Yes, this is wild country … especially in winter, when snowfall can come unexpectedly … and in feet, not inches.

Carbon County's seat is Red Lodge, where this barn is located, and named in honor of the Crow Indians. In their culture, the red lodge was a place of worship — they painted their council tepee with red clay. In fact, 23 Crow scouts fought with the US Calvary against their common enemy, the Sioux, in the Battle of the Little Big Horn, located on the Crow Reservation, just east of Billings. That was 1876. Nineteen years after Custer's Last Stand, Carbon County was formed.

Ephraim Kent emigrated with his family from Finland in the early 1900s and settled in Red Lodge, part of the large Finnish immigration of the northern states in the late 1800s. He began working in coal mines while his wife Fiina started a small dairy operation. All their children helped in delivering raw milk in buckets, and later bottles, to local customers. Despite the Great Depression, the Kents survived, following the Code of the West, and expanded their dairy business. However, when local laws forbade keeping cows in town, the family purchased land outside city limits in 1938. The next year the Kents decided to build a round barn. And they hired the best — Indiana's McNamees, legendary circular barn builders.

First, Ephraim, by this time retired, and his sons purchased an abandoned building in the town of Bear Creek and they salvaged materials, including wood joists, a decorative tin ceiling, and brick, taking care to clean each brick by hand. Ephraim and son Harry cut down two tall cottonwood trees and hand hewed two beams, which supported the main floor's ceiling. Using Finnish ingenuity, Ephraim made a plane — to finish the beams — out of a leaf spring from a car. They used a draw knife to fashion the 37 support posts.

Emery McNamee and his father Isaac (who taught him carpentry and the art of building a round barn), traveled with a construction crew in the early 1900s to build round barns. Their reputation took them not only to several western states but also to Saskatchewan, Canada, where they built many round barns in 1913, after which they settled in Roundup, Montana, where they continued building. After a few years, they returned to Indiana, where they kept busy until round barn building declined in the late 1920s and Great Depression hit in the 1930s.

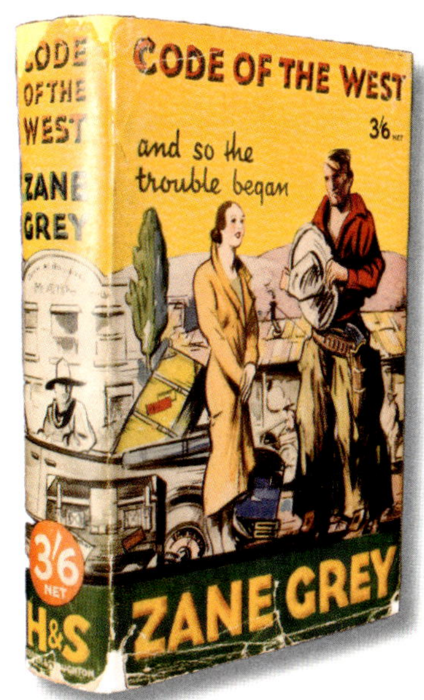

Code of the West *by Zane Grey. Courtesy of Abe Books*

Presumably because of their work near Roundup — word of mouth travels fast in the rural West — the Kents hired them to design their barn in 1939. At the time, Emery was 81 and probably returned with his own son to rekindle memories of earlier adventures. However, the Kents did the carpentry, cleverly using iron steam pipes that they salvaged from the West Side Mine in Red Lodge, bending them into curves for cow stalls, using a cottonwood tree and a truck for leverage. Locals observed that they displayed what the Finnish call "sisu," a term that connotes determination, perseverance, and fortitude. Although the traditional circular round barn called for a central silo, this one had only a grain bin because the short growing season in these parts was not ideal for corn. Grains — wheat, oats, and barley — could be dropped from the second-floor storage. Knowing the rigors of Montana's winters, the family chose brick, rather than wood, for the walls, which they also laid, even though masonry was a new experience for them. They finished construction in 1941, when 37 cows made it their new home.

The family used the barn to develop a robust dairy business, co-owned by the Kent brothers — farming, milking, and processing milk for local customers and stores. Eventually Armas and Sylvia bought out the other brothers and, in the late 1950s, signed an agreement to sell their raw milk to a dairy in nearby Wyoming, which, in turn, processed and distributed it throughout the region.

The 60-foot-wide barn was enough for a modest dairy herd but it also entertained the community by hosting barn dances in the second floor throughout the 1940s. Laminated wood benches, attached to the walls, were used for seating, presumably when the cowboys got tired. Cowgirls like to dance.

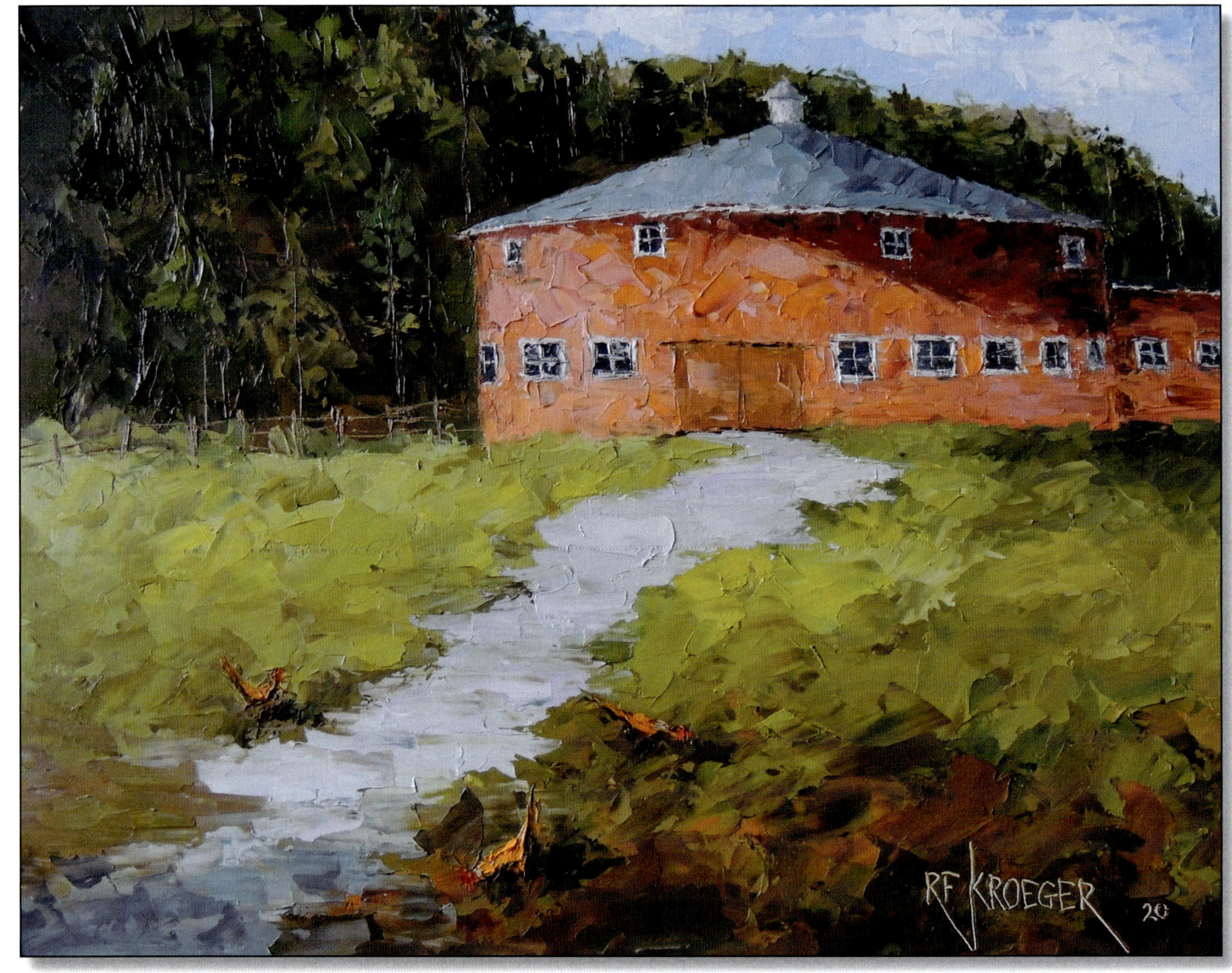

Versatile

After using the barn for dairy farming for 30 years, Armas and Sylvia Kent retired in 1969 and sold the barn two years later. Its versatility continued with its next owners, entrepreneurs Carm and Shirley Hampton, who saw an opportunity, made the purchase, and converted the barn into a gift shop and restaurant, The Round Barn Restaurant. Bonnie Porter rented the second story to sell antiques.

In 1974 ownership changed again: Carl and Jennie Hanson of Billings bought it and, hoping to attract the Nordic element (in 1910 the population of Red Lodge was a quarter Finnish), installed a Norwegian-styled smorgasbord, which they operated for 20 years. In the 1980s they altered the second floor for local theater productions. The name became The Round Barn Restaurant and Dinner Theater. Its adaptability continued.

Among the entertainers to grace the round barn's stage was The Ringling 5, whose "off-the-wall humor spills over into lively audience participation," according to the former website's advertising. Five members of the group are ranchers, one is a schoolteacher, and one is a feed salesman. The cost for dinner and show was $21, a pretty good bargain in the 1980s. Offerings included a barbecue and cowboy poetry. Ah, the West, where even cowpokes write poetry!

In 1994 Daniel and Marcee Farrar of Boise, Idaho, took over, retained the smorgasbord, but changed to a dairy theme. They kept the stage performances going and, historically minded, they successfully listed the round barn in the National Register. They also turned the second floor into a ski chalet, emphasizing breathtaking mountain views and nearby trout ponds. But they, too, sold the buildings. A 2004 real estate listing described the property: "the food is buffet style with seating in the round next to the original stanchions from the historical dairy barn. On a weekly basis, the theater hosted a variety of shows from dinner theater murder mysteries, theater productions, vaudeville, to nationally recognized musical artists." I wonder if that included The Ringling 5.

A Ford dealership came next — its red pole barn building still sits next to the round barn — but they also decided to sell, once more challenging the barn. Eventually the Good Lord got involved.

The Church of the Rockies has multiple locations in the region and chose the round barn to be its newest, as it calls its Red Lodge Campus. The public, formerly having enjoyed entertainment and meals in the Round Barn Restaurant and Dinner Theater, now gets God's messages every Sunday, giving the barn a new, and perhaps its best, purpose. The late Charles Kuralt, CBS traveling news commentator and author of *On the Road With Charles Kuralt*, his memoir of traveling through Americana, named highway 212, locally known as the Beartooth Highway, a road that passes by the Round Barn, as "the most beautiful drive in America." I'm sure that, if Charlie were still alive — and if he knew about the transition of this round barn from dairy farming to a restaurant/dinner theater and antique shop to a family smorgasbord-ski chalet to a Ford dealership to a Christian church — he would have simply used one word to describe it — versatile.

WYOMING

SHERIDAN COUNTY

America ... and Its County Fairs

Even though this octagonal barn was built in 1939 and, as such, does not have the antiquity of round barns built decades earlier, it merits attention not only because it is a rare stone octagonal barn (Only two others exist — Ohio and Missouri.) but also because it was built specifically for the Sheridan County Fair. County fairs represent agriculture in America and they trace back to 1807 when Elkanah Watson, a Massachusetts businessman who retired to a farm, organized the Berkshire County Fair, which is still held today in Pittsfield.

Watson urged farmers to showcase their livestock in public, where awards were given, pride was displayed, and community spirit uplifted. Socialization factored into the fair's popularity, especially because farm families often led solitary lives, working long hours and being isolated from their neighbors in rural settings. In time these gatherings spread to other villages in the region, culminating with the first state fair, held in 1841 in Syracuse, New York. Here, attendees not only saw champions in livestock and crops, they also learned new farming methods. The country's first state fair drew over 10,000 people. Recently (2019) the New York state fair attracted over one million; Minnesota's surpassed that with over two million visitors.

Over the years, county fairs have become economic engines, resulting in substantial revenue and entertainment to cities, large and small. The Ohio State Fair, held in the capital city of Columbus, brings in nearly 70 million dollars each year. County fairs, while not on this scale, likewise contribute to the economy. In Ohio, even though there are 88 counties, there are well over 90 county fairs. And, for some reason, fair leaders occasionally chose the round design for floral halls or barns that house exhibits and livestock sales on fairgrounds. Professor King's plans and the round barn complex of the University of Illinois may have contributed to this trend.

Interior, octagonal sale barn. Courtesy of Sheridan County Fair, Wyoming

The first fair in Sheridan was held in 1885 and, although records are sketchy, several buildings were built for the fair, including a floral hall, stables, and a grandstand. As the fair's popularity grew, more buildings were added. In 2011 The Sherdian County Fairgrounds Historic District was listed on the National Register. This included six buildings: a 1923 brick exhibit hall, three circa 1939 WPA-built sandstone buildings including this barn, horse stalls from 1950, and a frame barn built in the 1930s. The sandstone barn, also known as the Sale Barn, is the most significant of the lot.

Sheridan's fair grew quickly and in the early 1900s it included an Indian village set up by the Crow and Cheyenne tribes, a carnival, a Wild West show, horse racing, and a rodeo, which is still held today.

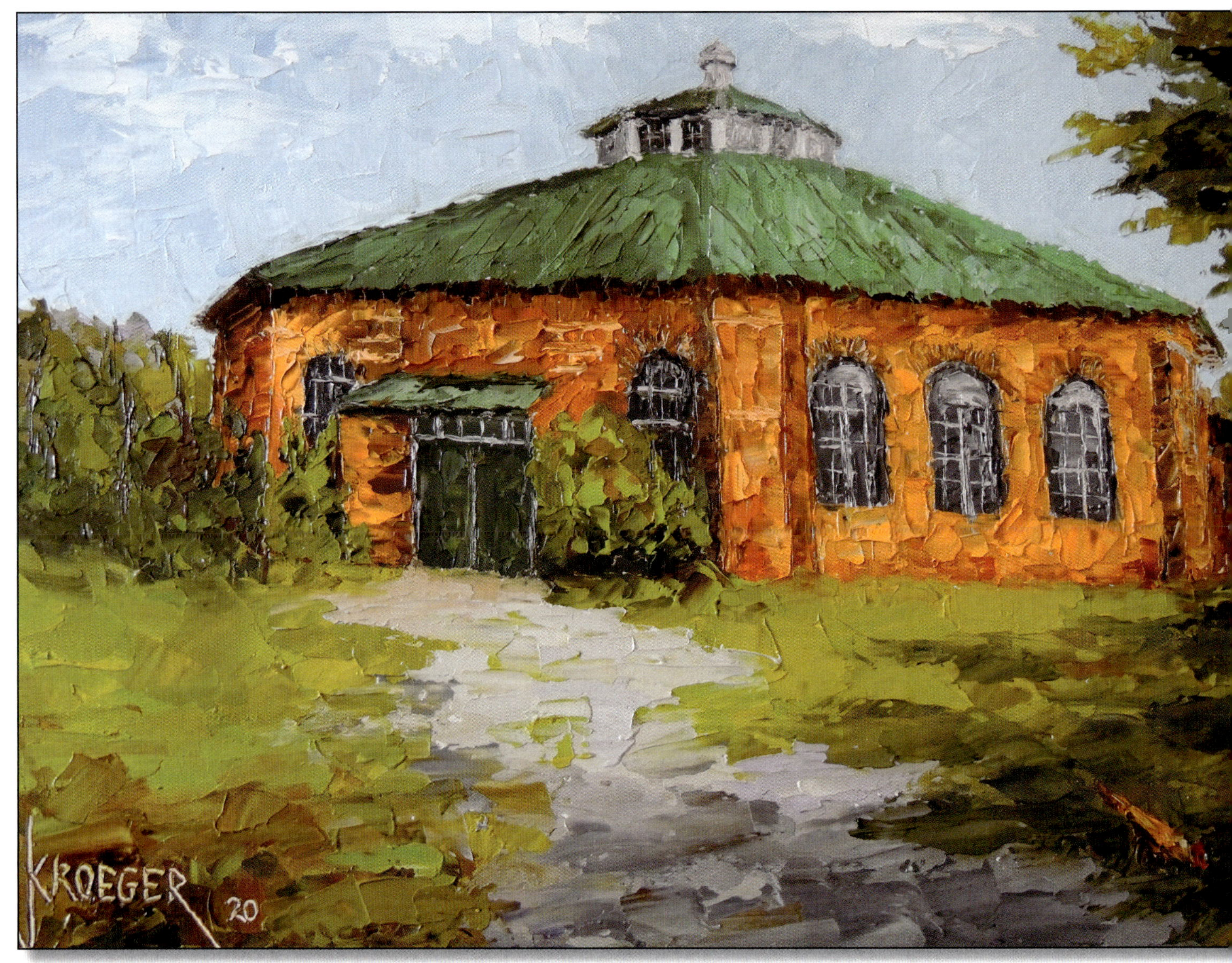

America ... and Its County Fairs

Eventually boys and girls clubs participated and evolved into the 4-H program. The county fair became the premier event of the region.

Wisely, the county took advantage of President Franklin Roosevelt's New Deal Program, an important part of the nation's recovery from the Great Depression, and secured funds to build this iconic barn. They were able to hire 53 men for the project: five stone masons, seven carpenters, two painters, 30 laborers, and a local architect, C. Walter Wiberg, who designed the barn. Though only one story, compared to two or three stories of most round barns, it's a testament to not only the architect but the men who built it. Its stone walls, 18-inches thick, are accentuated with stepped buttresses at each corner. At the top of the roof, a raised octagonal lantern provides natural illumination through six-light windows in each wall facet. The colors of the sandstone give a pleasing effect — rubble walls, composed of a reddish tint, contrast with the buff color of the coursed stone. Twenty-one steel windows in large arched openings allow plenty of light. Visitors enter through three pairs of double doors.

Originally, rubble stone walls, tinted red, surrounded the central sales area and its dirt floor. Today, livestock pens hold the animals for sale and are situated under tiered stands, which can seat up to 420. In 2013 a cement floor was added. The green metal roof, supported with steel trusses that radiate around the octagon, delights those folks who've never been inside a round barn. Metal grandstands, completed in 1992, have replaced WPA-constructed wooden structures.

True West magazine selected Sheridan as the "# 1 Western town in America" in 2006, an achievement, which is tied closely to its county fair. With a little luck, the sturdy stone walls of this impressive sandstone octagonal barn — as it approaches its century mark — should provide many more years of hosting its county fair.

NEW MEXICO

TAOS COUNTY

A Natural Curiosity

The truly circular barn at Ojo Caliente Mineral Springs, located about 50 miles north of Santa Fe, though built in 1924, has a history dating to the prehistoric era. Surrounding the barn and its famous hot springs are ruins of cities populated before the birth of Christ. Called "Posi," which translates to "village at the place of the green bubbling hot springs," the area was once a site where ancestral tribes built large pueblos and terraced gardens overlooking the springs. Thanks to the work of archaeologists Adolph Bandelier and Edgar Hewitt, evidence has revealed that thousands lived here until the 16th century — when the Spanish conquistadors arrived.

Searching for gold and the Fountain of Youth, the explorers found these hot springs instead and one of them wrote, "The greatest treasure that I found these strange people to possess are hot springs which burst out at the foot of a mountain ... so powerful are the chemicals contained in this water that the inhabitants have a belief that they were given to them by their gods. These springs I have named Ojo Caliente." This Spanish term for "hot eye" eventually came to mean a hot spring, which many claim has medicinal healing properties.

And, even though the Spanish, in their efforts to colonize and Christianize the natives, continued to live here for three centuries, it was not easy. Raids by Indian tribes, such as the Comanche, often drove white settlers back to safer ground in Santa Fe.

Another explorer, Zebulon Pike, under orders from General James Wilkinson, explored western lands, newly acquired in the 1803 Louisiana Purchase. On his second exploration, he discovered Colorado's now famous 14'er, Pike's Peak, and, continuing southwards to locate the source of the Red River, crossed into Mexican territory (now northern New Mexico). Captured by Mexican soldiers, Pike and his men were taken to Santa Fe but, on the way, they also visited these hot springs in 1807, which he termed "a natural curiosity."

After the Mexican-American war of 1846 and subsequent American acquisition of present-day New Mexico, many Spanish and Mexican land grants became nullified, allowing Antonio Joseph, who had moved here from St. Louis, to get control of the hot springs. He built a bathhouse in 1868 — now on the National Register — making this one of the first natural health resorts in the West. He added a hotel in 1895 so that guests could stay for extended periods and he founded a post office and a general store, where historic ledgers show that Kit Carson once bought supplies.

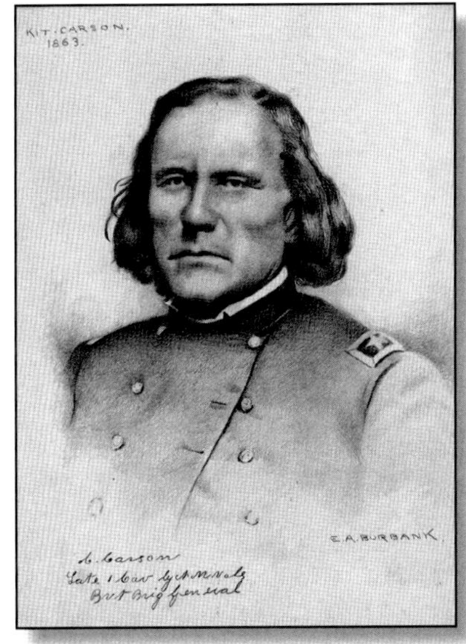

Kit Carson, 1863. Wikimedia Commons. Sketch by Elbridge Burbank

Though Antonio died in 1910, his widow Elizabeth continued to run the business, expanding it. Their only living son, Antonio F. Joseph, took the reins from his mother and built another hotel in 1917, also listed on the National Register. By this time business was good, thanks to New Mexico's statehood in 1912 and to improved roads, which allowed visitors easier access to the property. Realizing the need for food for hotel and spa guests, the owners built the round barn in 1924, principally for dairy cows, hay, and storage of in-season vegetables.

Why Antonio chose a round design remains a mystery, though he may have read about such barns in farming journals. Did he visit any in Kansas, the nearest state that had a modest representation of these barns? Did he know that experts had summarily dismissed the advantages of the round barns by 1920, their findings published in many agricultural journals of the time? Nonetheless, he built this barn in a true circle and, as such, it remains the only round barn in New Mexico and the only round barn with adobe walls in America. The hotel supplied milk and dairy products year round to hotel guests, as well as vegetables during the growing season.

The Josephs were prosperous enough during the 1920s to build this barn, a good sized one with a diameter of 66 feet and a hexagonal atrium rising to 65 feet. A full hay wagon could enter through large double doors and then exit through a narrow door on the opposite side. Though the barn didn't have a silo, hay was deposited through the haymow (the dormer was added after 1934) and into the second-floor loft, from where workers could drop it centrally to feed the cows, whose stalls lined the perimeter. The cupola — now with six fixed windows — provided light and the hexagonal air shaft assured adequate ventilation for the hay and livestock. A small shed was attached to serve as a milk cooling room.

However, over the years the hotel and spa changed ownership and weather and the elements began to take their toll. By 2000, the barn had begun to deteriorate: its

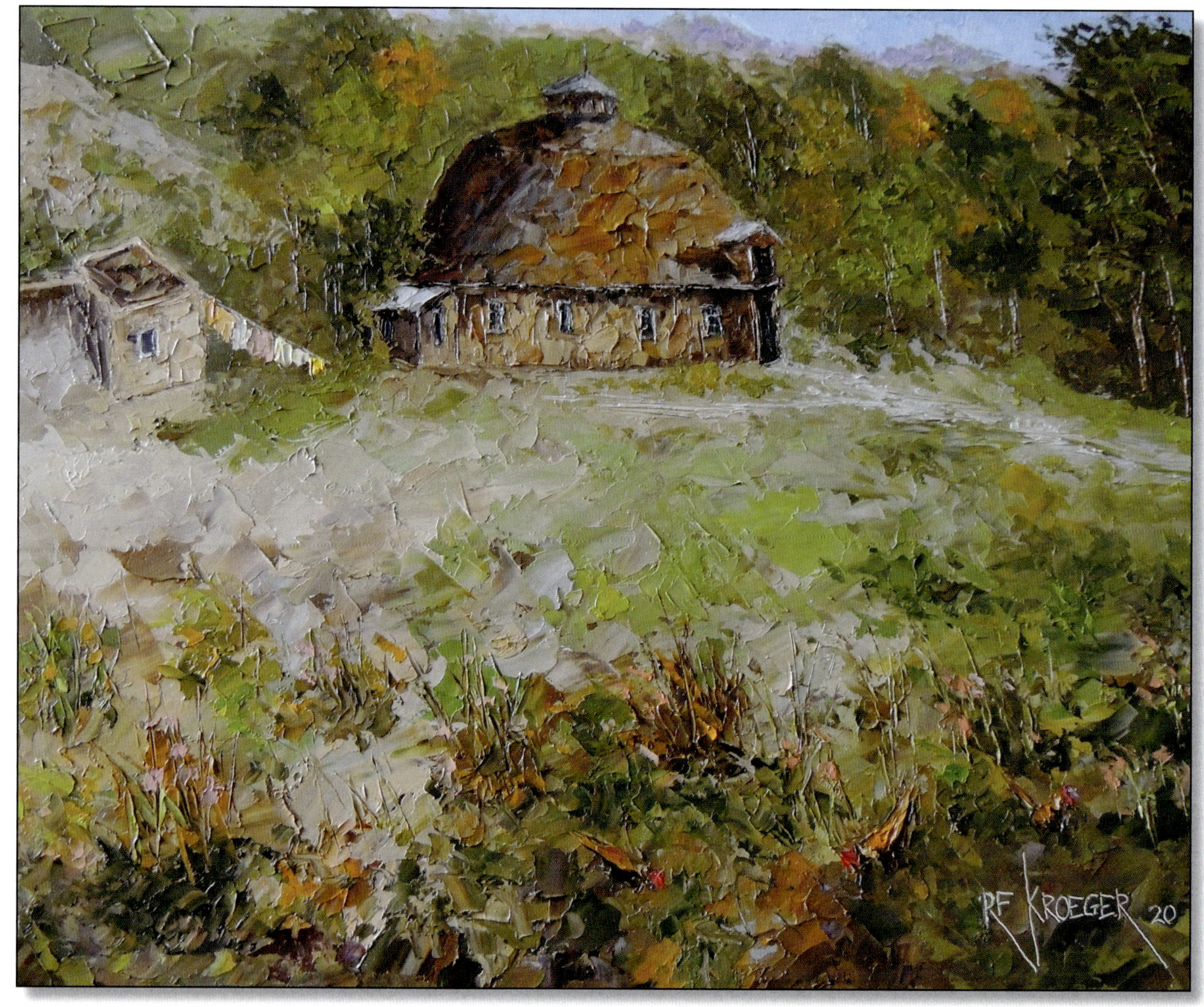

A Natural Curiosity

cupola had broken, the roof's missing shingles exposed the rafters, and the adobe walls had become stained. Fortunately, the new owner decided to save the iconic barn and added a new roof of 28,000 cedar shingles, new windows, a balustrade over the dormer hay mow, and new wooden doors. In 2003, the resort applied for and was granted a listing for the barn on the National Register. And, in 2014 the owners rejuvenated the farm, growing organic herbs, fruits, and vegetables on the two-acre plot.

Today the Ojo Spa Resorts of New Mexico own a property near Santa Fe as well as this one, which features thermal ponds and pools fed by cool artesian springs. The ownership has not only a business interest in the Ojo Caliente Mineral Springs but also a sense of history and stewardship in preserving the Southwest's only round barn as well as these hot springs, which merited praise in the words from Zeb Pike, "a natural curiosity."

12. FAR WEST

WASHINGTON

WHITMAN COUNTY

Jewel of the Palouse

This restored 12-sided barn lies in eastern Washington and southeast of Pullman, the seat of Whitman County, a region called "The Palouse." One of the most scenic areas of the state, the Palouse stretches into nearby Idaho and provides vast acreage of gently rolling treeless hills, which, thanks to ideal soil, has led to crop farming and, more recently, to vineyards. The Palouse, derived from pelouse, a French word for "land with thick grass," produces 95% of America's lentils and dry peas as well as 40% of Washington's wheat. Prior to 1850, when the only white people were fur trappers and gold prospectors passing through, it was the grassland of Native American tribes, hunters and gatherers. It must have been a sight: undulating hills of grass waving in the wind, interspersed with herds of antelopes and bands of roaming Indians.

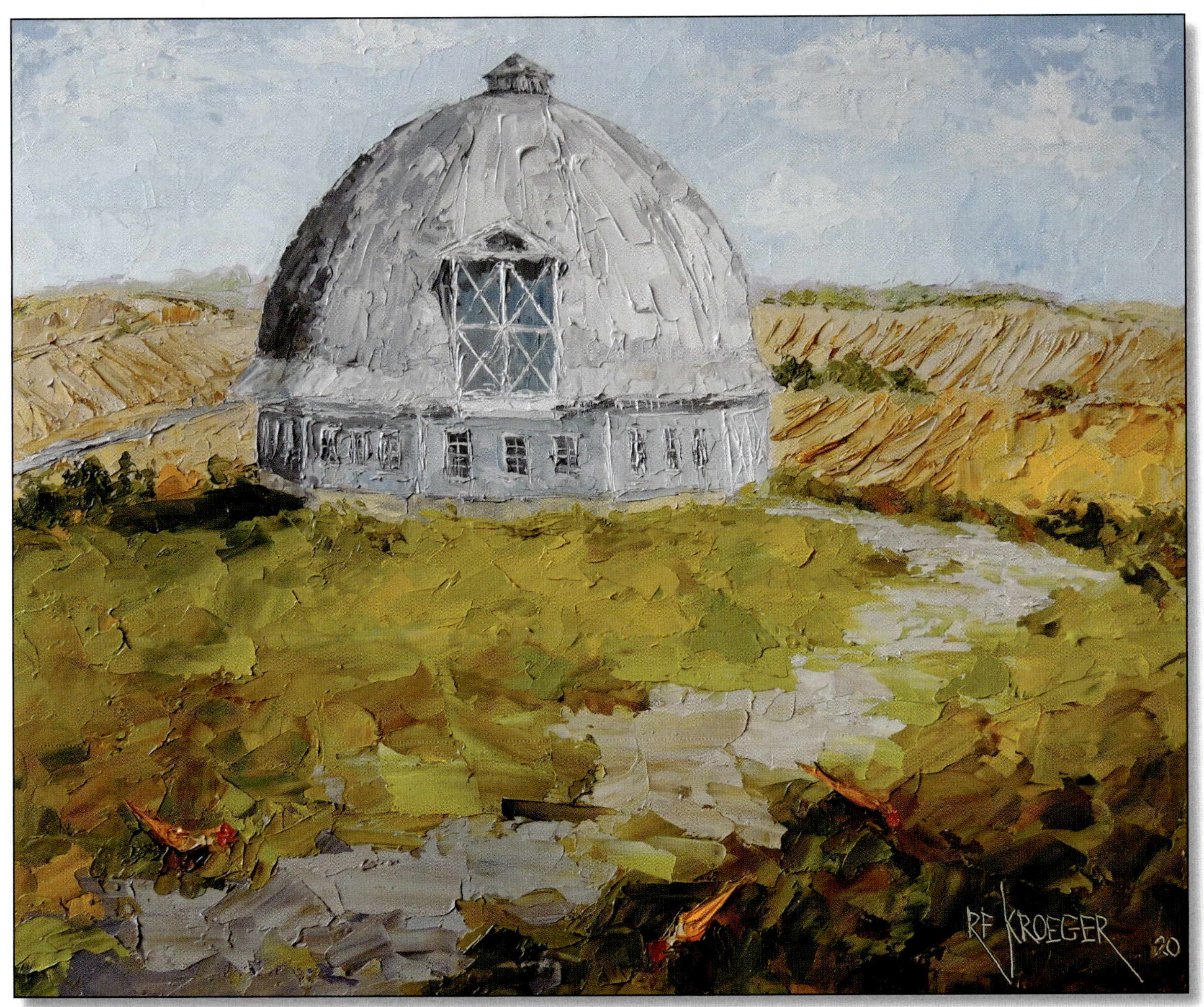

Jewel of the Palouse

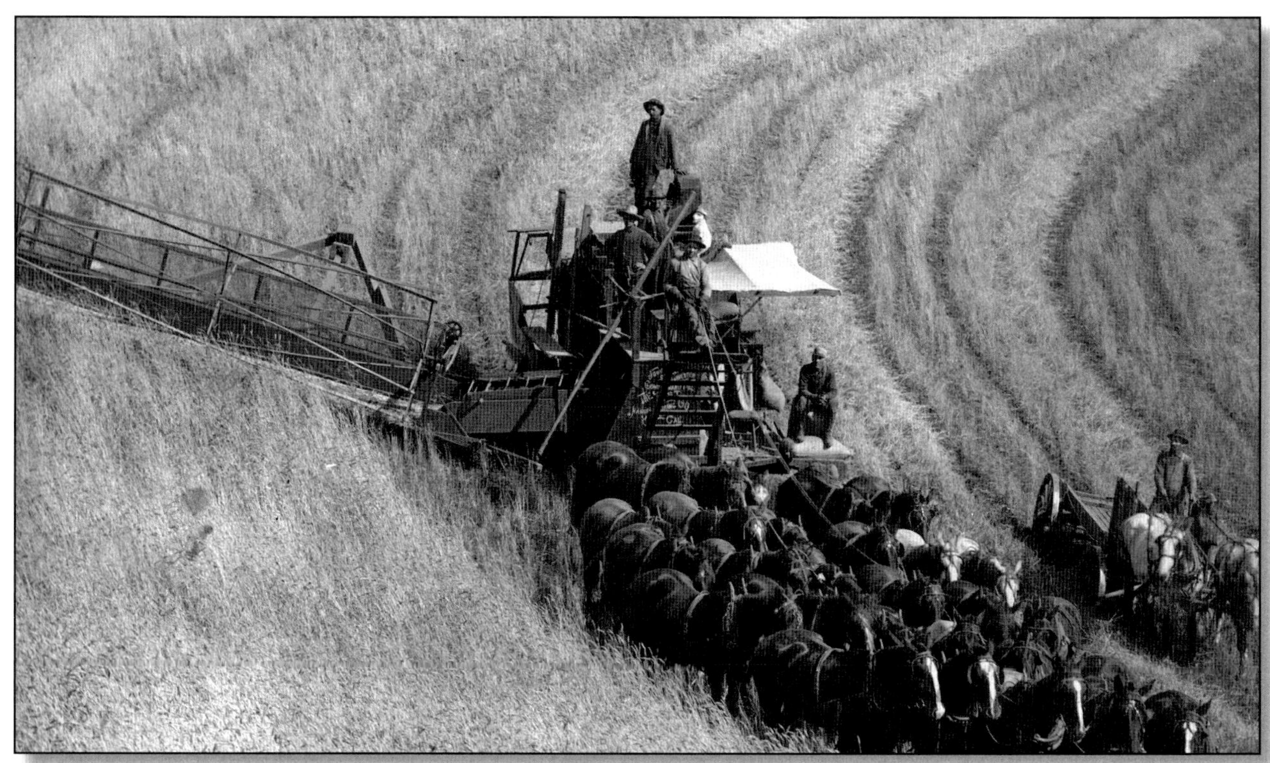

Farming on the Palouse. Courtesy of the Whitman County Historical Society

But, as elsewhere in the West, the settlers arrived and one of them, Thomas Andrew "Andy" Leonard, moved here from Pennsylvania in 1890 and started farming. He and his wife Kitty had three children and raised crops and livestock, using a traditional barn to house horses, dairy cows, hay, and grain. When the barn burned in 1917, Andy decided to replace it with a round one.

He made this decision after seeing round barns on his travels to Ohio, though he may have also seen some in Iowa, Illinois, and Indiana, where such barns were more abundant in the early 1900s. However, a 12-sided barn with a similar domed roof and distinctive dormers, built in 1901 by Richard Hall, also in Whitman County, may have been more influential than those he saw on his trip to the Midwest. A year earlier — in 1916 — Max Steinke, a farmer in Whitman County, erected another 12-sided barn, one with a domed roof and large dormers, whose work must have impressed Andy so much that he hired Steinke to design his barn. Andy chose to have the lower wall constructed with wood — opposed to concrete in the other two — so that he could add plenty of windows. Also, the dormer gable design in all three barns differed slightly. The central wooden-stave silo held straw and feed for the animals and a Louden manure carrier system ran on circular runners. The family also began raising thousands of chickens, though many other farmers raised wheat, not easy to harvest on the sloping hills of the Palouse.

In fact, a photo of a threshing team, courtesy of the Whitman County Historical Society, documented just what a major undertaking this was in the 1920s. The image shows five men sitting on a large combine, pulled by dozens of horses (often up to 40!), harvesting wheat on a hillside of about 30 degrees. Teams of up to 120 men and 320 mules and horses moved from one farm to another as crops were ready for harvesting. Large combines, such as these, were more suited to flat farm fields.

The Leonard barn, with a diameter of nearly 60 feet, featured an open first floor with 10 steel stanchions for cows and eight box stalls for horses. High above the hayloft, the self-supported roof, constructed with 12 large, curved bents, towered impressively. The coup de grace was the cupola, 45 feet above ground level, whose several large louvers provided ventilation.

However, the barn, sitting high on a hill and overlooking the treeless grasslands of the Palouse, was vulnerable to wind. Sadly, tragedy struck in 1946 when a 100-mph wind blew off the cupola, which was not replaced, allowing water to penetrate the cedar-shingled roof. The disaster signaled the end of the barn as the 12 Ponderosa pine trusses began to rot. Undaunted, Andy's son George continued farming, though he didn't replace the missing cupola.

When George retired from raising chickens, he began restoring his family's beloved barn and, by the time of his death in 1984, he had re-shingled almost half of the roof. Unfortunately, his descendants chose not to continue farming and leased the land to wheat farmers. Though the barn stored some farm equipment, it continued to deteriorate. Then, during the summer of 1985 two Washington State architecture students spent the summer researching the barn's history and drawing architectural plans. They entered their project in a historical survey competition and won first place. Buoyed by such interest, the family applied for and successfully obtained a listing on the National Register in 1987.

Years later, in 1992, the Washington Historical Preservation office noticed the importance of the round barn and labeled it as one of 10 endangered historic properties, but efforts to secure funding for restoration failed. However, when someone made an offer to buy the barn, the family declined and the Leonard Family Trust funded restoration, effectively keeping the farm and the iconic barn in family hands.

They began restoring the barn in 2000, which included building a new cupola, replacing all 12 trusses, adding a new shingled roof, replacing broken windows, rebuilding entry doors, and giving the barn a fresh coat of paint, all done to make the barn resemble its original appearance. In 2001, when the renovation was complete, a barn opening celebration attracted over 1,500 guests. Though today the family still owns the barn and presumably leases the farm, my letter to the family trust, located in California, was never answered. Regardless, the barn still sits high on a hill over endless fields of wheat and grassland, continuing to remain as "the Jewel of the Palouse."

OREGON

HARNEY COUNTY

The Cattle Barons

From a distance, this round barn looms as a tiny speck in vast sage-covered grasslands, set against a stunning backdrop of the snow-capped Steens Mountains. Built in 1883 by cattleman Peter French, it represents a colorful page in the history of the West.

In 1826 Antoine Sylvaille led a small party — the first white men to see this land — to trap beavers along local rivers, long before California (1850) and Oregon (1859) joined the Union. Yes, this was mostly Indian territory until the US Army began to herd the natives onto reservations.

Two decades later, about the time of the famous gold strike in California's Sierra Madre range, John William French — later known as "Pete" — was born in Callaway County, Missouri. In 1850 his father moved the family to northern California and began sheep farming. However, he soon found this rather dull and around 1870 he began

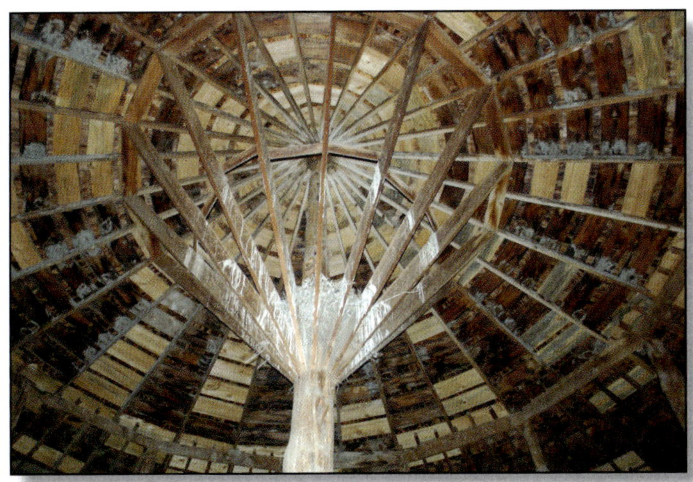

Interior of French barn. Courtesy of the Oregon Parks and Recreation Department

working on the cattle ranch of Dr. Hugh James Glenn, one of California's early cattle barons and wheat farmers. Originally from Virginia, Glenn earned a medical degree and served as a physician in the Mexican War. But his heart belonged to ranching.

French worked on the ranch with his father and, at 21, he registered to vote, listing his name as Peter, which was possibly bestowed on him by fellow workers, Mexican vaqueros. An industrious worker, Pete French became the son, in spirit at least, that Dr. Glenn never had — especially since his own children, raised indulgently, had no interest in manual labor. Quickly, Pete rose to the job of foreman on Glenn's ranch, which though large, did not have enough land to feed his herd. So, Dr. Glenn looked north into the Oregon Territory and selected French to lead his team of vaqueros on a cattle drive, taking 1,200 shorthorn cows into the high desert prairies of Oregon's Steens Mountains.

Young Pete French settled in the Blitzen Valley, where he acquired land, built fences and houses, and began raising beef cattle for Dr. Glenn, who by that time was known as "the Wheat King of the West." In his prime Dr. Glenn had an empire of 38 houses, 27 barns, 14 blacksmith shops, and one massive mansion, which author Giles French (no relation to Pete) described in his book, *Cattle County of Peter French*, as "a wreck, covered with overgrowing vines," a far cry in 1964 from its opulence in the late 19th century. There's no doubt that Pete French contributed to Glenn's success, raising cattle and driving them 200 miles east to market. His first sale, $7,157, was recorded in January, 1875.

But this was the Wild West, the land of heroes and desperadoes, the likes of Jesse James and Butch Cassidy and the Sundance Kid … and western justice. And so, it should come as no surprise that Glenn's empire came to an abrupt end, when, walking on the porch of his Jacinto Hotel in 1883, he was shot in the head by Huram Miller, a disgruntled bookkeeper, whom Glenn had recently fired. The *Oakland Tribune* reported the shooting, commenting that Glenn was "one of the remarkable men of his age." His estate, amounting to over one million dollars, was a huge one in those years. After Glenn's death and funeral, his heirs continued their profligate ways. On the other hand, Pete French returned to Oregon, where he formed the French-Glenn Livestock Company and established the Barton Lake Ranch.

Though he had built a rectangular barn in 1880, French, for some reason, built this round barn three years later, choosing a small hill for its construction, a site he claimed would be dry year round, keeping his horses well protected. Did he read agricultural journals, which might have described the octagonal designs of New York's Elliot Stewart, thousands of miles away? Did he somehow hear about the Shakers' round barn in Massachusetts or Nutwood's round barn in Ohio? The circular barn would not become publicized until the 1890s. Pete French must have had a keen imagination. Recent photos show the barn to be in excellent condition.

The barn, 100 feet in diameter, has an inner core of a mortared stone wall, and several centered posts (stripped juniper logs), which extend upwards to support the roof. There's no basement nor is there a second-story haymow, found in typical round barns. French built the barn, perhaps thinking the design would provide room for more horses than a conventional barn, and he planned to use it primarily to house his many horses during the Oregon winters. Outside the rock wall, the overhanging roof allowed wild horse training during the winters. Despite its unique construction, it's stood the test of time now for almost 150 years.

Prairie barns, also known as Western barns, had long, cascading roofs, sometimes nearly touching the ground, which allowed for more storage space, and perhaps resisted high winds better than a barn with a taller roof. A peak

Below: *The Cattle Barons*

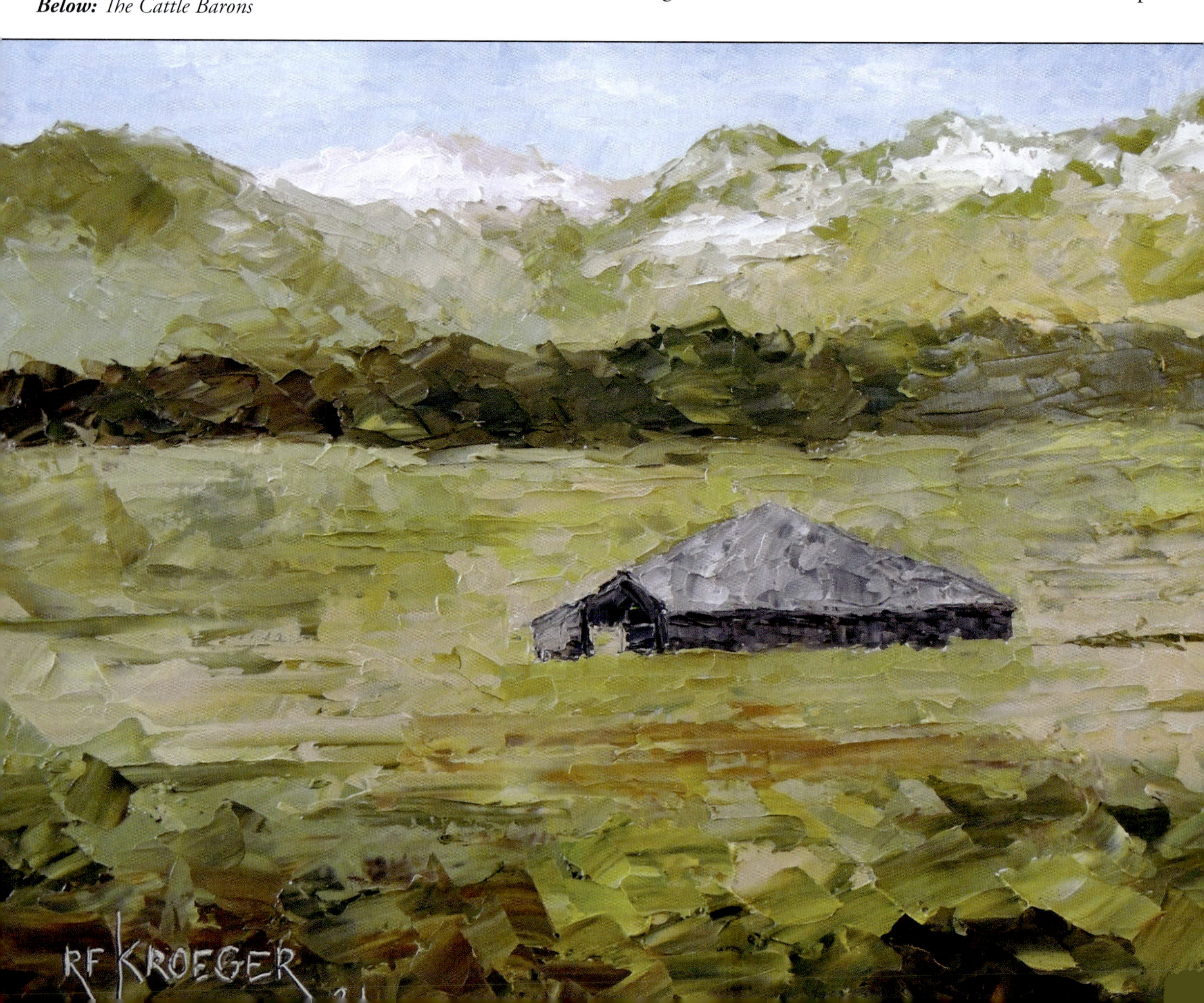

— above the hayloft opening — was also typical of the prairie barn, though it's hard to see in this painting.

French's empire, which he shared with Glenn's heirs, stretched for 130,000 acres of land, enough to graze over 30,000 head of cattle as well as 3,000 horses and mules. Business was good and French soon acquired more land and stock — 70,000 acres and 45,000 cattle. He also raised thousands of sheep for their wool, a throwback to his childhood days. Though small in stature, he ran a tight ship on this ranch but, as in the case of Dr. Glenn, was not without enemies.

After he returned from a business trip to Chicago on Christmas Day in 1897, French spent the evening with family in a festive party. But the next morning, he was shot in the head by an unhappy — and perhaps jealous — rancher. Peter French died instantly. He was 48. Incredibly, his assassin was found not guilty.

Over the decades, land ownership went through several owners and in 1908 President Theodore Roosevelt declared the nearby Malheur and Harney Lakes as a national animal refuge. Later in 1935 the owners sold another 64,717 acres to the government, which was added to the wildlife preserve. Today the Malheur National Wildlife Refuge encompasses over 290 square miles of wetlands in Oregon's high desert region and serves as habitats for over 320 bird species.

In 1946 the headquarters of Pete French's ranch burned, leaving the round barn as the only survivor of this era, and in 1969 the French family donated the iconic barn to the state of Oregon. It was listed on the National Register two years later. Today, the state park system maintains the old barn, one last monument to Peter French, a self-made cattle baron, often called "The Cattle King," one of a vanishing breed that tamed the West.

DOUGLAS COUNTY

Through a Looking Glass

When surveyor Hoy Flournoy charted this land in 1846, he observed that the beautiful green grass of the valley reflected light almost as well as a looking glass, the pioneer's term for a mirror. The name stuck and, in disregard for English teachers, the two words have remained joined together since the beginning. Today, the community of Lookingglass is a suburb of Roseburg with a population of 855.

In 1852 the Lookingglass Store — still existing and offering a shelf of two-cent candy — was built as the terminus for the Oakland to Lookingglass stage route. This was also the beginning of another famous stagecoach trail, the Coos Bay Wagon Road, a name that survives, also. This road connected Douglas County to Coos Bay, beginning in 1872. The stage line continued up to 1914. Indeed, not many grocery stores can claim being open for 170 years!

It was here that James Wimer built his octagonal barn — originally for cattle — in 1892. Moving here from Missouri, where he was born in 1856, he settled first in Murphy and then in Glide, where he ran dairy farms. He came to the Lookingglass valley in 1891 and purchased 40 acres of land. Wimer's descendants, the Shrum family, according to the National Historic Register listing, believed that Wimer himself shingled the roof with split cedar, though they didn't know how much more of the construction he did or why he chose an octagonal design.

A possible explanation is that Oregon State University, about 120 miles away, built its first teaching barn, an octagonal, in 1889. Though the college added a rectangular addition in 1892, the octagonal was the heart of the college's 180-acre farm until 1909, when a new rectangular-shaped barn was completed. Though the octagonal burned in 1924, it probably influenced farmers throughout the state.

Each side of the Wimer barn measures 31 feet and its roof, pitched at 45 degrees, spans 60 feet to the top of the octagonal cupola. A corrugated metal roof, now quaintly rusted with a tint of burnt sienna color, covers the cedar shingles. Originally, the barn's interior consisted of three octagons of cattle stanchions, the outer row being served from the hay loft by openings at the perimeter. Though the beams went through a sawmill, the connections were made with mortise and tenon joints and wooden pegs. Cedar timbers, resting on stone footings, have held up well, thanks to the protection of the metal roof.

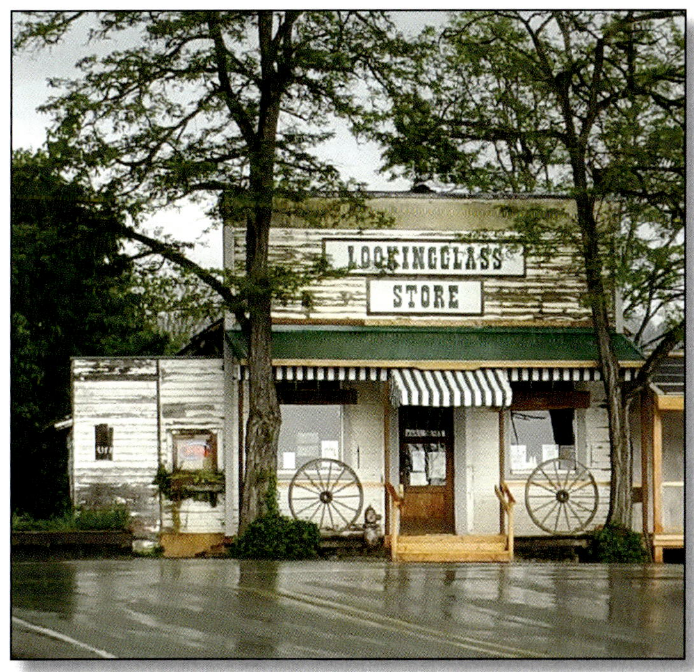

Lookingglass Store, 2022. Courtesy of Lookingglass Store, FB

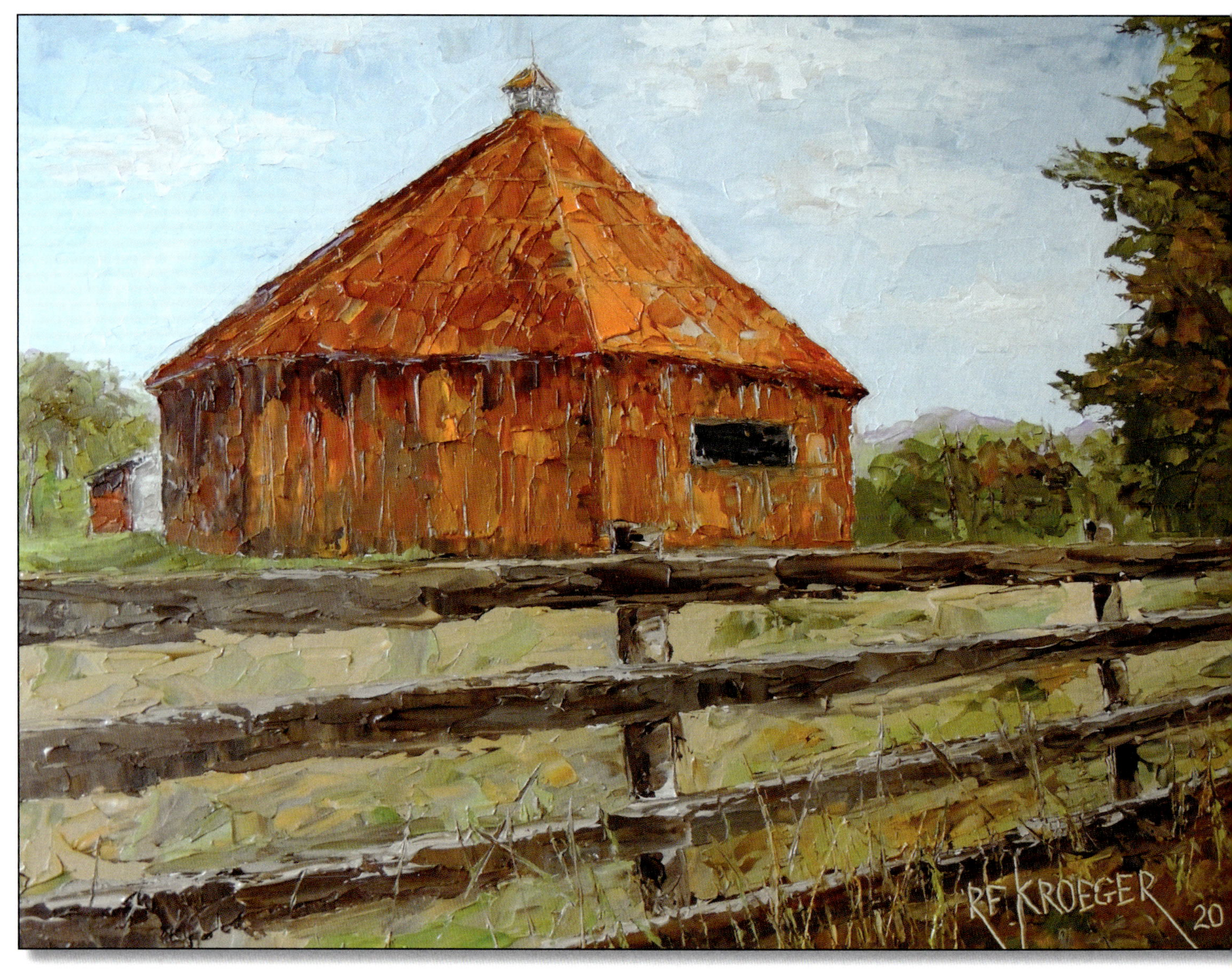

Through a Looking Glass

Though Wimer built the barn for cattle, he planted a prune orchard in 1892, which didn't fully produce until George Marsh purchased the farm three years later. Marsh expanded the orchard and around 1900 he removed the cattle stanchions to provide more room for fruit storage, as well as making other alterations for sheep raising. The orchards continued to produce until the 1960s, when the barn became a novelty instead of a functioning asset. The Marsh family, early settlers in this valley marketed their apples state-wide.

Current owners Ken and Nancy Bohon successfully submitted the application for listing in the National Register in 1985, a tribute to the early days of farming in this charming and fertile valley and to farmer James Wimer, who decided that a traditional design was not good enough for his barn, instead choosing an octagonal, which, in those days must have looked pretty good in a looking glass.

DOUGLAS COUNTY

The Claimant

Samuel D. Evans, born in Madison County, Ohio, wanted more land than he had in Ohio and, motivated by the Donation Land Claim Act of 1850, he traveled west to Oregon, settling in Douglas County in 1853. However, eight years later his decision to leave Ohio backfired when Indians killed him during a cattle drive to northern California. Such were risks of the Oregon pioneers.

Congress passed the Donation Land Claim Act of 1850 in hopes of attracting settlers into the Oregon Territory. Thousands took advantage of this free land offer — 320 acres to every unmarried white male citizen of 18 years or older and 640 acres to every married couple. Though the act included Americans who were half Indian and half white, it excluded full-blooded Indians and, in essence, was designed, via treaties, to move them from their ancestral lands and into reservations. For thousands of years over 60 tribes lived in the Oregon Territory and at least 18 languages were spoken. But, by 1855 there were three reservations and by 1879 there were three more.

However, in terms of bringing in settlers, the land act worked — over 7,400 land grants were issued under this law, which expired in late 1855. Interestingly, the law was one of the first to allow married women to hold land under their own name (In the case of a married couple, each would have half of the acreage).

The claimant's son, Samuel D. Evans, Jr., built this octagonal barn around 1900 and farmed the land, as his father did, until he died in 1933. The sawmill-cut beams, eight by eight inches square, and the post and beam construction suggest it was built, as the other seven octagonal barns in this county, at the turn of the century. Although Evans began raising cattle, he eventually used the barn for dairy.

And, though he was apparently a good farmer, he was also a bibliophile and assembled an impressive library of over 1,000 rare books. After his death, his heirs donated the collection to the Roseburg city library. From there the books went to the Douglas County library, where they're now kept. Although the painting's title could deservedly have gone to this book lover, the barn owner, instead it goes to his father, one of Oregon's founding families, who moved from Ohio for a new start, thanks to the opportunity to be a land claimant.

LANE COUNTY

An Immigrant's Dream

Though this circular barn was built between 1946 and 1949, well past the era of round barn construction, its uniqueness stems from its severely pitched roof and that it was built by an immigrant dairy farmer, who chose the design from a Midwest dairy magazine that promoted this as a more efficient design and less expensive to construct, compared to a rectangular barn. And, despite having deteriorated over the years, it earned a listing on the National Register in 2017, a coup for the current owners, Chris Mooney, Jr., and his wife Ellen.

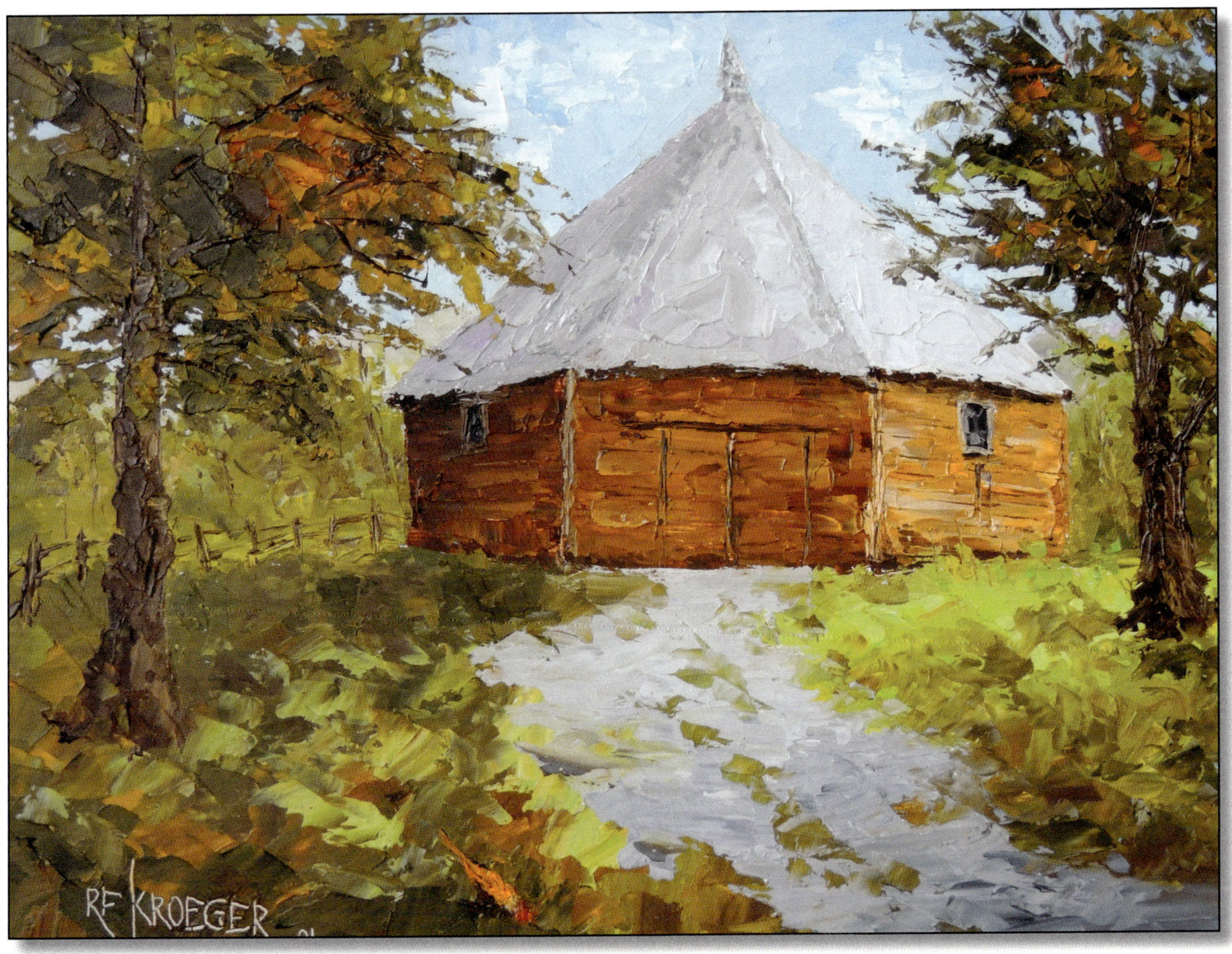

The Claimant

Located in Blachy, a small community three miles from the 300-acre Triangle Lake, which is also how this region of west-central Oregon is named, the farm sits in an area that's witnessed its share of history. Barely 50 years after Lewis and Clark reached the Pacific Ocean in the Oregon Territory, the Rogue River war broke out in 1855-1856, a conflict that stemmed from the influx of settlers from the Oregon Trail, many seeking gold in California. Known for its logging and lumber, the area was home to many sawmills, flour and grain mills, and a railroad with wooden rails. Six miles short of completion, its construction halted during the Great Depression. The round barn and part of the wooden railroad trestle are the only remaining remnants of this once bustling community.

The farm's story began when Yugoslavian immigrant Mike Sumich purchased 220 acres from James Pritchard in 1912. A year later he returned to Yugoslavia to get his parents and siblings, including John, who eventually built this barn. After the family set down roots in Blachly, it began a dairy operation. Over the decades — and through the Great Depression — they continued dairy farming, becoming financially successful enough to allow the siblings to live in separate housing. At 42, John married in 1939 and raised seven children with his wife LeEtta.

Though logging and timber come to mind when thinking about Oregon, in 1929 dairies were the economic engine of the state and the Sumich farm was one of them. The family enterprise must have been successful enough to prompt John to begin the round barn in 1946. According to his son Stanley, John saw a picture of a Midwestern round barn, which drew him to this design, even though, by 1920, many experts had refuted the economics of the round barn. Few were built after 1930.

To save money, he poured the concrete foundation himself, used aluminum for the roof — since it was inexpensive after WWII — and wood for the central silo. John dug the sand and gravel from nearby Lake Creek and cleverly used left-over logging cable for rebar. Bob Dodge, one of

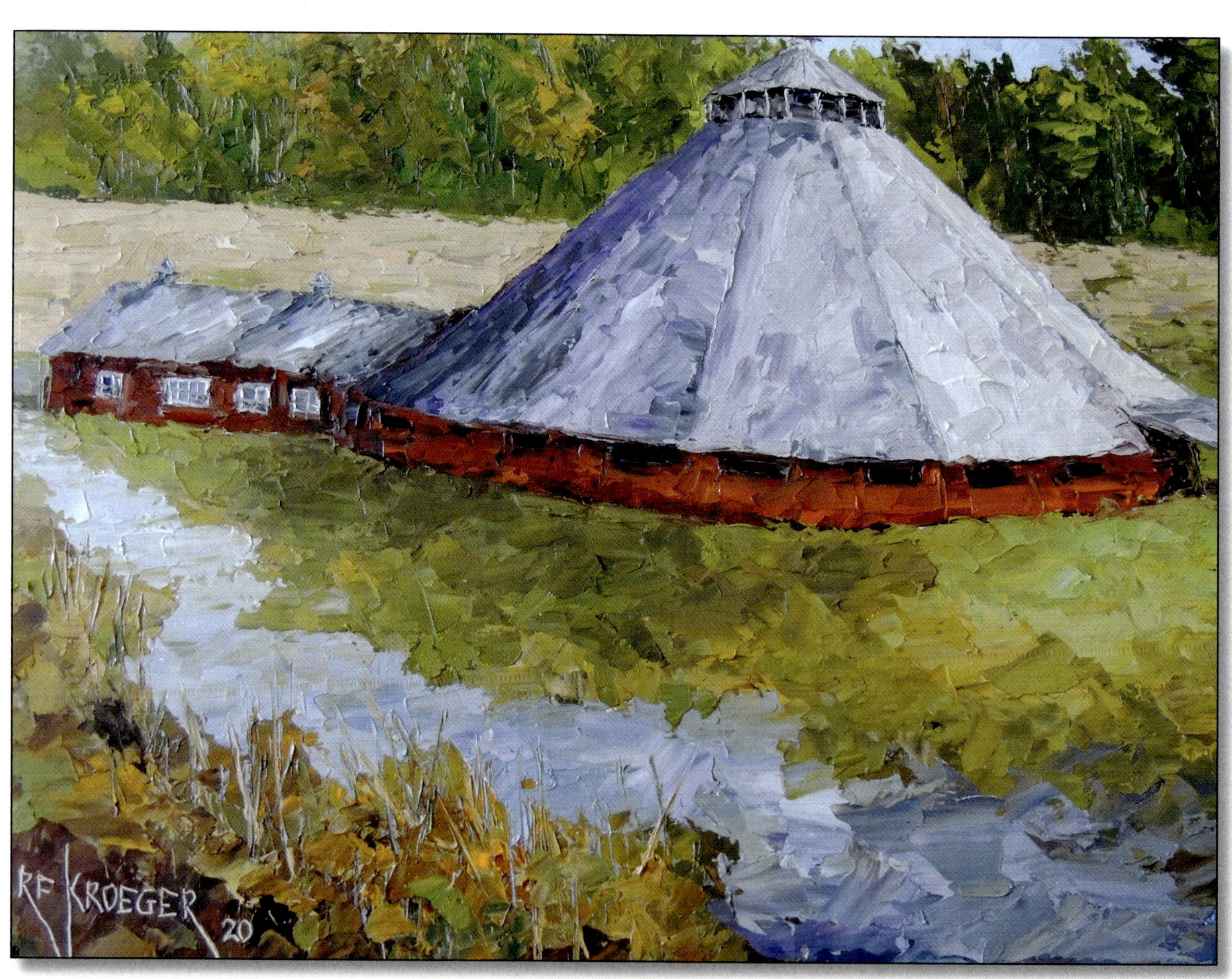

An Immigrant's Dream

the local laborers who worked on the barn, explained that many residents were curious about what he was building — over the course of three years — but the taciturn John said nothing. Finally, after the concrete pouring was finished, he explained his project.

He built 36 stanchions around a central silo and added a second-floor haymow for over 4,000 square feet of storage in this typical western barn. For waste removal, a 12-inch gutter allowed manure to collect, where it was shoveled into an overhead trolley, a standard structure in dairy barns. John also built a milk house, which the family had to live in when the farmhouse burned during construction years.

Numerous windows allowed light to filter into the barn and the steeply pitched roof and 30-foot overhang at the entrance provided protection during rain, a constant in Oregon. For a small dairy farm the barn was a decent size — 72 feet in diameter and 250 feet in circumference. The Grade A dairy required inspections monthly.

John Sumich operated the dairy for 15 years and sold it in 1965, the same year he died at the age of 68. Over the years, the farm changed ownership several times until the Mooney family purchased it. And taking an abrupt turn, the barn changed from housing dairy cows to housing Chinese Ringneck pheasants.

In 1989, owner Chris Mooney, Sr. got this idea from his grandson Shane, who was planning to raise 10 pheasants, not unusual in Oregon since about three dozen farms raise them. Chris, who ran a 130-cow dairy elsewhere, liked Shane's idea and decided to join him, but on a larger scale. He began by converting the barn into 24 pheasant pens and started with 150 birds, which gradually increased to 1,200, a supply he maintained from year to year. His idea turned to gold.

In this part of Oregon the pheasant population was declining and hunting spots were becoming scarce, which helped the Mooney project. Also, though the state pheasant hunting season was restricted to several weeks each fall, the Mooney's season lasted eight months — as the sign in front of the farm stated: *Round Barn Pheasant Ranch, August to March.* Hunters traveled here from Portland and Oregon City, some coming to "tune up" their dogs for hunting in central Oregon. However, the pheasant business came at a price.

The conversion of the barn caused structural damage to the haymow on the second floor, which will require replacement, especially since the floor helps support the conical roof, as do 12 vertical posts, which have also deteriorated. A winter storm in 2015 further damaged the aluminum sheeting, carefully constructed by Mr. Sumich in 1949. And, without a good roof, an old barn's days are numbered.

So, hoping to preserve this community landmark, co-owner Ellen Mooney created a GoFundMe website in 2016, hoping for donations to raise money to restore the barn. In 2017 they successfully listed the barn on the National Register and announced that they had formed a partnership with The Traveling Children's Heritage Museum. This partnership allows donations to qualify as a 501(c)(3) charitable donation for tax purposes. Their goal is to have the barn host summer local history camps for children of all ages and to educate them on the sustainability of agriculture and the timber industry, as well as how a farmer from Yugoslavia spent three years building this local landmark.

Though round barns represent far less than one percent of all old barns built, they are particularly attractive and sometimes, as in the case of this community, become local legends. In fact, it's the only documented true circular barn used for dairy in Oregon. And hopefully it will survive, though money is always an issue when preserving a barn that's lost its function. Sadly, recent photos show significant deterioration. Regardless of its future, it will remain recorded in this painting and essay, a tribute to John Pascal Sumich and his immigrant dream.

CALIFORNIA

SONOMA COUNTY

A Broken Heart

Adolph Weske, born in 1838 near Liegnitz in the province of Silesia, Germany, traveled around Cape Horn, arriving in California in 1850. He was 17 and ready for adventure, lured by tales of American riches — since gold was discovered here in 1848. He began mining with his older brother in Placer County, in a settlement founded by gold miners. Originally called Michigan City, it had its own post office in 1854 and by 1858 the town was shipping $100,000 worth of gold each month. Leland Stanford ran a store in the town from 1853 to 1855, was a successful merchant, became president of the Central Pacific Railroad, and later founded Stanford University. Michigan City was a place to strike it rich.

And Adoph did just that, earning an estimated $1,000 a day from the gold strike in the El Dorado Mother Lode area. After mining for a few more years and making a fortune, he moved to San Francisco, about 150 miles away, and became a businessman. Being a patriot, he enlisted in 1862 in the Second California Volunteer Cavalry and served as quartermaster sergeant, a position he held until the end of the Civil War.

After the war, Weske worked in San Francisco with the California Cracker Company, where he again had financial success. But homesick for his roots, in 1873 he returned to Germany and a year later married Betl Meyer. In 1885 he brought his family back to California, where he continued to ascend the ladder, becoming manager, superintendent and eventually president and principal stockholder of the California Cracker Company. After the company merged into the American Biscuit Company in 1888, he left the company, a departure that allowed him more time for other pursuits, including his other passion — trotter horses.

In the 1880s this former gold prospector-turned-business-executive-turned-millionaire purchased 240 acres in the foothills northeast of Windsor and built a substantial home for his family. And few years later in 1891 he hired Charles Mathison to construct a barn for his horses. And what a barn it was!

Though the reason he chose an octagonal shape may remain unknown, the barn's construction has been documented. The builder filled 17 train cars with virgin heart redwood, 52 kegs of square steel nails, and many rolls of steel rods. Inside the huge barn (105 feet in diameter) there were 50 horse stalls, six box stalls, two stalls for foaling, and, on the second level, tons of hay. A suspended stairway from the mezzanine led to the cupola, where Weske had a circular platform built so that he could watch his racehorses running on a mile and a quarter track surrounding the barn. This design resembled the brick Nutwood round barn of Champaign County, Ohio, built in 1858 for Absalom Jennings, another millionaire, who loved to watch his horses train. Perhaps that was Weske's inspiration. But unlike the Nutwood barn, Weske's also included a two-room apartment and fireplace, a bit dangerous for a barn, which, despite the threat of fire, has survived. He also built a quaint stone bridge, arching over the racetrack, so that his cattle could cross to pasture.

The cupola was no ordinary one. Above it sat a three-foot, 97-pound bronze weathervane, featuring a trotter, a sulky, and its driver. Also, though telephones were in use in the 1880s, Weske preferred passenger pigeons and built four rows of coops on a walkway near the cupola. To signal his ranch staff that he was leaving San Francisco, he'd release a bird upon departure, which carried the time that he'd arrive at the Windsor train station so that a driver would

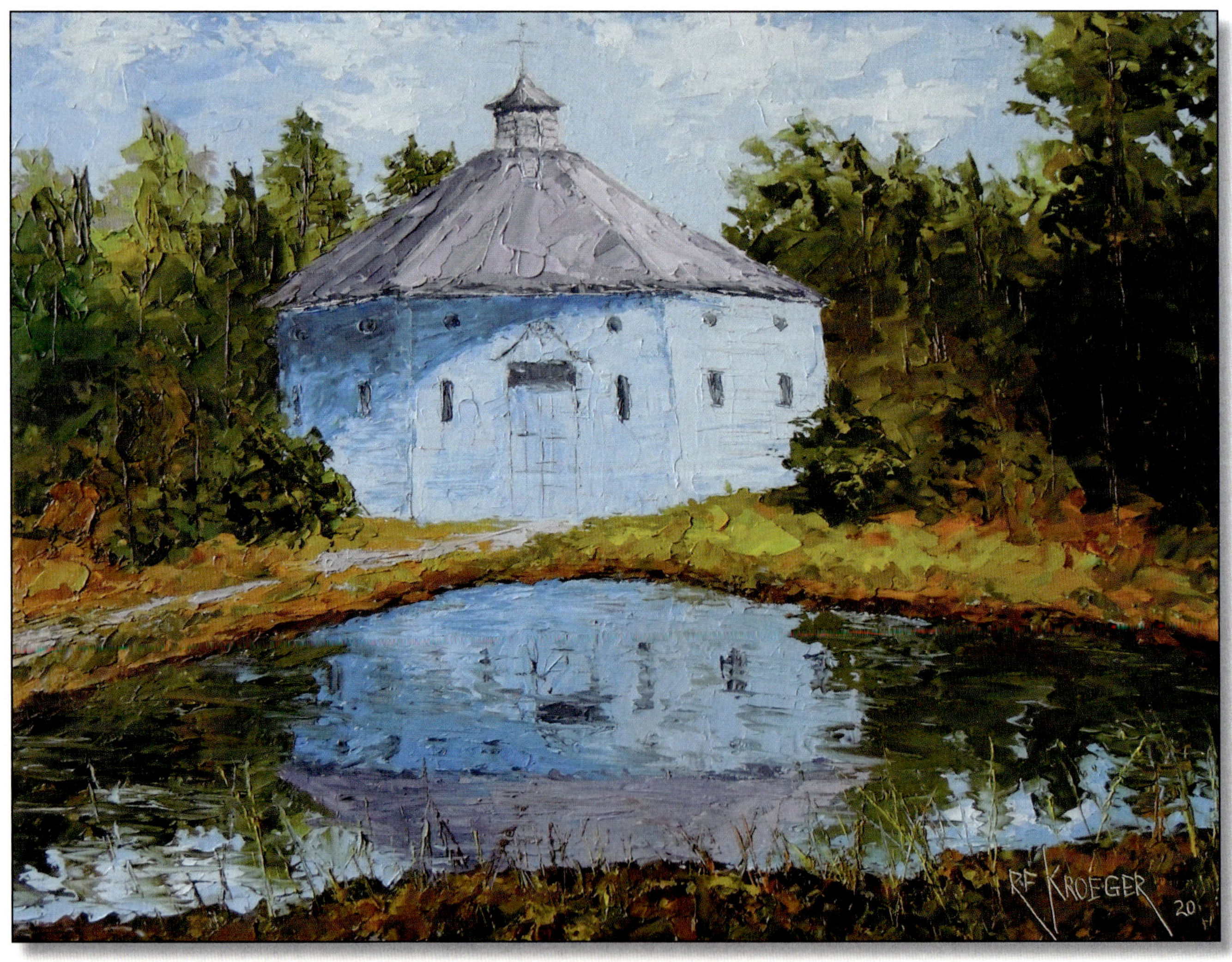

A Broken Heart

be there to pick him up. Shades of another round barn owner, John Hertz of Chicago.

However, bad luck entered his life when Black Prince, his favorite and prized stallion, died near the turn of the century. With a broken heart, he lost his fervor for horse breeding and moved back to San Francisco. His relatives took over the farm and, though otherwise healthy, Weske suddenly contracted pneumonia and died after a few days of illness in 1910. He was 72.

The estate, after family squabbles (his first wife claimed she had never signed divorce papers), sold it to Edwin and Bessie Richards, who also had ties to gold fever. This one involved the late 1890s Klondike gold rush in the Yukon, the famous one that drew over 100,000 prospectors, though only about a third reached the frozen tundra of Canada's Dawson City. A small percentage became wealthy, one of whom was Edwin Richards, who struck it rich, banking enough money to buy the Weske ranch and its iconic barn in 1911. They raised two children here.

After a certain Paul Meier bought the farm in 1945, it apparently became run-down and presented an opportunity to the next owners, Harold and Lorella Soderling and their sons, who took over in 1959. Historically minded, they restored the barn, returning it to its original colors, reminiscent of the Victorian 1890s. Their grand opening came in 1968 and featured a riding school.

In 1975 Michael Norreel, a 26-year-old Frenchman with an impressive resume as an international equestrian judge, trainer, and instructor, leased the barn and established the Center for Equestrian Arts. When a reporter asked why he chose an obscure corner of Sonoma County to start the biggest venture of his career, Norreel replied "You don't see a barn like this very often." For some reason, the barn has escaped being listed on the National Register.

But the center didn't last long and by 1987 Carol and Roy Applequist had become owners, choosing not to house horses in the barn, though they also continued restoring it. Following them, ownership became sketchy, beginning with the farm's sale in 2016 for $2.7 million, after an original listing of $3.3 million.

In December, 2020, it was again for sale and the real estate listing, especially at the bargain asking price of $2.1 million, should have tempted any horse lover: a 42-acre estate with a 12,000-square-foot round barn, a two-room office, an 150-foot show arena, paddocks and riding trails. A well produces 250 gallons per minute and there are 20 acres for a potential vineyard. Two custom built homes include a guest house and a main house with three bedrooms, as well as a pool, spa, and bathhouse. The property is gated and totally private, yet only five minutes from town and the Sonoma County wineries. The realtor also proposed possible uses, such as a winery, a tasting room, or a bed and breakfast. Such creativity!

Adolph Weske's barn has survived for over a century and offers a grand opportunity for yet another function. Hopefully when the next owners assume stewardship, they'll secure a well-deserved listing on the National Register, a recognition that would brighten the spirits of Mr. Weske and help ease the pain of his once broken heart.

Fountain Grove ... Utopia?

A map of the world that does not include Utopia is not worth even glancing at, for it leaves out the one country at which humanity is always landing.

— Oscar Wilde

California's northern Sonoma County, known for its vineyards, wineries, and the 19th-century Mission San Francisco Solano, has a population of close to half a million people, nearly as much as the entire population of Wyoming. From time to time, it's also known for devastating wildfires, one of which, in October, 2017, destroyed the 16-sided Fountain Grove barn, memorable for not only its shape but also for its story.

It centers around utopia, referring not to the book written by Sir Thomas More in 1516 but rather to a city of perfection where everyone is equal, happy, and prosperous. Unfortunately, as Shakespeare wrote in *Hamlet*, it's hard to avoid "the slings and arrows of outrageous fortune," a fact which, sooner or later, surfaces in many utopian communities. Fountain Grove was one of those.

The story begins with Thomas Lake Harris, born in 1823 to poor parents in England. When he was five, he moved with his parents to Utica, New York, and, after his father died, he was forced to help support his family when he was only nine. By 21, he had become a Universalist minister, got interested in mysticism, and started his first utopian commune in Virginia, which failed after two years. Back in England, he continued preaching and became a writer and a poet, earning enough money to once again return to the United States.

He established another community — the Brotherhood of the New Life — eventually settling in Chautauqua County, New York, where his followers began farming and growing grapes in vineyards. The commune was small — about 60 in number — and included five young Japanese students, one of whom, Kanaye Nagasawa, plays a major role in this story.

Born in Japan about 1852 and the son of a samurai, Nagasawa and 15 other young boys of the Satsuma clan were smuggled out of the country and sent to England to be educated and to learn western ways. Why smuggled? For over 200 years Japan had been isolationist and, though the older Japanese were satisfied with their lifestyle, some began to see that progress was inevitable. Commodore Perry, under orders from President Fillmore in 1853, sailed to Japan with several large warships, forcing Japan out of isolation and opening up ports for trade. In 1877 the Satsuma and other samurai clans staged their final rebellion against the massive army of Tokyo. It signaled the end of the samurai.

It's anyone's guess who decided to export the lads but whoever it was had ample funds for the long ocean voyage and university education. Though their parents must have known about the mission, they may not have been happy with it — Nagasawa's name was changed to protect his family since nearly all foreign travel was prohibited. Most of the students enrolled in Cambridge or Oxford but, the young Nagasawa, only 12 or 13, was sent north to Aberdeen, Scotland. There he met Laurence Oliphant, an English nobleman, who was a disciple of Thomas Harris. Oliphant brought Nagasawa and five other Satsuma students to the commune in New York. For a year — 1870 — Nagasawa, working in exchange for education, studied at Cornell. Though the other Japanese students returned home to share their knowledge with the samurai lord who paid for their trip, Nagasawa stayed with Harris and in 1875, at age 22, he accompanied his mentor to Sonoma County, where Harris, having heard about the climate of northern California, purchased 700 acres just north of Santa Rosa. Shortly after that he bought more land and planted a vineyard. The brotherhood was thriving.

By 1880 Nagasawa, who learned viticulture from Dr. John Hyde, a winemaker whom Harris brought along, was supervising the vineyards. Two years later, the Fountain Grove Winery was producing 70,000 gallons a year and, by 1884, the vineyard, now 1,700 acres, had cabernet, pinot noir, and zinfandel grapes. The small commune of only 30 people was selling its wine in New York and in the United Kingdom. And, the wines were winning medals.

But while Nagasawa was earning a name as a master vinter in a competitive area (by 1893 there were 23 vineyards and wineries in this district), Harris was apparently letting his utopian beliefs grow out of control. "America's best-known mystic," as Harvard-educated William James, regarded as the "Father of American psychology," described Harris, believed that "supernatural breathing" allowed man to communicate directly with God and that every soul is paired with a spiritual counterpart. He felt that it was necessary to have sexual relations with someone else to see if one's spirit lodged in that person. And, for some reason, he invited Alzire Chevaillier, a female writer and a reporter for the *San Francisco Chronicle*, to visit his commune. Perhaps he was trying to attract new recruits with media exposure but his strategy backfired when he offered to determine if his spirit resided in the attractive writer. She refused his offer of sex and she discovered other lecherous practices of Harris, eventually writing about them in several articles, which stirred up the public. This "brotherhood" wasn't unique; it was one of several other free-thinking communes in Sonoma County at the time, which continued to flourish despite the fall of the Harris experiment, the first utopian community in California.

Disgraced, Harris left the commune in 1892 and never returned. Next in line for leadership was Nagasawa, who assumed ownership of the business and expanded it, building not only beautiful stone wineries and redwood vats but also the 16-sided round barn, the flower of utopia. He hired local carpenter-contractor John Lindsay to erect the barn in 1899. Lindsay and Nagasawa may have been influenced by two other Santa Rosa round barns, the DeTurk (1870s) and the Mt. Weske (1891). Regardless, it was impressive. It sat high on a hillside with ample windows and an unusual globe-shaped cupola. And its red coat could be seen for miles. Initially, the brotherhood raised sheep and dairy cows, which may have prompted the barn's round design, but it also housed vineyard horses in its 28 stalls.

As the winery continued its success in the early 20th century, Nagasawa became famous, earning the title — in Japan — of "Wine King of California" and locally, because of his samurai heritage, of "Baron Nagasawa." Fortunately, the winery survived the earthquake of 1906 and a devastating phylloxera plaque of 1908, which prompted Nagasawa to replant the vineyards in 1912. Prohibition years were also difficult but the winery got through it by selling cooking sherry and grape juice. And, during these Roaring Twenties, Nagasawa must have convinced officials to turn their heads as he threw lavish parties, where award-winning wine flowed freely and influential guests included Thomas Edison and various Japanese dignitaries.

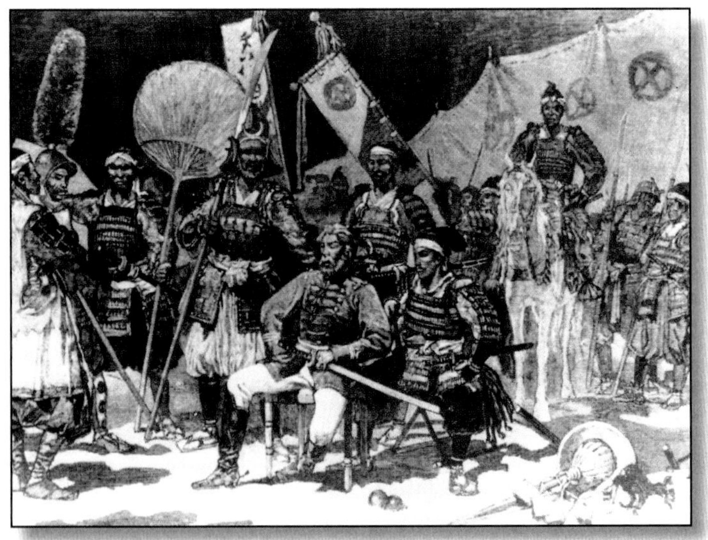

Saigo Takamori, last of the Samurai, with officers. Satsuma Rebellion, 1877. Wikimedia Commons, Le Monde Illustré

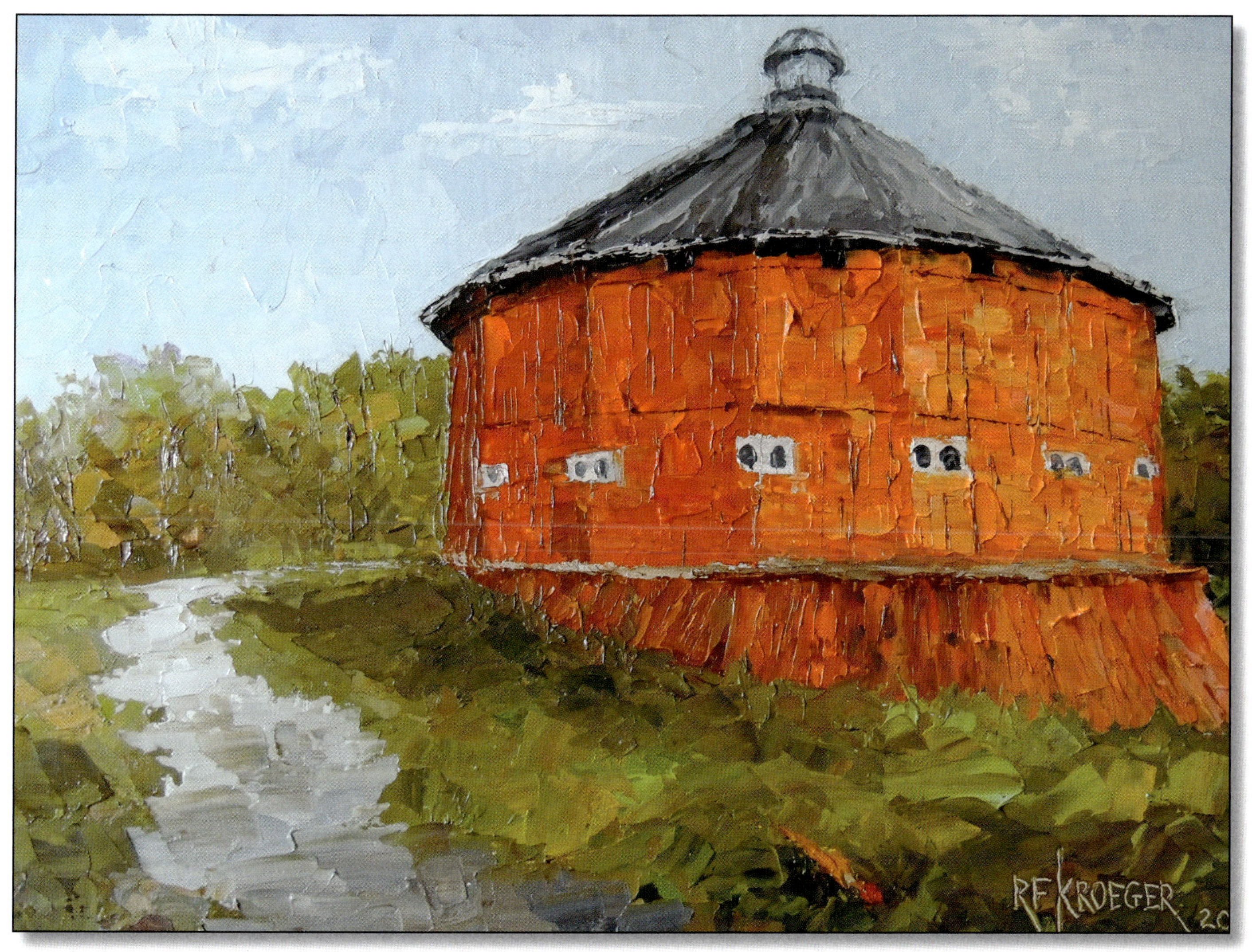

Fountain Grove ... Utopia?

When Nagasawa died in 1934, although he wanted the Fountaingrove estate (Nagasawa changed the name) to go to his descendants — including his American-born niece and nephew — he wasn't able to pass on this legacy, due to a law that prevented Japanese nationals from owning land in California. Instead, the property was sold in parcels and the barn and winery ended up in the hands of a widow and her German immigrant husband, Siegfried Bechhold. This German, somehow not understanding the heritage of the ranch and its iconic round barn, bears the infamy of having removed the vineyards and having turned the farm into a cattle ranch. He told his friends that he always wanted to be a cowboy. Furthermore, perhaps harboring a grudge against Russians, he placed a large sign on the road to the round barn, "Built by Russian Workmen," which, of course, was impossible since the Russians, who built nearby Fort Ross, had left the area in 1840. The sign remained for 25 years.

Over the years, the property changed hands and the buildings suffered the fate of disuse — with one building after another falling apart. In 1994 a report concluded that the property was eligible for inclusion into the National Register but no one bothered to submit it, which was a shame since it served as the first utopian commune in Sonoma County as well as being the brainchild of the first Japanese national to live permanently in the United States. By 2007 the handsome stone and redwood winery, though in disrepair and covered with graffiti, had survived, along with the barn, which was then owned by Angelo Ferro, a San Rafael businessman, who built the Fountaingrove Inn, a 124-room luxury hotel just below the hillside where Nagasawa's barn sat.

And then, as if to underscore the importance of submitting applications as soon as possible to the National Register, disaster struck. In October, 2017, wildfires spread through the county, taking human lives as well as Ferro's hotel and Nagasawa's round barn. Today, Thomas Lake Harris Drive, a road in a new housing development, remembers the commune's founder and Nagasawa Community Park, a 33-acre greenbelt, honors the famous Santa Rosa winemaker and builder of this memorable 16-sided barn, whose story provides another glimpse into early America.

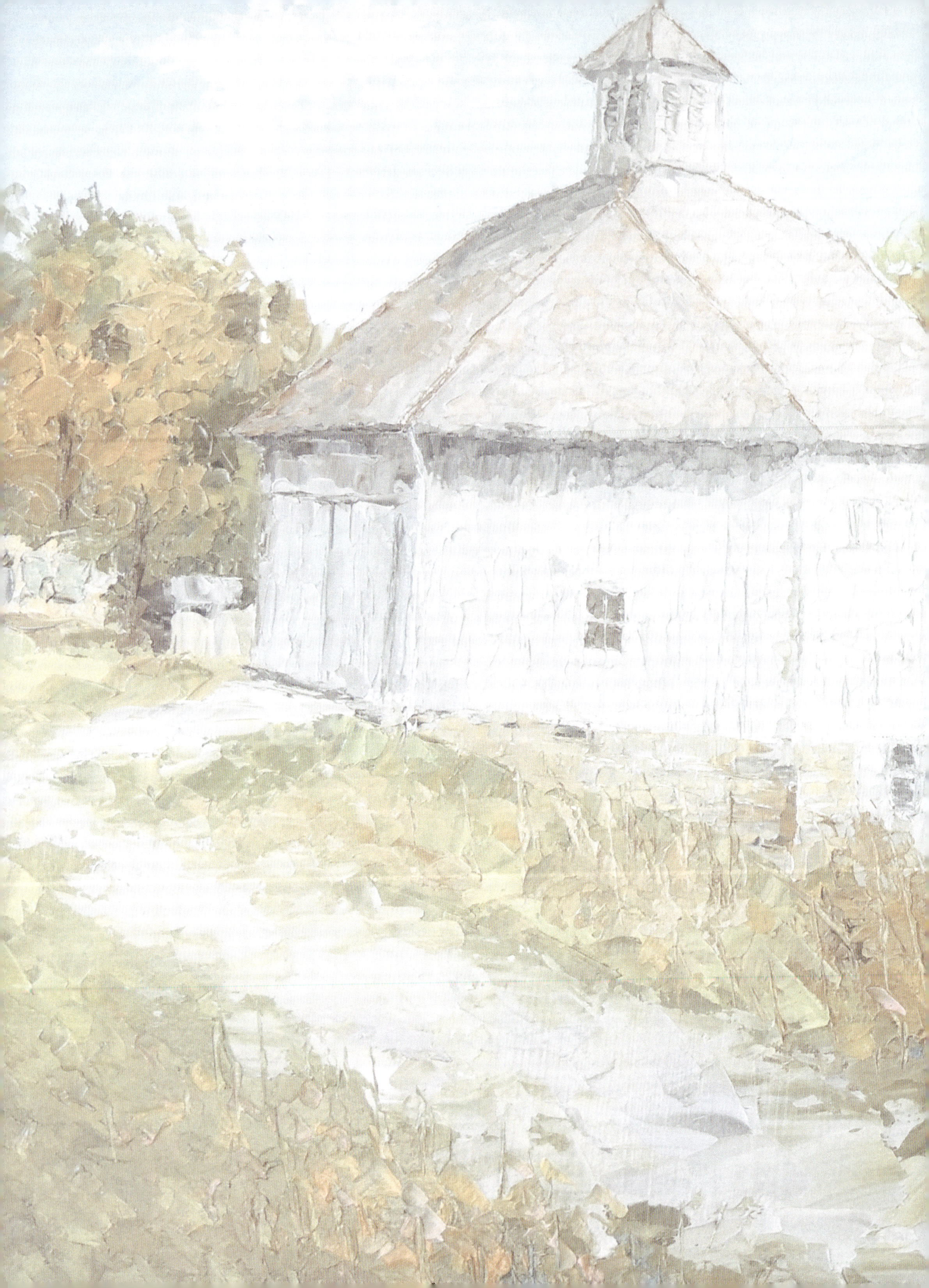

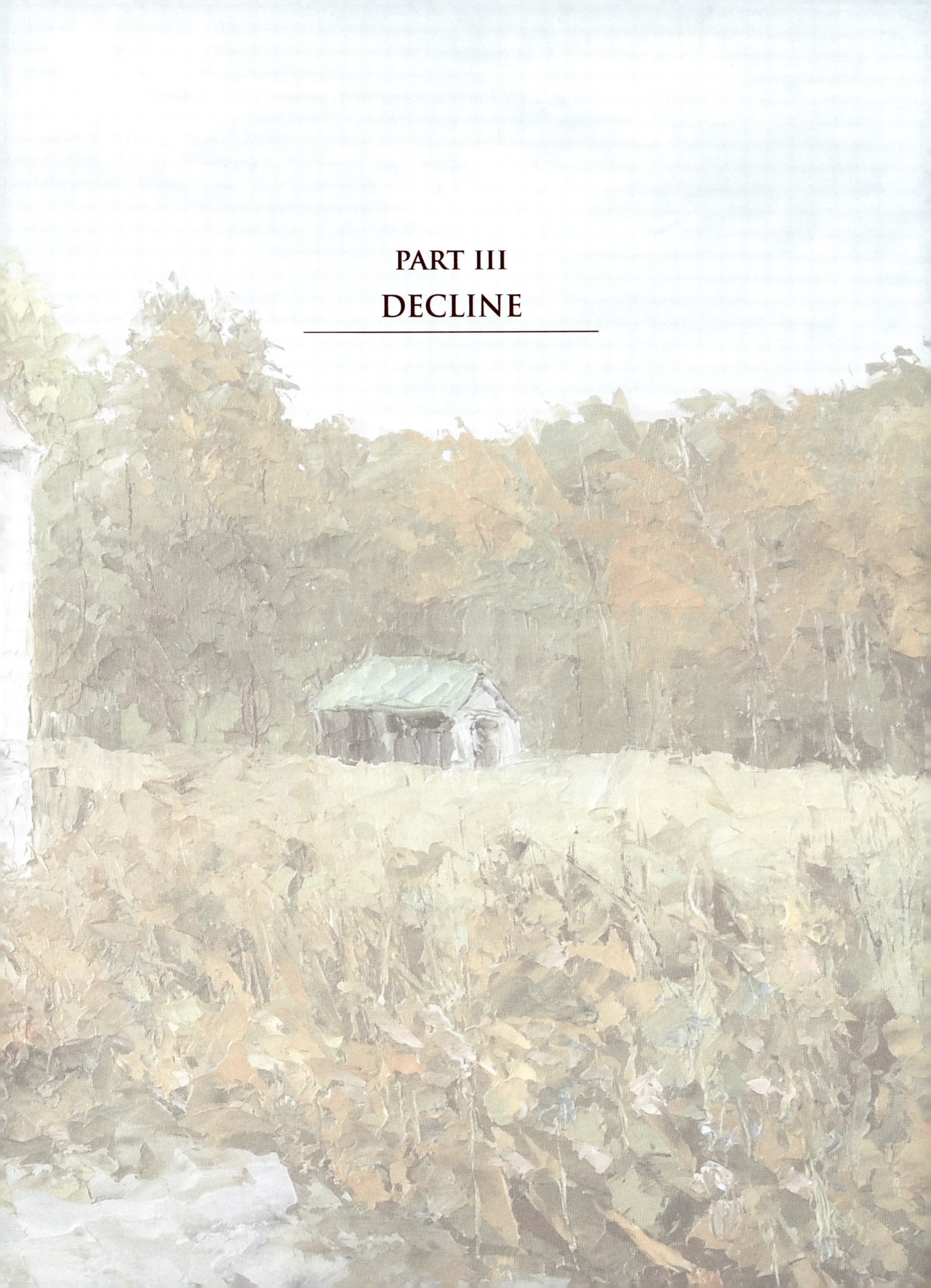

PART III
DECLINE

13. CRITICISM AND DECLINE

CRITICISM

Even as Wisconsin's Professor King publicized his round barn and central silo design, Elliot Stewart, who advocated the octagonal barn in the 1870s, finally admitted, in 1892, that a rectangular barn was easier to construct. Occasional criticisms about round barns followed in the 1890s, even as King's plans began to gain acceptance as Wisconsin shifted to a dairy state. Such articles continued despite the emergence of Indiana's round barn builders, and in spite of a supportive 1910 report by the University of Illinois. Round barn building was also flourishing in the corn belt of Iowa. This enthusiasm, though accepted by relatively few farmers, led to the golden age of round barns — between 1880 and 1920.

However, by and by, the agricultural press published more critical articles. In 1908, the influential *Hoard's Dairyman* published "Round or Rectangular Barns," which emphasized "the difficulty of getting sunlight into all parts of the stable" as well as the challenge of seeing all parts of the barn, the many extra steps in feeding, milking, and manure removal. This advice came from Wisconsin's own W. D. Hoard, the 16th governor of the state, who started this journal for dairy farmers in 1885. Hoard also founded the Wisconsin Dairymen's Association in 1871. His words carried weight with the farming community of the Midwest.

Dissatisfaction spread into Ohio. In 1906 the *Ohio Farmer* agricultural journal reported that one farmer explained that his small round barn cost six times more than a conventional one and that all he had left was "a large two-horse wagonload of small blocks."

In 1909, according to recent research by author John Hanou, the rift among Indiana's famous round barn builders may have caused many farmers in that state to opt for polygonal barns — instead of circular — in order to avoid lawsuits from Horace Duncan, whose 1904 patent for a self-supporting roof demanded payment from anyone using his roof design in a round barn.

Another insult came from a former agricultural student of Professor King, C.F. Doane, who left Wisconsin to work at the University of Maryland's experimental station in 1898. At that time, the station had a large round barn, which was subsequently taken down, as Doane complained that it was "not being worth the ground it encumbered." He also explained that round barns were being built on "misconceptions and lack of knowledge." His criticisms were published in "Round Barn Handicaps" in *Country Gentlemen 77*, 1912, and in "Round Barns Not Practical" in *Hoard's Dairyman*, 1914, adding more doubt to the practicality of these barns.

By now, many journals cited reasons why farmers should avoid building round barns: lack of adequate light and ventilation, hard to attach add-ons, wasted space in stall arrangements, central silo and haymow tough to fill, and wasted lumber due to curve cutting. Often a farmer, who wanted a round barn built, couldn't find carpenters to do the job, even if the farmer had blueprints.

In 1916, five years after Professor King died, University of Wisconsin researchers F.M. White and C.I. Griffith gave seven reasons why rectangular barns were superior to round ones, a sudden shift from where, only 15 years earlier, King had started the circular barn trend. After these negative comments, the university stopped promoting them. Despite this criticism, the University of Illinois published plans for round barns, declaring their experiment of 10 years a success, but it didn't help.

The final blow was the boom and bust in agriculture in the years of World War I. Farm production in France and other European countries suffered from the onset of war in 1914, which, along with the need to supply soldiers, sparked agricultural production in the United States. In the second half of the decade American farm products doubled and, with increased demand, costs for farmland and its crops and livestock rose dramatically. Wheat prices almost tripled in three years — the price of wheat rose from $.78 per bushel in 1913 to $2.12 per bushel in 1917, almost a 300 per cent increase. The government encouraged farmers to "Win the War with Wheat."

When the United States entered the war in April of 1917, four million young men were drafted, many from rural areas, thereby reducing manpower on the farm. But, even though others moved to cities for higher paying factory jobs, farms continued to produce. Farms rose in value as did open farmland and many farmers took advantage of these good days by borrowing money to increase their farms or start new ones. Between 1914 and 1919, 30 million new acres of land in rural America had become productive.

With farmers doing so well, manufacturers began to make new machinery, which started a keep-up-with-the-Joneses trend; gas-powered tractors were beginning to replace the horse and mule. In 1917 Henry Ford built the Fordson, a popular mass-produced tractor, which was as economical as his Model T car. If your neighbor had one, you needed one, too.

DECLINE

After the Treaty of Versailles and the end of the war in November, 1918, American farmers were still doing well, sending their products overseas — with no thoughts of slowing down production. Then came the bust, which experts failed to predict — the farms of Europe quickly recovered, lessening demand for American food, but farmers were still producing more food than Americans could eat. Supply overwhelmed demand. Farm prices fell and farmers had trouble making loan payments. In the corn state of Iowa, corn, which sold for 70 cents per bushel in the early 1920s, fell to 10 cents per bushel, a devastating plunge. Hog prices, formerly nine cents a pound, plummeted to three cents. Prices of other farm commodities dropped likewise.

In 1924 more than 2,500 farms were lost and by the end of the 1920s — which were roaring times in the cities but stinking times in rural towns and villages — many farmers were selling whatever they could, including personal belongings, equipment, and land they foolishly bought when prices were high. Banks foreclosed on many.

Then came the Great Depression. During these bleak days, farmers were even more watchful of their expenses and relatively few had enough money or courage to build a barn, let alone a round one. The arrival of electricity was another nail in the coffin. Although only about three percent of farms were electrified in the early 1930s, the passage of the Rural Electrification Act in 1935 provided funding for installation of electricity in American farmland. Eventually, barns got electricity and farmers realized that rectangular barns were much better suited to electrical use for milk machines and mechanical barn cleaners.

Eventually hay presses in barns evolved from the mid-1800s to portable machines that could be taken into the field, including one with a self-tie system, invented in 1936. Round barns were not conducive to stacking these — square hay bales fit much better in square corners, one more strike against round barn building. With progress in farm equipment, tractors and farm machines grew taller and wider and wouldn't fit into the small doors of not only round barns but many timber-framed rectangular barns as well.

However, despite the mounting evidence against the round barn, many survived into the 1940s and beyond, perhaps clinging to sentimentality. Others found new purposes, if they were fortunate enough to avoid disasters such as windstorms, tornadoes, fires … and to have owners who cared enough to maintain them.

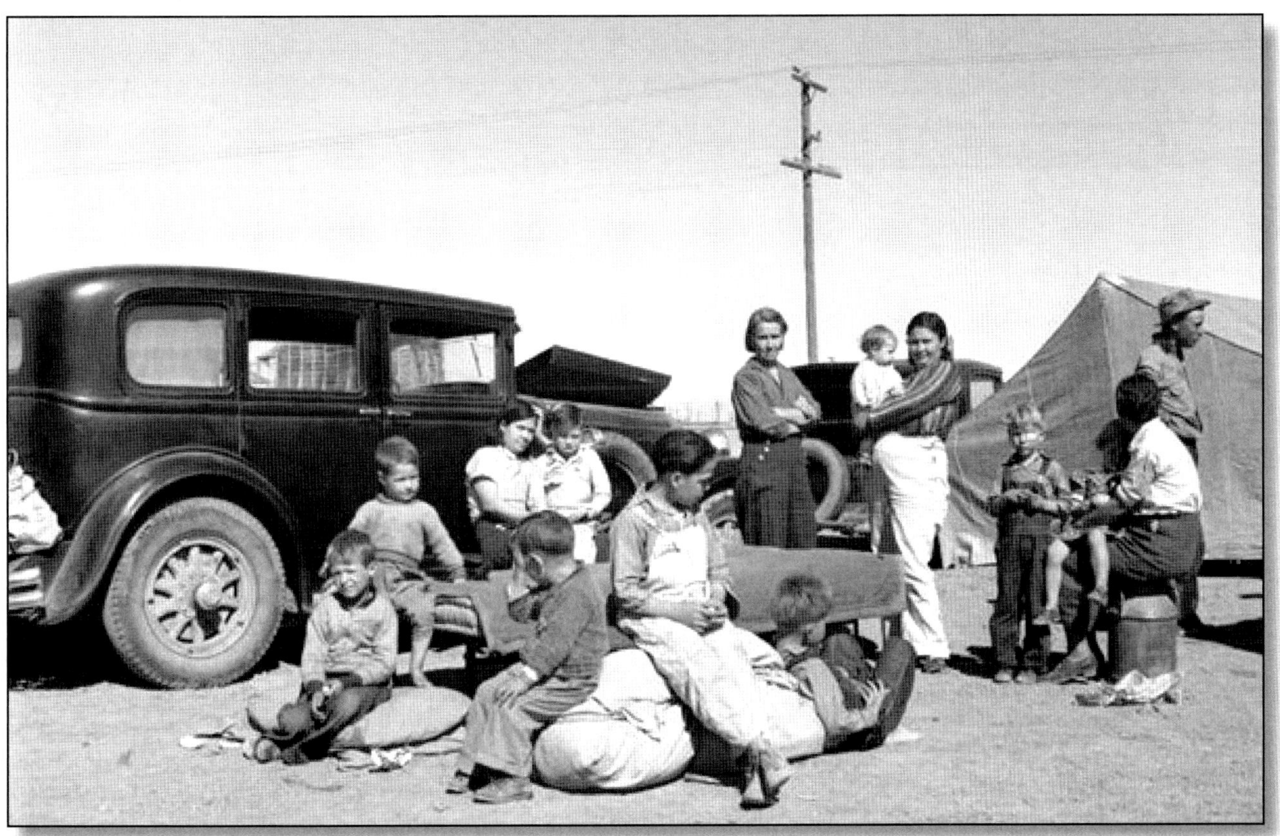

Migrants, Dust Bowl, 1930s. Wikimedia Commons, Dorothea Lange

14. DEATH AND REBIRTH

DEATH

The demise of round barns happens less frequently than that of old timber-framed barns since round barns are far less common. In Ohio, a state with over 70,000 farms, most of which still have a century-old barn hanging on, there are only about two dozen round barns left. A drive through any of the state's 88 counties will reveal old barns on the verge of collapse. In fact, many are lost each month.

Some succumb to fire, which has always been a threat to the farmer. Lightning can strike unexpectantly. In the old days, a fire brigade — with water buckets passed from hand to hand — might help, but not always.

Strong wind can be brutal, especially to the self-supporting roofs of round barns, which usually aren't anchored as well as those of traditional timber-framed barns. Many experts claimed that round barn roofs were highly resistant to damaging winds, which plagued the wide-open farm fields of the Midwest. In 1900 Indiana's McNamees built a round barn for John Whisler in Hancock County. When it survived a tornado that destroyed many homes and barns in the area, the McNamees used this in promotions, proclaiming that their round barns were "cyclone proof." However, in studying thousands of round barns, I've found the opposite to be more realistic; the self-supporting roofs are more vulnerable to wind damage than those of sturdy white oak-timber framed rectangular barns. And, of course, if a barn lies in the path of a twister, nothing can save it. In early March, 2022, a tornado leveled two large Ohio barns in Darke County. Heavy snow is another culprit, leading to roof collapse in wintry locations.

Suburban creep, both industrial and residential, spells doom for barns. Some developers simply raze barns in their way; others dismantle them for their lumber; and others move them, which happens when a concerned historical society or a historically minded town gets involved. In Lowell Soike's 1983 book, *Without Right Angles: The Round Barns of Iowa*, he described such an undertaking. Peter Tonsfeldt built a round barn in 1919 at the height of the WWI farm boom but unfortunately he overextended financially and lost the farm in 1928. The barn sat for years, publicly visible beside Route 3, and when the farm was auctioned in 1980, the townspeople of LeMars, a city of 10,000 in northwestern Iowa, became involved. After the purchaser of the farm offered the round barn to the local fair board, many stepped forward to pledge support for the expense of moving and relocating it. A year later, a truck and platform transported the round barn to its new home in the fairgrounds. Today, over 40 years later, the round barn is the showpiece of a pioneer village in the Plymouth County fairgrounds. Unfortunately, other round barns aren't as lucky.

Another factor that plays a role in deterioration is when the barn was sided horizontally, instead of vertically. Since the lumber had to be soaked to become flexible enough to be curved, it had a tendency to warp, especially if not maintained. And, when boards warp, leaving holes, water penetrates and causes timber to rot, just as in the case in a leaky roof.

REBIRTH

In 1987 the Smithsonian, together with the National Trust for Historical Preservation, launched a program called, "Barn Again!," which toured the country for a few years. Several states responded (Ohio, Wisconsin, Indiana, Michigan, Vermont, North Dakota) with similar programs, which also offered tips on preserving old barns. But, after spending thousands of dollars on restoration, what do you have? Answer — an old round barn that's not much good for anything except storage. And being old, it needs continual maintenance. But, for those owners who want to keep their round barns, there are many ways to give an old barn new life. Here are some of them.

EVENT CENTERS

Back in the 1950s and 1960s, most weddings took place in a church or synagogue. But times have changed and many folks today seem to prefer other venues: the beach, a foreign country, a back yard, and even a barn. In fact, getting married in an old barn has become so trendy that many enterprising barn owners have given this new purpose to their old barn. After all, a wedding in a round barn would be a unique experience, which appeals to young couples. In fact, Ohio has at least two of these — both octagonals — one in Miami County and one in Stark County.

Some round barn owners, entrepreneurs at heart, offer their barns for holding other events: family reunions, nonprofit fundraisers, corporate retreats. The list may continue to grow since many wish to return to the rustic smells of wood and hay, more appealing than buildings of concrete, steel, and glass.

MUSEUMS

Indiana's Fulton County, once home to 17 round barns, started a round barn festival and later converted a round barn into a museum. Built in 1924 for dairying, its roof fell victim to a tornado in 1989, which is when the owner donated it to the Fulton County Historical Society. After raising funds through grants and donations, the group restored and moved the barn to its property, where it serves as an agricultural museum in a pioneer village. Thousands pay visits every year to the iconic Shaker round barn in western Massachusetts, which educates visitors on Shaker life and agriculture. A replica of this barn in Cape Cod, built in 1969, doubles as a museum for 30 vintage automobiles, collected by the Eli Lilly family. The Amherst Historical Society has saved and restored an octagonal barn in northeastern Ohio, which will be used for agricultural farming education programs.

GOLF

Yes, round barns can be used for golf! Fulton County, Indiana, is home to another unique example of repurposing a round barn. In 2005, nearly a century after the Gerig round barn was built in 1915, the city-owned golf course became known as the Round Barn Golf Club at Mill Creek, thanks to its new pro shop — this round barn — which the city of Rochester renovated and transported onto the course. Yes, the routing of the holes had to change.

WINERIES

Another Fulton County round barn made its way to Baroda, Michigan, where it now functions as the Round Barn Winery. The 1912 Huffman round barn has found new life.

RELIGIOUS CENTERS

In Red Lodge, Montana, the Kent brick round barn has had more than its share of functions since it was built by Indiana's McNamees in 1939 — including a dairy barn, barn dance hall, restaurant, ski chalet, gift shop, smorgasbord, antique shop, dinner theater, Ford dealership, and, most recently, The Church of the Rockies. Who knows what's next?

One of the more fascinating repurposing has taken place in Canton, Stark County, Ohio, where the roller bearing giant, the Timken family, built a rare donut round barn circa 1894. Over the years, it fell out of family hands, was converted into a restaurant by a former NFL star, and is now being used as a synagogue, though its deteriorating condition warrants demolition, which would be an American tragedy.

REAL ESTATE VENTURES AND BUSINESSES

Some round barns have been converted into homes, apartments, and bed and breakfast enterprises. Others are now used in businesses, like the 1881 octagonal in Darrowville, Summit County, Ohio. Over the decades, after having been remodeled by an architect, it has been used for boat storage, an antique auction house, a meeting place for the Civil Air Patrol during WWII, offices of a mortgage company and, currently, a home for marketing and public relations professionals.

A 1924 circular barn, on its way to ruin and located in the ancient Ojo Caliente Mineral Springs, New Mexico, was fortunately saved and restored by a company that runs a spa-style resort. The Ojo Spa Resorts of New Mexico has preserved the last remaining round barn in the state.

Another business to find success in a round barn lies in Jackson County, Georgia. The 1913 Roncadori round barn has found use as a dairy barn and a furniture store. Since 1963 the family has been selling mattresses, calling their company, Round Barn Mattresses.

COUNTY FAIRGROUNDS

Floral halls in county fairgrounds throughout the country often took a polygonal shape and many date to the early 1900s. A few round barns were built for agricultural exhibits in county fairs, notably the rare stone octagonal sales barn in Sheridan County, Wyoming, and an attractive red circular barn, built in 1906 specifically for dairy cattle showings, which still delights visitors in Lancaster, Fairfield County, Ohio.

NEW CONSTRUCTION

Some historically minded groups have reconstructed round barns, including the most famous and what is America's first recorded round barn, the 16-sided threshing barn of President George Washington, built in 1794. Thanks to the Mount Vernon Ladies' Association and a generous $2 million grant from the W.K. Kellogg Foundation, Washington's round barn has been reconstructed and is part of his Mount Vernon legacy.

Another round barn enthusiast, Iowa's businessman Dick Schwab, has illustrated the infectious attraction of a round barn. His journey began in 1984 when a storm toppled some large trees on his rural property, about three miles northwest of Iowa City. Intrigued by the logs, he took them to a sawmill and eventually used them to build three rectangular barns from 1985 to 1987, but he wanted something different. "This rectangular, square stuff is kind of boring. Anybody can build rectangular barns," he said in a newspaper interview. So he began building round barns ... three of them ... out of stone quarried in Iowa. Finished with his first three, one circular, one 13-sided, and one 16-sided, Schwab built a large (100-foot diameter) event stone circular barn in 2008. Not finished yet, he built one even bigger in 2011 — 120 feet in diameter — with the same quarried stone. The latter two are used for events in a new park, called Cangleska Wakan, which is a Lakota name meaning "sacred hoop," referring to the interconnectedness of all things.

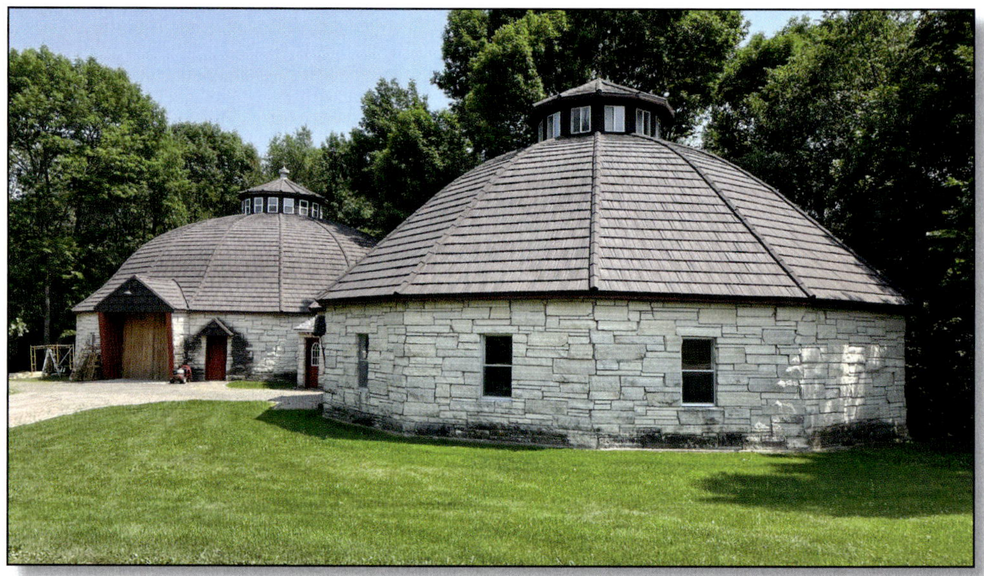

Dick Schwab round barns, Iowa. Courtesy of Johnson County Conservation Board

In 2018, the year Schwab and his wife moved to Wisconsin to be closer to family, they sold four of the round barns and the rest of their 100 acres — for $1.2 million below valuation — to the Johnson County Conservation Board, which plans to make it a pioneer village. It's not hard to understand why this round barn aficionado was named the local 2001 Man of the Year. He said that Soike's book, *Without Right Angles: The Round Barns of Iowa*, introduced him to round barns, even though he grew up on a farm without one in Minnesota. If awards were given for individuals building new round barns, he would take first honors.

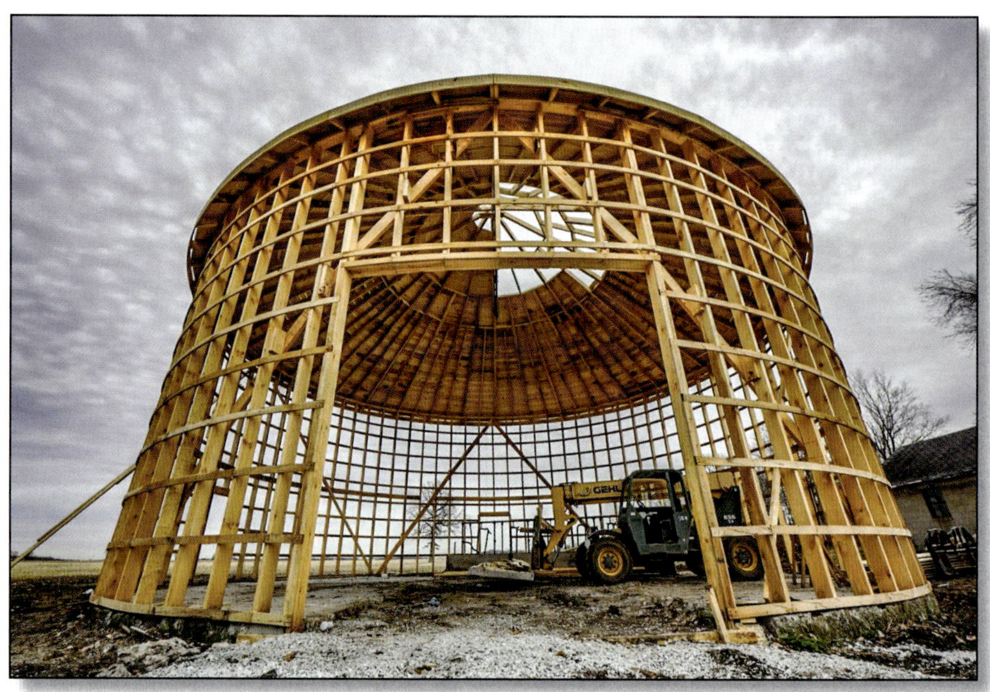

New round barn, Indiana, December, 2021. Courtesy of Scott Smith, Indiana Barn Foundation

Indiana, which at one time had over 260 round barns, more than any other state, has its share of round barn lovers. Brandon McClarnon built a new round barn by himself and others in 2009 in Hancock County. He plans to use this circular barn for his horses and antique tractors. Another Indiana resident, Larry Bauerle, decided to replace his round barn, which came down in a severe windstorm, with another round one! According to Scott Smith on the Indiana Barn Foundation Facebook page, he's rebuilding to the original barn specs. Started from scratch in the autumn of 2021, the barn was finished in 2022, another diamond in the crown of Indiana's round barn heritage.

However, of the 75 round barns in this book, most are owned privately and are used for storage or perhaps for family gatherings, which suggests a sentimental attachment, especially if the barn has been in family hands for many years. Likewise, old timber-framed rectangular barns continue to be cared for because of family memories and sheer love of historical preservation. If the owners can keep up with maintenance or if they can repurpose the old barns to make them financially viable, they'll continue to remind us of a bygone era of vintage Americana. And round barns comprise a fascinating part of that heritage.

AFTERWORD

Whenever an old barn catches fire or falls down, locals feel that a little bit of them disappears with the barn. In January, 2021, a barn scout from Hancock County, Ohio, called to let me know that his family barn burned down. Space heaters, put there during the cold winter to keep newborn calves warm, had sparked an electrical fire, a complete and tragic loss for this functioning barn, built in the 1890s. "But, Bob," he said tearfully, "at least we have your painting to remember it by," a statement that reinforced why I do this historic barn project.

What now? With my projects on round barns and Ohio barns completed, I will embark on another adventurous plan to capture another interesting niche of old barns, which will involve visiting several other states. However, I will continue to seek out barns in Ohio and Indiana, hoping to preserve them in paintings and essays — as well as using them to raise not only funds for nonprofits but awareness of the importance of the old "money maker." If a nonprofit — such as a historical society or 4-H — has interest in taking me on a tour of old barns in his or her county, I can be reached via the contact page at www.barnart.weebly.com. I also do an occasional commission of an old barn, if time allows.

I've been blessed to preserve the memories of these barns and I hope I can continue for many more years. After all, our American ancestry, whether we live in suburbs, cities, or farmland, has ties to old barns, going back hundreds of years and evoking the poetry of John Donne, written in 1624. "No man is an island entire of itself; every man is a piece of the continent, a part of the main." His words echo throughout the land, where old barns are vanishing, "And therefore never send to know for whom the bell tolls; it tolls for thee."

BIBLIOGRAPHY

Apps, Jerold W. 2010 *Barns of Wisconsin*. Madison, Wisconsin: Wisconsin Historical Society Press.

Arthur, Eric and Witney, Dudley 1981 *The Barn: A Vanishing Landmark in North America*. Toronto, Canada: Galahad Books.

Dregni, Michael, ed. 2002 *This Old Barn: A Treasury of Family Farm Memories*. Stillwater, Minnesota: Voyageur Press.

Endersby, Elric, Greenwood, Alexander, and Larkin, David 1992 *Barn: The Art of a Working Building*. New York, New York: Houghton Mifflin Company.

Falk, Cynthia G. 2012 *Barns of New York: Rural Architecture of the Empire State*. Ithaca, New York: Cornell University Press.

Fink, Daniel 1987 *Barns of the Genesee Country: 1790-1915*. Geneseo, New York: James Brunner, Publisher.

French, Giles 1964 *Cattle Country of Peter French*. Portland, Oregon: Binfords and Mort, Publishers.

Haney, Chuck 2007 *Big Sky Barns*. Helena, Montana: Riverbend Publishing.

Hanou, John T. 1993 *A Round Indiana: Round Barns in the Hoosier State*. West Lafayette, Indiana: Purdue University Press.

Hanou, John T. 2020 *A Round Indiana: Round Barns in the Hoosier State, Second Edition*. West Lafayette, Indiana: Purdue University Press.

Huger, Lucie F. 2001 *St. Albans: History and Folklore of a Missouri River Town*. Kirkwood, Missouri: Fairfield Publishing Company.

Hughes, Graham 1985 *Barns of Rural Britain*. London: The Herbert Press.

Jackson, Jacqueline D. 2011 *The Round Barn: A Biography of an American Farm*. Beloit, Wisconsin: Beloit College Press.

Leffingwell, Randy 1997 *The American Barn*. Osceola, Wisconsin: MBI Publishing Company.

Mohr, Marsha W. 2010 *Indiana Barns*. Bloomington, Indiana: Indiana University Press.

Noble, Allen G. and Wilhelm, Hubert G.H., eds. 1995 *Barns of the Midwest*. Athens, Ohio: Ohio University Press.

Roscoe, John 2019 *Minnesota's Round Barns*. Willmar, Minnesota: Lakeside Press.

Scott, Donald H. 1997 *Barns of Indiana*. Virginia Beach, Virginia: The Donning Company.

Schense, Deb, ed. 2008 *Barns Around Iowa: A Sampling of Iowa's Round Barns*. Iowa City, Iowa: Penfield Books.

Sloane, Eric 1954 *Eric Sloane's America*. New York, New York: Promontory Press.

Sloane, Eric 1965 *A Reverence for Wood*. Mineola, New York: Dover Publications.

Sloane, Eric 2001 *Eric Sloane's An Age of Barns*. Minneapolis, Minnesota: Voyageur Press.

Soike, Lowell J. 1983 *Without Right Angles: The Round Barns of Iowa*. Des Moines, Iowa: Iowa State Historical Department.

Steccato, Jeffrey 2019 *Barns Across America*. Buffalo, New York: Amherst Media.

Sommer, Robin L. 1997 *The Old Barn Book*. Barnes and Noble.

Skinner, John S., ed. *The American Farmer*, 1827. Volume 9, Number 3. Rural Economy, "Shakers' Barn." Baltimore, Maryland.

Triumpho, Richard 2004 *Round Barns of New York*. Syracuse, New York: Syracuse University Press.

Whitney, Charles W. and Gray, Pamela W. *Ohio Barns: Inside and Out*. Mt. Vernon, Ohio: Gray's Venture.

ABOUT THE AUTHOR

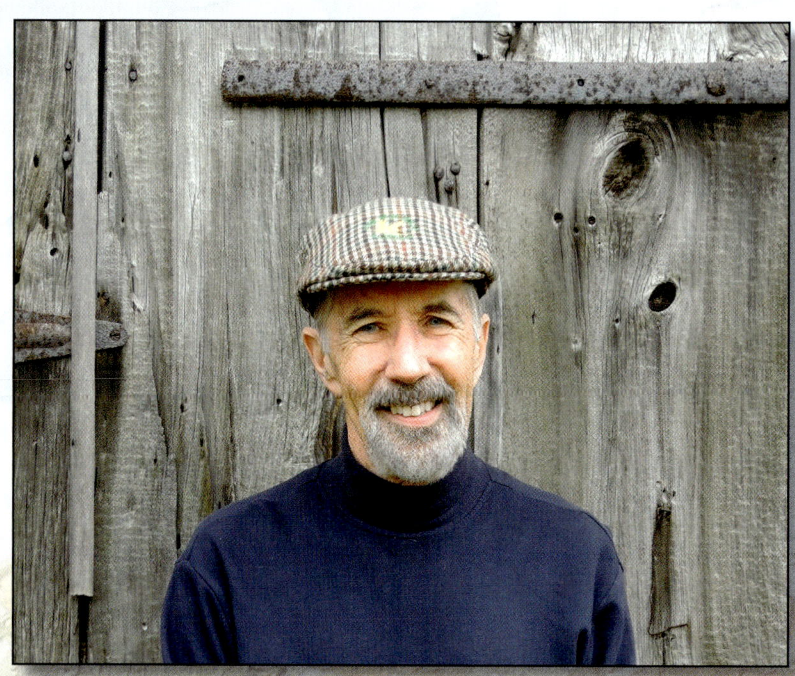

Robert Kroeger. Photograph, David Bimschleger

Dr. Robert Kroeger, a native of Youngstown, graduated from Ohio State University's College of Dentistry, served four years of active duty in the US Navy, ending with the rank of lieutenant commander. He and his late wife Brenda moved to Cincinnati where they raised five children and Dr. Kroeger practiced general dentistry from 1977 to 2010, when he retired. He and his wife Laura also live in Cincinnati, where they enjoy spending time with nine grandchildren.

Dr. Kroeger is a second-generation artist, though, unlike his father Francis, who held an art degree from Notre Dame, his professional art career blossomed later in life. Though he did not immediately follow in his father's footsteps, Robert's career as a dentist allowed him to study color values and facial esthetic principles in smile design. He is the author of *Historic Barns of Ohio*, a book that features a barn, its painting, and its essay in each of Ohio's 88 counties.

Dr. Kroeger has also written two books on dentistry and seven books on golf in Scotland, England, Wales, and Ireland, including *To The 14th Tee, The Links of Wales, The Golf Courses of Old Tom Morris, Golf on the Links of Ireland, Golf on the Links of England, Complete Guide to the Golf Courses of Scotland*, and *The Secrets of Islay*. This is his second book on old barns but hopefully not his last. He can be contacted via the website, www.barnart.weebly.com.

KROEGER '20

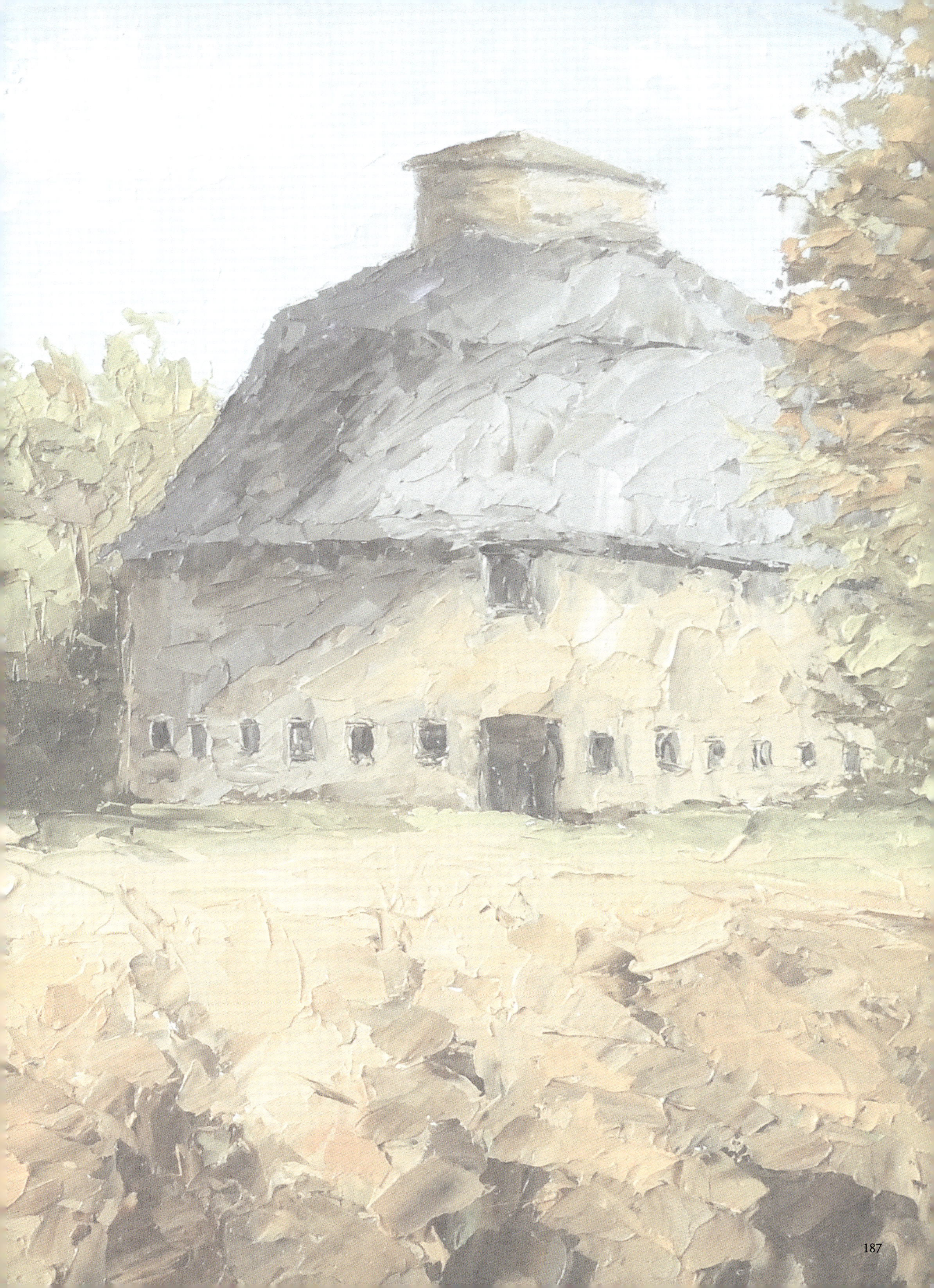

INDEX

D

E

F

G

H